GENDER AND IMMORTALITY

GENDER AND IMMORTALITY

HEROINES IN ANCIENT GREEK
MYTH AND CULT

Deborah Lyons

PRINCETON UNIVERSITY PRESS   PRINCETON, NEW JERSEY

Library of Congress Cataloging-in-Publication Data
Lyons, Deborah, 1954–
Gender and immortality : heroines in ancient Greek myth and cult /
Deborah Lyons.
p.   cm.
Includes bibliographical references (p.   ) and index.
ISBN 0-691-01100-1 (cl : alk. paper)
1. Greek literature—History and criticism.   2. Women and
literature—Greece.   3. Immortality in literature.   4. Women—
Greece—Mythology.   5. Sex role in literature.   6. Heroines
in literature.   7. Mythology, Greek.   8. Greece—Religion.
9. Cults—Greece.   I. Title.
PA3015.W65L96   1997
880.9′352042—dc20   97-19562

For my parents
and
for Fred

Contents

Illustrations

Acknowledgments

THIS BOOK has been long in the making, and I could not have written it without the generous help of family, friends, and colleagues. I begin with my teachers Froma Zeitlin, Richard Martin, and Robert Lamberton, who shepherded this work in its earlier form as a doctoral dissertation, and who have been generous with their advice and support ever since. For their encouragement and the inspiration provided by their work, I am indebted to Ileana Chirassi Colombo, Nicole Loraux, and Jean-Pierre Vernant. Deborah Boedeker and Gregory Nagy, once-anonymous reviewers for Princeton University Press, made many indispensible suggestions and saved me from many errors. Thanks are due also to the first editor of this book, Joanna Hitchcock, who believed in it before I did, to Marta Steele, for her patient and meticulous copyediting, and to Jeffrey Carnes, for his judicious indexing.

I have benefited enormously from the critical talents of Fred Bohrer and Moshe Sluhovsky, both of whom read the book in its entirety. Other friends whose contributions of various kinds were much appreciated along the way include Carla Antonaccio, Kathryn Argetsinger, Stefano Gallo, Carolyn Higbie, Andrea Jördens, Lisa Maurizio, June McCombie, Eric Miller, Deborah Modrak, Linda Reinfeld, and David Rosenbloom. For technical support at critical moments, I wish to thank Harry Barnes and David Sider, as well as Kevin Duval of Nota Bene.

I thank the associates of the Susan B. Anthony Institute for Gender and Women's Studies of the University of Rochester both for their interest in my work and for material support for my research. My thanks also to the Dean of the College of the University of Rochester for underwriting the cost of the illustrations. This project might never have gotten off the ground had it not been for the timely intervention of the American Association of University Women. During the researching of this book, I have incurred many pleasurable debts of *xenia*. For their hospitality, I wish to thank the faculty, students, and staff of the Department of the Classics of Harvard University and the Seminar für Klassische Philologie of the University of Heidelberg, as well as the director and staff of the American Academy in Rome. Special thanks go to Deborah Boedeker and Kurt Raaflaub, directors of the Center for Hellenic Studies in Washington, D.C., and to Ellen Roth, the Center's librarian, whose warm welcome made it not only possible, but also pleasant, to complete the innumerable small tasks required to complete this book.

Some debts are hard to put into words. My dear friends Nina Davis-Millis, Christopher Millis, and David Weinstock all know why their names are here. Finally, I dedicate this book to my parents, who were in on it from the beginning and to Fred, whose support and affection have lightened the end of the work.

Note to the Reader

IN SPELLING Greek names, I have tried to balance consistency with a desire not to baffle the reader unnecessarily. I have therefore used the familiar Latinized forms for names of authors and the best-known mythological figures (Sophocles, Aeschylus, Achilles, Helen), combined with a more consistent system of transliteration for all other Greek names (Telemachos, Kirke, etc.). The occasional compromise has also been necessary (e.g., Klytemnestra). Please note that I use *k* to transcribe the Greek letter *kappa*, but *ch* to transcribe the letter *chi*.

All unmarked translations from Greek and Latin are my own. In cases where a foreign-language secondary work is cited, quotations in English are also my translations. Greek texts are from the *OCT* editions except where noted.

The list of abbreviations at the front includes journals, compilations, and ancient authors most frequently cited in this book. All other abbreviations are according to the conventions established by Liddell, Scott, and Jones, eds., *A Greek-English Lexicon*.

Abbreviations

Journals and Compilations

AC	L'Antiquité Classique
AJA	American Journal of Archaeology
AJP	American Journal of Philology
AK	Antike Kunst
AW	Antike Welt
BCH	Bulletin de Correspondence Hellénique
BICS	Bulletin of the Institute of Classical Studies
CA	Classical Antiquity
CIG	Corpus Inscriptionum Graecarum
CJ	Classical Journal
CQ	Classical Quarterly
CR	Classical Review
CW	Classical World
FGrH	Die Fragmente der griechischen Historiker ed. F. Jacoby (Berlin/Leiden, 1923–64)
FHG	Fragmenta Historicorum Graecorum ed. C. Muller and T. Muller (Paris, 1841–51)
GRBS	Greek, Roman, and Byzantine Studies
HSCP	Harvard Studies in Classical Philology
HThR	Harvard Theological Review
IG	Inscriptiones Graecae
JHS	Journal of Hellenic Studies
LIMC	Lexicon Iconographicum Mythologiae Classicae
M-W	Fragmenta Hesiodea ed. R. Merkelbach and M. L. West (Oxford, 1967)
PMG	Poetae Melici Graeci ed. D. L. Page (Oxford, 1962)
PP	Parola del Passato
QUCC	Quaderni Urbinati di Cultura Classica
RE	Realencyclopädie der classischen Altertumswissenschaft
REA	Revue des études anciennes
REG	Revue des études grecques
RM	Rheinisches Museum
SEG	Supplementum Epigraphicum Graecum
SMSR	Studi e Materiali di Storia delle Religioni
TAPA	Transactions and Proceedings of the American Philological Association
YCS	Yale Classical Studies
ZPE	Zeitschrift für Papyrologie und Epigrafik

Ancient Authors Frequently Cited

Aesch.	Aeschylus
Alc.	Alcman

Ant. Lib.	Antoninus Liberalis
Apollod.	Apollodorus
AR.	Apollonius of Rhodes
Aristoph.	Aristophanes
Athen.	Athenaeus
Callim.	Callimachus
Cert. Hom. et Hes.	The Contest between Homer and Hesiod
Diod.	Diodorus Siculus
Eur.	Euripides
Hdt.	Herodotus
Hes.	Hesiod
Cat.	Catalogue of Women attributed to Hesiod
Theog.	Theogony
WD	Works and Days
Hesych.	Hesychius
Hom. Hymn	Homeric Hymns
Hyg. Fab.	Hyginus Fabulae
Lycoph.	Lycophron
Paus.	Pausanias
Plut.	Plutarch (see below for individual titles)
schol.	scholia (ancient commentaries)
Soph.	Sophocles
Theocr.	Theocritus
Thuc.	Thucydides

All others may be found in the *Oxford Classical Dictionary* or *A Greek-English Lexicon*, ed. Liddell, Scott, and Jones.

Plutarch Moralia: Titles of Individual Works

Amat. narr.	Love Stories
Apotheg. Lac.	Sayings of Spartans
De def. orac.	On the Obsolescence of Oracles
De frat. am.	On Brotherly Love
De gen. Socr.	On the Sign of Socrates
De Herodot. malig.	On the Malignity of Herodotus
De mul. virt.	On the Bravery of Women
Glor. Athen.	On the Fame of Athens
Parall.	Parallel Stories
Praec. coniug.	Advice to Bride and Groom
Quaest. conviv.	Table-Talk
Quaest. Gr.	Greek Questions
Quaest. R.	Roman Questions
Sept. sap. conviv.	Dinner of the Seven Wise Men

Plutarch Lives: Titles of Individual Works

Alcib.	Alcibiades
Arist.	Aristides
Rom.	Romulus
Them.	Themistocles
Thes.	Theseus

GENDER AND IMMORTALITY

Introduction

According to my Aunt Evanthia, the heroic age for
women in Greece was from the moment they were born
to the moment they died.
                            —Stratis Haviaras, *The Heroic Age*

Alas! if the heroine of one novel be not patronized by the
heroine of another, from whom can she expect protection
and regard?
                            —Jane Austen, *Northanger Abbey*

MALE VERSUS FEMALE and mortal versus divine: these fundamental oppo-
sites hold pride of place among the many binary oppositions that shape
ancient Greek thought. By situating heroines in relation to these two
categories, I aim to change the way we look not only at heroines, but also
at the very categories themselves.

This book proposes, first of all, that the heroine is a distinct religious
and mythic category, and one that so far has not received adequate attention; second, that heroines have a different relationship to immortality
than do heroes; and third, that the integration of heroines into our view
of Greek heroic myth and cult requires a new model of divine/mortal
relations based as much on reciprocity as on antagonism.

While the third of these propositions might seem to indicate adherence
to the tenets of so-called difference-feminism, to understand it in such a
way is to sentimentalize the concept of reciprocity. The reciprocity in
question is largely symbolic and has to do with the exchange of qualities
between male and female, and between mortal and immortal, in ways
that complicate these categories. That this interest in ambiguity is not a
purely modern innovation is shown by the lines from Heraclitus with
which I begin Chapter 3.

Despite this caveat, it will be obvious how much my choice of topic,
and my focus on issues of gender, owe to recent work in feminism. Some
readers may find fewer references to feminist theory than they would
like. I have, however, attempted, rather than situating my analysis within
one or another school of feminist thought, instead to present material
that will be of use to others working with this body of theory. It may be
helpful, however, to say something about one current debate in gender

theory—that over essentialism.[1] While I am generally persuaded of the largely constructed nature of gender-identity, the habit of thinking in essentialist terms is prevalent in ancient Greek culture and leaves its stamp on the material at hand. In this context, because I strive as far as possible to explicate native categories, it has been necessary to speak in what may seem to be essentialist terms about male and female, mortal and divine. I hope it will be clear that these essentialisms are the reflection of ancient Greek thinking rather than my own.

This book had its origin in a Ph.D. thesis entitled "Heroic Configurations of the Feminine in Greek Myth and Cult" (Princeton University, 1989), which was reportedly the only classics dissertation of its year whose title indicated treatment of women's or gender issues.[2] In the intervening years, interest in these topics has increased steadily, and interest in heroines in particular. New books by Brulé, Sourvinou-Inwood, and Dowden on the myths and rituals of girl's transitions were also published at about the same time.[3] Since then, Jennifer Larson has written an invaluable account of the cults of heroines.[4] Not until I began my revisions was I able to take advantage of this body of work, and in so doing, I have tried to strike a balance between recognizing adequately the work of my colleagues and overburdening my own book with cross-citations. Since my approach to the material is often quite different, and since I have not fundamentally changed my views since completing the thesis, I have stopped short of indicating every point of similarity or difference among our positions. I have, however, taken pains to acknowledge all debts.

As the two passages with which I began clearly show, in English usage *heroine* most often means a women of extraordinary qualities, or the female protagonist of a work of fiction or drama. The word *heroine* carries with it an unfortunate freight of associations, suggesting not a powerful being to be invoked and propitiated from beyond the grave, but a frail

---

[1] Classicists will find discussion of the debate on essentialism in David Halperin, *One Hundred Years of Homosexuality* (New York, 1990). For a useful critique of the artificiality of the debate, see Diana Fuss, *Essentially Speaking: Feminism, Nature, and Difference* (New York, 1989). See also John Boswell, "Concepts, Experience, and Sexuality," in *differences* 2 (1990) 67–87.

[2] Amy Richlin in the Women's Classical Caucus newsletter, 1990.

[3] Pierre Brulé, *La Fille d'Athènes: La Religion des filles à Athènes à l'époque classique* (Paris, 1987); Christiane Sourvinou-Inwood, *Studies in Girls' Transitions* (Athens, 1988); Ken Dowden, *Death and the Maiden: Girls' Initiation Rites in Greek Mythology* (London, 1989). Other relevant works that appeared around this time are P.M.C. Forbes Irving, *Metamorphosis in Greek Myths* (Oxford, 1990) and Emily Kearns, *The Heroes of Attica* (*BICS*, suppl. 57) 1989.

[4] Jennifer Larson, *Greek Heroine Cults* (Madison, 1995). Although it appeared as I was completing final revisions, I have tried, wherever possible, to provide readers with cross-references to this work, whose gendered analysis of Greek heroine cults complements my own gendered analyses of Greek heroine myths.

creature requiring rescue by none other than a hero. I decided not to circumvent this problem by the use of the phrase "female hero," since such a phrase reinforces the notion of the female as the special case, the other, the marked category, while the male remains unmarked, normative, universal. In English, a language in which gender is relatively unmarked, gender-specific forms like "poetess" can be rightly rejected as patronizing. In translating from Greek, a language with a high degree of gender specificity, it would be a distortion to deny the existence or significance of gender-marked terms. For these reasons, I have elected to use the word *heroine* as the female equivalent of the male *hero*, confident that it needs not rescue but a chance to speak for itself.

Throughout this work I will use the word *heroine* to mean a heroized female personage or recipient of heroic honors, and secondarily, as a female figure in epic, myth, or cult.[5] Expanding the notion of the heroic in Greek myth to include the feminine will mean considering and perhaps challenging traditional definitions of the hero, which have been largely constructed without reference to heroines.

The very notion of a "heroine" in Greek religious thought has been called into question, and not without reason. Our sources preserve no word for the concept before Pindar, and no single form of the word prevails in the history of the Greek language. It has been suggested that no real distinction exists between goddesses and heroines. Some of this is mere misogyny. In response to this line of argument, we may note Farnell's chivalrous exasperation: "We can repudiate the dictum of a recent unimaginative German writer, that all Greek heroines must have been originally goddesses because no woman could naturally become a heroine."[6] The unnamed German is easily refuted since he fails to account for the fact that women were heroized in the historical period.[7] Those who argue for the nonexistence of heroines on linguistic grounds are harder to refute.[8] Nonetheless, early texts such as the Hesiodic *Catalogue of Women*, as well as passages in Homeric epic, provide us with a working definition of a heroine *avant la lettre*, who is called "wife or daughter of a hero," and who is frequently also the mother of a hero. These figures are clearly set apart from other women and at the same time are distinguished from goddesses.

Those who would deny any clear distinction between heroine and goddess generally do so by contrast with the case of heroes. Greek religious ideology seems to demand a sharp division between hero and god,

---

[5] In so doing, I follow the usage of Angelo Brelich, *Gli eroi greci* (Rome, 1968). See discussion in Chapter 1 of this book.

[6] Lewis R. Farnell, *Greek Hero Cults and Ideas of Immortality* (Oxford, 1921) 56.

[7] See Farnell (1921) 420–26 for a list of historical heroes and heroines.

[8] See the discussion in Chapter 1 of Finley's remarks.

and this demand has been felt even by scholars writing in the twentieth century.[9] Hence the often repeated comment that, aside from Herakles, the *hērōs theos*, and Dionysos, the *theos hērōs*, the lines are hard and fast. Walter Burkert's view may be cited as a recent example:

> In Homeric terms heroes and gods form two quite separate groups, even though they share the nature of Stronger Ones in relation to man. The wall which separates them is impermeable: no god is a hero, and no hero becomes a god; only Dionysos and Herakles were able to defy this principle.[10]

These comments make no mention of any female counterparts and ignore the numerous heroines who make the transition to divinity, both familiar figures like Semele, Ino, Ariadne, and sometimes Iphigeneia, and the more obscure like Molpadia and Phylonoe. Even within the Homeric tradition, to preserve the limits of Burkert's discussion, we find the example of Ino, and perhaps Helen. In the words of Emily Vermeule,

> One of the archaic fictions was that the gulf between men and gods could not be crossed, 'the bronze heaven cannot be climbed' (Pindar, *Pythian* 10.27), but archaic myth was busy providing bridges, or, rather, a double ladder up which some creatures ascend toward immortality and others sink down to the darker mortal condition.[11]

In this book I shall have more to say about upward than downward mobility. Central to my project is the phenomenon of heroines whose myths tell of their transformation to goddesses. These figures may seem at first glance to undermine the integrity of the heroine as a distinct religious category. I believe, however, that the apparent contradiction they pose may be resolved if we take into account the ways in which such transformations are marked. I wish to explore the possibility that, although the distinction between heroine and goddess is clear, there is greater potential for female heroized figures to cross the mortal/immortal divide than for male ones. Although heroines are analogous to heroes in most respects, at the same time they, more regularly than heroes, challenge the well-defended barrier between the divine and the heroic, and by extension, the distinction between mortal and immortal. In structuring my study in this way, I hope not only to elucidate some particulars of Greek mythic thinking and cultic practice, but also to address a central issue of Greek religious ideology, the division between mortal and divine.

---

[9] A. D. Nock long ago pointed out that the distinction between heroic and divine *cult* was not as hard and fast as some scholars believed. See "The Cult of Heroes," *HThR* 37 (1944) 141–73.

[10] W. Burkert, *Greek Religion*, trans. J. Raffan (Cambridge, Mass., 1985) 205. That Herakles and Dionysos were paradigmatic in this regard in antiquity can be seen from a remark of Plutarch contrasting them with Apollo who was always immortal (*Pelopidas* 16.5).

[11] E. Vermeule, *Aspects of Death in Early Greek Art and Poetry* (Berkeley, 1979) 127.

CHAPTER ONE

Heroines and Heroes

"Hero" has no feminine gender in the age of heroes.
—M. I. Finley

WHAT, IF ANYTHING, IS A HEROINE?

The daunting judgment of a distinguished ancient historian that "'hero' has no feminine gender in the age of heroes" might appear to call into question the very phenomenon I propose to study here: heroines in ancient Greek myth and cult.[1] If there is no word for the female counterpart to the hero in the earliest times, how can we speak of the myths and cults of heroines without being anachronistic? How can we speak coherently of heroines at all?

Based on his observation that no word for *heroine* is attested in archaic Greek, Finley concludes that there is no female counterpart to the hero, that heroism, for the Greeks of the archaic period, is impossible for a woman. He makes this observation within the context of Homeric epic, where it is perhaps true. We must not allow this to deter us, however, given that the object of our study is not only *heroism* but rather the entire range of cultural meanings and practices associated with the *myths and cults of heroines*. I will argue, furthermore, that the "feminine gender" of *hero* is recoverable, if not in Homer, then in other archaic texts.

Homeric epic is famous for its silence on the topic of hero cult, but even so it can be made to yield some evidence. The opinion of earlier scholars such as Wilamowitz, Rohde, and Farnell, that hero cult was unknown to Homer or irreconcilable with the worldview of the poems, has been effectively challenged.[2] The most explicit references to cult are in the *Catalogue of Ships* in the *Iliad*, which mentions the tomb of Aipytos (2.604) and offerings to Erechtheus in the temple of Athena (2.546–51),

---

[1] M. I. Finley, *The World of Odysseus*, 2d rev. ed. (New York, 1978) 33. The title of this section calls for apologies to Stephen Jay Gould, "What, If Anything, Is a Zebra?" in *Hen's Teeth and Horses' Toes* (New York, 1983) 355–65.

[2] Ulrich v. Wilamowitz, *Homerische Untersuchungen* (Berlin, 1884); Erwin Rohde, *Psyche* (London, 1950 [Freiburg, 1898]); L. R. Farnell, *Greek Hero Cults and Ideas of Immortality* (Oxford, 1921). An early attack on these views can be found in R. K. Hack, "Homer and the Cult of Heroes," *TAPA* 60 (1929) 57–74.

but hints of cult may be found in other passages.[3] Nagy finds traces of hero cult in the treatment of the dead warrior Sarpedon in *Iliad* 16, suggesting that the tradition preserves knowledge even of practices that cannot be made explicit.[4] It has recently been argued that Homeric epic was directly responsible for the diffusion of hero cult, but this claim has not been universally accepted.[5] The generic requirements of epic limit its usefulness for an archaeology of hero cult, but it has a few things to tell us, not only about heroes, but about heroines as well. Other archaic texts are fortunately more forthcoming, and archaeological evidence shows that heroines are included in some of the earliest manifestations of hero cult.[6] The shrines of Pelops and Hippodameia at Olympia may be of great antiquity, early hero-reliefs show hero and heroine pairs, and a dedication to Helen is perhaps the earliest known Laconian inscription, dating from the second quarter of the seventh century.[7]

The difficulties posed by these kinds of early evidence must be confronted, insofar as they call into question the category of heroine as the female equivalent of hero. In the absence of a word for *heroine* in the earliest texts, we are forced to extrapolate, looking on the one hand toward figures such as the famous women (called "wives and daughters of the best men") whom Odysseus meets in the Underworld in *Odyssey* 11, and on the other hand to some of the more powerful female figures of myth, who in fact share many characteristics with male heroes. But "wives and daughters of the best men" may seem to be less than heroes, while figures like Ino-Leukothea, or Helen, for whom we have some of the earliest evidence, are at times worshiped as goddesses (*theoi*) and

[3] Erechtheus is also mentioned in *Odyssey* 7.80–81, where Athena is said to enter his *pukinon domon* (well-built house). The relationship with the goddess is clear, but the passage does not explicitly refer to cult honors.

[4] G. Nagy, *The Best of the Achaeans* (Baltimore, 1979), and "On the Death of Sarpedon," in *Approaches to Homer*, ed. Rubino and Shelmerdine (Austin, 1983) 189–217, now reprinted in different form in G. Nagy, *Greek Mythology and Poetics* (Ithaca, 1990) 122–42.

[5] The debate can be followed in A. Snodgrass, *The Dark Age of Greece* (Edinburgh, 1971) and *Archaic Greece* (Berkeley, 1980); T. Hadzisteliou Price, "Hero-Cult and Homer," *Historia* 22 (1973) 129–44 and "Hero Cult in the 'Age of Homer' and Earlier," in *Arktouros*, ed. G. Bowersock et al. (Berlin, 1979); J. N. Coldstream, "Hero-Cults in the Age of Homer," *JHS* 96 (1976) 8–17, and *Geometric Greece* (London, 1977).

[6] For an important reconsideration of early evidence for hero cult, see C. Antonaccio, *An Archaeology of Ancestors: Tomb Cult and Hero Cult in Early Greece* (Lanham, Md., 1995).

[7] Hadzisteliou Price (1979) 223–24 considers the Pelopeion at Olympia the "earliest reasonably well-attested heroon," along with the nearby Hippodameion (Paus. 6.20.7). Antonaccio (1995) 176 comes to a more negative conclusion. For the shrine of Helen and Menelaos at Therapne and its dedications, see H. W. Catling and H. Cavanagh, "Two Inscribed Bronzes from the Melenaion, Sparta," *Kadmos* 15.2 (1976) 145–57 and Antonaccio (1995) 155–66. For hero-reliefs, see below, p. 47.

hence seem to be more than heroines.[8] The category of heroine as female counterpart to the hero, poised neatly between mortal and immortal beings, seems threatened.

Despite Homeric reluctance to speak of hero cult, there are clear epic references to heroes who transcend their heroic status. The *Odyssey* refers to one of the most famous of all heroes, Herakles, in a way that emphasizes not his status as a heroized mortal, but his apotheosis.[9]

> Τὸν δὲ μέτ' εἰσενόησα βίην Ἡρακληείην,
> εἴδωλον· αὐτὸς δὲ μετ' ἀθανάτοισι θεοῖσι
> τέρπεται ἐν θαλίῃς καὶ ἔχει καλλίσφυρον Ἥβην,
> παῖδα Διὸς μεγάλοιο καὶ Ἥρης χρυσοπεδίλου.

> And after him I saw the powerful Herakles,
> or rather, his phantom; he himself among the immortal gods
> enjoys the feast, and has as his wife lovely-ankled Hebe,
> child of great Zeus and golden-sandled Hera.

> *(Odyssey* 11.601–4)

Strikingly similar treatment is accorded Leukothea, the divine apotheosis of the heroine Ino:

> Τὸν δὲ ἴδεν Κάδμου θυγάτηρ, καλλίσφυρος Ἰνώ,
> Λευκοθέη, ἣ πρὶν μὲν ἔην βροτὸς αὐδήεσσα,
> νῦν δ'ἁλὸς ἐν πελάγεσσι θεῶν ἒξ ἔμμορε τιμῆς.

> But then Kadmos' daughter, slender-ankled Ino, saw him—
> Leukothea, who once was a mortal endowed with human speech
> but now deep in the sea, has a share of honor among the gods.

> *(Odyssey* 5.333–35)

Although the reference to Herakles' phantom has been treated by some as an interpolation, no one has ever challenged the authenticity of the lines about Ino. We can conclude from this that Homeric epic (or at least the *Odyssey*) has no objection to speaking of heroes—once they have become gods, admittedly a rather exclusive company. The other conclusion to be

---

[8] As Isocrates says about Helen and Menelaos, they are worshiped not as heroes, but as gods (οὐχ ὡς ἥρωσιν ἀλλ' ὡς θεοῖς, *Praise of Helen* 10.63).

[9] Lines 602–4 were rejected by ancient critics as an interpolation, and many modern critics have held the same opinion. See F. Solmsen, "The Sacrifice of Agamemnon's Daughter in Hesiod's 'EHOEAE,'" *AJP* 102 (1981) 355nn. 6 and 7. Mark Griffith, "Contest and Contradiction in Early Greek Poetry," in *Cabinet of the Muses: Essays on Classical and Comparative Literature in Honor of Thomas G. Rosenmeyer,* ed. M. Griffith and D. J. Mastronarde (Atlanta, 1990) 206n.48 remarks that it hardly matters if the passage was interpolated, since "in either case, the effect of the existing text on the reader/listener is the same."

drawn is that the poet of the *Odyssey* is at least as willing to speak of divinized *heroines*, and to speak of them in a way that leaves no doubt about their originally human status. By the some token, the cults of heroines are not likely to have been any more foreign to the Homeric tradition than the cults of heroes.

The phrase "wives and daughters of the best men (*aristoi*)," which introduces the catalogue of heroines in the *Nekyia* (Underworld) section of the *Odyssey* (11.227), provides another clue. The women, who include Alkmene, wife of Amphitryon (266), and Ariadne, daughter of Minos (321–2), are identified by their male relatives, not only husbands and fathers, but also sons (e.g., Herakles 267–68). What is more, all of these male relations—fathers, husbands, sons—are heroes of myth and cult. As Nagy has shown, being "the best" is not merely a characteristic of heroes, but their defining feature. The heroes are the *aristoi*, the best, and *aristos* is the functional equivalent of *hērōs*.[10] To see the relevance of this to our elusive heroines, we may now turn to that other more extensive, although fragmentary, catalogue of female mythic figures, the Hesiodic *Catalogue of Heroines*.

> Νῦν δὲ γυναικῶν [φῦλον ἀείσατε, ἡδυέπειαι
> Μοῦσαι Ὀλυμπιάδε[ς, κοῦραι Διὸς αἰγιόχοιο,
> αἵ τότ' ἄρισται ἔσαν[
> μίτρας τ' ἀλλύσαντο [
> μισγόμεναι θεοῖσ[ιν

> Now sing about the race of women, sweet-voiced
> Olympian Muses, daughters of aegis-bearing Zeus,
> sing of those who were the best of their time
> who loosened their girdles,
> mingling in union with the gods

> (frg. 1 Merkelbach-West)[11]

The poet begins by asking the muses to sing of the *gunaikōn phulon*, the "tribe of women." In the fragmentary lines that follow, these *gunaikes* are described as "the best of their time" (*hai tot' aristai*) who "had intercourse with the gods" (*misgomenai theosin*). In other words, they are not ordinary women, but the same wives and daughters (and mothers) of heroes encountered by Odysseus in the *Nekyia*, along with others of similar mettle.[12] The poet of the *Catalogue*, however, in referring to them as *aristai*,

---

[10] Nagy (1979) esp. 26–41.

[11] The Greek text cited is that of R. Merkelbach and M. L. West, *Fragmenta Hesiodea* (Oxford, 1967). Brackets indicate missing text or conjectural readings.

[12] Another text that brings together male and female figures in an epic setting is *Hom. Hymn* 3 (Apollo) 160, in which the Delian maidens delight their audience by singing a

has given these figures an appellation that clarifies their heroic status. The word *aristai* shows that they are the counterparts of the heroic *aristoi* of the Homeric poems. A more complete examination of the linguistic field shows that Finley did not look far enough. Here, then, is the "feminine gender" of hero in the age of heroes.

The troublesome indeterminacy found in the earliest texts gives way by the early fifth century. By the time of Pindar at the latest, *heroine* is clearly a recognizable category. Pindar's use of the word *hērōis* (ἡρωῒς), in an ode written for Thrasydaios of Thebes, is generally taken to be the earliest extant example of a female equivalent of *hērōs* (ἥρως). Thrasydaios, according to the scholia, won two victories, one in the boy's footrace of 474, and one twenty years later. Most commentators assign this ode to the earlier victory. The word *hērōis* (gen. pl. ἡρωΐδων, *Pythian* 11.7) is unlikely to be a Pindaric invention, especially as it appears in an invocation, generally a conservative element in Greek poetry. A fragment of the Boiotian poet Corinna (*PMG* 664b = Campbell 664b) proclaims her subject as the "merits (or valor) of heroes and heroines" (εἰρώων ἀρετὰς / χειρωάδων).[13] If she was indeed a contemporary of Pindar, as the ancient tradition has it, this is further evidence for the diffusion of a female form of *hērōs* (at least in Boiotia) by the first quarter of the fifth century.[14] Indeed, the fragment from Corinna may be even older than the Pindaric ode, even if we do not accept the later date for the victory of Thrasydaios which it celebrates.

We may also approach the problem of the heroine by examining the criteria for establishing the status of male heroes. For a male hero, in the absence of archaeological evidence such as a named dedicatory inscription, we rely on textual evidence for myth or cult. Heroes are generally considered to be those who have one or more of the following attributes: heroic or divine parentage; a close relationship—erotic, hieratic, or antagonistic—with a divinity in myth; ritual connection with a divinity, such as a place in the sanctuary or a role in the cult; a tradition or evidence of a *hērōon* (hero-shrine) or tomb, sacrificial offerings, or other ritual observance. If we consider those figures generally numbered among male heroes, we will find these criteria to cover most instances. The next step is to see whether we can apply the same criteria to heroines.

As a test, let us consider some figures for whom we have the kind of

---

hymn about the women and men of long ago (μνησάμεναι ἀνδρῶν τε παλαιῶν ἠδὲ γυναικῶν / ὕμνον ἀείδουσιν, θέλγουσι δὲ φῦλ' ἀνθρώπων).

[13] The dialect form used by Corinna, *εἰρώας in the nominative, is not found elsewhere.

[14] Sources for Corinna: Plutarch *Glor. Athen.* 4, 347f–348a; Aelian *Varia Historia* 113.25; Paus. 9.22.3. See J. M. Snyder, *The Woman and the Lyre* (Carbondale, 1989) 41–54 and M. Lefkowitz, *The Lives of the Greek Poets* (London, 1981) 64–65.

archaeological evidence we spoke of above, and see whether the other criteria apply. Both Herakles and Helen have divine parentage, and both have ample evidence of cult.[15] Hyakinthos and Semele are united erotically in myth with divinities, and in each case there is the requisite cult evidence.[16] These two figures could fit equally well into our third category, that of ritual connection with a god, but we can supply other examples, such as Hippolytos and Iphigeneia.[17] This demonstrates the degree to which the various features of heroic myth and cult coincide, regardless of the gender of the heroized figure. Other heroes and heroines languish in comparative obscurity, and in these instances we do not have the evidence on which to base firm conclusions. We can, nonetheless, learn something about heroines by extrapolating even in circumstances in which we have less than complete documentation.

If "heroine" is clearly a recognized category by the early fifth century, it is also true that the category "hero" is an extremely expansive and inclusive one, which changes through time. The term *hērōs*, ostensibly more stable and tangible by virtue of its impeccable Homeric lineage, proves scarcely easier to define than its linguistically more elusive female counterpart. To put our problem in perspective, let us examine attempts by several scholars, all of whom have made considerable contributions to the field, to define *hero*. For Brelich, the hero is "a being venerated in cult and remembered in the myths of the ancient Greeks."[18] That he felt it necessary to defend this definition, stressing the essentially religious character of myth, was a reaction to prevailing tendencies in the study of Greek religion at the time. Kirk offers a more hesitant definition: heroes are "men who had a god or goddess as one parent or who at least walked the earth when such figures existed."[19] With time, the balance has shifted. Unlike Brelich, who is concerned to restore myth to its rightful place in the study of religion, Kirk, writing more than a decade later, takes the importance of myth for granted but is somewhat apologetic about cult, and about the fact that many of the heroes have only the most tangential relation to it.[20] Burkert recognizes two separate senses of

---

[15] For Herakles, see Chapter 2, n. 93; For Helen, see n. 7 above and Appendix. Also L. Clader, *Helen: The Evolution from Divine to Heroic in Greek Epic Tradition* (Leiden, 1976) 63ff.

[16] For Hyakinthos, see S. Eitrem, *RE* 9.1 (1914) 4–16. For Semele's *abaton*: Paus. 9.12.3; her tomb: Paus. 9.16.7. There is only late inscriptional evidence (3rd c. c.e.) for observances at her tomb (*SEG* 19.379 Delphi), but sacrifices are recorded for her in the ritual calendar of Erchia (*SEG* 21.541) discussed below.

[17] Hippolytos: Eur. *Hipp.* 1423ff.; Paus. 3.12.9—*hērōon*; 1.22.1—grave at Athens. Iphigeneia: Eur. *I.T.* 1462ff.; Paus. 1.33.1; 2.35.1; 7.26.5; Chapter 5 below.

[18] "Un essere venerato nel culto e ricordato nei miti degli antichi greci," *Heros: Il Culto greco degli eroi e il problema degli esseri semi-divini* (Rome, 1958b) 14.

[19] G. S. Kirk, *Myth: Its Meaning and Function in Ancient and Other Cultures* (London, 1970) 175.

[20] "The truth seems to be that cultic association and semi-divine ancestry were felt more

"hero," the first being a character in epic, and the second, "a deceased person who exerts from his grave a power for good or evil and who demands appropriate honour."[21] This two-part definition corresponds to the two parts of Brelich's formulation, but the substitution of "epic" for the broader category of "myth" is surprising, given the importance of myth in Burkert's own work.

If heroines, while retaining the right to be called by that name, deviate in various ways from standards of male heroism, it is also true that heroes themselves frequently do so. If female heroized figures frequently slip across the border into divinity, male heroes occasionally do so as well. In other words, although the mass of heroines act or react in ways that deviate from the male heroic norm, nothing they do—allowing for biological difference—is outside the range of possible behavior for heroes.

In what follows, I adopt a flexible definition of "heroine," which corresponds to Brelich's two-tiered definition of "hero." While I insist on the integrity of the category of hero/ine as a distinct religious and mythic phenomenon, I do not consider it to be a privileged one, and in this I follow the usage of the ancient Greeks themselves. While for the purposes of my study, I will admit to finding those heroines who figure in both cult and myth the most interesting, we do not always know who they are. For this reason, the operating definition must be the more inclusive one of "female figure in epic, myth, or cult." As we saw in attempting to bring the heroes of Homer into relation with the practice of hero cult, there is some overlap, and there would likely be more if both archaeological data and literary sources were more complete. Since there is no way of knowing what we are missing, it seems unwise to exclude anything that might allow patterns to emerge. To prevent this inclusivity from becoming imprecision, I will indicate the limits of available evidence for each heroine, signaling those places where conjecture has been allowed to exceed it.

ANCIENT WORDS FOR FEMALE HEROIZED FIGURES

All words used to indicate the female equivalent of hērōs (ἥρως) are in fact derived from this masculine form, which appears in the earliest extant

---

and more, from the time of Homer and Hesiod on, to be the hallmark of important heroes; but that many heroic figures of myth, and not only in the developed literary forms of the Iliad and Odyssey, just belonged to aristocratic families that traced their ultimate genesis to a god or goddess. Such heroes would normally have no individual cult, but were nevertheless conceived as belonging to a generation that still enjoyed the protection of the gods and shared, to a varying extent, their supernatural capabilities, in favoured cases their very blood." Kirk (1970) 176.

[21] Walter Burkert, Greek Religion, trans. J. Raffan (Cambridge, Mass., 1985) 203.

Greek literature. Although in Homer it refers exclusively to living beings, in Hesiod it already implies a recipient of local honor after death (*Works and Days* 159–72). As Chantraine notes, the antiquity of the cult of heroes is shown by the form *ti-ri-se-ro-ei* found on a Mycenaean tablet, which would correspond to **trisērōs*, an otherwise unattested form meaning "the very ancient hero."[22]

Various etymologies for *hērōs* have been proposed. Attempts to connect it with Latin *servare* (to preserve, protect) based on a postulated early Greek form **ηρω-*, are called into question by the discovery of the Mycenaean form mentioned above, which shows no trace of the expected *w*-sound. Chantraine considers more plausible the etymology favored by Pötscher, from the root **ser-* (or perhaps **ier-*), which would connect it with the goddess Hera, as well as with the noun *hōra* (ὥρα), "time, hour, ripeness," and the adjective *hōraios*, (ὡραῖος), "timely, ripe, marriageable." Pötscher argues, based on this etymology, that the hero is the young divine consort of the goddess, with whom he shares the quality of being "ripe for marriage."[23] O'Brien emphasizes the connection with the seasons (*Hōrai*) and the hero as one "who belongs to the goddess of the seasons."[24] Householder and Nagy argue that the hero's association with goddesses, and specifically with *Hēra*, is signaled not only by the etymology of *hērōs*, but also by the language of epic itself.[25]

The feminine form of this word appears for the first time relatively late and is never stabilized in Greek. As mentioned above, the earliest form, ἡρωΐς, -ΐδος (*hērōis, hērōidos*), found in Pindar (*Pyth.* 11.7) and Corinna (*PMG* 664b), remains the most common. This form also gives its name to a Delphic festival in honor of Semele.[26] The names of festivals are usually of great antiquity, which suggests, but cannot prove, that the word predated Pindar by many generations.[27] The form ἡρωΐνη (*hērōinē*)

---

[22] P. Chantraine, *Dictionnaire etymologique de la langue grecque* (Paris, 1968) 2:417. The Mycenaean tablet is PY Fr 1204. See John Chadwick and Lydia Baumbach, "The Mycenaean Greek Vocabulary," *Glotta* 41 (1963) 201, 250.

[23] See W. Pötscher, "Hera und Heros," *RM* 104 (1961) 302–55 for the etymology of ἥρως and its connection with Hera, as well as his "Der Name der Göttin Hera," *RM* 108 (1965) 317–20. D. Adams, "Ἥρως and Ἥρα," *Glotta* 65 (1987) 171–78, taking a different line, sees both words as linked to *Hēbē*.

[24] Joan V. O'Brien, *The Transformation of Hera: A Study of Ritual, Hero, and the Goddess of the "Iliad"* (Lanham, Md., 1993) 113–19.

[25] Fred W. Householder and Gregory Nagy, *Greek: A Survey of Recent Work* (The Hague, 1972) 51–52.

[26] Plut. *Quaest. Gr.* 12, 293c-d and Hesych. s.v. Σεμέλη.

[27] Our sources for the *Hērōis* are all late. Plutarch mentions it in connection with two other Delphic festivals, the *Charila* and the *Septerion*, which were celebrated in succession at eight-year intervals. Burkert (1983) emphasizes the antiquity of the *Septerion*, 127–28. Joseph Fontenrose, *Python: A Study of Delphic Myth and Its Origins* (Berkeley, 1959) 377–78,

appears in Aristophanes, Theocritus, Callimachus, and others, as well as in various inscriptions. In the Hellenistic period, the form ἡρώϊσσα (*hērōïssa*) is particularly popular.[28] This form is used to invoke the intriguing "Founder Heroines" ('Ἡρωϊσῶν Κτιστῶν, *IG* 9.2.1129) on an urn at Volos in Northern Greece. In addition to these, there are many other variations.[29]

This indeterminacy of form and the derivative nature of all words in Greek for "heroine" or "female heroized person" have led some, like Finley, to doubt the existence of heroines as a recognizable class. It can, however, be shown, as I have argued, that despite these linguistic variations, a coherent concept of the heroine can already be identified in the earliest Greek texts. The "wives and daughters of the best men" whom Odysseus meets in the Underworld, and the mothers of heroes whom Zeus lists among his conquests, as well as the women of the Hesiodic *Catalogue* are as much heroines as Achilleus, Odysseus, and Perseus are heroes. And once the word *hērōís* has entered the language, its use accords with expectation. Pindar, who uses it to refer to the daughters of Kadmos and Harmonia, addresses these heroines not only as members of a heroic family, but also as powerful beings worth invoking in a sacral context.

Nonetheless, words for "heroine" appear very rarely in classical authors. Aristophanes uses the word ἡρῷναι (*hērōinai*) to refer to the Clouds, but his meaning is unclear.[30] Epigenes, the writer of Middle Comedy, entitled one of his plays *Hērōínē*, but the few remaining fragments tell us nothing much about it.[31] Later authors who use these words include Plutarch, Lucian, and Strabo. Eventually, the terms *hērōís* or *hē-*

has his own take on the festival, translating *Hērōís* as "Mistress" and connecting it with the name Hera.

[28] We find ἡρῶσσαι in Apollonius of Rhodes (4.1309; 1323; 1358) and ἡρῳσσαι in Nicaenetus (*Greek Anthology* 6.225.1, 6), both referring to the daughters of Libya and Poseidon. For the cult of the Libyan heroines, see J. Larson, *Greek Heroine Cults* (Madison, 1995) 23. Callimachus uses the form ἡρῶσσαι at *Aitia* 66.1 but elsewhere uses ἡρωΐδας (*Hymn* 3.185) and ἡρωίνης (*Hymn* 4.161).

[29] Ἡρωίνη is contracted at times to ἡρῷνη and has the Lesbian variant ἡροῖνα, while ἡρώϊσσα is contracted to ἡρῶσσα. There is also the Cretan hapax, ἡρώασσα, and the second-century form ἡρυς found at Lilybaeum, "about which one can only speculate" (Chantraine [1968] 2:417).

[30] *Clouds* 315. The *hērōinai* are the *Nephelai* (Clouds) of the title. Is it possible that there is a play intended on the word *Nephelē* understood as the name of a woman? This name belongs to at least one heroine, the wife of Athamas and mother of Helle and Phrixos, as well as to the cloud made by Zeus to deflect Ixion from his lustful attack on Hera. The joke, if one is meant, is still not clear. The scholia are mostly concerned with metrical problems posed by the form, although Johannes Tzetzes does gloss it as "heroic women, wives of heroes," ἡρωϊκαί, ἡρώων γυναῖκες (schol. Aristoph. *Clouds* 315).

[31] They are preserved in Athenaeus *Deipnosophistai* 11.469c; 474a; 502e; II.417 Kock.

rōinē come to mean nothing more pronounced than "female protagonist or figure in epic." This is the case for Eustathius, who uses them generously in his commentaries on the *Iliad* and *Odyssey*. In this, his usage parallels the use of the word *hērōs* by the epic poets themselves. Eventually, *hērōs* and *hērōinē* become standard terms for the commemorated dead, frequently appearing in Roman funerary inscriptions of the imperial period.[32]

The same carelessness of usage is visible in the various titles given the Hesiodic catalogue. Although it was usually known as the *Gunaikōn Katalogos* (*Catalogue of Women*), the *Suda* cites it as the *Gunaikōn hērōinōn katalogos* and Tzetzes as the *hērōikē genealogia*, "the heroic genealogy," an ambiguous phrase that leaves some doubt about whose "heroism" is at issue.[33]

ANCIENT SOURCES FOR HEROINES

Where does one go to look for evidence of heroines? The sources consist of material remains—inscriptions, vase paintings, archaeological finds— as well as a great variety of literary sources. These writings range in date from the late eighth or early seventh century B.C.E. to the sixth century C.E. and include the disparate genres of epic, tragedy, guidebook, and lexicon. Not only is our evidence varied in kind, but it also concerns two partly separate matters: the stories told about heroines and heroes, and the cult practices enacted in their honor. The definition of myth and its relation to cult are difficult problems of long standing, which this study does not pretend to solve. In the material at hand, which deals with both myth and cult, the two will frequently be seen to be inextricably entwined. Nonetheless, there is a distinction to be made.

One way of expressing this distinction would be to borrow the terms applied by Jane Harrison to the Eleusinian mysteries, *legomena*, "things said," and *drōmena*, "things done."[34] Inscriptions tell us something about the *drōmena*, as do archaeological sites, when we know how to read them.

[32] A computer search of the corpus of Greek literature (*Thesaurus Linguae Graecae*) yielded less than 100 relevant matches for the search pattern "ηρωι-" of which 48 were found in Eustathius. Additional searches for forms with iota subscript yielded only 7 matches from four authors. A search of inscriptions and papyri yielded approximately five times as many references, almost all from Roman funerary inscriptions.

[33] I take *Gunaikōn hēroinōn katalogos* to mean something like "Catalogue of Heroine Women" rather than "Heroic Women," since *herōis* is not usually used adjectivally, but the distinction is perhaps not pronounced. See M. L. West, *The Hesiodic Catalogue of Women* (Oxford, 1985) 1f.

[34] See *Themis: A Study of the Social Origins of Greek Religion* (Cambridge, 1927) 42, 329 for τὰ δρώμενα and τὰ ἐπὶ τοῖς δρωμένοις λεγόμενα.

Our written sources generally concentrate on the *legomena*, the stories told about gods and heroic figures, which constitute the corpus of Greek myth. It is important to keep in mind, however, that much of what we know about ancient Greek cults and cultic practice comes from written texts, and that in these texts the distinction between myth and cult is frequently pushed to its limits. Here, in the grey area between myths of heroic exploits and descriptions of contemporary cultic practice, we find foundation myths attributing the establishment of these very cults to the heroes and heroines themselves. Thus we have not only myth that may or may not be the reflex of cultic practice, but also myth *about* that cultic practice, which strives to place it within the heroic context. In this way the hero acts as a pivotal figure, at times being heroized as a direct result of a role in the founding of a divine cult (as was the tragedian Sophocles).[35]

Sources for the myths of heroines range over many centuries, creating considerable difficulties of interpretation. Most important for this study are Homeric epic and the Homeric Hymns; the Hesiodic corpus, especially the *Theogony* and the *Catalogue of Women*; lyric poetry, especially Stesichorus and Pindar; tragedy, especially Euripides; Plutarch; Pausanias; Apollodorus; and Antoninus Liberalis. Ancient commentaries known as scholia provide much useful information. Some valuable citations come also from Byzantine and Alexandrian reference works from the fifth to the twelfth centuries C.E.[36] The earliest of these texts, by virtue of their antiquity, may be presumed to provide us with early versions, but the converse is not necessarily true, that later texts must give us only late versions.[37] Pindar, for example, frequently uses unfamiliar versions of myths, but these apparent innovations often turn out on further investigation to be earlier traditions he has chosen to revive.[38] Euripides, a known innovator, may play fast and loose with the plot but usually seems to conform to contemporary practices when he places an aetiology in the mouth of the deus ex machina at the end of so many of his plays.[39] A source like Pausanias reports both on the monuments he sees and on the

[35] He was honored as the *Hērōs Dexiōn* (the receiving hero) for giving house-room to the cult of Asklepios before a temple was built in Athens (*Etym. Mag.* 256.6). On his role see H. W. Parke, *Festivals of the Athenians* (Ithaca, 1977) 135.

[36] Hesychios' *Lexicon* was written in Alexandria in the fifth or sixth century. From Byzantium come the writings of Stephanus Byzantinus, a sixth-century grammarian; Photius' reading notes from the ninth century (known as the "Library"); the *Suda*, a tenth-century lexicon; the twelfth-century *Etymologicum Magnum*; and Eustathius' commentaries on Homer from the same period.

[37] See Brelich, *Gli eroi greci* (Rome, 1958) 23–77 for a detailed discussion of the many problems attendant on the use of ancient sources for myth.

[38] See G. Nagy, "Pindar's *Olympian* I and the Aetiology of the Olympic Games." *TAPA* 116 (1986) 71–88 and Nagy (1979) 71 on Pindar's conservatism.

[39] For the debate on this point, see below n. 53.

local traditions and cult practices surrounding them, both the *legomena* and the *drōmena*. That he is in fact a reliable witness about what he has seen has by now been well established.[40] From this, and from the care he takes to detail his own and other peoples' disagreement with these traditions, we can assume that he is equally reliable about what he has heard.

As the ancient myths and cults become more a focus of antiquarian interest than of piety, authorial emphases change. Later sources are less likely to manipulate the material for political or moral propaganda, although there are some exceptions. (Plutarch is as much a moralist as Pindar.) On the other hand they are more likely to shape it to suit the generic requirements of the project at hand. For example, a compiler of *katasterismoi* will obviously prefer versions of myths in which the heroine is transformed into a star, even when there may be other traditions of greater antiquity. Such a writer may have rewritten myths to fit his requirements, on the analogy of others he knows, but even this does not render a source useless.[41] The late Byzantine commentators and lexicographers are closer in years to our own time than to Homer, but they have nonetheless the benefit of a continuous tradition. Moreover, the genres of commentary and lexicon are inherently conservative, designed as they are to elucidate ancient data. Used with care, they can be illuminating.

The following discussions of specific sources and genres are intended both to provide a brief introduction to some texts that may not be familiar to all readers, and also to indicate my assumptions about the usefulness of these texts for the study of heroines. It includes some works used primarily as sources for the catalogue of heroines at the conclusion of this work.

CATALOGUE POETRY

The largest archaic source for heroines is certainly the Hesiodic *Catalogue of Women*, also known as the *Ehoiai*, from the repeated phrase ἤ'οἵη, "such a one [was] . . ." which introduces many of the heroines.[42] This

---

[40] C. Habicht, *Pausanias' Guide to Ancient Greece* (Princeton, 1985) uses recent archaeological excavations to corroborate Pausanias' assertions. Brelich (1958) 45ff. also considers Pausanias a reliable witness for local traditions.

[41] See P.M.C. Forbes Irving, *Metamorphosis in Greek Myths* (Oxford, 1990) 19–32 for a concurring view. He remarks (32), on the subject of one Hellenistic author, "Everything we have considered so far suggests that if Nicander is innovating he is at least doing it according to the rules and in a framework that does not belong just to his own times, and that therefore even his innovations would be a valuable source for the study of Greek myths."

[42] Merkelbach and West's edition (1967) has now been supplemented by the third edition of West's *Hesiodi Opera* (Oxford, 1990). See also West (1985) for discussion of the character of the work, its structure, and origins.

long (albeit fragmentary) genealogical poem, although in a class by itself, may be compared to other shorter pieces of catalogue poetry in the Homeric corpus, which are also fruitful sources.[43] One of these is the catalogue of gods who mate with mortals at the end of the *Theogony*, long recognized as a bridge to the *Ehoiai*.[44] The possibly interpolated, but certainly archaic, catalogue of heroines in the *Nekyia* (Underworld) episode of the *Odyssey* (11.225–332) is also of great interest, together with the scholia containing commentary by the fifth-century mythographer Pherecydes.[45] In this passage Persephone sends forth the "wives and daughters of the best men" (ἀριστήων ἄλοχοι . . . ἠδὲ θύγατρες, 227) to meet Odysseus. These women are not explicitly called heroines, but neither are their male connections called heroes. Moreover, the use of the key term *aristoi* has its counterpart in the use of *aristai* (frg.1 M-W), as discussed above. Most of their stories involve an encounter with a god, and the inevitable birth of a child. In a short space, Odysseus sees fourteen or fifteen women.[46] The passage reflects obvious delight in the stories for their own sake, as one might expect, considering that the narrator is none other than Odysseus himself.

Other comparable passages show a more purely genealogical interest, such as the brief catalogue of Zeus' erotic adventures in *Iliad* 14, or the *Catalogue of Ships* in *Iliad* 2, with its interest in dynastic information.[47] In this passage the spheres of men and women in the heroic age achieve their greatest point of contact. The role of women is to produce the sons who will be warriors. The woman's moment of crisis in childbirth is the logical precondition of the hero's moment of crisis on the battlefield. Later in

[43] G. McLeod, *Virtue and Venom: Catalogues of Women from Antiquity to the Renaissance* (Ann Arbor, 1991) 9, aims to analyze "all catalogues as attempts to express or critique cultural attitudes towards women." Unfortunately, despite this interesting approach, the sections on ancient Greek poetry contain inaccuracies that limit their usefulness.

[44] Although the *Catalogue* was traditionally considered the work of Hesiod, West (1985) believes that it cannot be the work of the poet of the *Theogony* (127). He argues for a sixth-century, Attic origin (130–36; 164–71). For a view of the Hesiodic corpus as emerging from a tradition of oral composition, see R. Lamberton, *Hesiod* (New Haven, 1988) 11–27.

[45] See West (1985) 127–30 on the connection between the *Theogony* and the *Catalogue of Women*. He also notes the similarity of the *Nekyia* passage with these texts (32 with n. 7).

[46] Tyro (235–59); Antiope (260–65); Alkmene (266–68); Megara (269–70); Epikaste (271–80); Chloris (281–97); possibly Pero, Chloris' daughter (whose story begins at line 287); Leda (298–304); Iphimedeia (305–20); Phaidra, Prokris, and Ariadne (321–25); Maira, Klymene, and Eriphyle (326–27).

[47] The heroines mentioned in *Iliad* 14 (discussed at length in Chapter 3) are Dia (317–18), Danae (319–20), Europe (321–22), Semele and Alkmene (323–25). In the *Catalogue of Ships*, we find the heroines Astyoche (513–15), Astyocheia (658–60), Aglaia (672), Alkestis (714–15), and Hippodameia (742–44). On the relation of the *Iliad*'s "little catalogues" to larger free-standing ones, see R. Hope Simpson and J. F. Lazenby, *The Catalogue of the Ships in Homer's Iliad* (Oxford, 1970) 166.

the poem, the pain of a wound suffered by Agamemnon is compared to the pain of childbirth.[48] In these texts sons and fathers are important, while heroines are treated quite summarily. Nonetheless, the archaic catalogues are helpful in trying to reconstruct the "prehistory" of the heroine.

From these early examples, it is clear that women have a place in heroic poetry as far back as that tradition is accessible to us. These wives and daughters of heroes are important for dynastic reasons, since they provide access to the divine lineage desired by any noble family. Here "biographies" of heroines are stripped to their essentials. In the few lines allotted each woman are the kernels of the more developed myths of seduction, concealment, and disaster that will be represented on vases, staged by tragedians, and eventually collected by the writers of mythological handbooks.

DRAMA

A look at the titles not only of extant tragedies, but also of lost ones shows how important a role was played by the myths of heroines. Figures like Iphigeneia, Medea, Elektra, Helen, and others are the eponymous protagonists of familiar tragedies. Among the lost works of the tragedians are numerous plays bearing the names of heroines.[49] Heroines also play an important role in plays named for the chorus or a male protagonist (e.g., Deianeira in Sophocles' Trachiniai, Phaidra in Euripides' Hippolytos). Sometimes doubt about the actual name of a lost play makes it unclear whether it was named after a female protagonist, a male protagonist, or the chorus: Aeschylus' Semele is also referred to as the Hydrophoroi, and Sophocles' Hippodameia may actually have been called the

---

[48] Iliad 11.268–72. This comparison is given a different emphasis by Euripides' Medea, who says, "I would rather stand three times in the front lines than give birth once." (ὡς τρὶς ἂν παρ' ἀσπίδα / στῆναι θέλοιμ' ἂν μᾶλλον ἢ τεκεῖν ἅπαξ, Medea 250–51). See N. Loraux, "Le Lit, la guerre," L'Homme 21.1 (1981) 37–67, now translated as "Bed and War" in The Experiences of Tiresias, trans. Paula Wissing (Princeton, 1995) 23–43. For a contemporary feminist analysis of this theme, see N. Huston, "The Matrix of War: Mothers and Heroes," in The Female Body in Western Culture, ed. S. Rubin Suleiman (Cambridge, 1985) 119–36, esp. 130–31.

[49] Known titles of plays by Aeschylus contain the names Alkmene, Atalanta, Europe, Helen (three titles), Hypsipyle, Iphigeneia, Kallisto, Penelope, and Niobe; Sophocles: Andromache, Andromeda, Danae, Erigone, Eriphyle, Hermione, Hippodameia, Iphigeneia, Kreousa, Nausikaa, Niobe, Polyxene, Prokris, Tyro, Phaidra, and possibly others; Euripides: Andromeda, Antiope, Hypsipyle, Ino, Melanippe (two titles), and Stheneboia.

Oinomaos.[50] These uncertainties point nonetheless to the importance of heroines in almost all tragedies, regardless of title. In fact, only one extant tragedy, the *Philoktetes* of Sophocles, has no female characters, and in many tragedies they are central.

While a general treatment of female characters in the Greek tragedians lies beyond the scope of this study, the female protagonists of tragedy are of interest to us insofar as they are representations of figures of myth and cult. That Greek tragedy deals almost exclusively with the myths of a few important heroic houses is well known. For our purposes, then, these works are valuable as instantiations of the myths. No myth exists in "pure form," but only in its versions—individual attempts to present, and of necessity to interpret, the themes at hand. The more innovative the poet, the farther away we may find ourselves from early mythic material. Poetic license in the plots of tragedy is not uncommon. Familiar examples are the Sophoclean *Antigone*, radically different from any earlier version, or Euripides' *Medea*, for the first time a deliberate murderer of her children.[51] Neither of these mythic innovations can, however, be assigned with complete confidence to the particular tragedian, who may not have been the first to present the myth in this form. Tragic poets may also, like Pindar, choose at times to exploit an old but less-known variant of the myth in question. Still, tragedians are rarely the sources of first resort for early versions. This is not, however, to dismiss the tragic texts as of no interest for this study. One feature of tragedy that is invaluable for the study of heroine cult, and of Greek religious practice in general, is the frequent use of an *aition*, a brief narrative establishing some religious rite or custom, to achieve closure. These *aitia* are usually put in the mouth of the deus ex machina, whose function it is to resolve the tragic conflict, to predict the future, and to establish cult.[52]

As I have said above, even for a poet like Euripides, whose use of the mythic inheritance is often inventive, the treatment of cultic practice is quite another matter. These cults are in some sense the common property

[50] See *Tragicorum Graecorum Fragmenta*, 2d ed., ed. A. Nauck with suppl. by B. Snell (Hildesheim, 1964).

[51] Sophocles' tragedy is the first extant text in which Antigone dies for the crime of burying her brother. *Iliad* 4.394, where Maion is said to be the son of Haimon, may reflect an earlier tradition in which they live to marry. For Medea, it is impossible to be certain that Euripides was indeed the innovator. See R. Seaford, "Dionysos as Destroyer of the Household: Homer, Tragedy, and the Polis," in *Masks of Dionysos*, ed. Carpenter and Faraone (Ithaca, 1993) 123n.38.

[52] See B.M.W. Knox, "The *Medea* of Euripides," *YCS* 25 (1977) 206. Nagy (1979) 279n.2 stressing the important distinction between explanation and motivation, defines an *aition* as "a myth that traditionally motivates an institution, such as a ritual."

of all Athenians (or all Greeks, where Panhellenic cult is concerned), and a fair degree of accuracy would be demanded by the audience.[53] Although Euripides uses the device of deus ex machina and cult aetiology more consistently than any other tragic poet, he is not the only one to do so.[54] The ending of Aeschylus' *Eumenides* provides the earliest extant example of cult aetiology in tragedy, and Sophocles uses the same technique at the end of the *Oidipous at Kolonos,* to predict the establishment of the hero cult there. The *aition* most important for us is the one at the end of the *Iphigeneia among the Taurians,* which specifies dedications to Iphigeneia at Brauron. Other *aitia* of particular significance are those that close the *Helen,* concerning the burial of Klytemnestra and the divinity of Helen.

While other dramatic forms also drew on the myths of heroines, too little has survived for these to be valuable sources here. The satyr-play at the end of a trilogy often burlesqued the same myths used in the tragedies that preceded it. Aeschylus' lost *Amymone,* for example, was a satyr-play. Comedy as well made use of this material, although often as a parody of a particular tragedy. Aristophanes wrote a play called the *Danaids,* while another practitioner of Old Comedy, Plato, wrote the *Europe, Io,* and *Nux Makra* ("The Long Night," a play about Zeus' encounter with Alkmene). We also have suggestive titles by other dramatists, but the use of mythological themes is more a characteristic feature of Middle Comedy, which exists only in fragments.[55] Philemon, a writer of New Comedy, seems to have continued the use of mythological themes with his *Neaira* and *Nux,* but the practice was on the wane. For visual evidence of this tradition, we can point to a comic scene of the birth of Helen on a fourth-century South Italian vase (figure 1).[56]

---

[53] The argument over the reliability of Euripides' descriptions of ritual continues. See R. Eisner, "Euripides' Use of Myth," *Arethusa* 12 (1979) 153–74 and Christian Wolff, "Euripides' *Iphigeneia among the Taurians*: Aetiology, Ritual, and Myth," *CA* 11 (1992) 308–34. Francis M. Dunn, "Euripides and the Rites of Hera Akraia," *GRBS* 35 (1994) 103–15 takes a particularly sceptical view, concluding that Euripides rewrites "not only character and legend but the 'real world' of cultural practice and belief." I am more in sympathy with Richard Seaford's cautions against underestimating Euripides' traditionalism, *Reciprocity and Ritual: Homer and Tragedy in the Developing City-State* (Oxford, 1994) 285n.21.

[54] W. S. Barrett, ed. *Hippolytos* (Oxford, 1964) 412 notes that every Euripidean play for which we possess a satisfactory ending, except the *Trojan Women,* ends with an *aition.*

[55] Some known titles for Old Comedy: Epicharmos' *Atalantai* and *Medea* (possibly by Deinolochos), Strattis' *Atalante* and *Medea,* and Theopompos' *Althaia* and *Penelope*; Middle Comedy: Alexis of Thurii's *Anteia* (possibly by Antiphanes), *Galateia, Helen, Hesione*; Antiphanes' *Alkestis, Anteia* (possibly by Alexis), *Omphale*; Euboulos' *Antiope, Auge, Europe, Laconians* or *Leda, Medea, Nausikaa, Prokris* (known to be a parody of a tragedy), *Semele* or *Dionysos*; Nikostratos' *Pandrosos*; Philetairos' *Atalanta*; Timokles' *Neaira.*

[56] *LIMC* s.v. "Helene" 5. See A. D. Trendall, *Phylax Vases,* 2d ed. (*BICS* suppl. 19) 1967, 27–28.

Figure 1 Comic scene of the birth of Helen, Apulian bell krater, c. 380–370 B.C.E. (Museo Archeologico, Bari 3899. Photograph Courtesy of Deutsches Archäologishes Institut, Rome).

PAUSANIAS

The second century C.E. travel writer, and a major source of information for ancient cult-sites and religious customs, has a great deal to say about heroines and their role in religious tradition and practice. I have already commented on his reliability, but since he is so frequently cited throughout this study, it is worth saying more about the nature of his contribution. In writing his *Description of Greece*, he is mainly interested in recording monuments and other sites of interest, and the local traditions about them. (He is only interested in Greek antiquities and does not even record contemporary Roman monuments.) As he travels around, he picks up not only many local versions of myths about known figures, but also traditions about local ritual observances. These traditions typically connect a familiar myth to some feature of the local landscape or history. In his chapter on Messenia, for example, Pausanias describes "a place on the coast regarded as sacred to Ino. For they say that she came up from the sea at this point" (4.34.4).[57] The pattern is to "bring the myth home" in some way, and then to use this point of contact as the aetiology for a local monument or observance.

Pausanias faithfully records local claims to the grave of a particular heroine along with the inhabitants' testimony about how she came to be buried there. At times he dissents from the local tradition, usually because he finds an opposing local tradition more plausible:

> [The Megarians] say that there is also a hero-shrine of Iphigeneia; for she too according to them died in Megara. Now I have heard another account of Iphigeneia that is given by the Arcadians, and I know that Hesiod, in his poem *A Catalogue of Women*, says that Iphigeneia did not die, but by the will of Artemis is Hecate . . .[58] (1.43.1)

The insistence on finding the correct location befits a guidebook, but it also emphasizes a central feature of hero cult, its necessarily local, place-bound quality. The efficacy of the heroine or hero as helper emanates directly from the physical remains. The most explicit example in Pausanias concerns the dispute about where to bury the bones of Alkmene (1.41.1), which brings to mind Herodotus' accounts of struggles over the bones of the heroes Orestes (1.67–8), or Adrastos and Melanippos (5.67).[59]

As in the passage cited above, Pausanias often bases his judgments about the authenticity of local tradition on something he has read. The works he cites most in this connection are Hesiod, Homer, Pindar, Stesichorus, and other lyric poets. He also makes extensive use of otherwise unknown local writers, both poets and historians. Thanks to his reading habits, Pausanias is a major source for modern reconstructions of both the *Catalogue of Women* (*Ehoiai*) and the Great Catalogue (*Megalai Ehoiai*) attributed to Hesiod.[60]

---

[57] Trans. W.H.S. Jones and H. A. Ormerod, *Pausanias' Description of Greece*, vol. 2 (Cambridge, Mass., 1920). Pausanias himself reports a conflicting tradition at 1.42.7, where the Megarians claim that it was on *their* shores that Ino was washed up. See Gregory Nagy, "Theognis and Megara: A Poet's Vision of His City," in Thomas J. Figueira and G. Nagy, *Theognis of Megara: Poetry and the Polis* (Baltimore, 1985) 79–80 on this variant tradition.

[58] Translation adapted from Jones.

[59] See D. Boedeker, "Hero Cult and Politics in Herodotos: The Bones of Orestes," in C. Dougherty and L. Kurke, eds., *Cultural Poetics in Archaic Greece: Cult, Performance, Politics* (Cambridge, 1993) 164–77.

[60] See Habicht (1985) 132–34, 142–44, on Pausanias' literary tastes and sources of information.

Pausanias frequently speaks of the tombs of mythic women, but only occasionally mentions cult observances connected with them, and it is hard to say if they are in fact hero-shrines (*hērōa*). Pausanias uses the word only occasionally, in most cases preferring the word *mnēma*, or "memorial," with its overtone of commemoration.[61] He frequently uses the word *taphos* (tomb or burial) interchangeably with *mnēma*, to avoid repetition, which he is at greater pains to do than classical Greek authors. He also uses these two terms in alternation (presumably to preclude the idea of a joint burial), when he describes the graves of those who, hostile to each other in life, are nonetheless buried in close proximity.[62] In fact, we know very little about the form of hero-shrines, and particularly about heroines' shrines. A recent work on three temples to Artemis in Attica argues against the notion of an architectural feature common to all, an inner room that has been called the *adyton*, with a common function in honor of the heroine Iphigeneia. Even in this case, in which there is some archaeological evidence, interpretation is difficult.[63]

In Pausanias, mention of heroines is not limited to burial but may include dedications and offerings to them, or the dedications or festivals they themselves established in honor of the gods. Occasionally, the object Pausanias discusses is not only a monument but itself a carrier of mythic information. There are two works of art of particular relevance for heroines, each of which he describes at length. These are the "Kypselos chest" in the temple of Hera at Olympia (5.17.5–5.19.10), and Polygnotos' paintings of the *Ilioupersis* (Sack of Troy) and the *Nekyia* (Odysseus' visit to the Underworld) at Delphi (10.25–31), great pictorial summaries of myths of gods and heroes which we know only from his descriptions. Several mythic scenes are also shown on the throne at Amyklai (3.18.9–16). Pausanias only rarely uses works of visual art to support his arguments, tending rather to see them as objects requiring interpretation, although he is at great pains to record the information they contain.[64]

---

[61] In Pausanias only the following heroines are explicitly said to have a *hērōon*: Andromache (1.11.2), Ino (1.42.7), Iphigeneia (1.43.1), Hyrnetho (2.28.7), Kyniska (3.15.1), and Plataea (9.2.7).

[62] For example, he speaks of the tomb (*taphos*) of Phaidra, located near the monument (*mnēma*) of Hippolytos (2.32.4). In the same way, at 2.21.7, he distinguishes the grave (*mnēma*) of Gorgo from that (*taphos*) of Gorgophone, who, as the daughter of Perseus, is presumably opposed to her by reasons of etymology as well as lineage. (Her name, "Gorgonslayer," commemorates her father's most famous exploit and calls ironic attention to their proximate burial.)

[63] See M. B. Hollinshead, "Against Iphigeneia's Adyton in Three Mainland Temples," *AJA* 89 (1985) 419–40.

[64] For a reconstruction of Kypselos' chest, see K. Schefold, *Myth and Legend in Early Greek Art*, trans. A. Hicks (New York, [1966]) 72–73. See also H. A. Shapiro, "Old and

Pausanias' descriptions are accompanied by a great deal of mythological commentary, which is almost always concretely bound to the physical context. His goal is to describe a landscape, and it is a landscape marked by the works of mortals. But it is also a landscape inhabited by gods and heroes, and most of the human monuments he describes are attempts at communication with the divine, part of the dialogue between mortal and immortal which is an essential feature of Greek religion. Given a general tendency to translate female mythic figures into natural phenomena (e.g., the Pleiades) or features of the landscape (e.g., Niobe), it is instructive to note that for Pausanias they are also firmly embedded in a physical space that is decidedly human in origin.[65]

OTHER GRAECO-ROMAN SOURCES

Sources from the Hellenistic period and beyond fall in general into two main categories: works that are primarily antiquarian in character, like that of Pausanias, and those that deal exclusively with mythology. Among the antiquarian writings, the works of Plutarch, dating from the end of the first to the beginning of the second centuries C.E., are particularly important. Especially valuable for our purposes are the *Quaestiones Graecae* (Greek Questions), and some of the lives, particularly those of mythic figures, like the *Life of Theseus*. Innumerable valuable citations from ancient texts otherwise lost are preserved for us by Athenaeus, whose collection of table talk, the *Deipnosophistai* (Sophists at Dinner), dates to the end of the second century C.E.

Notable among the mythological works is the *Bibliothēkē* (Library), which bears the name of Apollodorus. Apparently compiled in the second century C.E., it is a compendium of familiar myths along with some unusual variations. The considerably more erratic and idiosyncratic *Fabulae* of Hyginus (2nd c. C.E.) provide intriguing variants, but one is often hard-pressed to know what to make of them. This work shows the Alexandrian influence in its organization into headings such as *Qui filios in*

New Heroes: Narrative, Composition, and Subject in Attic Black-Figure," *CA* 9 (1990) 138–40. On Polygnotos, see M. D. Stansbury-O'Donnell, "Polygnotos' *Iliupersis*: A New Reconstruction," *AJA* 93 (1989) 203–15.

[65] F. Pfister, *Der Reliquienkult im Altertum* (Giessen, 1909) 1:328–65, lists natural phenomena connected with heroes. These are for the most part not the results of actual transformations but are landmarks connected with and occasionally created by the heroes themselves. Heroines are frequently associated with springs, which they create either deliberately, like Atalante striking her spear against the rock (Paus. 3.24.2), or inadvertently, like the weeping Niobe (Pherec. in schol. T *Iliad* 24.617). For Niobe herself as a rocky outcropping, see Paus. 1.21.3. See Forbes Irving (1990) passim.

epulis consumpserunt (Those who ate their children for supper), and the unfortunately missing *Quae immortales cum mortalibus concubuerunt* (Goddesses who slept with mortals). The Hellenistic interest in collecting and codifying myth also led to the development of specialized genres, among which the two most useful for the study of heroines are the books of *Katasterismoi* and Metamorphoses. The former genre, accounts of catasterism, i.e., transformation into constellations, goes back at least as far as Eratosthenes (3rd c. B.C.E.), although the fragments that survive under his name are apparently not genuine. The Metamorphosis tradition can be traced at least as far as the second-century poet Nicander, although this part of his work does not survive. Ovid takes off from this tradition in his *Metamorphoses*, although his poem transcends the dry nature of the genre. More typical is the work of the same name by Antoninus Liberalis, a writer of the second or third century C.E. who frequently cites Boios or Nicander as his source.[66]

We have alluded above to the problems inherent in the use of these materials for our study. Works centered around metamorphosis or catasterism naturally tend to emphasize the most dramatic aspects of heroic mythology, those involving crises in the mortal sphere which can only be resolved by drastic divine intervention, usually resulting in the translation to another sphere. In such contexts the solution to the problem of mortality is translation into the animal or vegetable world, with species-continuity replacing the continuing life of the individual, or transformation into astronomical phenomena whose enduring nature is obvious.

These specific interests act to narrow the range of action available to a mythic figure. Female figures are especially prone to this kind of presentation, perhaps because of their limited sphere of action in the world outside of myth.[67] Orion becomes a constellation, but this is only a small part of his very rich mythic tradition. By contrast, many heroines, deprived of the ability to defend themselves, can hope for nothing better than a transformation as a way out of present difficulties. For those who would interpret mythic treatment of the heroine, such material is especially problematic. That heroines are frequently transformed in this manner is a point to which I will return.[68] On the other hand, once books of metamorphoses become popular, these transformations of heroines may take on a certain decorative nature that obscures the degree to which we are in the presence of authentic mythic material.

[66] For a discussion of this tradition, see Forbes Irving (1990) 19–36.

[67] F. I. Zeitlin, "Configurations of Rape in Greek Myth," in *Rape*, ed. S. Tomaselli and R. Porter (Oxford, 1986) 122–51, 261–64 (notes) explicitly connects metamorphosis with the woman's flight from sexual violence (123).

[68] See Chapter 3, below, pp. 96, 101.

CATEGORIES OF HERO AND HEROINE

For many scholars of Greek religion, the starting point for understanding hero cult is the proper categorization of heroes. There has been no more enthusiastic or influential proponent of this approach than Farnell. In *Greek Hero Cults and Ideas of Immortality*, he offers the following categories: 1) heroes and heroines of divine origin or hieratic type, with ritual legends or associated with vegetation ritual; 2) sacral heroes and heroines; 3) heroes of epic and saga; 4) cults of mythic ancestors, eponymous heroes, and mythic oecists [city-founders]; 5) functional and culture-heroes; 6) cults of real and historic persons.[69]

The list of categories, some based on origin and some on function, recalls Borges' Chinese Encyclopedia, in which the classifications "animals belonging to the Emperor" and "animals which from a distance resemble flies" are given equal weight, and the frame of reference constantly shifts.[70] It is nonetheless of great interest as an attempt to describe hero cult and a potential source of information about heroines, compiled by a scholar of profound learning. Unfortunately, the conclusions one can draw from Farnell's work are somewhat limited by the incompleteness of his data. Several of Farnell's categories overlap, and the arbitrary assignment of a figure to one group or another is often unsatisfying, while some heroines whom we would expect to find are excluded. In almost every category, heroes outnumber heroines by a significant margin, as might be expected. Only in the first group, "heroes and heroines of divine origin or hieratic type, etc.," is this trend reversed. Here female figures outnumber male, approximately two to one. Although this finding is suggestive, certain features of Farnell's organization seriously limit the value of his categories. Why, for example, is Helen placed among the "heroes of epic and saga" when she might equally well be considered a hero of divine origin? Why does Penelope appear neither among heroes of epic and saga, nor anywhere else? For that matter, why is Klytemnestra omitted? Hippodameia, here among the ancestors, eponymous heroes, and oecists, could also be placed among sacral heroines as founder of the *Heraia* (for it is in this category that Farnell has placed Physkoa, whom Pausanias mentions almost in the same breath). And where is Aithra, whose role in the cult of Athena Apatouria ought to give her a place? Many eponymous heroines mentioned by Pausanias are omitted from the list of ancestors, eponymous heroes, and oecists. The task of classification is a difficult one, and one can only regret that Farnell did not make explicit his principles of inclusion.

[69] Farnell (1921). See discussion throughout, and the lists on pp. 403–26.

[70] Jorge Luis Borges, *Other Inquisitions*, trans. Ruth L. C. Simms (New York, 1968) 103.

The problem lies partly in the necessity of integrating information that, leaving aside tremendous variations in antiquity and reliability, simply does not always answer the same questions. How are we to harmonize myth or saga recounting the adventures of heroes and heroines as living beings, with local tradition about the acts of these figures in religious contexts, as founders of cults and festivals, as well as the evidence of honors accorded these figures after their death? This information may take the form of aetiologies of the classical period, or of local traditions recounted by Graeco-Roman antiquarians, or it may come to us from the realia—inscriptions, temples, or other dedications. A heroine of epic like Helen may be the recipient of both heroic and divine cult honors, as we know from a combination of extant inscriptions and local traditions from different parts of the Greek world. Choosing an original version or meaning is futile, and it is therefore usually impossible to assign a single "value" to any heroic figure.

The least ambiguous of Farnell's categories is that of "real and historical persons." While the individual figures, for the most part, fall outside the scope of this study, some useful inferences can be drawn. This list contains 93 heroized individuals, of whom 13 are female. This ratio certainly corresponds to our expectations, given the restricted role of women in the Greek world. Accordingly, the heroines in this list are mainly Hellenistic queens and hetairai. The exception is the poet Sappho, who like other poets of the archaic and classical periods, received heroic honors.[71]

Pfister, writing a decade before Farnell, makes less of an attempt to categorize types of heroes. His interest is in the cult of relics of heroes (and its similarity to the cults of Christian saints), and so he concentrates on the nature of the remains, and their location. He does list graves of eponymous heroes, but it is interesting to note that none of the heroines in the list appears in Farnell's list of eponymous figures. His larger list of hero-shrines accompanied by a tomb includes figures from four of Farnell's six categories, as well as some, like Penelope, whom Farnell omits entirely. His most inclusive list of heroes' graves includes those of 80 heroines, of whom only 23 coincide with Farnell's 52 nonhistorical heroines.[72]

[71] See Farnell (1921) 367 on the cult of Sappho on Lesbos. For poets as heroes, see Brelich (1958) 320–22 and Nagy (1979) especially 279–308. Other female poets who might have received cult honors are Telesilla and Corinna, who are not mentioned here. See Paus. 2.20.8–9 for the bravery of Telesilla, and the relief commemorating it, and 9.22.3 for the tomb of Corinna.

[72] Pfister's list of heroes' graves seems to include every instance in which Pausanias records a *mnēma* or a *taphos* (two words he uses almost interchangeably for "grave"). Farnell applies a more complicated, and at times elusive, standard. For eponymous heroes and heroines, see Pfister (1909) 1:279–89; for hero-shrines with tomb, Pfister (1912) 2:450–55; for graves of heroes and heroines, 2:627–40.

The approach of Brelich, instead of seeking to establish the "essential nature" of the hero, examines roles and functions, recognizing that they may be multiple and overlapping. He considers heroes in their relation to a number of mythic and religious themes, both as figures in myth or epic taking part in a variety of relationships—social, familial, and religious—and as the focal points for cults embodying many of the diverse aspects of Greek ritual practice. In considering the relation of a particular hero to healing, to choose one example, he discusses in turn the hero as a healer in myth, and the role of healing in the cult of that hero. His approach stresses both the importance of the distinction and the necessity of bringing together the two kinds of evidence.[73] This is an especially important point for the study of heroines, as will become clear if we look at two areas of heroic activity—invention and city-founding. The prestige of both these kinds of activities derives from the special honor accorded to those who did something for the first time.[74] So pervasive was the interest in "being the first," that it has been said that in Greek culture, "everything had to have an 'inventor.'"[75]

The range of action permitted heroines in myth is perhaps not as restricted as the actual scope of women's lives in the archaic and classic periods.[76] It is, however, more limited than that allowed male heroes. Let us start with the example of city-founding. Founders of cities, as we know, are often honored with burial in the agora and other observances. These honors, also given to mythic and historical ancestors and legislators, were the most notable exception to the general Greek prohibition against burial within the city, and one that lasted until the end of Greek antiquity.[77] The sacral aspect of city-founding is reflected in myth and in

[73] See Brelich (1958) 79 for elucidation of this principle; 113–18 for its application to healing. See also Deborah Lyons, "Manto and *Manteia*: Prophecy in the Myths and Cults of Heroines," in *Sibille e linguaggi oracolari*, ed. I. Chirassi Colombo and T. Seppilli (Pisa, forthcoming).

[74] See Brelich (1958) 27 for the importance of the first time; 166–77 for the hero as *protos heuretes*, "inventor" or "originator."

[75] M. Robertson, "Adopting an Approach I," in *Looking at Greek Vases*, ed. T. Rasmussen and N. Spivey (Cambridge, 1991) 4.

[76] The topic of the position of women in archaic and classical Greece lies for the most part outside the scope of this study. For an account of the debate on seclusion, see I. Savalli, *La Donna nella società della Grecia antica* (Bologna, 1983), and M. Arthur, "Review Essay: Classics," in *Signs* 2.2 (1976) 382–403. Overviews of women's economic and legal status include D. M. Schaps, *Economic Rights of Women in Ancient Greece* (Edinburgh, 1979); R. Just, *Women in Athenian Law and Life* (London, 1989); and R. Sealey, *Women and Law in Classical Greece* (Chapel Hill, 1990).

[77] Roland Martin, *Recherches sur l'agora grecque* (Paris, 1951) 194–95. F. de Polignac, *La Naissance de la cité grecque* (Paris, 1984) 132, argues that these founder-tombs need not all have been new installations. Some may have been ancient burials rediscovered and attributed to hero-founders. See Antonaccio (1995).

religious practice.[78] It is also the case that glorious enterprises could be made more glorious by the imprimatur of a heroic name, in which case the foundation of a city becomes just another deed easily inserted into the hero's busy program. For these reasons it is difficult to decide if one becomes a hero by founding a city, or if one founds a city because one is a hero and that is what heroes do. When all we have is the name of an eponymous hero, of whom we have heard nothing before, it is tempting to assume that the hero has been trumped up for the occasion.[79]

This indeterminacy has particular consequences for our interpretation of eponymous heroines. Given the unlikelihood of a woman having led a colonial expedition, we do not expect to find many heroines as city-founders, nor do we. The inscription in honor of the "Founder Heroines" (*Hērōissai Ktistai*, mentioned above) is suggestive, but relatively late in date, and its use of the plural may also signal a symbolic collectivity rather than any specific historical figures. The degree of women's participation in Greek colonization is a matter of debate.[80] Pausanias has two examples of female oecists: Leprea, founder of Lepreus (5.5.5), and Antinoe, daughter of Kepheus (8.8.4), who in obedience to an oracle and guided by a snake, moves the city of Ptolis to a new site. Antinoe, by virtue of not being eponymous, may appear the more convincing of the two. Her foundation story, moreover, is carefully buttressed by sacral and mystical details that would make female participation more palatable. What is more, Pausanias' account suggests that she may have received heroic honors for her role, as he tells us that her tomb was to be found among other famous graves near the theater in Mantineia (8.9.5).

Pausanias provides other examples of eponymous heroines, particularly in Boiotia, where the cities are more often named for women than men (9.1.1), but he gives them no explicit role in foundation.[81] He also

---

[78] See Marcel Detienne in the *Annuaire. Ecole pratique des Hautes Etudes* 94 (1985–86) 371–80, on Apollo as the city-founding god. For the role of Delphi in colonization, see H. W. Parke and D.E.W. Wormell, *The Delphic Oracle* (Oxford, 1956) 1:49–81; Joseph Fontenrose, *The Delphic Oracle* (Berkeley, 1978) passim; Carol Dougherty, *The Poetics of Colonization: From City to Text in Archaic Greece* (New York, 1993).

[79] According to Martin (1951) 195, the eponymous hero is "le produit d'une réfection de la tradition religieuse" (the product of a remaking of the religious tradition) in response to internal political events or major external ones. De Polignac (1984) 132ff. also suggests that sometimes it was necessary to invent the mythic founder.

[80] See A. J. Graham, "Religion, Women and Greek Colonization," in *Religione e città nel mondo antico* (Rome, 1984) 293–314.

[81] Heroines who give their names to cities include Abia, Alalkomenia, Amphissa, Andania, Araithyrea, Arene, Arne, Boura, Dyme, Eirene, Ephyre, Harpina, Helike, Hyrmina, Ismene (?), Kombe, Kyrbia, Kyrene, Lampsake, Larisa, Larymna, Messene, Mothone, Mykene, Myrine, Nemea, Nonakris, Oichalia, Oinoe, Physkoa, Psothis, Side, Sparte, Tanagra, Thebe, Therapne, Thespia, Thisbe, Thyia (2), Triteia. Others are said to

considers somewhat critically the tradition of an eponymous Mykene (2.16.3–4), citing both "Homer in the *Odyssey*," i.e., the *Nekyia* in book 11, and the *Great Ehoiai* as sources, and rejects the idea of a male eponym Mykeneus son of Sparton, on the grounds that although the Laconians have a statue of Sparte, they would be very surprised to hear of a Sparton. Here we have a chance to see the material evaluated not by modern notions of plausibility, but by local, more or less ancient ones. From Pausanias' discussion we see that while female founders of cities, mythic or not, may have been rare, the idea of an eponymous heroine caused no trouble. Indeed, in instances such as this, a female eponym could be more credible than a male one, if the sources concurred.[82]

Perhaps our best evidence for the political and religious importance of an eponymous heroine comes again from Pausanias, in his account of the founding of Messene in 369 B.C.E. after the liberation of Messenia by Epaminondas. The importance of Messene the daughter of Triopas for the community called by her name is both religious and political. She, together with Polykaon, was supposed to have consecrated the precinct of Zeus on Mt. Ithome and for this reason was given heroic honors (4.3.9). While the role of cult-founder is a more frequent one for heroines than that of city-founder, Messene was also given at least a symbolic role in the refoundation of the Messenian polity.[83]

As Pausanias describes the ritual surrounding the foundation of the city, it is here that Messene assumes preeminence. When the Messenians summoned the heroes to return to their midst, Messene was first and foremost, and only the hero Aristomenes was summoned with greater enthusiasm (4.27.6). Pausanias also records among the sights of Messenia the temple of Messene and her image of gold and Parian marble (4.31.11).

Few if any heroine-inventors are recorded. I have found only three. According to a certain Agallis, a learned Corcyraean woman, Nausikaa invented ball-playing (Athenaeus 1.14d). This is a perfect example of Robertson's dictum: as the first to appear playing ball in Greek literature (*Odyssey* 6.100), she must be its inventor. The other examples are rather obscure. Boudeia is associated with the invention of the plough (schol. *Iliad* 16.572). She is also known as Bouzuge, a talking name (Ox-Yoke) apparently related to this invention (schol. AR. 1.185), but the exact na-

---

give their names to demes (Aglauros, Hekale, Melite), tribes (Hyrnetho, Milye), and the gates of Thebes (Elektra). On the eponymous heroines of demes, see E. Kearns, *The Heroes of Attica. BICS* suppl. 57 (1989) 101–2.

[82] Pfister (1912) 2:279–89, lists about 60 examples of graves of eponymous heroes, 10 of whom are actually heroines.

[83] The subject of heroines as cult-founders is discussed in Chapter 5 (with appendix). See Carolyn Dewald, "Women and Culture in Herodotus' *Histories*" in *Reflections of Women in Antiquity*, ed. Foley (New York, 1981) 91–125, especially p. 110–12; 122.

ture of her contribution is unclear. The third example, Phemonoe, is doubly important as the first Pythia and the inventor of hexameter (Paus. 10.5.7). But as with city-founding, myths of invention may attract heroines even if only as passive participants. One such tradition links a heroine to the invention of writing. According to Skamon in his fourth-century book on inventions, the alphabet was named by its inventor, Aktaion king of Attica, in honor of his daughter Phoinike who died young.[84] In this instance, the letters gain prestige from the name of the princess, while in turn giving honor to her.

In our investigation of the nature of heroes and heroines, two questions alternately claim our attention: "What do heroes do?" and "What does one do to become a hero?" The relationship between these two questions is complicated by the fact that we are dealing with a phenomenon that is already old at the time of our first sources, and that continues to be vigorous into the late Hellenistic period. This means not only that the old traditions about heroes are being maintained, and that observance continues, but that new heroes are still being made throughout the period in which many of our sources were written. It is difficult to say exactly when hero cult ceased in antiquity, especially since it can be seen to reappear in the form of emperor cult in certain parts of the Greek east.[85] There are those who would even see its survival in the Christian cult of saints.[86]

It seems likely that the Greeks were generally comfortable with a flexible notion of what heroes were and did, and that this notion allowed a certain amount of revision and reevaluation backward and forward in time. The earliest and most venerable source of information about heroes was the *Iliad*, perhaps supplemented by other epics and especially the Hesiodic Catalogues, and it was easy to extrapolate the behavior of later heroes on the basis of these poems. If the Greeks knew their city-founders as the inhabitants of heroic tombs in the agora, then obviously founding cities was something heroes did. Some of this flexibility comes from the fact that, although in the historical period people could only be heroized after their death, the earliest traditions about heroes concerned people who were very much alive.

---

[84] *FGrH* 476 F 3 = Photius and *Suda* s.v. Φοινικήϊα γράμματα. See J. Svenbro, *Phrasikleia: An Anthropology of Reading in Ancient Greece*, trans. J. Lloyd (Ithaca, 1993 [Paris, 1988]) 8–9, 82–86.

[85] On cults of emperors, see S.R.F. Price, *Rituals and Power: The Roman Imperial Cult in Asia Minor* (Cambridge, 1984).

[86] Pfister, for example, follows pagan examples with Christian ones throughout his study of *Reliquienkult*. It is precisely in the matter of relics that the comparison is most tempting. See P. Brown, *The Cult of the Saints* (Chicago, 1981) 5–6 for a critique of this idea.

The prestige offered by a heroic ancestor or antecedent is clear, but when an invention or other "first" is ascribed to a hero the prestige is in some sense reciprocal, as with the *Phoinikeia grammata*. The same holds true for the establishment of a religious institution: on the one hand, the heroine is magnified by her role in founding a festival or dedicating a temple, and on the other, so important an undertaking as temple-foundation must, of necessity, have been carried out by an important personage. There is little to be gained by trying to establish the order of these events, but taken together they give us a very clear idea of what the Greeks expected of their heroes once they had made them.

What, specifically, did the Greeks expect of their heroines? That is the question to which we now turn, examining both the place of heroines in the ritual life of the individual and the community, and the cultural meanings of the myths told about them.

CHAPTER TWO.

Heroines and Mortals

Aretaphila, of Cyrene, was not born long years ago, but
in the crucial times of Mithridates; she displayed, however,
a bravery and an achievement which may well rival the
counsel of the heroines of olden time.
—Plutarch *On the Bravery of Women* 255e,
trans. F. C. Babbitt

EXEMPLARY HEROINES

What was the significance of heroines for Greeks of the archaic and classical periods? We cannot hope to arrive at a single answer, since cultural
meanings shift and change over time, as do the sources of available information. I have already argued that we can only hope to make sense of the
category of heroine (or hero for that matter), by treating it as a distinct
mythic and religious category, not reducible to any other. The phenomenon of heroic myth and cult becomes nonsense when one tries to reduce
these figures to gods (faded) or mortals (elevated), yet it can only be fully
understood with reference to these categories. While the remaining chapters explore several facets of relations between the heroic and the divine
spheres, this chapter concerns the interaction of heroines and mortals.
What did the living expect from heroines? What did they give and what
did they hope to get in return? I will attempt to answer these questions by
examining the ritual practices associated with heroines, the honors they
were given, the names by which they were known, the myths told about
them, and the representations of those myths in poetry, prose, and even
on objects of daily use. All of these elements can help create a more
complete picture of the cultural significance of heroines.

Despite the centuries that separate them, Homeric epic and Athenian
tragedy each appeal to the idea of the heroine as exemplary, a standard of
comparison. While the Homeric passage that comes most readily to
mind emphasizes the cleverness and beauty of the heroines, the tragic
examples stress extremity—the horrible crimes committed by or against
them. In each case the exemplary heroine is something of a straw
woman, set up only to be knocked flat by the superior virtue or the
greater enormity of the object of the comparison. But there is a further

twist—the figure to whom the heroines of old are compared and found
wanting is herself a heroine. Let us look at some examples.

In the second book of the *Odyssey*, Antinoös rebuts Telemachos, who
has just called for justice and aid against his mother's suitors, currently
eating him out of house and home. This spokesman for the suitors invokes Penelope's cleverness and the trick she uses to confound their
hopes:

τὰ φρονέουσα ἀνὰ θυμὸν, ἅ οἱ πέρι δῶκεν Ἀθήνη
ἔργα τ' ἐπίστασθαι περικαλλέα καὶ φρένας ἐσθλὰς
κέρδεά θ', οἷ' οὔ πώ τιν' ἀκούομεν οὐδὲ παλαιῶν,
τάων αἳ πάρος ἦσαν ἐϋπλοκαμῖδες Ἀχαιαί,
τυρώ τ' Ἀλκμήνη τε ἐϋστέφανός τε Μυκήνη·
τάων οὔ τις ὁμοῖα νοήματα Πηνελοπείη
ᾔδη· ἀτὰρ μὲν τοῦτο γ' ἐναίσιμον οὐκ ἐνόησε.

She may rely too long on Athena's gifts—
talent in handicraft and a clever mind;
so cunning—history cannot show the like
among the ringleted ladies of Akhaia,
Mykene with her coronet, Alkmene, Tyro.
Wits like Penelope's never were before,
but this time—well, she made poor use of them.

(*Odyssey* 2.116–22 trans. Fitzgerald)[1]

Skill in weaving and cleverness are both properly identified as the gifts of
Athena, and elsewhere (*Iliad* 9.389–90, e.g.) these talents cause women to
be compared to goddesses, but here the comparison is to "those who were
before," the heroines of old.[2] And these are an illustrious company—
the eponymous heroine of the city of Agamemenon, the mother of the
great Panhellenic hero Herakles, and Tyro, less well known to us, but
recognizable to the epic audience as the mother of Pelias and Neleus, and
whose story is told in some detail in the Catalogue of Heroines in the
Underworld (*Od.* 11.235–59). Alkmene is also mentioned in the catalogue (266–68), but otherwise none of these heroines reappears in the
Odyssey. They are part of the body of basic knowledge that a listener
would bring to an epic performance. It is interesting that while Penelope
is famous for her cleverness, precisely because of the weaving-trick to

---

[1] R. Fitzgerald, trans., *Homer. Odyssey* (Garden City: N.Y., 1963).

[2] See Marylin A. Katz, *Penelope's Renown: Meaning and Indeterminacy in the Odyssey*
(Princeton, 1991) 4–5 on this passage and on Penelope as "exemplar of her sex." Although
G. Nagy, "Mythological Exemplum in Homer," in *Innovations in Antiquity*, ed. Hexter and
Selden (New York, 1992) 311–31, prefers to speak of "exempla" rather than exemplars, his
article is relevant here.

which Antinoös refers, the heroines held up as standards are not (as far as we know) famous for any particular cleverness. Like heroes, heroines are expected to be exceptional in wit and beauty, by definition smarter and more beautiful than ordinary women.[3]

There is a mild irony in the comparison of Penelope with "heroines of old," since for the audience of epic, as for us, she herself is certainly also a "heroine of old," even if she belongs to a later heroic generation. A second-century B.C.E. epitaph from Didyma, calling Gorgo, the deceased woman, the "Penelope of the Ionians," shows that this heroine retained her power as a model through time.[4] In fact, Penelope with her un-weaving of the shroud remains a byword for cleverness throughout classical antiquity, and beyond. Antinoös' speech contains one more twist in the play of comparisons. After comparing Penelope favorably to the heroines of old for her intelligence (noēmata), he undercuts this compliment, saying that this time she has misused it. While the trick of the loom is perhaps more successful in narratological terms than in practical ones, the poem itself vindicates Penelope's cleverness, suggesting that she is not only more than the equal of the heroines of old; she is the equal of the cleverest of heroes, the wily Odysseus.

Tragic choruses often resort to comparisons with events from the mythic past in an attempt to come to terms with the horror they see unfolding before them. In Sophocles' Antigone, when the protagonist is walled up in her tomb, the women of the chorus grope for previous examples of others so ill-treated, choosing two heroines and one hero. They recall the fates of Danae (944), Lykourgos (955), and finally Kleopatra, the cast-off first wife of Phineus who is ill-treated by his second wife (966). In a fragment from Euripides' lost Hypsipyle, the chorus responds to the eponymous heroine's apparent lament about being far from home and in reduced circumstances by calling to mind the wanderings of Europe and Io and their happy endings. She seems unwilling to be consoled and speaks in her turn of the tragic fate of Prokris, who was killed by her husband. The text is too fragmentary to make clear the exact relevance of Prokris, but the overall mood of lamentation is established.[5]

In Euripides' Medea, when the women of the chorus hear the cries of

---

[3] Jeffrey Henderson, "The Cologne Epode and the Conventions of Early Greek Erotic Poetry," Arethusa 9 (1976) 164 cites Odyssey 15.418 for the "epic ideal of feminine beauty," which includes stature. Here the ideal woman is καλή τε μεγάλη τε καὶ ἀγλαὰ ἔργα ἰδυῖα (beautiful, tall, and skillful in glorious crafts).

[4] W. Peek, "Die Penelope der Ionerinnen," Athenische Mitteilungen 80 (1965) 160–69.

[5] G. W. Bond, ed. Euripides. Hypsipyle (Oxford, 1963) 76, suggests that Hypsipyle envies Prokris for having someone to mourn her death, while she herself is alone. The relevant fragments are I.iii-iv. See also D. L. Page, ed., Select Papyri, vol. 3: Literary Papyri (Cambridge, 1970) 3:86–89, lines 55–98.

Medea's children as she kills them, they express their horror by searching for mythological precedents. Only one comes to mind:

μίαν δὴ κλύω μίαν τῶν πάρος
γυναῖκ' ἐν φίλοις χέρα βαλεῖν τέκνοις·
'Ινὼ μανεῖσαν ἐκ θεῶν, ὅθ' ἡ Διὸς
δάμαρ νιν ἐξέπεμψε δωμάτων ἄλη·
   πίτνει δ' ἁ τάλαιν' ἐς ἅλμαν φόνῳ
   τέκνων δυσσεβεῖ,
ἀκτῆς ὑπερτείνασα ποντίας πόδα,
δυοῖν τε παίδοιν συνθανοῦσ' ἀπόλλυται.
   τί δῆτ' οὖν γένοιτ' ἂν ἔτι δεινόν; ὦ
   γυναικῶν λέχος
πολύπονον, ὅσα βροτοῖς ἔρεξας ἤδη κακά.

> Of one alone I have heard, one woman alone
> Of those of old who laid her hands on her children,
> Ino, sent mad by heaven when the wife of Zeus
> Drove her out from her home and made her wander;
> And because of the wicked shedding of blood
> Of her own children she threw
> Herself, poor wretch, into the sea and stepped away
> Over the sea-cliff to die with her two children.
> What horror more can be? O women's love,
> So full of trouble,
> How many evils have you caused already!
>
> (1282–92 trans. Warner)[6]

As with the example from Homer, these comparisons reenact a mythic moment, placing it in relation to the heroic past in such a way as to emphasize the immediacy of the current myth.[7] By referring in this way to distant heroic times, the playwright creates the illusion that what is happening on stage is contemporary, far removed from the horrible precedents of the ancient mythic past. The claim of singularity in the *Medea* passage, the insistence that there is "only one" precedent (a debatable claim), makes the myth presented stand out in relief.[8]

Did Greeks of the archaic period actually compare themselves to the

---

[6] Translation by Rex Warner, *Euripides I*, ed. D. Grene and R. Lattimore (Chicago: University of Chicago Press, 1955).

[7] For the relevance of Ino to Medea's situation, see Robert Eisner, "Euripides' Use of Myth," *Arethusa* 12 (1979) 158–59.

[8] The myths of Prokne and Philomele, Agave, and the daughters of Minyas all provide examples of mothers who kill their children. See Appendix under the individual names.

figures of myth? Were the ancient heroines a standard of comparison for fifth-century Athenian women? There are few examples indeed, but these may serve to illustrate why there are not more. Let us take two very different uses of the figure of Helen, one from lyric poetry and the other from comedy. Sappho's fragment 16 (Lobel-Page = 16 Campbell) says that the most beautiful thing is whatever one loves, and proceeds immediately to invoke the name of Helen. Many have assumed that Sappho intended Helen as an answer to the question of "what is most beautiful," but most recent interpretors, able to see Helen not only as object but also as agent, have insisted on reading through to the end of the sentence, where it is clear that Sappho is interested in Helen not merely as an object of desire, but also as an actor following through on her own desire for Paris.[9] In the second example, the protagonist of Aristophanes' *Lysistrata* meets general resistance to the idea of a sex-strike to end the war until the Spartan Lampito recalls that Helen was able to use her physical charms to good purpose in turning away the anger of Menelaos, who threw away his sword when he saw her bare breasts.[10] This episode is very popular in Attic vase-painting, but Lampito has put her own spin on it, and one well-suited to needs of the moment. On the Attic vases, Helen is always shown fully clothed (figure 2).[11]

In these two instances, female speakers cite the myths of heroines as positive models for their own situations. But Aristophanes' women are comic creations, while Sappho is a lyric poet using mythological references to poetic effect. It is perhaps not coincidental that these references are made by a woman with considerably more autonomy than those of fifth-century Athens, and by a playwright representing, however satirically, a group of women attempting to claim greater autonomy than their society allowed. In these examples the heroine is not a passive victim of the desires of others but instead prevails on account of the desire she

[9] See John J. Winkler, "Double Consciousness in Sappho's Lyrics," in his *The Constraints of Desire* (New York, 1990) 176–78; N. Austin, *Helen of Troy and Her Shameless Phantom* (Ithaca, 1994) 51–68. For an overview of earlier interpretations, see G. W. Most, "Sappho Fr. 16.6–7 L-P," *CQ* 31 (1981) 11–17. Elsewhere, Helen is clearly marked as object of desire, rather than desiring subject, when Sappho uses her as standard of comparison for a beautiful woman: "(not even) Hermione (seems to be) like you, and to compare you to golden-haired Helen (is not unseemly)" (frg. 23 Campbell restored, with his translation).

[10] Ὁ γῶν Μενέλαος τᾶς Ἑλένας τὰ μᾶλά πα / γυμνᾶς παραϊδὼν ἐξέβαλ', οἰῶ, τὸ ξίφος (*Lys.* 155–56: "Well, you know Menelaos caught one glimpse of Helen's apples and dropped his sword.") Cf. Eur. *Andr.* 627–31.

[11] For other representations of Helen, see *LIMC* s.v. "Helene," 260–277. The scene may also be depicted on a stele in the Sparta Museum (Sparta 1) c.600–570. See M. N. Tod and A.J.B. Wace, *Catalogue of the Sparta Museum* (Rome, 1968 [Oxford, 1906]); M. Pipili, *Laconian Iconography of the Sixth Century* B.C. (Oxford, 1987) 30–31, cat. no. 87.

Figure 2 Helen and Menelaos, Attic bell krater, Persephone Painter,
c. 440–430 B.C.E. (Toledo Museum of Art 67.154).

provokes, or else follows her own desire. More commonly the heroine is invoked as a paradigm of passive suffering, in proverbial phrases like "the sorrows of Ino" and the "sufferings of Niobe."[12]

At times, particularly in Homeric epic, a speaker will cite a heroic myth as a precedent for a particular course of action. In these examples the behavior of heroines can even be seen as an appropriate model for a Homeric hero. In the embassy to Achilles, Phoinix attempts to persuade Achilles to relent by retelling how Meleager was induced to relent from his anger by the entreaties of his wife Kleopatra (*Iliad* 9.590ff.). While Achilles is asked to identify with Meleager, Phoinix implicitly equates himself with Kleopatra. A more explicit example comes in the last book of the *Iliad* (24.602ff.), when Achilles urges Priam to eat by reminding him that even Niobe after the death of all her children

[12] For Ino, see below n. 102. For Niobe, see Apostolius 12.11 under Νιόβης πάθη in *Corpus Paroemiographicum Graecorum* vol. 2, ed. E. L. Leutsch and F. G. Schneidewin (Hildesheim, 1958).

Figure 3 Heroines at Home, Attic red-figure pyxis, attributed to a follower of Douris, c. 455–445 B.C.E. (British Museum BM E 773).

paused from her mourning long enough to take nourishment. Achilles himself has only recently broken his own long fast, so the comparison to the heroine Niobe is perhaps meant for both of them and need not be seen as the imposition of a female role on an aged and vulnerable enemy.[13]

These examples give an idea of the extent to which heroines as well as heroes are used as models for correct behavior even among heroes. Our sources do not allow us to say to what extent these models were used by ordinary people in their everyday lives, although they do show us heroic and tragic characters, acting like "ordinary people," making such connections. Another kind of evidence shows that it was possible to assimilate heroines to Athenian women in their everyday life. A pyxis in the British Museum (figure 3) shows Iphigeneia standing in a doorway, while Danae approaches with a jewel box. Inscriptions identify the other women as Helen, Klytemnestra, and Kassandra.[14] In more quotidian settings, it may be easier to find examples of heroines as paradigms of nega-

---

[13] On the Meleager passage, see R. P. Martin, *The Language of Heroes* (Ithaca, 1989) 81. For Achilles and Priam, see R. Seaford, *Reciprocity and Ritual: Homer and Tragedy in the Developing City-State* (Oxford, 1994) esp. 159–60.

[14] *LIMC* s.v. "Iphigeneia" 32 = "Helene" 380.

tive behavior. The speaker in a fourth-century law-case calls his step-mother a "Klytemnestra" to embellish a charge that she has killed his father (Antiphon 1.17). A later literary example shows how a heroine could also provide a model to be surpassed. In a poem in the *Greek Anthology*, Hipparchia the Cynic compares herself to Atalante. The point of comparison is the masculine style of life they each adopted, but Hipparchia is confident that her choice of a philosophical life is more worthy of fame than a life spent hunting.[15] In any case, the idea of the heroine as a standard of comparison is well documented in Greek literature.

FIRE FOR IODAMA: THE WORSHIP OF HEROINES

If heroines could serve as models for ordinary mortals, they also played an important role in daily ritual. Not only did they receive dedications to mark moments of transition in the lives of individuals; they were also the recipients of regular sacrifices at community expense. Dedications to heroines took as many different forms as did sacrifices to heroes.[16] These offerings might be animal or vegetable, burnt or unburnt. They might be personal items, statues, or other objects. They might even take the form of a performance, like the choruses dedicated to Physkoa and Hippodameia at Olympia (Paus. 5.16.66–67). Dedications were made at a place associated with the heroine, such as a tomb or other sanctuary. At times a heroine was honored in more than one place, although usually the various sanctuaries were each considered by the local inhabitants to be the true site of the tomb. In rare cases a heroine might actually have multiple sanctuaries of different character. Frequently, the heroine was honored in the sanctuary of a goddess with whom she was closely associated.

A heroine might also be commemorated at other sites associated with her myth, such as her *thalamos* (bedchamber), like Semele (Paus. 9.12.3–4) and the daughters of Minyas (Paus. 2.25.9). A road in Orchomenos was named after Niobe (*IG* 7.3170.6–7). Objects associated with heroines were also placed in temples. Among these were the statues dedicated by Theseus in memory of Ariadne (Paus. 9.40.3–4; Plut. *Thes.* 21), Hippodameia's couch (*klinē*) at the Heraion in Olympia (Paus. 5.20.1),

---

[15] Antipater of Sidon, *Anthologia Palatina* 7.413, discussed in J. M. Snyder, *The Woman and the Lyre* (Carbondale, 1989) 107–8.

[16] A classic, if dated, treatment of dedications to the gods and heroes is W.H.D. Rouse, *Greek Votive Offerings* (Cambridge, 1902). For more recent treatments, see *Gifts to the Gods*, ed. T. Linders and G. Nordquist (Uppsala, 1987) and J. Larson, *Greek Heroine Cults* (Madison, 1995).

the cup that Zeus gave Alkmene (Athen. 11.475c), Leda's egg at the shrine of the Leukippides in Sparta (Paus. 3.16.1), and countless other objects.[17] Heroines were also associated with features of the natural landscape, such as the spring into which Glauke jumped when burned by Medea's poisons (Paus. 2.3.6), the one that arose when Atalanta struck the ground with her lance (Paus. 3.24.2), or the straits of the Hellespont, where Helle drowned. In most cases, however, there is no evidence of cult-offerings at these places.[18]

Just as in some hero cults, dedications to heroines could be ruled by ritual prohibitions against certain kinds of offerings or participation by certain groups.[19] The heroine or goddess Molpadia-Hemithea accepted offerings of hydromel, a mixture of water and honey, but wine was forbidden.[20] The worshiper must also have had no contact with pigs. These prohibitions were explained in antiquity by the myth that Molpadia and her sister killed themselves in shame at having allowed pigs to spoil their father's wine (Diod. 5.62). Plutarch, who is very fond of these ritual prohibitions, tells us that slaves and Aitolians are forbidden to enter the sanctuary of Leukothea at Chaironeia. His explanation is based on an episode in the myth of Ino, concerning her jealousy over a slave-woman from Aitolia (*Quaest. R.* 16, 267d).[21] When the ritual requires the sacrifice of a live victim, it is not uncommon, as in the cults of goddesses, to find that the animal is specified as female, although there does not seem to be a hard and fast rule that the gender of the victim match that of the

---

[17] Rouse (1902) 318–21, on Theseus' dedication, also 391–93; F. Pfister, *Der Reliquienkult im Altertum* (Giessen, 1909) 1:332ff. on relics and 1:365–68 on *thalamoi*.

[18] Heroines who bear the names of bodies of water, like Kastalia and Ismene, are considered by some to be nymphs who infiltrated heroic genealogies. Whatever their origin, once they become part of heroic myth, they take on the characteristics of heroines. (Other figures whose names are associated with springs: Akidousa, Amymone, Arene, Arsinoe, Kleite, Makaria, Peirene, and Physadeia; with seas: Myrto, Gorge, and Hyrie; rivers: Dirke, Herkyna; lake: Bolbe.) See Pfister (1909–12) 1:328–65, on heroines' associations with natural phenomena. On the usually clear distinctions between heroines and nymphs, see Larson (1995) 18–19.

[19] See J. W. Hewitt, "Major Restrictions on Access to Greek Temples," *TAPA* 40 (1909) 83–91; Robert Parker, *Miasma* (Oxford, 1983) 81–84; Susan Guettel Cole, "*Gunaiki ou Themis*: Gender Difference in the Greek *Leges Sacrae*," *Helios* 19 (1992) 104–22, especially 105–7.

[20] A similar prohibition against wine is also specified for the Hyakinthides, daughters of Erechtheus, in fragments of Euripides' *Erechtheus*. See C. Austin, *Nova Fragmenta Euripidea* (Berlin, 1968) frg. 65.83–89 and comments by Larson (1995) 102.

[21] Plutarch also tells us that flute-players were not allowed into the shrine of Tenes, nor was it permitted to mention Achilles there (*Quaest. Gr.* 28, 297d-f), and that women could not enter the grove of the hero Eunostos of Tanagra (*Quaest. Gr.* 40, 300d-301a). As with the examples of heroines, his explanations are based on details of the hero's myth.

divinity honored.[22] At times a pregnant victim was required, as for Pelarge, the founder of the cult of the Kabeiroi at Thebes (Paus. 9.25.8). Similarly, women offered a pregnant sheep to the Eumenides at a shrine near Sikyon (Paus. 2.11.4).

Although generalizations can be made about heroic sacrifice, our sources often give particulars of highly personalized votive dedications, providing a sample that is undoubtedly weighted toward the nonperishible and the unusual. Fortunately, we are not exclusively dependent on these descriptions, since the archaeological record gives us precise knowledge of actual dedications. From Sparta alone, we have examples ranging over almost the entire period of which we speak. A bronze aryballos and sacrificial fork inscribed to Helen date to the late seventh century, while a relief dedicated to Alexandra, showing a female figure in three-quarter profile playing the kithara, is from the first century B.C.E or later.[23]

The varied character of heroic dedications reflects in part the difference between regular yearly sacrifices on the day appointed by the sacrificial calendar, and those dedications that accompanied the passage of certain crucial transitions—rites of passage—in the life of the individual.[24] Young Megarian women on the eve of marriage offered libations and a lock of hair to Iphinoe, who died before she could marry (Paus. 1.43.4).[25] This is a common form of dedication, as Pausanias points out, mentioning the offerings made by the Delian maidens to Hekaerge and Opis. The same honor is promised by Artemis to Hippolytos, another figure who fails to complete the passage to maturity: "Unyoked girls will cut their hair for you before marriage."[26] Childbirth, another crucial transition in women's lives, is commemorated by a dedication to Iphigeneia at Brauron:

---

[22] See Larson (1995) 29–39. Some reflection of gender symmetry may be seen in a decree of the cult of Bendis (*IG* II² 1361) specifying that certain parts of female victims go to the priestess, and of male victims, to the priest. Translated in L. Bruit Zaidman and P. Schmitt Pantel, *Religion in the Ancient Greek City*, ed. and trans. P. Cartledge (Cambridge, 1992) 88–89.

[23] For offerings to Helen, see chapter 1, n. 7. For the relief, see Tod and Wace (1968 [1906]) no. 441; G. Daux, "Chronique des Fouilles 1967: Péloponnèse," *BCH* 92 (1968) 817 for the dating; *IG* 5.1.26 for the inscription; also Georgia Salapata, "Pausanias 3.19.6: The Sanctuary of Alexandra at Amyklai" [abstract of 1990 AIA talk] *AJA* 95 (1991) 331 and C. Antonaccio, *An Archaeology of Ancestors* (Lanham, Md., 1995) 181–82.

[24] See Arnold van Gennep, *The Rites of Passage*, trans. M. Vizedom and G. Caffee (Chicago, 1964).

[25] See Ken Dowden, *Death and the Maiden* (London, 1989) esp. 1–3, 63, together with criticisms by Larson (1995) 73–74.

[26] κόραι γὰρ ἄζυγες γάμων πάρος / κόμας κεροῦνταί σοι (Eur. *Hipp.* 1425–26.) In Aeschylus' *Libation Bearers* (6), Orestes makes a similar dedication to the river Inachos upon his return to Argos, and Artemis also receives locks of hair from young women at the Apatouria (Hesych. s.v. Κουρεῶτις).

οὗ καὶ τεθάψῃ κατθανοῦσα, καὶ πέπλων
ἄγαλμά σοι θήσουσιν εὐπήνους ὑφάς,
ἃς ἂν γυναῖκες ἐν τόκοις ψυχορραγεῖς
λίπωσ' ἐν οἴκοις.

When you have died and are buried,
they will dedicate robes as an adornment for you
the painstaking webs that women leave behind
in their houses when they die in childbirth.

(Euripides *Iphigeneia among the Taurians* 1464ff.)

In this example also, the ritual marks the failure to negotiate a transition, in this case by the dedication of the clothes of women who have died in childbirth. This time, however, the failure does not occur in the heroic sphere, but in the mortal one.[27] Plutarch, in his *Life of Theseus*, records a version of the myth of Ariadne in which she dies in childbirth on Cyprus. A sacrifice is performed there in her honor, on the second day of the month Gorpiaios, on the occasion of which one of the young men imitates the cries of a woman in labor (20.3–4). Although Plutarch appears not to credit this story of *couvade*, the specific date for the ritual suggests that the Cypriots took it seriously. As with Iphinoe, a sacrifice is made in honor of a figure who fails to make the transition. In all of these cases, the sacrifice is apotropaic, and is intended to ward off the fate of the mythic figure from the one who makes the offering.

Helen is another heroine whose cult may be associated with female life transitions, although in this case we have only the sketchiest indication of ritual practice. A story is told by Herodotus (6.61–62) about an ugly baby girl born to a prominent Spartan family. Every day its nurse took it to the shrine at Therapne and laid it in front of the image of Helen, while praying for its ugliness to be removed. One day a woman appeared, stroked the baby's head, and said that the child would grow up to be the most beautiful woman in Sparta, which came to pass. In fact, the woman was so beautiful that her first husband lost her to the king of Sparta. Calame notes that Helen's function is to render the girl beautiful *for marriage* and that she succeeds almost too well.[28] Offerings to Helen at the

---

[27] Christian Wolff has argued, in a paper delivered at the APA 1987 annual meeting, that Euripides distorts the actual custom, whereby women who *survived* childbirth dedicated their garments. Parts of that paper are quoted by Richard Hamilton, *Choes and Anthesteria* (Ann Arbor, 1992) 119. Wolff has returned to the topic in his article "Euripides' *Iphigeneia among the Taurians*: Aetiology, Ritual, and Myth" *CA* 11 (1992) esp. 319–24. See Chapter 1, n. 53.

[28] Claude Calame, *Les Choeurs de jeunes filles en Grèce archaïque* (Rome, 1977) 1:341–44, maintains that the account reflects ritual practice. Pausanias mentions the same episode (3.7.7).

shrine at Therapne have been discussed above, but their relation to female rites of passage, if any, is not clear.

Other unusual observances include the fireless annual rites for Dirke, the location of whose tomb was known only to the Hipparchs at Boiotia (Plut. *De gen. Socr.* 5, 578b-c). To these we may contrast the daily offering to Iodama, at the temple of Athena Itonia also in Boiotia. Here, as Pausanias tells us, fire was placed on Iodama's altar by a woman who three times announced that Iodama was alive and demanded fire ('Ἰοδά-μαν ζῆν καὶ αἰτεῖν πῦρ, 9.34.2). This is a rare case in which the ritual formula accompanying an offering to a heroine is preserved. It is interesting also because it suggests a figure in need of frequent appeasement. While there are numerous angry heroes who require expiatory or placating sacrifices, Iodama is the only heroine of this kind who comes to mind.[29]

THE HEROINE IN THE RITUAL CALENDAR

As we have observed, many of the sacrifices and dedications mentioned above are performed by individuals on occasions of personal and social significance—rites of passage like marriage or childbirth. Others, such as the one to Ariadne, occur on a specific day every year. Events of this kind are part of the ritual calendar of a particular city-state or region. Several examples of these sacrificial calendars have survived, most from Attica.[30]

The calendar of the Marathonian Tetrapolis, which dates from the early fourth century, specifies sacrifices for heroes and their accompanying heroines.[31] While most of the heroes are identified either by name or location, the heroines are not.[32] From the same period comes the calendar of Erchia, also in Attica, which is known as the Greater Demarkhia.

---

[29] Larson (1995) 134 observes that "the anger of the heroine is less likely to be emphasized than that of the hero." I omit treatment here of the many "bogeywomen" like Lamia or Mormo, who were believed to threaten children (or used to ensure their good behavior), because they are generally quite distinct from heroines. For these figures, see S. I. Johnston, "Penelope and the Erinyes: *Odyssey* 20:61–82," *Helios* 21 (1994) 137–59.

[30] J. Mikalson, *The Sacred and Civil Calendar of the Athenian Year* (Princeton, 1975); D. Whitehead, *The Demes of Attica* (Princeton, 1986) 185–211. For heroines in Attic calendars, see Larson (1995) 26–42.

[31] For the text, see *IG* II².1358, first published by R. B. Richardson, "A Sacrificial Calendar from the Epakria," *AJA* 10 s. 1 (1895) 209–26. A translation is published in *Sources for the Study of Greek Religion*, D. G. Rice and J. Stambaugh, eds. (Missoula, 1979) 113–15.

[32] For example, at B7, line 105 we find ἡρωίνηι οἶς (a sheep to the heroine). See G. M. Quinn, *The Sacrificial Calendar of the Marathonian Tetrapolis*, Ph.D. dissertation, Harvard University, 1972, esp. 28–29, 121. Larson (1995) 29, 33 notes the lower value and status of offerings to heroines.

Here, in addition to two sacrifices "to the Heroines" (*Herōinais*) in the months of Metageitnion and Pyanopsion, we find an offering of a goat to Semele by a college of women, in the month of Elaphebolion.[33]

The sacrificial calendar of the Attic deme of Thorikos (400–350 B.C.E.) records a yearly sacrifice to the heroine Prokris, listed right after her husband, Kephalos (*SEG* 33.147 col.I.16–17). The same calendar also lists sacrifices to Thorikos and the heroines of Thorikos (18; 30), to Hyperpedios and his heroines (48–49) and Pylochos and his heroines (50–51).[34] In most cases the hero receives a victim, while Prokris and the groups of unnamed heroines are each honored with a table of offerings (*trapeza*).[35] Alkmene and Helen also receive animal sacrifices (l.37–38). That male heroes commonly received sacrifices together with their often-unnamed heroines or wives is indicated also by a notice from Pausanias (1.34.3) that the sanctuary of Amphiaraos at Oropos had an altar, part of which was dedicated to "the heroes and the wives of heroes." Pausanias also gives us another example from Elis where libations are poured to the Elean and Aitolian heroes and their wives (ἥρωσι καὶ γυναιξὶ σπένδουσιν ἡρώων, 5.15.11–12).[36] The practice of honoring heroine and hero pairs with ritual meals is also commemorated in votive objects, ranging from reliefs to figurines.[37] Among the earliest of these are Laconian hero reliefs dating from the seventh and sixth centuries, showing pairs tentatively identified as Agamemnon and Kassandra or Klytemnestra, and Helen and Menelaos.[38]

Heroines as well as heroes are tied into the ritual calendar by being honored as part of the festival of a god. Pausanias tells how the Phliasians

---

[33] *SEG* 21.541. Sacrifices to the heroines: E 3–4 and A 19; to Semele: A 45. G. Daux, "La Grande Démarchie: Un Nouveau Calendrier sacrificiel d'Attique (Erchia)," *BCH* 87 (1963) 603–34; F. Sokolowski, *Lois sacreés des cités grecques* (Paris, 1969) no. 18, with commentary; Mikalson (1975); Larson (1995) 30–31.

[34] In another part of the inscription, sheep are offered to the heroines of Koroneia in Boiotia. See G. Daux's publication of the inscription, "Sacrifices à Thorikos," *Getty Museum Journal* 17 (1984) 145–52; also his "Le Calendrier de Thorikos au musée J. Paul Getty," *AC* 52 (1983) 150–74.

[35] E. Kearns, *The Heroes of Attica* (*BICS* Suppl. 57, 1989) 136 analyzes the patterns found in the various locations: in Marathon we find one hero and one heroine; in Thorikos, one hero and a group of heroines; in Erchia, single heroes and unrelated groups of heroines; Larson (1995) 41 emphasizes "male-female polarity" in these groupings and discusses husband-wife pairs in hero cult (78–84).

[36] Richardson (1895) 219, suggests that the sacrifice to the *Herōinē* ('Ηρωίνη) may refer to Hekale, in which case the hero would be Theseus (219). See comments of Larson (1995) 28.

[37] For an excellent discussion of the importance of heroic couples on votive objects, see Larson (1995) 43–57, who notes that the tendency toward male-female polarity is more important than the specific relationship.

[38] See Rouse (1902) 5–29; Pipili (1987) 30–31.

look toward their tombs while calling the children of Aras, Araithyrea and her brother Aoris, to the libations that begin the mysteries of Demeter (2.12.5).

Occasionally, a heroine is honored by her own festival. Plutarch tells us of a group of three festivals that took place at Delphi every eight years, two of which are dedicated to heroines. The second of these festivals is called *Herōis*. The heroine in question is Semele, and the events include mysteries that Plutarch supposes to be connected with her evocation, the "calling up" from the Underworld (*Quaest. Gr.* 12, 293d).[39] The third of them, the *Charila*, is named after a young girl who is a kind of *pharmakos* figure. Humiliated, she hangs herself, and the festival is proclaimed by way of expiation (293d-f).[40] We know also of the existence of a festival called the *Ariadneia* at Oïnoe in Lokris (*Cert. Hom. et Hes.* 234–35). Pausanias describes an annual celebration at Olympia in honor of Hippodameia:

> There is within the Altis by the processional entrance the Hippodameium, as it is called, about a quarter of an acre of ground surrounded by a wall. Into it once every year the women may enter, who sacrifice to Hippodameia, and do her honor in other ways. The story is that Hippodameia withdrew to Midea in Argolis, because Pelops was very angry with her over the death of Chrysippus. The Eleans declare that subsequently, because of an oracle, they brought the bones of Hippodameia to Olympia. (6.20.7 trans. Jones)

This passage gives the location, some indication of the rite, and a foundation myth of sorts but it is very sketchy on the details. We shall see other cases in which rites enacted by women are described in similarly sketchy terms.

On Crete the *Inacheia*, a festival in honor of Ino, is celebrated. On Samos and Teos there are festivals, the *Leukothea* or *Leukathea*, honoring her under her other name. Festivals frequently give their names to months. To choose an example from hero cult, the festival of the *Hyakinthia* gives its name to a month in many parts of the Greek world. The prevalence of cities with month-names like *Leukatheōn* (Chios and Magnesia) or *Leukathiōn* (Lampsakos) suggests that a festival in honor of Leu-

---

[39] See Hesych. s.v. Σεμέλη. See also J.-A. Hild, "Herois," in *Dictionnaire des antiquités*, ed. Daremberg and Saglio.

[40] On Charila and her festival, see G. Nagy, *Best of the Achaeans* (Baltimore, 1979) 92–93. J. Fontenrose, *Python: A Study of the Delphic Myth and Its Origins* (Berkeley, 1959) sees her as a "spirit of drought and famine" (459) later transformed "from a demoness into a humble girl of the people" (460). I find far more persuasive the suggestion of J. Larson (1995) 15, 140–43 that scapegoats like Charila, and the sisters Auxesia and Damia, ought to be seen in connection with heroines who become sacrificial victims.

kothea was widespread throughout the islands and the coast of Asia Minor, at least in Hellenistic times.[41]

Because of the hero's inevitable mortality, many heroes and heroines are honored with ritual lamentation. The oldest known example of this may be the "Linos-song" on the shield of Achilles (*Iliad* 18.570).[42] Some heroic festivals are made up of two parts, with a shift from lamentation to celebration, as at the Hyakinthia and the Cypriot festival of Ariadne. This phenomenon may be related to forms of worship that combine elements of divine and heroic cult, as was the case for Herakles and for Ino-Leukothea, whom the people of Elis honored as both goddess and heroine. When they consulted with Xenophanes, he told them, "If they consider her a goddess, then they should not mourn, but if human, then they should not sacrifice."[43] (Xenophanes, who held unorthodox religious views, clearly did not believe in the cult of heroes.) In these examples the object of worship is honored at times as a hero, and at times as a god. Occasionally a city-state decides to change its form of worship once and for all, as did the citizens of Lampsakos, according to Plutarch: "They rendered heroic honors to Lampsake at first; later they voted to offer sacrifice to her as to a goddess, and so they continue to do."[44]

This example reminds us that heroines had an important civic role to play. While this role was usually signaled by sacrifices specified in the local calendars, heroines also received sacrifices, analogous to those marking off personal transitions, at moments of crisis or transition for the entire community. We have already discussed the invocation of the heroine Messene at the foundation of the city of Messene, which took place in 369 under the auspices of Epaminondas. This leader may have been particularly aware of the political value of such manifestations, since he is also said to have sacrificed to Skedasos and his daughters before the battle of Leuktra in 371.[45] Invocations to heroines in times of war are rather rare, but the Athenian ephebes may have called on Aglauros in their oath that

[41] For Crete: Hesych. s.v. Ἰνάχεια; Teos: *CIG* 3066.25. For the Hyakinthia, see Eitrem, "Hyakinthos," *RE* 9.1, 8. For the month-names of Chios, Magnesia, and Lampsakos, see Eitrem, "Leukothea," *RE* 12.2, 2296.

[42] Whether Linos is the name of the mourning song or of the one mourned is debated. See Abert, "Linos," *RE* 13.1 (1926) 715–17; Reinhard Häußler "λίνος ante Λίνον?" *RM* 117 (1974) 1–14. Other ancient traditions about Linos: Hdt. 2.79; Paus. 9.29.6–9.

[43] εἰ μὲν θεὸν ὑπολαμβάνουσι, μὴ θρηνεῖν, εἰ δ' ἄνθρωπον, μὴ θύειν. (Xenophanes 21.11.13 Diels-Kranz = Arist. *Rh.* 1400b5), also attributed to Lykourgos by Plutarch *Apotheg. Lac.* 26. 228e. See Chapter 4 for similarities in the worship of Ariadne.

[44] *De mul. virt.* 255e, trans. F. C. Babbitt, *Plutarch's Moralia* (London, 1931).

[45] These young women, according to local myth, had been raped by Spartans, and cursed Sparta before killing themselves in shame (Paus. 9.13.5–6). Sometimes the young women are said to be daughters of Leuktros, apparently the eponymous hero of Leuktra. See Leuktrides and Molpia in the Appendix.

was made in her sanctuary (Plut. *Alcib*. 15.4), and an Athenian drinking song (Athen. 15.694) gives Pandrosos credit for helping bring victory over the Persians. These few examples of heroines invoked in moments of civic crisis may be compared to the numerous myths of young girls sacrificed, like Iphigeneia, on the eve of battle, or like Makaria and the Hyakinthides, to save a besieged city.

Other ritual forms commonly associated with heroes, such as games and oracles, are found less often in connection with heroines, but they do occur. Ino, as so often the exception, had agonistic games at Miletos, according to Conon (*Narr*. 33) and may also have had a share in the Isthmian games, principally dedicated to her son, Melikertes-Palaimon. She is also credited by Pausanias (3.26.1) with having an oracle, at Thalamai in Laconia, where prophecy was conducted by incubation, although other ancient sources disagree. Plutarch (*Agis* 9) calls the titulary of the oracle Pasiphae and provides three possible identifications for this figure, none of them compatible with Pausanias' view—Kassandra, Daphne, or a daughter of Atlas.[46] Incubation is also associated with healing cults, like that of Asklepios, and in fact the techniques of oracular and healing cults have much in common. Nonetheless, heroines are not usually associated with healing, except insofar as they are associated with childbirth.[47] Aside from this, the tradition discussed above, in which Helen at Therapne "cures" a baby girl's ugliness, is the nearest thing to a healing function we find for a heroine.

Mysteries, in general associated with divinities, also figured in the cults of heroines, as we noted in the case of the festival *Hērōis*. Once again, Ino appears to be among the heroines honored in this way. She may have a place in the mysteries of Samothrace, although the evidence is uncertain. The scholion to Apollonius of Rhodes 1.916–18 tells of Odysseus' initiation into these mysteries, which protect the initiate against shipwreck. This may be solely inspired by the passage in *Odyssey* 5 in which Ino's *krēdemnon* (veil) rescues Odysseus from drowning and does not necessarily grant Ino a place among the Samothracian divinities, known

[46] See Appendix under Pasiphae. See also Cicero *de Divinatione* I.43.96. For Kassandra's identity with Pasiphae and more importantly with Alexandra, see J. Davreux, *La Légende de la prophétesse Cassandre* (Paris and Liège, 1942) 88–96. See also D. Lyons, "Manto and *Manteia*: Prophecy in the Myths and Cults of Heroines," in *Sibilli e linguaggi oracolari*, ed. I. Chirassi Colombo and T. Seppilli (Pisa, forthcoming).

[47] See Kearns (1989) 19. See Chapter 5 for the connection of Iphigeneia and Molpadia-Hemithea with childbirth. Epione, the wife of Asklepios, and his daughters Akeso, Iaso, Hygieia, Panakeia, and Aigle seem to be honored as minor divinities. Except for Aigle, their names are derived from words for healing and they seem to be little more than deified abstractions. One heroine, Alexida (Defender), is the ancestor of the *elasioi* (averters), who have the power to avert epileptic attacks (Plut. *Quaest. Gr.* 23, 296f.).

as the Kabeiroi. A much later source, Libanius, writing in 362 C.E., defends his friend Aristophanes by comparing him with those who have committed real crimes: profaning the mysteries of Ino and her son, of the Kabeiroi, and of Demeter.[48] It seems clear from his text that Libanius regarded these as three distinct cults.

THE NAMING OF HEROINES

As we have seen, it is not essential to know the name of a heroine before offering sacrifices to her. All the same, there are very few unnamed heroines in Greek cult, far fewer than there are unnamed heroes, and they are almost always collectivities, groups of figures, often sisters, subsumed under a single identity. Even more than for male heroes, there is a marked preference for naming those you honor or honoring those you can name.[49] In poetry, moreover, the names of heroines have a certain talismanic importance, as when Kleopatra's genealogy and her mother's nickname are given great attention in Phoinix's speech in *Iliad* 9. When the aim of the poetry is genealogical, female figures almost always are named. For reasons I discuss below, it does not necessarily matter if the names assigned are supported by tradition. Despite this arbitrariness, the names of heroines are a rich source of information, to which we now turn.[50]

The names of heroines are for the most part made up of the same elements used to construct hero names, elements that can be interpreted as Greek nouns or adjectives and whose meaning is transparent.[51] What most distinguishes them from the names of heroes is the extent to which they are both variable and repeatable. The heroines of two different myths may have the same name, while the heroine in two versions of the same myth will have a different name. On the other hand, a few of the

---

[48] *Oration* 14, 65. Nonetheless, he has been blamed for creating a mistaken impression that Ino had some connection with the mysteries of the Kabeiroi in Samothrace. Clearly, however, this impression, whether mistaken or not, has a much longer history, as we see from the scholiast. See also G. Nagy, "Theognis and Megara: A Poet's Vision of His City," in *Theognis of Megara: Poetry and the Polis*, ed. Figueira and Nagy (Baltimore, 1985) 79–80.

[49] For anonymous heroines, see Larson (1995) 22, 26–27. She emphasizes their numbers, but these are mostly members of groups, or the consorts of heroes, themselves often anonymous. The stand-alone, unnamed heroine seems to be a less common phenomenon.

[50] On heroic names in general, see Max Sulzberger, "Ὄνυμα ἐπώνυμον: Les Noms propres chez Homère et dans la mythologie grecque" *REG* 39 (1926) 381–447, which is more useful than for its examples than for its eccentric thesis. See now C. Higbie, *Heroes' Names, Homeric Identities* (New York, 1995).

[51] For a discussion of the meanings embedded in heroic names, see Nagy (1979) esp. 69–93, 102–15.

most familiar figures have names that are significant and distinctive. This apparent contradiction reflects the two poles of the heroine's situation: to be little more than a name in a genealogy, or to be distinct, to suffer, sometimes even to achieve immortality. This tension between the generic and the specific is inherent in the paradoxical nature of female *kleos* and elucidates the connection between gender and the transcendence of mortality.

A heroine's name may seem to be the most arbitrary of signs, a mere genealogical place-holder, as for example when Apollodorus (2.4.5) identifies the mother of Amphitryon as either Astydameia, Laonome, or Hipponome. Meanwhile, Astydameia is the name of at least two other heroines. Oidipous' mother is sometimes named Iokaste and sometimes Epikaste, but here the common element suggests the possibility that we may discover some continuity of identity.

At times the variations become dizzying, as in the following example: there are no less than three heroines called Polykaste, one of whom, also called Periboia, is identified as the mother of Penelope by Apollodorus (3.10.6; cf. schol. Lycophr. 511). Nestor and Eurydike (also known as Anaxibia) have a daughter Polykaste who appears in the *Odyssey* where she bathes Telemachos (3.464ff). According to the Hesiodic *Catalogue of Women*, this Polykaste bears Telemachos a son, Perseptolis (frg. 221 M–W), while a later tradition (*Cert. Hom. et Hes.* 39–40) makes her Homer's mother, also called Epikaste, who should not be confused with the mother of Oidipous, who *is* confused with the mother of Agamedes and Trophonios (schol. Aristoph. *Clouds* 508), who also sometimes goes by the name of Iokaste. And so on.

At other times it is the repetitiveness more than the variability of the names that makes them seem less than distinctive, an impression sometimes heightened by their transparent meaning. Kreousa and Medousa, the feminine counterparts of Kreon, "ruler," and Medon, "lord, guardian, mindful one" are commonly used as the names of kings' daughters.[52] The name Eurydike (Broad Justice) belongs to so many heroines, most of them wives of kings, that it becomes generic, possibly expressing some sort of hope about the relationship between kingship and justice. Other common names are Klymene, Hippodameia, and Astyocheia, suggesting aristocratic concerns such as fame, horse-taming, and the defense of citadels—in fact, a whole *Iliad* in miniature.[53]

[52] As with heroes' names, heroine names may indicate some quality of the parent, usually the father. As Pausanias says of Gorgophone, daughter of Perseus, "You understand right away when you hear it" (2.21.7). See the discussion of the name Iphigeneia in Chapter 5.

[53] Nagy (1979) 102ff. discusses the epic themes in the name Patroklos and others.

While these names are the female counterparts to hero names like Klymenos, Hippodamas, or Astyanax, what distinguishes them is the frequency with which they are recycled. This is not the case with heroes, among whom the appearance of two of the same name usually requires that they be distinguished in some way, most often by patronymic. The two heroes called Aias are by turns differentiated from, and assimilated to, one another. Aias (Ajax) the son of Telemon and Aias son of Oileus are distinguished from each other, either by patronymic or as the "greater" and "lesser." The son of Oileus is also called the Lokrian Aias, and at times they are referred to in the plural as the *Aiantes*.[54] When heroines are identified by patronymic, it is to indicate their place in the larger heroic genealogy, not to distinguish them from other heroines. Heroines can also be identified by their husbands or even their sons. The grammarian Diomedes gives the examples of Helena Menelais and Althaia Meleagris.[55]

Unlike heroes, heroines almost invariably lose their specificity and identity when they acquire a collective name, and these collective names are not based on their own. Although there is more than one Hippodameia, we do not find references to the "Hippodameiai."[56] (Admittedly, unlike heroes of the same name, they never have an occasion to act in tandem.) A plural name indicating more than one heroine denotes a collectivity, usually named after the father: Danaids, Hyakinthides, Kekropids, Minyades, or much more rarely after the mother: Niobids, Pleiades. A few groups of sisters are even known by the name of their brothers: Meleagrides, Phaethonides. As Claude Calame has noted, these forms in -*id* or -*ad* mark off a feminine collective, whether a group of mythic sisters or women who band together to serve a god, and they imply subordination as well as geographical or familial connection.[57] While some groups, like the Kekropids (daughters of Kekrops) Aglauros, Pandrosos, and Herse, have distinct names and identities, often members of collectivities do not. Even the names of collectivities can be inter-

---

[54] The dual form *Aiante* (Αἴαντε) has been variously interpreted. G. S. Kirk, *The "Iliad": A Commentary*, vol. 1 (Cambridge, 1985) at *Iliad* 2.406 considers it ambiguous, while Richard Janko in vol. 4 (1992) at 13.46 emphasizes that it originally meant Aias and his brother Teukros. At 13.681 he refers to "Homer's pervasive and creative misunderstanding" of this term.

[55] Diom. *Ars grammatica* 1 = Ibycus 290 Campbell. Neither of these examples is free from irony, if we consider the troubled relationships to which they refer.

[56] The comedy *Atalantai* (Atalantas) possibly by Epicharmos, of which we know little more than the title, is the closest I have found to a counter-example. Minor divinities, on the other hand, do have a tendency to multiply, e.g., "Eileithyiai." See J. Rudhardt, *Notions fondamentales de la pensée religieuse et actes constitutifs du culte dans la Grèce classique* (Geneva, 1958) 91ff., on the fragmentation of divine identity.

[57] Calame (1977) 70–71.

changeable: the Hyakinthides are the daughters of Hyakinthos, who sacrifice themselves for their city, but the name can also indicate the daughters of Erechtheus, some of whom suffer a similar fate.[58]

Not only the names themselves, but even the elements of which they
are made, emphasize their interchangeability. I have already mentioned
several examples of names that share an element, but in fact most heroine
names are made up of two elements that can be recombined almost infinitely: Eury-dike, Eury-anassa, Iphi-anassa, Iphi-aneira, Dei-aneira, Deidameia, Lao-dameia, Lao-dike, and so on. Names with only one element
often indicate physical beauty or connection to the natural world (Aglaia,
Kallisto, Phaidra). Others are eponyms, the names of cities or other
places (Amphissa, Nemea, Tanagra).[59] Theophoric (god-bearing) names
are rare among heroes, but even more so among heroines.[60]

As what I have called genealogical placeholders, heroines in the catalogues may not always *have* names, nor are their names consistently used,
even when they do exist. As mothers of heroes, the rank and file of
heroines have only the most contingent identity. When Zeus recites his
list of conquests (*Iliad* 14.313–28, discussed further in Chapter 3), he
identifies the women by the names of their husbands or fathers, and only
occasionally by their own names, while the names of their heroic male
offspring are carefully recorded: Ixion's wife, who bore Peirithoös;
Danae, daughter of Akrisios, who bore Perseus; the daughter of Phoinix,
who bore Minos and Rhadamanthys; Semele and Alkmene, who bore
Dionysos and Herakles; Demeter and Leto. The mothers of divine offspring at least are guaranteed mention by name, but only the goddesses
merit mention by name without their children.

The Hesiodic *Catalogue of Women* almost always assigns names, but
they are often not distinctive. In many cases, even when the myth is
familiar from other sources, the name assigned a female figure may be
unique to this text. This suggests that the specificity of the name is less
important than the appearance of genealogical thoroughness or the aes-
thetic pleasure offered by the flow of heroic-sounding names. For example, the heroine Chlidanope is, according to West, "a colourless figure
with an artificial name, serving only to make a genealogical link."[61] The
apparent "misinformation" created by an ad hoc name is actually mini-
mal, since descent is only rarely reckoned through the female line. Even
when a family traces its lineage to the union of a mortal progenitor,

---

[58] See Kearns (1989) 62–72 on these apparent patronymics, which she believes actually
refer to specific qualities of the sisters so named.

[59] See Chapter 1, nn. 81 and 82.

[60] In this category Sulzberger (1926) 399 counts only Hera-kles, and names beginning in
Dio- and Arē-. Among heroines this would yield only Dia, Diogeneia, Diomedeia, and
Diomeneia.

[61] M. L. West, *The Hesiodic Catalogue of Women* (Oxford, 1985) 88.

usually a woman, with a god, the exact identity of her female descendants may be beside the point.[62]

In direct contradiction to this principal of generic names for generic figures, most of the best-known heroines, like most heroes, have names that are theirs alone. Ariadne, Ino, Semele, Niobe, Danae, and Iphigeneia are all names associated with one heroine only.[63] Not only are these names unique, they also tend to deviate from the pattern of composition mentioned above. Instead of being made up of two transparently intelligible roots, most of these names consist of one root and are of uncertain etymology. In this way, they escape the interchangeability that is doubly determined for so many other heroines.[64] These are some of the heroines whose stories we know best, and theirs are stories of disaster—rape, abandonment, and death, sometimes at the hands of the gods whose children they bore. Meanwhile, other women listed in the catalogues as bearing the offspring of the gods manage to reintegrate themselves into mortal life, afterwards bearing purely mortal children to tolerant or credulous husbands. These heroines get a line or two in the catalogue, but that is all, because they essentially *have no story*.[65] It is this quality of having no story that saves them for a return to everyday life.[66]

Having no story, as we know from Achilles' dilemma (*Iliad* 9.412–16),

[62] The list in Apollodorus' *Library* (2.1.5) of the Danaids and their spouses-for-a-day is instructive. The need for specific names for fifty women and fifty men strains the author's resources. Several Danaids share the same name, and many names familiar from other contexts are recycled here. These include extremely common heroine names like Elektra, Kleopatra, and Eurydike, as well as less common ones like Hyperippe and Anaxibia. Another interesting feature is the pairing of women and men with matching names: the Danaids Klite, Sthenele, and Chrysippe marry Klitos, Sthenelos, and Chrysippos.

[63] Occasionally an ancient mythographer or a modern scholar argues for the existence of two Ariadnes (Plut. *Thes.* 20 citing the view of the Naxians) or Iphigeneias (H. Lloyd-Jones, "Artemis and Iphigeneia," *JHS* 103 (1983) 87–102). These efforts are designed to resolve discrepancies between mourning and celebration in the cult of Ariadne or mortal and immortal elements in the myth of Iphigeneia. The "discrepancies" arise from the intrinsic tensions between mortality and immortality from which the myths derive their significance. In none of these cases is it necessary or even useful to postulate the existence of two heroines of the same name.

[64] Iphigeneia is an exception here, because of the legibility of her name, and the early form Iphimede, which is itself not unique. I include her in this account because she is mostly known as Iphigeneia, a name that refers only to her. See discussion in Chapter 5.

[65] G. McLeod, *Virtue and Venom* (Ann Arbor, 1991) 13, remarks that these heroines "play no active role in their own stories."

[66] Interestingly, Sandra M. Gilbert and Susan Gubar in *The Madwoman in the Attic* (New Haven, 1979) 25, 34, describe the distinction between monstrous villainesses and idealized selfless women in nineteenth-century English and European literature as the difference between having and not having a story. Cited in Toril Moi, *Sexual/Textual Politics* (London, 1985) 58. The terms have changed only slightly in our own era. At the time of the Prince of Wales' engagement to Lady Diana Spencer, it was said of her that she had "a history but no past" (*New York Times*, March 22, 1981).

is the trade-off for a long and happy life, although it would be misleading to suggest that these heroines actually exercised any choice in the matter. The choice offered Achilles in *Iliad* 9 between *nostos* (homecoming) and *kleos* (glory) is a choice no heroine is ever offered.[67] But it is true, as Helen herself knows (*Iliad* 6.357–8), that having a story, which means suffering, also means having a name and having *kleos* for all time. She is undoubtedly the only heroine to exhibit a conscious relation to *kleos*. Without being allowed to exercise choice in anything, she does manage to have *nostos* as well as *kleos* (although the domestic scene presented in *Odyssey* 4 suggests that both *nostos* and *kleos* are somewhat compromised). But Helen's myth is unusual in a number of ways, and the ability to survive having a story may be only one more proof of her divinity.

In the *Odyssey*, where the equation is rather different, both *nostos* and *kleos* depend on having a name and living up to it, as George Dimock has shown. Odysseus' name is his fate, and it is only by remembering that name, and remembering to act in a way that is appropriate to it, that he is able to remember the day of his return.[68] According to this code, therefore, a heroine may have a name that is in fact *no name*, because it is not distinctive and carries no *kleos*. Few heroines are allowed the scope of action necessary to achieve *kleos* on their own, and often they achieve it instead through the actions of others. Still, one and the same rule binds a hero like Odysseus or Achilles and the anonymous heroines of the catalogues: having no name means having no story.

Not only do heroines like Medea or Ariadne have a story and an identity guaranteed by names that belong to no one else, there are also heroines with no less than two distinctive names. These are the ones whose stories culminate in apotheosis, and whose transition to immortality is marked by a change of name. Ino becomes Leukothea, Semele becomes Thyone, Molpadia becomes Hemithea, and Iphigeneia becomes either Einodia, Hekate, Molpadia, or Orsiloche.[69] Heroes more rarely achieve apotheosis, and when they do, they retain their original names.[70]

When Herakles is transported to Olympos and made immortal, the change is commemorated not by a change of name but of spouse. Leav-

[67] On Achilles' choice, see Nagy (1979) 102. On female *kleos*, see Katz (1991).

[68] George E. Dimock, "The Name of Odysseus," in *Essays on the "Odyssey"* ed. Charles H. Taylor (Bloomington, 1963) 54–72.

[69] Leukothea (*Od.* 5.333f.); Thyone (*Hom. Hymn* 1 (Dionysos) 20–22); Hemithea (Diod. 5.62–63); Einodia (Hes. frg. 23a 26 M-W); Hekate (Paus. 1.43.1= Hes. frg. 23b M-W); Orsiloche (Ant. Lib. 27).

[70] Here the main exceptions are boy-heroes like Melikertes-Palaimon. I would argue, however, that child-heroes, who are almost exclusively male, have a different relationship to immortality than do adult male heroes. Their fates are most closely bound to, and most closely resemble, the fates of their mothers or other important female figures in their myths, who are givers of life and would-be givers of immortality. This complex topic deserves further treatment, and I plan to return to it in the future.

ing Deianeira to live up to the etymology of her name as the "man-destroyer," he marries Hebe (Youth), whose name is a transparent guarantor of his new status as *athanatos* (deathless) and *agēraos* (unaging). This is a completely different relation to naming than anything we see among the heroines. Exchanging the man-destroying wife for the goddess of endless youth, he has changed his fate by changing not his own name, but the name of his spouse. At the same time, Herakles' own name calls attention to his status as an embodiment of female *kleos*, but it is the *kleos* of a goddess (Hera-kles), quite a different matter.

Dionysos, the other male hero who most conspicuously achieves immortality, preserves his name, but again the change is registered among the women around him. His mother Semele, his aunt and nurse Ino, and his wife Ariadne all become divine, and the first two receive new names, as I have already mentioned. (Interestingly, Ovid, perhaps inspired by the transformations of the other heroines, gave Ariadne the new name Libera.)[71]

What conclusions can be drawn about the nature of female *kleos*? In thinking about the mute, inglorious heroines of the catalogues, it is tempting to recall what Thucydides tells us Perikles said about the *kleos* of women: it consists in their not being spoken of at all.[72] But it would be anachronistic to apply this dictum to the archaic texts we have been considering. Indeed, in these texts, women both good and bad are spoken of constantly. The *kleos* of Penelope, for example, is a theme that dominates the second half of the *Odyssey*.[73] But Klytemnestra, too, receives both mention and perhaps even cult.[74] She and Medea are evidence for the complete amorality with which fame is generated. A heroine who keeps quiet, not complaining when raped by a god, will never become a subject of song for generations to come. Her name will be forgotten, or even worse, multiplied to the point of meaninglessness. If she does something really horrible—kills her children or husband, for example—no one will ever stop speaking of her.

Sometimes, however, it is enough merely to suffer something horrible

[71] *Fasti* 3.511–12. Discussed below, Chapter 4.

[72] That Perikles' remarks in the funeral oration (2.45) were based not only in ideology but also in practice is shown by D. Schaps, "The Woman Least Mentioned: Etiquette and Women's Names," *CQ* 27 (1977) 323–30. He shows that the orators generally named only women who were dead, of low repute, or associated with the speaker's opponents. J. Bremmer, "Plutarch and the Naming of Greek Women," *AJP* 102 (1981) 425–26, describes Plutarch's difficulties in recovering the names of important women in writing his *Lives*, concluding that "the Athenian custom of avoiding naming living respectable women had rendered even the names of the mothers of their most important statesmen into oblivion."

[73] Katz (1991) explores the ambiguities inherent in the situation of even a virtuous figure like Penelope, arguing that she cannot be understood apart from her apparent opposite, Klytemnestra.

[74] See above, p. 47 with n. 38.

in order to attain a name, a story, *kleos*, whatever we wish to call it. Most of our examples fit into this more passive paradigm. From this state of affairs, there arises the contradiction with which we began. Cut off from mortal or heroic spheres of action, these heroines are far less likely to achieve *kleos* through any action of their own but are paradoxically more likely to achieve it by making the leap to immortality.

THE HEROINE'S BIOGRAPHY: TRANSGRESSION AND TRANSFORMATION

Pausanias, in his description of the Akropolis of Athens, mentions two statues by Deinomenes: "Io, the daughter of Inachos, and Kallisto, the daughter of Lykaon, who have exactly the same story, to wit, love of Zeus, wrath of Hera, and metamorphosis, Io becoming a cow and Kallisto a bear." (1.25.1 adapted from Jones). These words provide an excellent point of departure, summing up as they do one of the most common patterns of myth for a heroine. In what follows we shall see to what extent Pausanias' formula fits the material, and where it needs to be expanded. No epic texts present us with the "career" of a heroine in the way that Achilles' and Odysseus' careers are the subjects of Homeric epic. Although each has in some sense a female foil, a Helen or a Penelope, these heroines are the focus of dramas of character rather than of action.

Various attempts have been made to summarize the life of the "standard" hero. It may be useful to review a few of them before turning to the biography of the "typical" heroine. Otto Rank, at the time very much under the influence of Freud, published *The Myth of the Birth of the Hero* in 1914. In a very short space he summarizes the myths of heroes and extracts a pattern which he then subjects to psychological analysis: "Summarizing the essentials of the hero myth, we find the descent from noble parents, the exposure in a river, and in a box, and the raising by lowly parents; followed in the further evolution of the story by the hero's return to his first parents, with or without punishment meted out to them. It is very evident that the two parent-couples of the myth correspond to the real and the imaginary parent-couple of the romantic fantasy."[75]

Despite the limitations of his approach, Rank identified an important

---

[75] *The Myth of the Birth of the Hero*, trans. Robbins and Jelliffe, reprinted in *In Quest of the Hero*, ed. Robert A. Segal (Princeton, 1990) 62. This volume also contains Lord Raglan's *The Hero* and a useful introduction by Segal.

heroic story-pattern, and his formulation of it has been quite influential even among those more concerned with myth than with psychology. A similar pattern as presented by Lord Raglan in 1936 has twenty-two steps, not all of which appear in the life of a single figure.[76] Central to the plot he outlines is the uncertainty of the hero's birth, the ambiguity of his parentage, a period of exile, a triumphant return, and a mysterious death. Unlike Rank's account, Raglan's steps cover the entire life-cycle of the hero.[77] It is easy to think of heroes who cannot be fit into the mold, but the story Raglan tells about heroic myth fits often enough to be compelling. For our purposes, it will be interesting to see which of these patterns are called into question by a study of the myths of heroines. A different approach is taken by G. S. Kirk, who instead of trying to identify the heroic story-pattern, inventories important mythic themes under two headings: "Commonest themes in Greek (mainly heroic) myths" and "Special, unusual or bizarre themes." Despite his rejection of the story-pattern approach, he illustrates his method with the Oidipous myth, one that fits particularly well into the Rank or Raglan model.[78]

A survey of typical elements of the heroine's story suggests that often it is a piece of the hero's story told from another perspective. This is the case in large part because many heroines *are* heroines by virtue of being mothers of heroes. For the hero, the uncertainty of his birth is a temporary setback from which he recovers. This very uncertainty may ultimately be a source of strength, or even a part of the hero's standard equipment. As Pausanias observes about the Phocian hero Parnassos, "Like the others who are called heroes, he had two fathers: one they named as the god Poseidon, the other a man called Kleopompos" (10.6.1). But the same event from the point of view of the heroine who bears him may represent the crisis of her life. As Brelich remarks, "To have a child by a god obviously creates complications in a woman's life, especially if she is a virgin [i.e., a *parthenos*, an unmarried woman], like Danae or Auge, but even if she is married, like Tyro; and these complications also affect the situation of the newborn hero."[79] However problematic for the young hero, these conditions never result in his destruction; for the mother, however, destruction is a real possibility. Koronis and Semele do not even survive to give birth. In such myths, the heroine takes on a purely metonymic function, by which the whole woman comes to be represented exclusively by her childbearing abilities, that is

[76] See *The Hero*, in Segal (1990). The pattern is presented on p. 138 and is then worked out with reference to a number of Greek heroes and others.

[77] Segal (1990) xxiv compares the two schemes.

[78] G. S. Kirk, *Myth: Its Meaning and Functions in Ancient and Other Cultures* (London, 1970), 187–89; 194–96; Oidipous myth, 190.

[79] Angelo Brelich, *Gli eroi greci* (Rome, 1958) 297.

to say, her womb. More frequently, the pregnancy, once it comes to light, is the occasion for harsh treatment of some kind, whether by the heroine's father, or other relatives, or by a jealous god. The attempt on the life of the infant hero (Raglan's item no. 6) is accomplished in one of two ways. Either the woman's enraged father orders the exposure of the unwanted baby hero with or without his mother, or the mother herself, fearing parental wrath, conceals her pregnancy and exposes the baby. (In Greek myth, as in actual practice, exposure is preferred to outright attempts on the baby's life.) In either case the actual or expected hostility of the baby's grandfather drives the plot. This familiar theme of generational conflict is sometimes motivated by the device of an oracle predicting disastrous consequences for the heroine's father resulting from the birth, as in the myth of Danae.[80] The potential threat is made explicit in the myth of Antiope, whose father dies as soon as he learns of his daughter's union with a god.[81] At other times it is the heroine's father's outraged morality that motivates the action, or the sense that paternal prerogative has been flouted.

The heroine's part of the story may in fact begin with the conception and end with the birth of the hero. In any case, the events surrounding each make up the two crises in the myths of many heroines. These are the two moments most often depicted on Attic vases, which show either the pursuit or rape by a god (e.g., Oreithyia pursued by Boreas or Herse by Hermes—figure 4) or the expulsion of the heroine and her baby (e.g., Danae watching as the carpenter prepares the chest in which she will be put to sea—figure 5).[82] The vase-paintings make visible and explicit the peculiar family dynamics hinted at in written accounts. Fathers stand by impassively while daughters are pursued or punished, and mothers, almost always absent from the texts, here make gestures of impotence and horror.[83] The heroine's defenselessness may be clear, but she cannot count on paternal protection any more than the baby hero can.[84] Fathers

---

[80] Danae's father Akrisios has received a prophecy of his own death at the hands of his daughter's son. A similar prophecy motivates the Oidipous myth, although here the generational conflict is more direct. This is a common folktale motif, to be found also in the Irish story of Deirdre.

[81] A. Scafuro, "Discourses of Sexual Violation in Mythic Accounts and Dramatic Versions of 'The Girl's Tragedy,'" *differences* 2.1 (1990) 131.

[82] Scenes of pursuit are discussed and illustrated in S. Kaempf-Dimitriadou, *Die Liebe der Götter in der attischen Kunst* (Berne, 1979). See also P. Brulé, *La Fille d'Athènes* (Paris, 1987) 291–97 for Oreithyia and Herse; and W. R. Agard, "Boreas at Athens" *CJ* 61 (1966) 241–46.

[83] An impassive Erechtheus watches Herse's abduction on a krater by the Syracuse painter (L.A.Cty.Mus.50.8.6), figure A, discussed by Brulé (1987) 296–97. Akrisios looks self-righteous on the hydria in Boston (figure 5).

[84] As Scafuro (1990) points out, most accounts of abduction do not distinguish between

Figure 4 Hermes pursues Herse, Attic red-figure Column Krater, Syracuse painter, *c.* 470–450 B.C.E. (Los Angeles County Museum of Art, William Randolph Hearst Collection 50.8.6).

are far more likely to punish daughters for suffering rape than to protect them.[85] An exception of sorts can be seen on a pyxis of about 470 (*Camb. 10. 1934*) on which Zeus chases Aigina while her two sisters Harpina and Korkyra run to their father Asopos for protection. Aigina, however, is on her own.

This hostility or indifference to daughters in both written and pictorial representations points to the theme of generational conflict once again,

---

coercive and consensual sex between gods and mortal woman, precisely because the woman's volition was of little interest. As a result, Greek writers tend to treat all women as guilty, with the notable exception of Euripides, particularly in the *Ion*.

[85] The punishments, or attempts to avoid them, frequently involve getting put to sea. See Appendix under Aerope, Chione, Rhoio.

Figure 5 Danae and the larnax, Attic red-figure hydria, Gallatin Painter, c. 490 B.C.E. (Boston MFA 13.200). Francis Bartlett Fund. Courtesy Museum of Fine Arts, Boston.

since it is through these daughters that succession occurs. Fathers, however loathe to cede their powers to the younger generation, cannot avoid doing so. Akrisios can no more prevent Danae from bearing the child who will overthrow him than the fifth-century Athenian father can (respectably) avoid giving his daughter in marriage. Meanwhile, mothers, despite their occasional appearances on the vases, are without power to protect their daughters. Even the goddess Demeter could do little to protect her divine daughter Persephone. The mother-daughter connection is very rarely addressed in heroic myth. Pindar invokes his Theban heroines as the daughters of Harmonia, and Aeschylus has Agamemnon address Klytemnestra as "Daughter of Leda," (Λήδας γένεθλον, *Ag.* 914) but in general the connection is weak. Moreover, the mother who looks on in horror at her daughter's rape may have suffered a similar fate. We have only to think of Leda herself and her daughter Helen, or of Oreithyia and Chione.

Only rarely does the unfortunate heroine receive protection or vindication from the divine lover who caused the trouble. Instead, she must often suffer any number of indignities before her own son comes of age and champions her, as Perseus does Danae. (Antiope and Tyro are rescued by pairs of sons and Aithra by her grandsons.) The solidarity of

mortal son with mortal mother corresponds to a lack of solidarity between the divine lover and mortal beloved.[86] For some heroines, like
Semele, only posthumous vindication is possible. While the divergence
of interests of the hero's parents is a fairly constant feature of Greek hero-
myths, it is neglected by both Rank and Raglan, who tend to treat both
the "real" parents as a unit.

If we work from the heroine's beginning, looking for correspondences
with the hero's story, we find few indeed. Let us consider for example
the items associated with the birth of the hero. In Raglan's schema these
would be "4) The circumstances of his conception are unusual, and 5) He
is also reputed to be the son of a god." How many myths about the births
of heroines can we find? Only Helen has a distinctive (and divine) conception, and her birth from an egg is the most strikingly nonhuman
among heroes' births. (See figure 1).[87] Helen is the only mortal daughter
of Zeus.[88] Several of the other Olympians, particularly Poseidon, have
mortal daughters, but they tend to be obscure.[89] Instead of beginning
with her own birth, the myth of the typical heroine begins with the conception of a heroic son. So completely is her story entwined with his that
it is coextensive with the part of his career beginning with his birth and
ending with the trials of prowess that mark his coming of age.[90] The
story of Herakles, the most typical of heroes, and his mother Alkmene,
conforms to this model.

This is, however, only one type of heroine story, even if the most
prevalent. Heroines whose myths do not conform to the "mother of the

[86] Larson (1995) 60 observes that "Even in the case of heroines whose sons are fathered
by gods, the cult association tends to be with the son and not with the god who fathered
him (Alkmene-Herakles, Semele-Dionysos, Psamathe-Linos)."

[87] For Helen's egg, see Athen. 2.57f.; Bethe, "Dioskuren," RE 11.1 (1905), 1113. For
additional vase paintings of the birth of Helen from the egg, see LIMC s.v. "Helene" 1–13.
Klytemnestra is generally considered to be the daughter of Tyndareos. See Appendix under
Leda.

[88] L. Clader, Helen: The Evolution from Divine to Heroic in Greek Epic Tradition (Leiden,
1976) 54, observes that Helen is the only mortal called Διὸς κούρη (an epithet she shares
with Athena, Artemis, and Aphrodite), as well as being the only female heroic child of
Zeus. Indeed her status is ambiguous and she is at times considered divine.

[89] Some of his daughters: Aithousa, Eirene, Euadne, Lamia, Rhode. Ares is father of
Alkippe, and of the Amazons Penthesilea and Antiope. Harmonia, who may be a goddess,
is said to be the daughter of Ares or Zeus, as is Milye. Dionysos, the least paternal of the
gods, is credited in one version with fathering Deianeira, but this is a minority opinion.

[90] Although I do not fully share her views of female difference, I find helpful Carol
Gilligan's aptly titled article, "Woman's Place in Man's Life-Cycle," in Feminism and Methodology, ed. Sandra Harding (Bloomington, 1987) 57–73, especially her observations on the
necessary maleness of the child in the writings of psychologists (63) and the way in which
women exist in men's lives as nurturers and caretakers (67). In the writings she examines, as
in the heroic myths, children are assumed to be male, while women are necessarily
mothers.

hero" pattern are frequently virgins who for one reason or another are prevented from embarking on adult female life. They are shown at the moment of crisis, which takes the form of parental opposition to marriage (Hippodameia, the Danaids), personal aversion to marriage (Atalante), or the need for a sacrifice of some sort which stands in for marriage, as in the cases of virgin-sacrifice in time of war (Makaria, Iphigeneia). In the tragic tradition, these sacrificed virgins are often referred to as "brides of Hades."[91] In other cases the crisis in a heroine's myth is the collapse of marriage. These myths, in which the heroine is supplanted by another wife, frequently involve infanticide, as with Ino, Medea, and Prokne and Philomele.[92]

There is at least one heroine whose myth does not merely complete that of a hero but actually competes with it in scope and breadth of action. Ino is one of the few heroines to translate transgressions against her into transgressive behavior against others. The origin of her troubles, however, is not the birth of an illegitimate child, but the assumption of the role of nurse for her sister's illegitimate baby, Dionysos. (In other versions it is her husband's abandonment of her that sets the plot in motion.)

We have already had occasion in Chapter 1 to speak of Herakles and Ino in the same context. A point-by-point comparison will show how similar is the career of Ino to that of Herakles, the hero's hero. Ino, an exception among heroines, demonstrates that the heroine has the potential for a career reminiscent of male heroic ones. One may object that Ino, because she becomes a goddess, is already set apart from heroines. This, although undeniable, is no less true of Herakles, whose apotheosis in no way diminishes his claim to heroic status, for he continues to receive heroic cult alongside divine cult.

Unlike Herakles, whose many adventures have been organized into a more or less coherent narrative, Ino's myths appear to fall into several contradictory patterns, in which she is either victim or victimizer. We know that Herakles was worshiped all over the Greek world. Both the appeal of his myth and its diffusion contributed to a "rationalization" of the material. In the case of Ino-Leukothea, although she was widely worshiped, this process was never completed. Whereas the Ino-Leukothea myths seem a jumble of conflicting fragments, the Herakles myths were unified into a sort of canon at least by the mid-fifth century.[93] If we look

---

[91] See H. J. Rose, "The Bride of Hades," *CP* 20 (1925) 238–42 for a brief discussion of the homology of marriage and death in Attic customs and in myth. Also, R. Seaford, "The Tragic Wedding," *JHS* 107 (1987) 106–30.

[92] See J. Fontenrose, "The Sorrows of Ino and of Procne," *TAPA* 79 (1948) 125–67.

[93] H. A. Shapiro, "Heros Theos: The Death and Apotheosis of Herakles," *CW* 77 (1983) 10 considers Sophocles' *Trachiniai* the first continuous account of Herakles' life (although Aristotle in the *Poetics* 1451a16ff. uses the life of Herakles as an example of a theme that does

more closely, however, this difference begins to dissolve. Not only are there many similar plot elements, but even the confusions in plot resemble one another. Ino's place in the order of Athamas' wives is fluid, but then so is the order of Herakles' marriages and their relation to his labors.

To begin with, both figures are descended from the gods. Herakles is the son of Zeus and a mortal woman, while Ino is the daughter of Kadmos, a mortal but kingly father, and Harmonia, herself the daughter of Aphrodite and Ares, and perhaps a goddess in her own right. What is more, they each have an especially close connection with another divinity, for better or worse. Herakles, as the child of one of Zeus' other loves, has the support of his father but also the enmity of Hera throughout his life. But the relationship is ambivalent, and by the time of his apotheosis, Hera is no longer hostile but gives Herakles her daughter as a wife.[94] Ino, at the death of her sister, takes on the nursing of the baby Dionysos and so incurs the animosity of Hera as well.[95] The theme of nursing occurs in the Herakles material as well, but there it is the ostensible enemy Hera who is tricked into giving her breast to the infant Herakles. Here is an example of the asymmetry that biology creates and custom enforces. Heroines, as women, are so consistently associated with the maternal function that the mythic material never shows them as infants in need of sustinence. The one exception, the suckling of Atalante by a bear, suggests that she is unnatural and serves to show how much she is like a male hero. She is, after all, the only woman to participate in the voyage of the Argo and the Kalydonian boar-hunt. The heroic infant is, by definition, male.[96] This is replicated in vase-painting, where we find heroes in their infancy and childhood, but not heroines. The few young heroines found on vases are easily explained. Helen, always anomalous, is shown emerging from her egg, looking more like a miniature woman than a baby. The young Antigone and Ismene appear on vases illustrating Sophocles' Oidipous Tyrannos, where they represent not so much mythic figures as characters in the drama.[97]

To return to our comparison, we note then that both characters are dogged by the hostility of Hera, and on each of them it has a similar

not form a unity). See also K. Schauenburg, "Herakles unter Göttern," Gymnasium 70 (1963) 113–33 and plates.

[94] See the extended discussion of Hera and Herakles in Chapter 3.

[95] For this triangulation effect, see Chapter 3. The implications of Ino's relation to Dionysos are discussed at length in Chapter 4, "Dionysiac Heroines."

[96] It is interesting to compare the remarks of Gilligan (1987): "Once again it turns out to be the male child—the coming generation of men like George Bernard Shaw, William James, Martin Luther, and Mahatma Gandhi—who provide Erikson with his most vivid illustrations" (63).

[97] See L. Burn, "Vase-Painting in Fifth-Century Athens," in Looking at Greek Vases, ed. Rasmussen and Spivey (Cambridge, 1991) 123 for a discussion of depictions of child heroes on vases, all of them male. See LIMC s.v. "Helene," "Antigone."

effect. Madness, at least in some versions of the Ino myth, is the reason for the murder or attempted murder of her children. Herakles' murder of his children while stricken with insanity sent by Hera is an ancient part of his story, although there is some variation in chronology.[98] Ino has no *ponoi* (labors) to carry out but must undergo difficulties in her marital life. Each of them is forced at some point to assume the role of a social inferior. Herakles must dress as a woman and play the servant for Omphale, while Ino, banished from her own house by her divorce from Athamas, returns in the guise of a servant girl.[99] Her disguise allows her to enact the revenge that may be purely an act of sexual jealousy, or a way to save her children, depending on the version in question. Either she plots to kill the second wife's children or tricks her into killing her own instead of Ino's. Herakles is driven to violence by erotic desire, in the sacking of Oichalia, and felled by the jealousy of his wife Deianeira. Each of these figures experiences and inflicts suffering because of *eros*, although the violence of the heroine is provoked by jealousy, while the hero uses violence as a means to satisfy his desires.

Finally, each of these mortal figures dies under ambiguous circumstances that lead to immortality. Herakles dies on a mountain top, and by the purging effect of fire, achieves immortality on Olympos.[100] Ino plunges downward from a cliff, and through contact with water suffers a sea-change into the marine goddess Leukothea. We should not be surprised that Herakles does not get a new name, since this phenomenon is largely limited to women and children. These violent and unusual deaths lead to a diffusion of cult that is uncommon for heroes.[101] From the remarks made earlier in this chapter, it should be apparent that also in cult-observance, Ino is set apart from other heroines and shares in kinds

[98] The madness of Herakles goes back at least to the *Kypria* (Proklos p. 18. Kinkel) and the murder of his children is to be found in Stesichorus (fr. 230 *PMG* = Paus. 9.11.1–2). See Shapiro (1983).

[99] This seems to have been the plot of Euripides' *Ino* as recounted by Hyginus. On Herakles as "slave, woman, and madman," see Nicole Loraux, "Herakles: The Super-Male and the Feminine," trans. R. Lamberton in *Before Sexuality*, ed. Halperin, Winkler, and Zeitlin (Princeton, 1990) 24, reprinted in *The Experiences of Tiresias* (Princeton, 1995) 116–39.

[100] For the purging of mortality by fire in sacrificial practice, see J.-P. Vernant, "At Man's Table: Hesiod's Foundation Myth of Sacrifice," in *The Cuisine of Sacrifice among the Greeks*, ed. M. Detienne and J.-P. Vernant, trans. Paula Wissing (Chicago, 1989 [Paris, 1979]) esp. 21–43; W. Furley, *Studies in the Use of Fire in Ancient Greek religion* (New York, 1981) 5–6.

[101] For extensive information on the cult of Herakles in Boiotia, see A. Schachter, *Cults of Boiotia*, *BICS* suppl. 38.2 (1986) 1–37, who concludes that his cult at Thebes remained that of a hero (see pp. 20 and 21 n.1). Worship of Herakles was, however, by no means confined to Boiotia. The mass of evidence is imposing. See O. Gruppe, "Herakles," *RE* suppl. 3, especially 910–1015, for the diffusion and nature of Herakles' cult. The cult of Ino-Leukothea is discussed above and in Chapter 4.

of honors usually limited to male heroes. As we have already mentioned, each was the recipient of both heroic and divine honors. Furthermore, each was in antiquity almost a byword for excessive suffering. Herakles' reputation as the suffering hero led to his later equation with Jesus as a prototypical "Man of Sorrows," while *Inous achē* (the sorrows of Ino) was a proverbial expression.[102]

The designation "hero" carries with it no particular moral weight. Heroes are under no obligation to behave well, and in fact they often engage in transgressive behavior. They are frequently rapists, murderers, and challengers of the gods—guilty, in short, of every kind of hybris—and their myths often culminate in criminal acts beyond the scope of ordinary mortals. They offend, like Herakles or Oidipous, against their most intimate family members, or like Lykaon or Ixion, against the gods. The typical heroine is transgressed against rather than transgressing, and that transgression usually takes the form of rape or attempted destruction of offspring.[103] Like heroes, however, heroines may also commit terrifying crimes. Klytemnestra and Medea, paradigmatically evil women in Greek culture, are no less heroines for all that.

In conclusion let us return to the topic of transformation touched on earlier in this section. As noted above, in myths of heroines the crisis is frequently resolved by some kind of metamorphosis.[104] Metamorphosis is not limited to mortals, but for the gods it is usually a manifestation of power and a deliberate strategy. Proteus and Thetis metamorphose to avoid capture. Zeus frequently changes shape to carry out his seductions. This strategy is not always effective: both Proteus and Thetis are eventually taken. When Demeter becomes a horse to escape the lust of Poseidon, he takes on the form of a stallion and rapes her. The gods, however, control metamorphosis, and so for them it is self-inflicted and temporary, while for mortals, it is almost always imposed from without.[105] They may, as Io did, eventually regain human form, but usually the change is permanent, turning them into natural phenomena, wildlife or parts of the landscape. Finally, metamorphosis may be, as for Aktaion, a prelude to destruction.

While male figures do undergo metamorphosis, this kind of resolution

---

[102] See G. Karl Galinsky, *The Herakles Theme* (Totowa, N.J., 1972) 202–5, 228n.39. *Suda* s.v. Ἰνοῦς ἄχη. See also Zenobius 4.38, *Paroemiographi Graeci*, ed. Thomas Gaisford (Osnabrück, 1972). The similar phrases ἀχέεσσιν Ἰνου[ς and Ἰνους παθήμα[σι appear in a fragment of Ibycus with commentary (fr. 282b iii Campbell).

[103] See P.M.C. Forbes Irving, *Metamorphosis in Greek Myths* (Oxford, 1990) 69, on women as passive victims of male lust, who are nonetheless themselves transformed. He remarks that "[i]n myth women are continually punished for being raped."

[104] See F. Dupont, "Se reproduire ou se mètamorphoser," *Topique: Revue freudienne* 9–10 (1971) 139–60.

[105] Only the heroine Mestra has the power to change shape at will. See Appendix.

is particularly common in myths of heroines. In some familiar examples, Prokne and Philomele are transformed into birds, and Kallisto into a bear. Niobe becomes a rock, Daphne a tree, the Pleiades a constellation. Analysis of the evidence presented by Forbes Irving shows that heroines undergo metamorphosis more often than heroes.[106] This phenomenon may owe something to a tendency, found in many cultures, to equate the feminine with nature.[107] Many of these myths focus on transitional moments such as the change from virginity to mature sexuality, a passage that for women is attended by a far greater degree of danger and physical change.[108] The frequent transformations of heroines seem to reflect an awareness of the more radical physical and social transformations that occur at critical moments in the lives of women.

In the myths, metamorphoses are performed by the gods, to resolve a crisis or prevent a crime, or to assuage the grief of a victim. It is often unclear whether the transformation is a reward, a rescue, or a punishment.[109] Most striking among these metamorphoses are the ones that turn a mortal into an immortal.[110] Even this can be ambiguous, for becoming immortal may only mean being turned into a star. At times, however, the transition to immortality involves a total transformation, in which the heroine becomes a goddess and takes on a new name, as when Iphigeneia, "by the will of Artemis," becomes Hekate (Paus. 1.43.1, quoting Hesiod). Investigation of the intricate relation between mortal and immortal, hinted at in this enigmatic passage and elsewhere made more explicit, forms the basis for much of what follows.

[106] Forbes Irving (1990) passim. Exceptions are myths found only in later authors, and in the category of insects, reptiles, and sea creatures, where males outnumber females 7:6. In the striking case of metamorphosis into plants, females outnumber males 17:2.

[107] Simone de Beauvoir made this point in *The Second Sex*, trans. Parshley (New York, 1953). For a systematic treatment of the problem in anthropological terms, see Sherry B. Ortner, "Is Female to Male as Nature Is to Culture?" in *Women, Culture, and Society*, ed. Rosaldo and Lamphere (Stanford, 1974) 67–87.

[108] See A. Carson, "Putting Her in Her Place: Women, Dirt, and Desire," in Halperin, Winkler, and Zeitlin, eds. (1990) 135–69.

[109] Forbes Irving (1990) makes it clear that this depends in part on the genre of the work and in part on the nature of the transformation. In tragedy, metamorphosis may be "a compromise with some harsh reality" (17). More often the transformation reflects "the negative side of the link between animals, women, and sex" as a punishment for sexual transgression (66), while transformation into a bird is more ambiguous (112).

[110] Here Forbes Irving and I part company. He does not believe that transformation is "a narrative motif which is interchangeable with motifs such as death (or apotheosis)" (195–96).

CHAPTER THREE

Mortals and Immortals

ἀθάνατοι θνητοί, θνητοὶ ἀθάνατοι, ζῶντες τὸν
ἐκείνων θάνατον, τὸν δὲ ἐκείνων βίον τεθνεῶτες.

Immortals are mortal, mortals immortal, living the
others' death, dead in the others' life.
—Heraclitus (frg. 62 Diels-Kranz trans. C. H. Kahn)

BETWEEN MORTALITY AND IMMORTALITY

A defining feature of heroic figures is their similarity and proximity to
the gods, with whom they are intimately but ambiguously connected.
Numerous myths detail the relations of heroes and heroines with gods
who are their parents, lovers, or protectors, and not infrequently their
enemies. Much has been written about the relations of gods and mortals,
but little about the role of gender in determining the character of these
interactions. Not only can such a role be demonstrated, but this demon-
stration will also help to define the category of heroine, causing it to
stand out in sharper relief.

This chapter analyzes the structure of relations between heroized and
divine figures in Greek myth and cult. After a discussion of several passages of early Greek poetry about relations between mortals and immortals, we proceed to an overview of these relations as they appear in myth.
Although this chapter is structured as an analysis of mythic patterns, cult
evidence will be introduced wherever possible. Often fragmentary, and
serving different purposes from the mythic accounts, this evidence at
times allows for a more nuanced reading of the mythic material. In particular the concept of "ritual antagonism" discussed below centers on the
relationship between myth and cult. In order to bring issues of gender to
the foreground, I examine in turn god-hero, goddess-hero, god-heroine,
and goddess-heroine pairs.

If a close relationship with the gods is one of the most characteristic
features of the hero, certainly the other, even more marked, is the fact
of mortality. As has been frequently observed, heroes are distinguished
from most other mythic beings by their "obligatory relationship with
death."[1] Death defines the difference between god and hero, and death

---

[1] For the hero's "rapporto obbligatorio con la morte," see I. Chirassi Colombo, "Heros
Achilleus—Theos Apollon" in *Il mito greco*, ed. Gentili and Paione (Rome, 1977) 231. See

is the source of the inequality inevitable in any relationship between them.

This inherent inequality between those subject to death and those who are not provides many of the myths with their tragic denouement. These pairings, even when characterized by the affective relations of parenthood, erotic love, or friendship, are nonetheless highly charged with ambivalence and are often marked by hybris and betrayal reflecting an underlying rivalry between the participants. Even ostensibly positive relationships may have a background or undertone of hostility.[2] Where the identity of the two figures is closest, the relationship is cast in even more explicitly hostile terms. Some heroes have both a divine protector and a divine antagonist who simultaneously represent the opposing tendencies of closeness and antagonism.

The opposition between hero and god may be presented as enmity of the god toward the hero or as presumption or hybris on the part of the hero. The myth of Herakles revolves around the hatred of Hera for the son of Zeus by a mortal woman, a hatred that the hero himself has done nothing to incur. Odysseus' troubles with Poseidon stem from the blinding of Polyphemos, an act committed in self-defense. Odysseus' conduct in this episode shows incautious arrogance, but not deliberate defiance of Polyphemos' father, the god Poseidon. Frequently, then, the enmity of a god seems, if not unmotivated, at least undeserved. Some heroes, on the other hand, openly challenge the god. The *theomachos*, the hero who dares to fight with a god, is a recurring theme in the *Iliad*. The hybris he represents is more often threatened than carried out, but he exists as a cautionary figure to whom both gods and mortals refer. Apollo warns Diomedes (5.440–42), Patroklos (16.707–9), and Achilles (22.8–13) against continuing to oppose him on the battlefield. Dione comforts Aphrodite after her encounter with Diomedes by saying that those who fight the gods do not live long:

> ὅττι μάλ' οὐ δηναιὸς ὃς ἀθανάτοισι μάχηται,
> οὐδέ τί μιν παῖδες ποτὶ γούνασι παππάζουσιν
> ἐλθόντ' ἐκ πολέμοιο καὶ αἰνῆς δηϊοτῆτος.

> Not long for this world is he who fights with the gods,
> nor will his children at his knees cry out "Papa"
> when he returns from terrible battle.

> *(Iliad 5.407–9)*

---

also A. Brelich, *Gli eroi greci* (Roma, 1958) 80–90; G. Nagy, *Best of the Achaeans* (Baltimore, 1979).

[2] See J. S. Clay, *The Wrath of Athena* (Princeton, 1983) passim. I find her presentation of this phenomenon more convincing than her application of it to the relationship between Athena and Odysseus.

Shortly thereafter (6.130ff.), Diomedes himself repeats the lesson to Glaukos, citing the cautionary tale of Lykourgos, who dared to challenge the god Dionysos, with predictable results.[3]

The *theomachos* continues to be a significant figure throughout Greek myth and literature.[4] Heroic opposition to the gods takes various, often less physical forms. Occasionally these transgressions are inadvertent, as when Philoktetes accidentally treads on ground sacred to Chryse, but more often they are reckless or even deliberate. Atalante and her husband defile the grove of Zeus by having intercourse there; the daughters of Proitos refuse to worship Dionysos, staying home while all the other women celebrate his rites.[5] Other forms of hybris include challenging the divinity to some sort of contest, or boasting to exceed her at whatever activity is most typically hers. Thus Orion claims to be a better hunter than Artemis; his wife Side challenges Hera to a beauty contest.[6]

Whether the offense is deliberate or not, the opponent of the gods is liable to pay with her life. Death frequently comes to heroes at the hands of the gods, as in the story of Lykourgos told by Diomedes. Nor is overt hostility a necessary component of these myths. The theme of accidental killing (*phonos akousios*) may be invoked to explain why, for example, Apollo kills his beloved Hyakinthos.[7] Since gods kill even heroes of whom they are very fond, one may suspect that the killing is the essential element and that the myths of hostility have grown up around this central fact.

RITUAL ANTAGONISM

When these myths are read in the light of cultic evidence, a more complex and even contradictory pattern emerges. While a heroine is frequently represented as the object of a particular god's hostility, the cult evidence shows her co-existing in close proximity with that same divin-

---

[3] G. A. Privitera, *Dioniso in Omero e nella poesia greca arcaica* (Rome, 1970) 53–74; R. Seaford, *Reciprocity and Ritual: Homer and Tragedy in the Developing City-State* (Oxford, 1994) 316.

[4] J. C. Kamerbeek, "On the Conception of θεομάχος in Relation to Greek Tragedy," *Mnemosyne* s. 4, I (1948) 271–83.

[5] For Atalante, see Appendix. For the Proitides, who in some versions offend Hera, see Hesiod frg. 131 M-W = Apollod. 2.2.2; Pherec. in *FGrH* 3 F 114.

[6] On the theme of agon between gods and mortals, I. Weiler, *Der Agon im Mythos* (Darmstadt, 1974). For Side, see Apollod. 1.4.3. For Orion, see *Od.* 5.121–24, as well as Apollod. 1.4.3–5, where the challenge is to a game of discus-throwing. Here also his crime is rape. See Brelich (1958) 260–64 for this feature of heroic hybris.

[7] See Brelich (1958) 89 for a discussion of the deaths of heroes. He discusses involuntary homicide for the most part as a feature of heroic, not divine, behavior, but see p. 359 for Apollo as a killer of heroes.

ity, sharing a sanctuary, a festival, and sometimes even a name. Ancient texts offer more than a few examples of heroic tombs in the temples of gods.[8] Pfister, who has collected many of these references, lists four ways that ancient writers account for this apparent violation of the usual taboo against introducing reminders of human mortality into a sanctuary of a god. The hero was either a cult-founder or priest of the god; or a son, protégé, or beloved of the god; or was buried in the temple as a kind of expiation; or finally, performed some extraordinary service to the community.[9] These explanations cover much of the ground but leave unexplained those instances, such as the burial of Erechtheus in the sanctuary of Poseidon in Athens, which unite two figures presented as hostile to one another in myth.[10]

Scholars of Greek religion have come to varying conclusions about the meaning of this bewildering complex of associations, depending on the particular theories they hold about the origin of heroes as a class. Since heroes occupy an intermediate (though not mediating or intercessory, *pace* Farnell) position between gods and mortals, many attempts have been made to explain this category by reducing it to a development of one of the other two.[11] Thus heroes are either real human beings elevated or gods demoted. The first of these positions is sometimes identified as "euhemerist," after the writer of the late fourth or early third century who imagined that the gods were merely extraordinary human beings glorified after death. The "neo-euhemerists," similarly, imagine a once-living human being lurking behind *heroic* myths and cult practices, although they would reject such explanations if applied to the gods. Farnell, who in seeking the origin of a heroic figure frequently rejects "invention by the poet" in favor of "reality," is probably the last great proponent of this explanation. The "faded god" theory, advanced by Usener among others, is no longer in fashion, although it is occasionally and convincingly revived not as a global explanation, but in order to clarify a particular mythic figure.[12]

Until recently scholars have sought exclusively historical explanations

---

[8] Pausanias has Aigyptos (7.21.13), Hippolytos (1.22.1), Kallisto (8.35.8), Orestes (3.11.10) all buried in, or next to, a temple. See also the list of Clem., *Protr.* 3.45.1.

[9] F. Pfister, *Der Reliquienkult im Altertum* (Geissen, 1912) 2:450–57.

[10] For Erechtheus, see R. Parker, "Myths of Early Athens," in *Interpretations of Greek Mythology*, ed. J. Bremmer (London, 1987) 202f.

[11] L. R. Farnell, *Greek Hero Cults and Ideas of Immortality* (Oxford, 1921) 371 suggests that heroes who were originally priests or cult-founders, or who were buried in the temple of a divinity, might "play the rôle of mediators or intercessors with the higher power, thus fulfilling part of the function of the mediaeval saint in Christian theology." I know of no evidence to support this claim.

[12] H. Usener, *Götternamen* (Bonn, 1948). For Helen's divine origins, see L. Clader, *Helen: The Evolution from Divine to Heroic in Greek Epic Tradition* (Leiden, 1976) 72–82.

for this discrepancy between hostile relations in myth and co-existence in cult, sometimes attempting to establish the priority of one figure over the other. Particularly perplexing are cases in which the god bears the hero's name as an epithet. Has the god taken his name from the hero, or is the hero a back-formation resulting from a detached, and personified, epithet of the god?

One of our best witnesses for ancient cult, although a latecomer, Pausanias offers us many examples of hero-name epithets for gods, and it would be interesting to know how he resolved this problem for himself. Unfortunately, he is inconsistent or perhaps feels no need for a unified explanation. He attributes the name of the temple of Athena Aiantis to a dedication by the hero Aias (1.42.4), that of Hera Bunaea to its foundation by a hero Bunus (2.4.7), and that of Artemis Knagia to the hero Knagos, who induced her priestess to run away with him and bring the cult-image along (3.18.4–5). He also cites a temenos of Zeus Messapeos, named after a priest of Zeus by that name (3.20.3). Nonetheless, he insists that Kalliste is an epithet of the goddess Artemis and refuses to repeat another explanation he has heard (1.29.2), even when the sanctuary of this goddess is located above the burial mound of the heroine Kallisto (8.35.8). In 2.35.1 he mentions the temple of Artemis "surnamed Iphigeneia" at Hermione, again with no attempt at explanation, although elsewhere he speaks of Iphigeneia as distinct from Artemis.

On the subject of Artemis and Iphigeneia, Farnell himself explicitly changed sides.[13] Although he is willing to entertain the possibility of an original identity between god and hero, his hypothesis does not expand to accommodate any ambivalence in the relationship as expressed in myth. For him, hostility in myth is positively a counter-argument against any relationship of identification. Time and again, he brings up, only to reject it, the idea that the two might coincide. For example, between Athena and Telemonian Aias he finds not "intimacy" but "occasional discord," and on the subject of Helen, he says, "We might with Herodotus regard her as a double of Aphrodite; but far from the legend justifying such an approximation of the two, it suggests at times an antagonism between them."[14] Marie Delcourt, on the other hand, sees the tension between hostility and identity as proof of a historical process. In her discussion of the role of Pyrrhos in the cult of Apollo at Delphi, she takes him to be a local daimon eclipsed by the arrival of a Panhellenic deity, and reduced thereby to the role of *paredros* (consort). She com-

---

[13] Farnell (1921) 56ff. Having put forth the notion that Iphigeneia was the original goddess in *The Cults of the Greek States* (Oxford, 1896) 2:438–41, here he inclines to the view that she is a heroized priestess.

[14] Farnell (1921) 309, 324.

ments that legends of heroes conquered by gods generally include an element of antagonism, which is not found in cult, where the two figures are honored side-by-side.[15]

Attempts to understand these phenomena historically have followed two divergent paths. Either the myth of hostility between god and hero has been taken as the trace of an actual conflict between the "indigenous," possibly pre-Greek cult of a hero or local divinity and the invading cult of a Dorian, Panhellenic, or non-Greek god;[16] or the myth of hostility has been interpreted as arising from a misunderstanding caused by the burial of the god's priest within the temple precinct.[17] Each of these theories may be plausible in specific cases but betrays its weakness when generalized. The first theory assumes a model of constant cultural conflict, while providing a slot for the favored bogeyman of the moment. Thus Apollo may be Dorian or Lycian, but he is always an invader. Theories of this kind tend to be short-lived.[18] Even if the model of cultural conflict is not to be completely discounted, its workings are perhaps more subtle than some scholars have allowed. Burkert has observed that the model of the "iron curtain" is less apt than one of peaceful co-existence.[19] The second theory, that earlier burial practices were misinterpreted, assumes a lapse of cultural memory that is highly unlikely. In all periods city-founders and others honored by the city were buried in public places where tombs were otherwise forbidden. A hero's tomb in a temple would not by itself suggest a violent end at the hands of the resident divinity, but instead high honor.[20]

Similar explanations are advanced in cases where a god and hero share a name. When a goddess bears the heroic name as an epithet, like "Artemis Iphigeneia," the goddess Artemis is said to have taken over and

---

[15] M. Delcourt, *Pyrrhos et Pyrrha: Recherches sur les valeurs du feu dans les légendes helléniques* (Paris, 1965) 45–46.

[16] For this theory as applied to Hyakinthos and Apollo, see B. C. Dietrich, "The Dorian Hyakinthia: A Survival from the Bronze Age," *Kadmos* 14.2 (1975) 133–42. See also J. Mikalson, "Erechtheus and the Panathenaia," *AJP* 97 (1976) 141–53.

[17] Delcourt (1965) 45–46.

[18] W. Burkert, "Apellai und Apollon," *RM* 118 (1975) 21, cites evidence that Apollo was in fact a foreign god to the Lycians. His epithet Paian appears on Linear B tablets, suggesting an early presence for Apollo in Greece. See W. Burkert, *Greek Religion* trans. John Raffan (Cambridge, Mass., 1985); M. Ventris and J. Chadwick, *Documents in Mycenaean Greek*, 2d ed. (Cambridge, 1973) 311–12, doc. 208. Dionysos was similarly held to be a late-arriving foreigner, until his name was found on two Linear B tablets, demonstrating his presence in Greece from an early date (127, 411).

[19] Burkert (1975) 17. See also J. Chadwick, "Who Were the Dorians?" *PP* 31 (1976) 103–17.

[20] See Roland Martin, *Recherches sur l'agora grecque* (Paris, 1951) 194–201; F. de Polignac, *La Naissance de la cité grecque* (Paris, 1984) 132ff.

absorbed the cult of a local goddess Iphigeneia. This explanation harmonizes with the cultural conflict theory above. But "Iphigeneia" the heroine has also been explained as a personification of the epithet of Artemis, which had become detached from the goddess to live a life of its own. Here again we are asked to fall back on the explanatory power of misunderstanding. This may be an appealing solution for modern scholars faced with scant information, but it would be a mistake to project our own frustrations onto the ancient Greeks, who had access to the syntax, as it were, of their own complex polytheism.[21] The traditions evolve through time, it is true, but they do so according to that syntax, the internal logic of the system. To explain the salient features of hero cult as a series of misunderstandings is to underestimate the Greek mythic and religious imagination and to overestimate our ability to explain things by reference to their origins.

The search for a unified explanation has largely gone out of fashion, clearing the way for a necessary redefinition of the problem. Nilsson cheerfully accepts the varied nature and origins of heroes.[22] Brelich, indicating a direction that has since proved productive, rejects altogether the quest for the origin of the hero in favor of a more purely phenomenological approach. He argues for the construction of a morphology founded on the known evidence, rather than on preconceptions about the nature of heroes.[23]

The ritual significance of the antagonism between mortal and immortal has been elaborated by Burkert, Nagy, and others. For Burkert, the polarity between god and hero is expressed in the idea of the hero as both mirror-image and sacrificial victim.[24] Nagy's understanding of the intersection between ritual and myth is reflected in the term "ritual antagonism," which he considers "a fundamental principle in Hellenic religion." In his words, "antagonism between hero and god in myth corresponds to the ritual requirements of symbiosis between hero and god in cult."[25] Such phenomena occur most often when the god and the hero are similar in nature, and thus usually of the same sex. Instances

---

[21] Burkert (1985) 218, in an eloquent comment on the limits of our own understanding of the Greek material, says that "the language of polytheism can only be learned passively."

[22] "Eine sehr bunte und gemischte Gesellschaft verschiedenen Ursprungs" (a very motley and mixed company of various origins), M. Nilsson, *Geschichte der Griechischen Religion* (Munich, 1967) 1:185.

[23] Brelich (1958) 16–20.

[24] "Der Heros als umdunkeltes Spiegelbild des Gottes in der unauflöslichen Polarität des Opfers," Burkert (1975) 19. This theme is also central to his book *Homo Necans* (Berkeley, 1983). The issue of hero as ritual substitute is particularly relevant to the discussion of the sacrifice of Iphigeneia in Chapter 5.

[25] Nagy (1979) 120.

such as the hostility of Apollo toward Achilles so central to the plot of the *Iliad* come readily to mind.[26] In the case of Hera and Herakles, although the myths tell of enmity, the names of the participants themselves hint at a different story, as we shall see.

The heroes, when we first encounter them in epic, are men and women who lived in an age when the gods still mingled freely in human lives: on the battlefield, at table, in bed. Strictly speaking, by the "dramatic" time of the Homeric poems, the gods no longer share meals with mortals, since that ended with the sacrifice of Prometheus.[27] Nor do they usually still mate with them. Nonetheless, it is clear from the number of heroes of divine parentage that such events had taken place in the very recent past.[28] That Plato has Socrates derive *hērōs* (ἥρως) from *erōs* (ἔρως), from the love of gods for mortal women and of mortal men for goddesses, shows that this association retained its force.[29]

The heroes who receive particular mention in the epic tradition are those whose special qualities attract the notice of the gods. These *isotheoi* or *antitheoi* are, by virtue of strength, beauty, and cleverness, worthy partners of the gods in love and war.[30] Worthy, but not truly equal, as we see from the depressing regularity with which these encounters end in disaster for the mortal. (For the gods there are no disastrous endings.) As we have noted above, this similarity to the gods is doubly dangerous, because it attracts their jealousy as well as their admiration.

The way the gods themselves feel about these encounters is also clearly

---

[26] See Chirassi Colombo (1977). Nagy (1979) 143–47 discusses the "thematic and formal convergences" between these two figures, as well as those between another hostile pair, Athena the goddess of the city, and Hector, whose function as bulwark of Troy is revealed in the name of his son Astyanax, as well as in his own.

[27] The sharing of meals with the gods, from the time of Prometheus, is purely symbolic. See F. Pfister, "Theoxenia," *RE* A10 (1934), 2256–58.

[28] The *Homeric Hymn to Aphrodite* has been interpreted as indicating the end of an era of mating between gods and mortals. The encounter of the goddess with Anchises results in the birth of Aineias, a hero of the Trojan war, but it does not lead to the immortalization of the human lover. The time for such transformations is presumably over. See Peter Smith, *Nurseling of Mortality* (Frankfurt, 1981). Clay (1983) also makes this point explicitly, 142n.22. The absence of apotheosis may, however, be more a reflection of generic convention, the "realism" of epic.

[29] Πάντες δήπου γεγόνασιν ἐρασθέντος ἢ θεοῦ θνητῆς ἢ θνητοῦ θεᾶς. ἐὰν οὖν σκοπῇς καὶ τοῦτο κατὰ τὴν Ἀττικὴν τὴν παλαιὰν φωνήν, μᾶλλον εἴσῃ· δηλώσει γάρ σοι ὅτι παρὰ τὸ τοῦ ἔρωτος ὄνομα, ὅθεν γεγόνασιν οἱ ἥρωες, σμικρὸν παρηγμένον ἐστὶν †ὀνό-ματος† χάριν *Crat.* 398d: "All of them sprang either from the love of a god for a mortal woman, or of a mortal man for a goddess. Think of the word in the old Attic, and you will see better that the name *heros* is only a slight alteration of Eros, from whom the heroes sprang." Trans. Jowett in *The Collected Dialogues of Plato*, ed. E. Hamilton and H. Cairns (Princeton, 1966).

[30] To Robert Lamberton I owe the observation that the term *antitheoi* was "conveniently misread in late antiquity (by Christians and Pagans alike) as 'opposing the gods, impious.'"

mapped out in the archaic texts. At times, mortals are erotic conquests to be listed in comic fashion (cf. Zeus' catalogue of mortal lovers in *Iliad* 14). In other instances, usually when the relationship is parental, the mortal is cherished and protected, like Aineias (*Iliad* 5.312ff.), or deeply mourned, like Sarpedon (*Iliad* 16.433ff.). Aphrodite's words in *Homeric Hymn* 5 (198–99) are the most explicit statement of the gods' distress at contact with mortality:

τῷ δὲ καὶ Αἰνείας ὄνομ' ἔσσεται οὕνεκα μ'αἰνὸν
ἔοχεν ἄχος, ἕνεκα βροτοῦ ἀνέρος ἔμπεσον εὐνῇ

His name will be Aineias, because of the terrible (*ainos*) pain which I felt, falling into the bed of a mortal man.[31]

MORTALS AND IMMORTALS: THREE KEY PASSAGES

The passages discussed in this section present episodes of erotic or hostile contact between gods and mortals, and in so doing, shed light on an ideological problem central to Greek religious thought, the necessity and difficulty of maintaining the boundaries that separate and define these two classes of being.

ZEUS' EROTIC CATALOGUE: *ILIAD* 14.313–28

Ἥρη, κεῖσε μὲν ἔστι καὶ ὕστερον ὁρμηθῆναι,
νῶϊ δ' ἄγ' ἐν φιλότητι τραπείομεν εὐνηθέντε.
οὐ γάρ πώ ποτέ μ' ὧδε θεᾶς ἔρος οὐδὲ γυναικὸς
θυμὸν ἐνὶ στήθεσσι περιπροχυθεὶς ἐδάμαυσεν,
οὐδ' ὁπότ' ἠρασάμην Ἰξιονίης ἀλόχοιο,
ἣ τέκε Πειρίθοον, θεόφιν μήστωρ' ἀτάλαντον·
οὐδ' ὅτε περ Δανάης καλλισφύρου Ἀκρισιώνης,
ἣ τέκε Περσῆα, πάντων ἀριδείκετον ἀνδρῶν·
οὐδ' ὅτε Φοίνικος κούρης τηλεκλειτοῖο,
ἣ τέκε μοι Μίνων τε καὶ ἀντίθεον Ῥαδάμανθυν·
οὐδ' ὅτε περ Σεμέλης οὐδ' Ἀλκμήνης ἐνὶ Θήβῃ,
ἥ ῥ' Ἡρακλῆα κρατερόφρονα γείνατο παῖδα·
ἡ δὲ Διώνυσον Σεμέλη τέκε, χάρμα βροτοῖσιν·
οὐδ' ὅτε Δήμητρος καλλιπλοκάμοιο ἀνάσσης,
οὐδ' ὁπότε Λητοῦς ἐρικυδέος, οὐδὲ σεῦ αὐτῆς,
ὡς σέο νῦν ἔραμαι καί με γλυκὺς ἵμερος αἱρεῖ.

---

[31] Here, the name Aineias is treated as if derived from αἰνός (*ainos*), "terrible, awful."

Hera, you may go there later,
but now come, let us turn to lovemaking.
For never did such desire for goddess or woman
ever flood over me, taming the heart in my breast,
not even when I loved Ixion's wife,
who bore Peirithoös, the gods' equal in counsel;
nor slim-ankled Danae daughter of Akrisios,
who bore Perseus, most renowned of men;
nor the daughter of far-famed Phoinix,
who bore Minos and godlike Rhadamanthys;
nor even Semele or Alkmene in Thebes—
one bore stouthearted Herakles;
the other, Semele, bore Dionysos, joy for mortals;
not for Demeter, the fair-haired queen
nor for glorious Leto, nor even for you
has such sweet desire ever taken me!

A comically self-aggrandizing attempt at seduction, and the first example of a genre culminating in Leporello's aria in Mozart's *Don Giovanni*, Zeus' list of conquests reveals something of sexual politics on Olympos, but even more about relations between mortals and immortals.[32] In a carefully structured catalogue, the objects of Zeus' previous desires are listed in a progression from mortal women who bear mortal offspring to goddesses who bear children immortal like themselves.[33] Inevitably, each one of these encounters results in a child, for "the beds of the gods are not unfulfilled" (*ouk apophōlioi eunai / athanatōn*, Od. 11.249–50).

The catalogue consists of a series of pairs. First are mortal women who bear mortal children: Dia, the wife of Ixion (317–18), mother of Peirithoös, and Danae, the daughter of Akrisios, mother of Perseus (319–20). Each heroine is clearly identified by a family affiliation, although in the case of Dia, not by name. The heroes themselves, the sons of Zeus, are clearly named. Next come Minos and Rhadamanthys, sons of Europe, the daughter of Phoinix (321–22). Again, the heroine is identified only by family affiliation—here a patronymic and the names of her sons. She is mortal, as are her sons. They do, however, live on in the Underworld as judges, a position that allows them a share of power and thus a special

---

[32] Although this passage has been suspected as an interpolation, no one has ever suggested that it was not an authentic piece of early Greek poetry. For this reason, it is useful for our purposes. See R. Janko, *The Iliad: A Commentary* (Cambridge, 1991) vol. 4, 201–3.

[33] See M. L. West, *The Hesiodic Catalogue of Women* (Oxford, 1985) 94 and Hesiod, *Theogony,* ed. and commentary (Oxford, 1966) 39 on the differing principles of organization that govern the *Catalogue of Women* and the end of the *Theogony,* where descending order of status prevails.

relation to death. The next pair, Herakles and Dionysos, are introduced in chiastic order after the names of their mothers, Semele and Alkmene (323–25). These two are the paradigmatic examples of mortals who cross the divide to divinity, although they are represented very differently in the tradition, which stresses the mortality of Herakles and the immortality of Dionysos. These divine offspring lead to the final pair.

Here, however, our expectations are thwarted, for the next two names, of the goddesses Demeter and Leto, are not followed by the names of their divine offspring at all. This transition from heroines to goddesses, among the loves of Zeus, leads up to Hera herself, in line 327, at which point the symmetry breaks down. In the transition from divine offspring to divine lovers, the pivot is Semele, whose name is mentioned a second time, in the same line in which her son Dionysos is called "a joy for mortals" (charma brotoisin). Semele is the only female figure in this catalogue who was worshiped as both heroine and goddess, and her pivotal placement in the catalogue corresponds to her ambiguous position in cult.

An examination of this list reveals that the sons of Zeus stand out among heroes in their relation to death, progressing in pairs toward immortality. Peirithoös and Perseus, although great heroes, do not transcend the barrier of mortality.[34] Minos and Rhadamanthys become more powerful in death than in life, as the judges of the underworld. Herakles is transported to Olympos and immortalized, although he never quite ceases to be, simultaneously, a hero. The history of his worship is complicated and includes both heroic and divine elements. Most notably, Dionysos becomes a god, losing all taint of mortality. His extraordinary second birth from the thigh of Zeus is perhaps the source of his ability to make the transition. Despite the unusual status of these sons of Zeus, they are in no way spared the tribulations of heroic existence. Herakles, in fact, suffers far more than most heroes.

Although Peirithoös and Perseus are lowest on the ladder to immortality, and there is no evidence of divinization or cult for them, some features of their myths unite them in their relation to mortality. The *Odyssey* (11.631) seems to provide our earliest allusion to Peirithoös' ill-conceived attempt, abetted by Theseus, to steal Persephone from Hades to be his bride.[35] The attempt fails and Peirithoös must stay in Hades, while Theseus returns. Although Perseus never attempts a *katabasis*, or trip to the Underworld, his helmet of invisibility connects him with Hades, perhaps reflecting an original meaning or folk etymology of Hades

[34] There is an apparently late tradition that Perseus became a star (Hyginus *Fab.* 224). This is, however, rather different from true immortality.

[35] Cf. Pausanias 9.31.5 citing Hesiod.

as *Aïdēs*, "the invisible one."[36] Even more relevant is his resistance to the cult of Dionysos, which results in physical violence and even the murder of the god.[37] If these traditions about Perseus are old enough to be relevant to our reading of this passage (also of indeterminate age), they suggest an interesting conclusion. The mortal offspring of Zeus with which his catalogue begins are not only *theomachoi* but are also opponents of Zeus' divine offspring, Persephone and Dionysos, one of whom is named and the other alluded to in this very catalogue. In these myths the rebellious quality of the hero is distilled—Zeus' mortal sons cherish murderous or lustful designs against Zeus' immortal offspring and try to bridge the unbridgeable gap between them through rape and homicide. Ultimately, the structure of Zeus' catalogue presents a hierarchy from mortal to divine and reveals the peripheral place of both heroines and goddesses in that system.

LYKOURGOS AND DIONYSOS: *ILIAD* 6.130–43

οὐδὲ γὰρ οὐδὲ Δρύαντος υἱός κρατερὸς Λυκόοργος,
δὴν ἦν, ὅς ῥα θεοῖσιν ἐπουρανίοισιν ἔριζεν·
ὅς ποτε μαινομένοιο Διωνύσοιο τιθήνας
σεῦε κατ' ἠγάθεον Νυσήιον· αἱ δ' ἅμα πᾶσαι
θύσθλα χαμαὶ κατέχευαν, ὑπ' ἀνδροφόνοιο Λυκούργου
θεινόμεναι βουπλῆγι· Διώνυσος δὲ φοβηθεὶς
δύσεθ' ἁλὸς κατὰ κῦμα, Θέτις δ' ὑπεδέξατο κόλπῳ
δειδιότα· κρατερὸς γὰρ ἔχε τρόμος ἀνδρὸς ὁμοκλῇ.
τῷ μὲν ἔπειτ' ὀδύσαντο θεοὶ ῥεῖα ζώοντες,
καί μιν τυφλὸν ἔθηκε Κρόνου πάϊς· οὐδ' ἄρ' ἔτι δὴν
ἦν, ἐπεὶ ἀθανάτοισιν ἀπήχθετο πᾶσι θεοῖσιν·
οὐδ' ἂν ἐγὼ μακάρεσσι θεοῖς ἐθέλοιμι μάχεσθαι.
εἰ δέ τίς ἐσσι βροτῶν, οἳ ἀρούρης καρπὸν ἔδουσιν,
ἆσσον ἴθ', ὥς κεν θᾶσσον ὀλέθρου πείραθ' ἵκηαι.

Nor did Lykourgos, the powerful son of Dryas
live long, who fought against the heavenly gods,
that time when he chased the nurses of raving Dionysos
down the sacred hill of Nysa; for they all
threw their wands on the ground, struck
by the ox-goad of murderous Lykourgos

---

[36] W. Leaf, *The Iliad*, ed. and commentary (Amsterdam, 1971) on *Iliad*. 5.845. See Stanley A. Pease, "Some Aspects of Invisibility," *HSCP* 53 (1942) 26.

[37] Schol. T. *Iliad* 14.319. Pausanias 2.20.4 and 2.22.1 describe the tombs of the women who came to Dionysos' aid.

and Dionysos, terrified, dived into the sea-swell,
and Thetis received him, frightened, in her lap,
for a powerful trembling seized him at that man's cry.
And then, the easy-living gods were angered at him
and the son of Kronos made him blind. Nor did he
live long after that, hated by all the gods.
And so I would not wish to fight with the blessed gods,
but if you are mortal and eat the fruit of the earth
come near so that I may send you the quicker to destruction.

Diomedes tells Glaukos the story of Lykourgos' attack on Dionysos to explain why he will not fight before assuring himself that he faces a mortal opponent. An exchange of genealogies establishes that the heroes are linked by the friendship of their grandfathers. They decline to fight, and instead renew their bond with an exchange of armor. The episode is an extraordinary display of the power of guest-friendship (*xenia*), but for our purposes its interest lies in the exemplary tale with which it begins. Lykourgos' downfall belongs to the myths of resistance to Dionysiac worship, and here we see how closely related ritual antagonism and hybris can be. Diomedes' point is clear. "It's dangerous to fight the gods—look at what happened to Lykourgos. But once I know you are mortal, look out!"

It is interesting that in this version of the resistance myth, the mortal is actually able to provoke fear in the god, as well as in his mortal associates. We notice, moreover, that Lykourgos' punishment comes to him not directly at the hands of the god he has offended, but from the other gods, and explicitly from Zeus. This may be due to the marginal status of Dionysos in the *Iliad*.[38] In any case, the effect is to suggest the physical equality of god and mortal, or perhaps even to diminish the god who can be scared by a mortal. Apollo's warnings to Achilles and Patroklos not to challenge him in battle similarly hint that a mortal might upset the balance of fate by winning such a contest. While Greek myth generally tends to suppress the idea that a mortal might physically overcome a god, here we see traces of the idea that the hierarchy of power is neither self-evident nor immutable.[39]

THE *HOMERIC HYMN TO APHRODITE*

The *Homeric Hymn to Aphrodite* is an essential text for our understanding of *eros* between gods and mortals and its treatment in the tradition of

---

[38] See Privitera (1970) 13; Seaford (1994) 328–30.
[39] See discussion below of the contest between Idas and Apollo for Marpessa.

early Greek poetry.[40] Aphrodite's power is specified as the ability to force the gods to mate with mortal women.[41] It is for this reason that Zeus desires to humble her, precisely by forcing her in turn into the same kind of relation. Her encounter with Anchises emphasizes this issue once again. The shepherd's first thought is that he is in the presence of a goddess, and he is careful to address her in the form of a prayer (92–102). When his fears have been allayed, Anchises declares that no one, neither man nor god, can keep him from the immediate consummation of his passion. This consummation brings together the two terms *goddess* (*thea*) and *mortal* (*brotos*) so that they are side-by-side in the line as well as in the bed.[42] Once Aphrodite has actually revealed herself, Anchises is terrified, as well he might be.[43] He knows that men who sleep with goddesses fare badly and begs her to spare his manhood. (Impotence is a frequent sequel to such encounters.)[44] She comforts him and tells two stories about love between mortals and gods. The fate of Ganymede (202–14) suggests that there can be a happy resolution of such relations. But the fate of Tithonos (218–38), a mortal lover condemned to live forever without eternal youth, is clearly meant as a cautionary tale. If Aphrodite offers this story as an explanation of her abandonment of Anchises, it is a rather feeble one. One may wonder why she does not simply remember to avoid Eos' mistake and ask Zeus to grant her lover both immortality and eternal youth. This formula is after all rather standard.[45]

[40] On the hymn, see J. S. Clay, *The Politics of Olympus: Form and Meaning in the Major Homeric Hymns* (Princeton, 1989) 152–201; C. P. Segal, "The *Homeric Hymn to Aphrodite*: A Structuralist Approach," *CW* 67 (1974) 205–12, and Smith (1981). For the background of the poem, see *Inni omerici*, edition and commentary by F. Càssola ([Milan], 1975) 227–52.

[41] πυκινὰς φρένας ἐξαπαφοῦσα / ῥηϊδίως συνέμιξε καταθνητῇσι γυναιξὶν (Deceiving his shrewd mind, she easily made him mate with mortal women), 38–39, cf. 50–52.

[42] The proximity of the two terms in the original can only be preserved at the cost of a certain artificiality in English: "Unwittingly he lay with an immortal goddess, mortal man though he was" (ἀθανάτῃ παρέλεκτο θεᾷ βροτός, 167). At *Iliad* 2.821 we find a similar collocation recounting Aineias' parentage: Ἴδης ἐν κνημοῖσι θεὰ βροτῷ εὐνηθεῖσα (the goddess having lain with a mortal in the folds of Mt. Ida).

[43] For Near Eastern influences on this episode, see Robert Mondi, "Greek Mythic Thought in the Light of the Near East," in *Approaches to Greek Myth*, ed. Edmunds (Baltimore, 1990) esp. 147–48. These influences do not make the text any less relevant for our analysis of ancient Greek religious ideology, for as Edmunds remarks in his introduction to Mondi's article, "[W]hat is diffused from one people to another is not the whole parcel but only that aspect or those aspects which at a given time are wanted and acceptable." (142)

[44] See Clay (1989) 182–83.

[45] Cf. Hesiod's *Theogony*, where Zeus makes Ariadne *athanaton kai agērōn* (949), and Herakles is made *apēmantos kai agēraos* (955). In the *Odyssey* he is *athanaton kai agēraon* (5.136), discussed below. In this passage, Kalypso makes it clear that she knows better than to make the same mistake as Eos. Clay (1989) 190 argues that Aphrodite is unwilling to ask Zeus for any favors.

But from its beginning this text is concerned with defending boundaries. This it accomplishes in part by obsessively defining and redefining them. The poem is remarkable for the density of repetition of words for mortal (*thnētos, katathnētos, brotos*) and immortal (*theos, athanatos*), which occur altogether seventy-two times in 293 lines. Every actor is clearly defined and given the appropriate tag. In lines 50 to 52, these terms are piled up, as gods mate with *mortal* women who bear them *mortal* sons, and goddesses mate with *mortal* men. In each case some form of *katathnētos* is used. While it is true, as Segal observes, that the hymn is concerned with mediating the two categories of mortal and immortal, it also seems that this need for mediation is established through a kind of exacerbation of the contrast.[46]

Aphrodite emphasizes that her passion for Anchises has brought her pain (*achos*, 199), and that it is a reproach (*oneidos*, 247) to lie with a mortal:

αὐτὰρ ἐμοὶ μέγ' ὄνειδος ἐν ἀθανάτοισι θεοῖσιν
ἔσσεται ἤματα πάντα διάμπερὲς εἴνεκα σεῖο . . .

But there will be great shame for me among the immortal gods
for all time to come, on account of you . . .

(*Homeric Hymn to Aphrodite* 247–48)

These are the feelings induced in an immortal by too close contact with a mortal being, and hence with mortality.[47] And unlike the *penthos* of Tros at the loss of his son, her pain cannot be assuaged by gifts from Zeus. This pain and shame will be commemorated in the name given to the child, discussed above. That there will be a child goes without saying, for the beds of goddesses are apparently no more likely to be "unfulfilled" than those of gods. Meanwhile, the problem of boundaries and category separation will be solved by a series of mediating and distancing manoeuvres. First of all, the baby Aineias will be placed in the care of foster mothers, *kourotrophoi*, who will care for the child until he reaches a certain age.[48] These are to be nymphs, a special kind of nymphs unknown to any other text, who are neither ordinary mortals nor precisely immortal (259).[49] In this way the sharp line separating Aineias' parents from one

---

[46] Clay (1989) 193 notes that two opposing sets of terms, *mortal/immortal* and *subject to age/unaging*, are at work throughout the poem, but especially in lines 257–73.

[47] This could be compared to the lament of Thetis at *Iliad* 18.429–34 that she alone has been forced into marriage with a mortal. For the importance of this theme for the poem as a whole, see L. Slatkin, "The Wrath of Thetis," *TAPA* 116 (1986) 1–24, and now, *The Power of Thetis: Allusion and Interpretation in the "Iliad"* (Berkeley, 1991).

[48] He will also be removed from contact with his father, as Segal (1974) 209 observes.

[49] Segal (1974) 209 and Smith (1981) 92–95ff. for significance of the nymphs.

another will be mitigated to a certain extent, although there is never any doubt that the child will be mortal.[50]

The other feature of the story minimized in this way is the maternity of the goddess. The physical ramifications of childbearing are completely elided in this account. Here once again are the traces of a fear, seen elsewhere in Greek myth, of divine female fertility, and specifically a fear of the offspring of goddesses.[51] Both Metis and Thetis must have their reproductive threat in some way neutralized, and in the case of Metis, the solution involves the usurpation of the childbearing function by Zeus. More often the maternity of a goddess is simply displaced, as we see, for example, in the kourotrophic role of Athena in the Erichthonios myth.[52]

Finally, Aphrodite warns Anchises against bragging (*epeuxeai*) about having slept with her and threatens him with Zeus' lightning bolt if he does. She herself has gotten into this trouble as a result of bragging (*epeuxamenē*, 48) about her powers over the gods. Anchises will not be able to resist doing the same, and he will suffer the punishment. The poem seems to preserve traces of a version in which Anchises becomes a victim of the goddess, directly or indirectly, as do many other *paredros* figures. Eustathius (commenting on *Iliad* 12.98) reports a tomb of Anchises on Mt. Ida, to which shepherds brought offerings. Pausanias, however, reports (8.12.8–9) that the inhabitants denied that Anchises was buried there, and even if he was, divine retribution is not necessarily implied.[53]

To sum up, these three texts share a preoccupation with the necessary differences in the human and the divine condition, and the dangers inherent in any kind of rapprochement between the two. Erotic and hostile contact are equally dangerous, for if Dione (or Diomedes) knows that the man who fights with the gods does not live long, Anchises is just as sure that the man who lies with a goddess will not flourish. With these paradigmatic passages as a backdrop, we turn now to an examination of heroic and divine interactions which interrogates the consequences of the gender of the participants.

[50] See Slatkin (1986) and (1991) on the inability of goddesses to pass on immortality to their children.

[51] See F. I. Zeitlin, "The Dynamics of Misogyny: Myth and Mythmaking in the *Oresteia*," in *Women in the Ancient World: The Arethusa Papers*, ed. Peradotto and Sullivan (Albany, 1984) esp. 178–80, 189–90n.21.

[52] See N. Loraux, *The Children of Athena: Athenian Ideas about Citizenship and the Division between the sexes*, trans. Caroline Levine (Princeton, 1993 [Paris, 1984]), especially 58–59. On kourotrophic figures see T. Hadzisteliou-Price, *Kourotrophos: Cults and Representations of the Greek Nursing Deities* (Leiden, 1978), together with Loraux's well-founded criticisms (71n.175).

[53] Càssola (1975) 243 discusses the implications of Pausanias' testimony.

GODS AND HEROES

Relations of gods and male mortals in myth may be parental or erotic, or neither, and they may fit anywhere along the spectrum of patronage and enmity. Where cult evidence is available, it usually conforms to the model traditionally interpreted as displacement of the hero by the god—in other words, that tension between identity and hostility referred to as ritual antagonism.

Zeus, the father of gods and mortals, engenders more heroes on mortal women than does any other god. The exuberant paternity of Zeus is an essential part of his characterization in myth, but the multiplicity of claims is also partly explained by the universal desire for a local or family connection to the god. For present purposes, however, we will bracket the question of the role of propaganda in the development of myth, since even the most flagrant examples are constructed according to an essentially conservative mythic pattern. As we have seen, when Zeus catalogues his exploits with mortal women, he enumerates the heroes born from those unions—Peirithoös, Perseus, Minos, Rhadamanthys, Herakles, and Dionysos (*Iliad* 14.317–25). Clearly the making of heroes is an important element in his affairs.

Zeus cares for his mortal sons, but often his power to help them is limited. In the case of Herakles, he must contend with the implacable enmity of his wife Hera. She also persuades him not to rescue Sarpedon, on the grounds that it will upset the balance of things and all the other gods will blame him. Although he cannot save Sarpedon, he takes special care in the handling of the body and sends Sleep and Death to carry him home.[54]

The one clear example of an erotic relationship between Zeus and a hero has come down to us in the *Homeric Hymn to Aphrodite*, a text explicitly concerned with the issue of *eros* between gods and mortals.[55] The rape of Ganymede results in his being installed on Olympos among the gods and granted immortality. As has been noted by Pfister, myths of translation (removal to Olympos or some other location) usually correspond to the absence of a tomb or any other proof of death.[56] And yet, there is a tradition that Ganymede was buried near the temple of Zeus.[57]

[54] *Iliad* 16.440–457. See Chapter 1,n.4.

[55] In one version of the rape of Chrysippos, the abductor is Zeus instead of Laius, but the attestations are few, and in the case of Clement, suspect. Cf. Praxilla, frg. 751 Campbell = Athenaeus 13.603a; Clem. Al., *Protr.* 2.33.5.

[56] Pfister (1912) 2:481.

[57] T. Schol. *Iliad* 20.234; *Suda* s.v. Μίνως. See the discussion in Pfister (1912) 2:451. This tradition does hint at Zeus' responsibility, while absolving him of blame.

The *Homeric Hymn* makes much of his immortality, in contrast to the inevitable mortality of Anchises. Why then this conflicting tradition?

In most, but not all, versions of the myth, Ganymede is raped, either by Tantalos, Minos, or Zeus himself.[58] Another persistant feature of his myth, burial in the temple of Zeus, occurs independently of the aggressor's identity, as for example in the scholia to *Iliad* 20.234, where Tantalos is the rapist. In another version Ganymede has been sent to make a sacrifice to Zeus Europaios and dies on the way, again finding burial in the temple of Zeus.[59] Since erotic relations between a god and a hero often hint at ritual antagonism, as with Hyakinthos, it is striking that in no surviving version does Zeus directly cause the death of the young man, even inadvertently. Only in this last-mentioned case, in which Ganymede dies in the service of the god, does Zeus have any responsibility, however indirect. Nonetheless, a clear connection is made between Zeus and Ganymede, whether erotic or not, and in contexts suggestive of cult.

For Zeus, there are relatively few explicit examples of ritual antagonism. The "father of gods and men" is the most apt of all the gods to stand in parental relation to mortal men, and overt hostility to heroes is relatively rare. His majesty makes him relatively immune to trivial challenges, such as those that occasionally worry the other gods.[60] Under his jurisdiction, however, fall the major acts of hybris such as Ixion's attempt to rape Hera, or Asklepios' raising of the dead.[61] Heroes who run afoul of Zeus are often engaged in inherently subversive acts, the success of which would attack the very foundations of the mortal/immortal distinction.

The relations of Apollo with mortal men fall more clearly into the pattern of ritual antagonism. Nagy has in fact articulated this principle with specific reference to Apollo and Achilles, a hero who has been characterized as Apollo's "Doppelgänger" by Burkert.[62] Here very close identification of hero and god coincides with implacable hostility, ending when Apollo helps to bring about Achilles' death. Following the work of Delcourt, Nagy has also discussed the process by which Pyrrhos-Neoptolemos, the son of Achilles, becomes the hero of Delphi, entering into the same relation of ritual antagonism with Apollo as his father be-

[58] P. Friedländer, "Ganymedes," *RE* 7.1 (1912) 737–49.

[59] *Suda* s.v. Ἴλιον.

[60] Brelich (1958) 262 cites the rare example of Salmoneus who poses as Zeus, lord of the lightning bolt, although, one imagines, not for long.

[61] Ixion: Pindar *Pyth.* 2.21–48, Aesch. *Eum.* 717–18, etc. For Asklepios' punishment: Pindar *Pyth.* 3.55ff., Eur. *Alk.* 3–4, 122ff.

[62] Nagy (1979) 62–64 and throughout; Burkert (1975) 19.

fore him.[63] The antagonism is partly displaced in the case of Hyakinthos, the young hero whom Apollo loves and accidentally kills while they compete at throwing the discus. Hyakinthos' cult is closely tied to that of Apollo and has been shown to conform to a pattern linking Apollo to a number of mostly prophetic heroes at different cult-sites.[64]

Although the erotic part of the Hyakinthos myth has most appealed to the imagination of poets such as Ovid, Schachter argues that it is a nonessential element. He cites examples in which the hero is either priest or son of the god, as evidence that the fact of a connection between mortal and god is more important than the nature of the connection. This kind of structural analysis can be useful, but taken alone, it risks eliminating some of the interesting specificity that enlivens the myths. Sergent notes that Apollo is involved in more homoerotic relations than any other god.[65] In the case of Dionysos, as I argue below, the god's erotic choices are revealing. Why should not the same be true of Apollo? In the end the choice between "essential" and "nonessential" may be a false one. Mythic narrative necessarily expresses relationships in personal terms, while cult depends on other kinds of associations, arising from the physical proximity of two shrines, or the encroachment of one cult on the other and their eventual reconciliation. But cult geography may also be the expression of a *conceptual* link between two figures. The narrative requirements of myth demand that there be some sort of relationship between god and mortal, while allowing a great deal of variation about the details. Nonetheless the specifics of the relationship can still reveal something about the figures involved.[66]

In the relations of Poseidon with heroes, a different pattern emerges. Apart from the single homoerotic relation with Pelops, to which Pindar alludes in the same ode in which he speaks of the rape of Ganymede (*Olympian* I), the most notable connections are with Odysseus and Erechtheus.[67] Both of these relationships conform to the pattern of ritual

---

[63] Delcourt (1965) 37–43; Nagy (1979) 119–21.

[64] For Hyakinthos, Paus. 3.19.3f.; Eur. *Helen* 1465ff., Apollod. 3.10.3, etc. See A. Schachter, "A Boeotian Cult Type," *BICS* 14 (1967) 1–16; Dietrich (1975). Mikalson (1976) has attempted to extend this type into the area of Athenian cult as well, taking it out of the specific sphere of Apollo.

[65] B. Sergent, *Homosexuality in Greek Myth*, trans. Goldhammer (Boston, 1986) 85ff. connects this with Apollo's role in initiation in an interesting work whose claims at times exceed the evidence. Plutarch in his *Life of Numa* 4.8 lists the following *eromenoi* (beloveds) of the god: Phorbas, Hyakinthos, Admetos, and Hippolytos of Sikyon (see Sergent, 150ff.)

[66] For example, Larson, *Greek Heroine Cults* (Madison, 1995) passim makes a strong case for the importance of familial relations in the cults of heroines.

[67] See Sergent (1986) for a different view of the importance of homerotic relations between gods and heroes. Nagy ("Pindar's *Olympian* 1 and the Aetiology of the Olympic

antagonism, with a myth of opposition and a cult geography suggesting identification. In each case the hero is caught in the cross-fire between Athena and Poseidon.[68]

Dionysos has few sons and no protégés. He most frequently enters into hostile relations with figures who oppose the spread of his worship. We have already discussed Lykourgos, who for Homer is the paradigmatic *theomachos*, as well as Perseus. To these we may add Pentheus, whose disastrous encounter with Dionysos is the subject of Euripides' *Bacchae*.[69] This opposition stems from Dionysos' unique mythic role as the permanent stranger, always arriving, bringing with him a new kind of intoxication and a new way of worshiping. The arrival of the cult of Dionysos in any Greek city presupposes a myth of opposition; or put another way, the foundation myth of the cult of Dionysos in any Greek city must include the element of opposition. Even when the relation of the god to his hosts is friendly, it has a disastrous effect, as for example, in the Attic myth of Ikarios and Erigone.[70] Unlike Apollo, Dionysos does not have a heroic double, a figure who threatens the god by virtue of close resemblance. The enemies mentioned above, Pentheus, Perseus, and Lykourgos, could theoretically fit into this pattern, but the sources do not encourage this interpretation. These heroes do not particularly resemble the god, and their hostility always occurs in the context of resistance to his cult.[71] Unlike Zeus or Apollo, moreover, Dionysos has virtually no homosexual adventures. There is only the strange (and as always somewhat suspect) report by Clement of Alexandria that the god promised to submit sexually to Prosymnos in return for directions to the Underworld, a promise that, due to Prosymnos' death, could only be fulfilled symbolically.[72] We will to return to these anomalies of the god Dionysos in considering his relations with heroines.

Games," *TAPA* 116 [1986] 71–88) finds in Pindar's telling of the myth a fusion of two equally traditional versions. See also T. K. Hubbard, "The 'Cooking' of Pelops: Pindar and the Process of Mythological Revisionism," *Helios* 14 (1987) 3–21.

[68] See Mikalson (1976).

[69] Pentheus first appears in Hekataeus (frag. 31) and in pictorial art, on a psykter in Boston (MFA 10.221), red figure, attributed to Euphronios, c. 520/510. See *LIMC* s.v. "Galene" II. Paintings in the oldest sanctuary of Dionysos in Athens apparently showed Pentheus and Lykourgos paying for their hybris toward the god (Paus. 1.20.3).

[70] See M. Massenzio, *Cultura e crisi permanente: La "Xenia" dionisiaca* (Rome, 1970). For sources for this myth, see Erigone in the Appendix.

[71] Euripides, with great psychological insight, recasts the antagonism between Dionysos and Pentheus in personal terms, playing on their potential similarity as Pentheus is beguiled into assuming the effeminacy of dress he had despised in Dionysos. See F. I. Zeitlin, "Playing the Other: Theatre, Theatricality, and the Feminine in Greek Drama," *Representations* 11 (1985) 63ff., now in a revised version in *Playing the Other: Gender and Society in Classical Greek Literature* (Chicago, 1996) 305–74.

[72] *Protrepticus* 2.34.3–4. Cf. Paus. 2.37.5, where there is no hint of sex. See Burkert,

GODDESSES AND HEROES

The *Homeric Hymn to Aphrodite* and the speech of Kalypso to Hermes in *Odyssey* 5.117ff. catalogue the different outcomes of an erotic encounter between a mortal and a goddess.[73] If the story of Aphrodite and Anchises is relatively benign, the mating of Eos and Tithonos comes to a sinister conclusion. Kalypso's speech to Hermes in *Od*. 5.117–44 serves quite a different purpose, since she is bent on proving the jealousy of the gods toward goddesses who mate with mortals:

Σχέτλιοί ἐστε, θεοί, ζηλήμονες ἔξοχον ἄλλων,
οἵ τε θεαῖς ἀγάασθε παρ᾽ ἀνδράσιν εὐνάζεσθαι
ἀμφαδίην, ἤν τίς τε φίλον ποιήσετ᾽ ἀκοίτην.

Oh you vile gods, in jealousy supernal!
You hate it when we choose to lie with men—
immortal flesh by some dear mortal side.
                    (*Odyssey* 5.118–20, trans. Fitzgerald)

The effect of this is to give the goddess a point of view that harmonizes with that of mortals. She provides the examples of Eos and Orion, Demeter and Iasion, and concludes with the argument that her rescue of Odysseus and her intention of making him deathless and unaging (*athanaton kai agēraon*) give her rights over his future. A comparison of her examples with *Theogony* 965ff. is instructive. Here we find, among others, Demeter and Iasion (969–74); Eos and not Orion, but Tithonos (984–85); Aphrodite and Anchises (1008–10); and finally, Kalypso herself paired with Odysseus (1017–18). It is striking that the *Theogony* passage omits the negative elements of these stories and emphasizes instead the offspring of these couples, children like gods (*theois epieikela tekna*). Thus there is no mention of Iasion's killing by Zeus, nor of the shriveled old age in which Tithonos must eke out his immortality, nor the laming of Anchises, nor, of course, the grief of Kalypso at Odysseus' departure. The comparison does in fact highlight the difference between her own case and those she cites. Odysseus is never made to pay for his proximity to a goddess, and perhaps this is due in part to her relatively low status

---

Homo Necans, trans. Peter Bing (Berkeley, 1983) 70. Ovid, in the *Fasti* 3.409–14, tells of the love of Dionysos for one Ampelus, after whom the vine takes its name. Frazer in his edition (Hildesheim, 1973) 3:95, remarks that "the myth is threadbare, for the name Ampelos is simply the Greek word for 'vine.'"

[73] On a pattern of relations between goddesses and mortals, see D. Boedeker, *Aphrodite's Entry into Greek Epic* (Leiden, 1974) 64–84. and Slatkin (1986) 5–6. For specifically erotic relations, see E. Stehle, "Sappho's Gaze: Fantasies of a Goddess and Young Man," *differences* 2.1 (1990) 88–125.

compared to the Olympians. That mating with a goddess can be read as hybris is clear from the later reinterpretation of Iasion's connection with Demeter as a rape punished by Zeus (Apollod. 3.12.1).

We have already alluded to the relationship between Hera and Herakles, which provides one of the best illustrations of ritual antagonism.[74] The events in the myth of Herakles are motivated by the unrelenting hostility of Hera toward Zeus' illegitimate son. Her efforts to eliminate him begin with his babyhood. Nonetheless, the etymology of his name as "the glory of Hera" is unmistakable, at least as the Greeks understood it.[75] Not only that, the later part of his story includes a reconciliation on Olympos in which Herakles marries Hera's daughter Hebe. At the Heraion in Argos, Pausanias (2.17.6) saw a relief depicting this marriage, which takes place under the protection of Hera. Even more confounding is the story that Athena tricked Hera into suckling the baby Herakles, and that this was the origin of his immortality, although Hera is supposed to have pushed him away when he bit her.[76] The breast-feeding story can be taken as evidence of an original bond between the two figures, or as an explanation for the goddess's hostility.[77] It has been postulated, by Pötscher and others, that the original state of affairs was a close relation between the two and that the myths of hostility result from a later misunderstanding.[78] But, as Burkert, Nagy, and others have shown, the paradoxical commingling of hostility and affinity permeates heroic myth. Misunderstanding may have helped this paradox to arise but cannot be a sufficient explanation for its persistence.

The companionship of a goddess may help a man, as Aphrodite helps

[74] G. Dumézil, *The Stakes of the Warrior*, trans. D. Weeks (Berkeley, 1983 [Paris, 1971]) 124–31.; W. Pötscher, "Der Name des Herakles," *Emerita* 39 (1971) 169–84; N. Loraux, "Herakles: The Super-Male and the Feminine," trans. R. Lamberton in *Before Sexuality*, ed. Halperin, Winkler, and Zeitlin (Princeton, 1990) 40–48, rept. in *The Experiences of Tiresias* (Princeton, 1995) 116–39.

[75] Joan V. O'Brien, *The Transformation of Hera: A Study of Ritual, Hero, and the Goddess in the "Iliad"* (Lanham, Md., 1993) 119 glosses the name as "he who wins fame from Hera." The suggestion that the name actually derives from the Near Eastern Erragal or Nergal "rests on uncommonly slippery grounds," according to Walter Burkert, "Oriental and Greek Mythology," in Bremmer (1987) 17.

[76] Diod. 1.24 and 4.9.6ff. for the outlines of the story; Lycoph. 1328 for Hera's suckling as the origin of his immortality. O'Brien (1993) discusses Hera as nurse of heroes and monsters, as well as the goddess Thetis (66–9; 93–111), and reproduces an Etruscan mirror that shows Hera nursing Herakles (109), without linking this tradition to that of the breast-wound, which she discusses elsewhere (189n.32).

[77] Loraux (1990) 48 calls them "adversaries too well-matched to get along without each other" and suggests further that "each of them is placed in confrontation with the element of the *other* sex contained within the adversary."

[78] Pötscher (1971); also his "Der Name der Göttin Hera" *RM* 108 (1965) 317–20 and "Hera und Heros" *RM* 104 (1961) 302–55. See also Burkert (1985) 210, Loraux (1990).

her son Aineias, and Athena, her mortal counterpart Odysseus. Aphrodite rescues not only her son but also her favorite Paris from danger on the battlefield. In Paris's case, her assistance serves to lead him into folly and destruction, but she continues to protect him as long as it is in her power to do so. Athena's relationship with Odysseus, whatever measure of ambivalence there may be, is founded on affinity. As the poet of the *Odyssey* has her say:

> ἀλλ' ἄγε, μηκέτι ταῦτα λεγώμεθα, εἰδότες ἄμφω
> κέρδε', ἐπεὶ σὺ μέν ἐσσι βροτῶν ὄχ' ἄριστος ἁπάντων
> βουλῇ καὶ μύθοισιν, ἐγὼ δ' ἐν πᾶσι θεοῖσι
> μήτι τε κλέομαι καὶ κέρδεσιν·

> No more of this, though. Two of a kind, we are,
> contrivers, both. Of all men now alive
> you are the best in plots and story-telling.
> My own fame is for wisdom among the gods—
> deceptions, too.

> (*Odyssey* 13.296–99, trans. Fitzgerald)

There is room for both hero and goddess in this system, since each is best in the appropriate class—all mortals (*brotōn hapantōn*) and all gods (*pasi theoisi*), respectively. Thus the rivalry between them is defused and Athena's aid allows Odysseus' safe return home.

While the companionship of Athena is usually positive, that of Artemis can be fatal. Every bit as virginal as Artemis, Athena is nonetheless rarely involved in the enforcement of virginity, or the rules governing the leaving of it, and plays only a small role in initiation for boys or marriage rites for girls.[79] Artemis, on the other hand, embodies a vigilant and defensive virginity, which she expects from her followers as well. This characterization of the goddess is the mythic reflex of her role in cult as the goddess under whose sign the transition to adulthood or marriage is most frequently made.[80] Prolonged contact with this "embodiment" of feminine independence is destructive for men, who cannot negotiate an acceptable path between it and their own sexuality. Orion, once a companion of Artemis, is destroyed by the goddess, whom he has offended by boasting or an attempted rape.[81] Hippolytos is destroyed because his

---

[79] See C. Calame, *Les Choeurs de jeunes fille en Grèce archaïque* (Rome, 1977) 235 for Athena's limited role in initiation.

[80] Two of the cults of Artemis concerned with the transitions of women's lives, those at Brauron and Mounichia, will be discussed in greater detail in Chapter 5. For rites of *proteleia* associated with marriage, see Burkert (1983) 62–63 with n. 20.

[81] While the rape version predominates, some versions of the Orion myth make this into a classic tale of human presumption, in which the mortal claims equal skill with the god, in

exclusive devotion to Artemis leads him to offend Aphrodite.[82] They err in opposite directions, Hippolytos in his rejection of adult sexuality, and Orion on the other hand because of a violent and immoderate sexuality directed, moreover, toward an inappropriate object. Sexual trangression, whether rape or inadvertent voyeurism, brings about Aktaion's destruction by Artemis, despite her close friendship with his mother.[83] Taken together, these myths point clearly to the danger of even apparently friendly contact with Artemis for men. Companionship with her is ultimately incompatible with mature male sexuality.

The companionship of Hippolytos with Artemis is the other side of the coin from his opposition to Aphrodite. This relationship takes the classic form of hostility in myth and identity in cult. The prologue of the *Hippolytos* tells us of a temple to Aphrodite *epi Hippolutōi*. We also have the testimony of Pausanias for the temple of Aphrodite Kataskopia, which commemorates Phaidra's destructive passion for Hippolytos.[84]

GODS AND HEROINES

Heroines and gods mostly come together for erotic and procreative purposes. The heroic genealogies are full of the fruits of these encounters, as are accounts of local traditions passed down to us by Pausanias and others. These sources often preserve only the divine parentage, and a name for the mother, who may have no independent mythic existence. Nor does the tradition distinguish much between rape, seduction, and consent on the part of the heroine in question.[85] All the male Olympians (with the exception of Hephaistos) are ascribed paternity in varying degrees bearing little relation to their depiction as lovers in myth and art.[86] Poseidon, who is almost never protrayed as a lover, appears to be the

---

this case in hunting. See J. Fontenrose, *Orion: The Myth of the Hunter and the Huntress* (Berkeley, 1981) 5–20.

[82] His destruction arrives by a rather circuitous route. See W. Burkert, *Structure and History in Greek Mythology and Ritual* (Berkeley, 1979) 112, on the "curiously complicated method Aphrodite uses to take her revenge."

[83] The more familiar version, memorably recounted by Ovid, has Aktaion accidentally coming upon the goddess while she bathes, but Stesichorus apparently knew another, in which he was punished for an erotic attempt on Semele (frg. 59 *PMG* = Paus. 9.2.3–4).

[84] Hippolytos: *IG* IV 754; Paus. 1.22.1. For his cult, see the preface to W. S. Barrett's *Euripides. Hippolytos*, ed. and commentary (Oxford, 1964) 3–6.

[85] See Adele Scafuro, "Discourses of Sexual Violation in Mythic Accounts and Dramatic Versions of 'the Girl's Tragedy,'" *differences* 2.1 (1990) 126–59. Pierre Brulé, *La Fille d'Athènes: La Religion des filles à Athènes à l'époque classique* (Paris, 1987) 289 lists as "recidivist" rapists Hermes, Apollo, Zeus, and to a lesser degree Boreas.

[86] On fifth-century Attic vase-painting, Zeus is by far the most active pursuer of women. See S. Kaempf-Dimitriadou, *Die Liebe der Götter in der attischen Kunst* (Berne, 1979) 22.

most prolific. Zeus, who is always successful in his pursuit, and Apollo, who rarely is, are credited with a roughly equal number of offspring, while Hermes and Ares are assigned less than half as many.[87]

The catalogue of Zeus' affairs in *Iliad* 14 has affinities with a passage in the *Theogony*, which recounts the wives of Zeus. The lines that deal with Semele and Alkmene (940–44) are particularly close to the *Iliad* passages, also emphasizing the offspring of the unions. Typically, the child of the god is male. Zeus' catalogue mentions only male heroic offspring and then trails off, omitting the names of the divine children, both male and female, of Demeter and Leto. The only heroine whose father is said to be Zeus is Helen, and her status is equivocal and unique. In general, the Olympians seem to engender male children, but none so consistently as Zeus. The other gods do occasionally father daughters who reflect some aspect of their father's nature: Apollo is said to be the father of several prophetic figures, while Ares is the father of Amazons.[88] Diodorus Siculus goes so far as to maintain that in at least one instance Zeus high-mindedly pursued a heroine entirely for the purpose of making children, and not because of any erotic desires on his part (4.9.3).

Apollo's erotic encounters are particularly ill-starred and usually have a rather sinister outcome. We have only to think of Kassandra, Koronis, and Daphne, to name a few, to see that here the heroine's pattern of transgression and transformation is in full force.[89] Despite some differences, many of the story lines are quite similar, centering around a heroine who rejects a sexual relationship with the god. Kassandra, having agreed to accept Apollo as a lover, thinks better of it, and for this is cursed with the disbelief of all who hear her prophecies. Koronis is killed for betraying her divine lover for a mortal husband, and Daphne is willing to accept total loss of her humanity to avoid the union. Koronis' fiery death may be compared with that of Semele, especially since in each case the divine father sees fit to rescue his child from the burning body of the mother. These rejections of Apollo are at times characterized as a kind of hybris, although one that is passive in nature. As we have observed earlier, it is this passive type of hybris which is most commonly associated with the heroine. She has little power to oppose a god, and her crimes are mostly those of refusal—refusal to sacrifice, or refusal to submit sexually to the god.

[87] Exact numbers are impossible to come by. See Appendix for examples.

[88] Apollo is said to be the father of Phemonoe, the naiad Chariklo, and the Leukippides. Ares is the father of the Amazons Antiope (2), Hippolyte, Melanippe (possibly three names for the same figure), Otrere, and Penthesilea, of Alkippe, Milye, and of Harmonia, who may be a goddess. Heroines said to be daughters of Poseidon include Euadne, Rhode, Thoösa (2), Aithousa, Eirene, and Lamia. Hermes is not mentioned as the father of daughters, so far as I have been able to determine.

[89] See Chapter 2; Appendix under Kassandra, Daphne; J. Davreux, *Le Légende de la prophétesse Cassandre* (Paris, 1942).

The only god who repeatedly has nonerotic contacts with women is Dionysos. Taking on a part of the hero's biography, he returns to Thebes to defend the honor of his mother, as the character of Dionysos explains in the prologue to Euripides' *Bacchae*. Many of the myths of resistance to his cult involve the defiance of women, usually groups of sisters, like the daughters of Kadmos, who deny their sister Semele's claim to have borne the child of a god, and the Minyades, all of whom suffer madness as the price of refusing his worship. In both cases the madness leads to the murder of one of their children. On the other hand, Dionysos is frequently accompanied by a band of women who worship and defend him, as in the Lykourgos passage or in the *Bacchae*.

The one explicitly erotic relationship with a mortal woman consistently ascribed to him is that with Ariadne, who is among the heroines who are also honored as goddesses.[90] We may note that she shares this characteristic with the heroines who are closely connected with Dionysos in nonerotic ways, namely his mother Semele and his nurse Ino. It is interesting that Dionysos is the only male divinity whose nature seems to contain within it elements of the feminine. This is shown in vase-painting, where his long hair and dress assimilate him to the maenads who follow him.[91] We have already remarked on this god's unusual relationship to mortality. Dionysiac cult temporarily breaks down the barriers of the self, allowing the worshiper to partake of the power of his divinity. As I will argue at greater length in Chapter 4, one might say that Dionysos' relation to his female followers involves an exchange, in which he partakes of their femaleness and they of his immortality.

GODDESSES AND HEROINES

When Achilles rejects Agamemnon's offer of marriage to one of his daughters, he sketches the features of a desirable wife in these terms:

κούρην δ' οὐ γαμέω Ἀγαμέμνονος Ἀτρεΐδαο,
οὐδ' εἰ χρυσείη Ἀφροδίτῃ κάλλος ἐρίζοι,
ἔργα δ' Ἀθηναίῃ γλαυκώπιδι ἰσοφαρίζοι·

---

[90] There are a few others that appear to be purely local traditions, most notably Physkoa, mentioned by Pausanias (5.16.6) as the lover of Dionysos and his first worshiper, in whose honor a chorus of women was established at the Heraea. Pausanias takes this to be an ancient Elean tradition.

[91] E. Simon, *Festivals of Attica* (Madison, 1983) 90–91; F. Frontisi-Ducroux and R. Lissarrague, "From Ambiguity to Ambivalence: A Dionysiac Excursion through the 'Anakreontic' vases," in Halperin, Winkler, and Zeitlin (1990) 211–56. See now also Michael Jameson, "The Asexuality of Dionysus," in *Masks of Dionysus*, ed. Carpenter and Faraone (Ithaca, 1993) 44–64.

> I would not marry the daughter of Agamemnon, son of Atreus,
> not even if she rivaled golden Aphrodite in beauty,
> and were as skilled in handiwork as Athena,
>
> (*Iliad* 9.388–91)

That a woman should be compared to a goddess is at once natural and dangerous. The gods are always available as the highest standard of comparison for mortals, and such comparisons frequently occur in the Homeric poems. Odysseus meeting Nausikaa suggests, with perhaps unequal measures of flattery and caution, that he is addressing a goddess. When, however, the individual makes him or herself the object of such a comparison, this is hybris. It is precisely the attempt to approach the conditions of divinity that brings mortals into difficulty. At the same time, as we will see in Chapter 4, an identification between goddess and heroine at times serves as the central focus for both myth and ritual.

In general the distinctive features of the Olympian goddesses signal the ways in which mortals will come into conflict with them. Athena is most often challenged in contests of skill in crafts and martial arts, while Hera's rivals claim equal marital happiness or they claim Zeus himself. The specificity breaks down, however, when it comes to beauty, for although it is clearly the province of Aphrodite, it is not hers alone. Side is punished for competing with Hera in beauty (*peri morphēs*), while Medousa, the wife of Pisidos, is killed by Athena for a similar challenge (*peri kallous*). Andromeda is left to the depradations of a sea-monster because her mother Kassiopeia had dared to compare her own beauty to that of the Nereids.[92] These small-scale beauty contests may call to mind the Judgment of Paris, in which the contestants *peri kallous* were Hera, Athena, and Aphrodite.[93] From its conclusion we know that goddesses are not eager to share their reputation for beauty even with one another.[94]

Not all relations between goddesses and heroines are purely competitive or hostile. Heroines, like heroes, may have a goddess for a protector. When Hypermestra is acquitted of impiety for disobeying her father's orders to murder her husband, she honors Aphrodite, although the relationship is never presented as a personal one (Paus. 2.19.6; 2.21.1). In

[92] Side (Apollod. 1.4.3); Medousa, Andromeda (Apollod. 2.4.3). See Weiler (1974) 100–114 for an extended discussion of the theme of contests of beauty and skill between goddesses and heroines.

[93] *Kypria* (Proclus p. 17 Kinkel). See also *Iliad* 24.25ff., which may refer to the episode; Apollod. *Ep.* 3.2, etc.

[94] Despite the omission of Artemis from this contest, necessary for reasons of plot, beauty is clearly not an inessential attribute for her, since she has the cult title *Kalliste*, "the most beautiful," and an antagonistic double Kallisto.

fact, here the heroine is shown acting like an ordinary mortal saved from disaster. On the rare occasions when the goddess intervenes personally, the assistance may be double-edged. The terrifying scene between Helen and Aphrodite in *Iliad* 3 shows how ambiguous and even sinister such a relationship can be. Yet the Helen who is bullied and threatened by Aphrodite may also be seen as a hypostasis—a double—of the goddess.[95]

Rarely is the relationship between heroine and goddess described as a bond between friends or companions. What would it mean to be a friend of a goddess? In those few cases where the language of *philia* is used, consideration of the mythic context renders this language ironic. A *scolion* (drinking song) quoted by Athenaeus credits the Attic heroine Pandrosos with bringing victory over the Persians, because of her friendship with Athena (*hōs philēn Athēnan*), but omits mention of the destruction that befell her and her sisters at the hands of the goddess.[96] A fragment of Sappho (frg. 142 L-P) calls Niobe and Leto true companions (*hetairai*), pointing to a time before Niobe's hybris shattered their friendship, with grim consequences for her family.[97] The irony only suggested in these examples resounds clearly in Callimachus' hymn, "The Bath of Pallas." Chariklo, Teiresias' mother, is Athena's much-loved and constant companion (5.57–67). Even so, many tears awaited her, although she was a very pleasing companion (*katathumion hetairan*) to the goddess (68–69). The tears will be the result of Athena's harsh punishment of Chariklo's son when he inadvertently sees the goddess naked. This last example makes explicit the inequality of the situation. Mortals cannot help giving offense, either directly or through the actions of their families, and when they do, prior friendship with the offended divinity offers no protection.

Athena and Hera most often come into conflict with heroines who are in some way rivals, and with whom there are no bonds of affection.[98] We have already alluded to Hera's rivalries with the various lovers of Zeus, whom she persecutes in a variety of interesting ways, often involving metamorphosis.[99] What can be seen in human terms as the wife's jealousy of the mistress can also be read more abstractly as a kind of ritual

---

[95] Clader (1976) 12–13; also 54 on the sharing of epithets by these two figures.

[96] 15.694d skolion 5. The phrase ὡς φίλην Ἀθηνᾶν may be an intrusive gloss. See the remarks of C. B. Gulick, ed., *Athenaeus, The Deipnosophists* (Cambridge, Mass, 1941) 7:221 note b. Perhaps this verse reflects the version in which Pandrosos alone of the sisters obeyed Athena's injunction not to look in the basket that contained the baby Erichthonios (Apollod. 3.14.6).

[97] This fragment is discussed at greater length at the beginning of Chapter 5.

[98] For an exception, see Myrmex in the Appendix.

[99] Some transformations for which Hera is responsible: Io—cow; Aedon—nightingale; Kallisto—bear; Antigone—stork; Galinthias—weasel. See the individual Appendix entries.

antagonism. These heroines, by sleeping with Zeus and bearing him sons, act out the role of "wife of Zeus," which by rights belongs to Hera. Thus assimilated to her, they invade her sphere of action as wife and in some sense threaten her sovereignty. Her power resides in her exclusive claim to marriage with Zeus. That jealous protection of her position is not unjustified is shown by Pausanias' comment (2.31.2) that he could not bring himself to believe that Semele had died, since she was the wife of Zeus. The degree to which Hera is associated with marriage, not only as wife of Zeus, but as the goddess of marriage is made clear by her punishment of Aedon, who claimed to be happier in marriage than the goddess herself.[100] That union with Zeus involves assimilation to Hera becomes particularly clear in the myth of Io, who was a priestess of Hera before she caught the eye of Zeus.[101]

Athena's relations to heroines, as we have noted, tend to fall into the agonistic category. The areas of contention are the *technai* (arts, skills) of weaving and of war. Athena, as we might expect, shows her greatest hostility to women who challenge her in contests of skill at handiwork or martial arts. The story that comes most readily to mind in this context is that of Arachne, who challenges Athena to a weaving contest and is turned into a spider. Although its earliest appearance is in the *Metamorphoses* of Ovid (4.5–145), the tale is commonly assumed to go back to a Hellenistic model and could be even older.[102] A similar story with more ancient attestation is that of Iodama, apparently a priestess of Athena, who challenges the goddess and meets with death at her hands. According to one version, the arena of competition is the armed dance, the *pyrrhikē*. According to Simonides, Iodama and Athena are actually sisters, both being daughters of Itonos. Another similar story is told about Pallas, the daughter of Triton, whose death Athena caused indirectly while they were practicing martial arts. In Apollodorus' account Pallas is also a sort of stepsister of Athena, who is being raised by Pallas' father Tritonos.[103] These sibling relations between goddess and mortals are ex-

---

[100] For Hera as wife, see Pötscher (1961, 1965). Also Calame (1977) 209–24, who remarks that her marriage with Zeus constitutes "the paradigm of all human marriages" (209). For this version of Aedon's myth, see Ant. Lib. 11.3 with the comments of Burkert (1983) 185. Earlier versions are similar to the myth of Prokne; see Appendix.

[101] The theme of identification of a goddess and her priestess will be considered in Chapter 5.

[102] Wagner, "Ariadne," *RE* 2.1 (1895) 367, thinks the story ancient. Weiler (1974) 100–101, adduces as evidence for its antiquity a Corinthian aryballos dated to ca. 600 (Corinth Museum, CP 2038), for which see G. D. Weinberg and S. S. Weinberg, "Arachne of Lydia at Corinth," in *The Aegean and the Near East, Studies Presented to Hetty Goldman*, ed. Saul S. Weinberg (Locust Valley, N.Y., 1956) 262–67, pl. 33 and fig. 1. The *LIMC* article on "Arachne" stresses, however, the absence of any securely identified depiction of this myth.

[103] For Iodama: Simon. (*FGrH* 8 F 1.1 = schol. Lycoph. 335) and Paus. 9.34.1. See

traordinary, not least for the genealogical and theological difficulties they would create if taken seriously. Nothing similar is found between gods and heroes, nor for any other goddess. The sibling relationship may provide a way to express a closeness and similarity that in its male versions would more likely be expressed as an erotic connection.

While relationships between goddesses and female mortals do not usually have happy endings, those involving Artemis are particularly likely to end in disaster—and it is always the same disaster of sexual transgression. These are in essence stories about the wrong way to make the transition from virginity to marriage, which is to say, by means of illicit relationships that do not allow for the ritual appeasement of the goddess who presides over this transition. Whether the transgression is inadvertent does not matter. Thus a heroine like Kallisto, a companion of the goddess who is seduced or raped by Apollo, may be punished by Artemis.[104] These particular connections often end in death for the heroine.

Here the conventional role of Artemis in bringing death to women must be considered. Artemis is associated with the correct time for transitions in women's lives, including childbirth and death.[105] Andromache's mother is killed in her father's halls by Artemis (*Iliad* 6.428). When Penelope wishes for death (*Od.* 20.61f.), it is to Artemis that she appeals. When Odysseus encounters his mother in the Underworld, she tells him (*Od.* 11.198–99) that she did not die by the arrows of Artemis, as if that would be the normal course of events. In the myth of Niobe, it is Apollo who kills the male children and Artemis who kills the female ones (*Iliad* 24.603–6). The same goddess also presides over transitions in social status, which may themselves be enacted as a ritual death.[106]

The case of Iphigenia, to be discussed further in Chapter 5, constitutes an exception to the paradigm of sexual trangression. Unlike the heroines just mentioned, Iphigeneia remains a virgin. She is not held directly responsible for her destruction, nor does that destruction come directly at the hands of the goddess. It is rather her father's transgression

---

Gunning, "Iodama," *RE* 9.1, 1839–41. For Pallas: Apollod. 3.12.3; Tzetzes, schol. Lycoph. 355, which also mentions Iodama. The similarity of the names Triton and Tritonos suggests contamination between the two stories. See Burkert (1983) 67.

[104] See Appendix for Kallisto. Among the other heroines said to have been killed by Artemis are Ariadne, Laodameia, and Koronis. An interesting case is the priestess of Artemis Triklaria who defiles the temple by making love with Melanippos. See Appendix under Komaitho, and J. Redfield, "From Sex to Politics: The Rites of Artemis Triklaria and Dionysos Aisymnētēs at Patras," in Halperin, Winkler, and Zeitlin (1990) 114–34.

[105] H. King, "Bound to Bleed: Artemis and Greek Women," in *Images of Women in Antiquity*, ed. A. Cameron and A. Kuhrt (Detroit, 1983) 119–22.

[106] See A. van Gennep, *The Rites of Passage*, trans. Vizedom and Caffee (Chicago, 1964) 75 on the ritual death of the initiate. On the distinction between physiological and social transitions, see p. 46. See the extended discussion in Chapter 5 of this volume.

that conforms to type and destroys her. Indeed, in some versions Agamemnon is said to have offended Artemis by boasting, like Orion, of his hunting skills. Meanwhile, the theme of marriage enters in the form of the ruse he uses to induce his wife to bring his daughter to Aulis, where she is in fact to be sacrificed. It is almost as if Artemis wishes Agamemnon to compound his crimes by misuse of the delicate transitional state of the young girl from virginity to marriage. Artemis' rescue, Iphigeneia's subsequent role as priestess and cult-founder, and her apotheosis introduce the theme of identification of goddess and heroine, which will be taken up at greater length in Chapter 5.

THE HEROIC DILEMMA: BETWEEN ANTAGONIST AND PATRON

As we have seen, a hero or heroine may occasionally be caught in the crossfire between a divine antagonist and a divine protector. Not surprisingly, these arrangements correspond to antagonisms among the gods, which often reflect local cult traditions. For example, Athena and Poseidon, whose battle for Attica is a staple of the local tradition there, are on opposing sides vis-à-vis Erechtheus and Odysseus.[107] Although Clay has suggested that there is ambivalence in the relationship between Odysseus and Athena, her role as Odysseus' supporter nevertheless places her in clear opposition to Poseidon in the *Odyssey*. Her connection with Erechtheus is commemorated in the *Iliad* (2.547–49).[108]

An erotic connection with a god, even one inclined to be generous, may bring the mortal into direct conflict with some other divinity. Semele, Io, and Alkmene, all lovers of Zeus, find themselves the object of Hera's hatred. Even in cases where the erotic element is only implicit, such as Hippolytos' exclusive connection with Artemis, a conflict may arise.

Hera and Zeus are as famous for their marital strife as for their marriage. Burkert notes that discord between the divine couple has many

---

[107] For this contest, see Hdt. 8.55, Plut. *Them.* 19, Paus. 1.24.5; Apollod. 3.14.1.

[108] Mikalson (1976) adheres to the model of cultic displacement: Poseidon displaced Erechtheus, but then Athena displaced them both. Others read the contest not as the record of a historical displacement of Poseidon's cult, but rather a justification for the disenfranchisement of women. See S. Pembroke, "Women in Charge," *Journal of the Warburg and Courtauld Institutes* 30 (1967); P. Vidal-Naquet, "Slavery and the Rule of Women in Tradition, Myth and Utopia," in *Myth, Religion and Society*, ed. R. Gordon (Cambridge, 1981) 187–200; Loraux (1984). D. Castriota, *Myth, Ethos, and Actuality: Official Art in 5th-Century B.C. Athens* (Madison, 1992) 145–51 applies the work of these authors to an interpretation of the west pediment of the Parthenon.

reflections in cult, among them the three temples of Hera at Stymphalos, each one dedicated to a different phase in her development. These were *Pais*, the girl; *Teleia*, the wife; and *Xēra*, the widow. The local tradition associates this last not with literal widowhood but with a quarrel and separation from Zeus (Paus. 8.22.2). Another interesting cultic manifestation of the hostility between Zeus and Hera discussed by Burkert is the Boeotian festival of the Daidala at Plataea, in which a wooden "wife of Zeus" is burned. The accompanying myth tells of a trick to induce Hera to appear by dressing up a wooden plank and staging a "wedding" in which Zeus was to have married "Plataia" or "Daidala."[109] This myth, analogous to the other myths of persecution by Hera referred to above, has been interpreted as an attempt at harmonizing a local tradition about the wife of Zeus with the Panhellenic one.[110]

Another triangle occurs for heroic figures caught between Artemis and Aphrodite, by virtue of their representing fundamentally opposing tendencies. Some heroines who are caught between these two divinities are Helen, Ariadne, Polyphonte, and Hypermestra.[111] Not surprisingly, a devotee of one of the two goddesses, because of the mutually exclusive nature of these attachments, incurs the wrath of the other goddess, as is the case, for example, with Hippolytos. When confronted with his inattention to the goddess Aphrodite, Euripides has Hippolytos reply, "To each their own, for gods and mortals" (ἄλλοισιν ἄλλος θεῶν τὲ κἀνθρώπων μέλει, *Hipp.* 104). The violence of the goddess's response teaches that this seemingly reasonable stance is untenable for mortals, although it very accurately reflects the behavior of the gods. For normal worship of the gods as practiced by ordinary mortals is inclusive and follows a prescribed pattern.[112] The worshiper, while honoring all the gods, falls under the jurisdiction of particular ones at moments of transition from one state to another. A mortal who chooses to worship, and thereby to emulate, only one of the gods neglects the all-important and dangerous transitions of life, particularly those having to do with maturation, and risks coming to resemble that god in a way that is perilous.[113] Thus it is not

[109] Burkert (1985) 133–35. S. Mizera, *Unions Holy and Unholy: Fundamental Structures of Myths of Marriage in Early Greek Poetry and Tragedy* (Ph.D. dissertation, Princeton University, 1984) 11–17.

[110] See also W. D. Furley, *Studies in the Use of Fire in Ancient Greek Religion* (New York, 1981) 201–10.

[111] For Ariadne's connection with Aphrodite, see Calame (1977) 226–27; Boedeker (1974) 44. For Helen, Polyphonte, and Hypermestra, see Appendix. Polyphonte's story sounds like that of Kallisto reversed.

[112] See Burkert (1985) 216f.

[113] See van Gennep (1964) for the perceived danger of transitional states and the ritual means to mitigate that danger as practiced in a number of cultures.

surprising that the patron god does not always choose to save the protégé from the anger of the slighted divinity.[114]

That such difficulties are not always chosen by the mortals themselves might be illustrated by the story of the Judgment of Paris, who, for all his shortcomings, is emblematic of the human dilemma in dealing with the gods. It is tempting to moralize his choice, but only because we are ignorant of what troubles might have resulted had he slighted Aphrodite. Here the point is not simply that everything happened in accordance with the will of Zeus, but that it is regularly pleasing to the gods to entrap mortals in situations in which they cannot win.

We have seen that for female characters in Greek myth, the range of action is decidedly more limited than for heroes and the price of stepping out of line, higher. While connection with a god, whether erotic or not, may be beneficial to a hero, who may prevail and be exalted under divine tutelage, similar contact for heroines is almost always disastrous, resulting in transformation often of a radical and unwelcome kind. For example, an Apulian vase in the Getty Museum shows Kallisto staring in horror as her hands grow furry and become paws, in a particularly eloquent portrayal of the horrors of metamorphosis (figure 6).[115] These images call into serious question the consolatory value of the many transformations by which Greek myths resolve an impasse. As we observed in Chapter 2, the heroines who manage to survive these experiences are those who *have no story*. Heroines rarely have a choice of whether or not to have a story, or whether or not to sleep with a god. One of the few to have such a choice is Marpessa, who when allowed to choose between Idas and Apollo (each of whom had in turn carried her away by force, it should be noted), chooses the mortal over the god.[116] An implicit choice is, however, made by Koronis, who takes a mortal lover or husband after her impregnation by Apollo. Her right to self-determination has not been agreed to by the god, whose vengeance is swift and terrible.

In the remaining two chapters, we consider several interactions between heroines and divinities that deviate in some measure from these restrictive patterns, giving greater scope of action to female mythic fig-

---

[114] Burkert (1985) 216 cites Artemis' words at lines 1328–30 of the *Hippolytos* in this connection.

[115] See A. D. Trendall, "Callisto in Apulian Vase-Painting." *AK* 20 (1977) 99–101 and plates 22, 1–5.

[116] This seems to be a later rationalization of an earlier story in which the mortal defeats the god in a physical contest for the woman, according to J. Tamburnino, "Marpessa," *RE* 14.2, 1916–17, who points to *Iliad* 9.557–64, in which there is clearly a contest of arms. The struggle is also depicted on a red-figure psykter by the Pan Painter c. 480 (Munich, Antikensammlungen 2417), illustrated in J. Boardman, *Attic Red Figure Vases: The Archaic Period* (London, 1975) n. 338. See Marpessa in Appendix.

Figure 6 Kallisto becoming a bear, Apulian red-figure Chous, close to Black Fury Painter, c. 370–350 B.C.E. (J. Paul Getty Museum, Malibu, California 72AE 128).

ures and expanding to some degree the range of mythic roles for women. Chapter 4, on Dionysiac heroines, returns to the subject of gods and heroines, while a detailed treatment of goddesses and heroines, as exemplified by the case of Artemis and Iphigeneia, is taken up in Chapter 5.

CHAPTER FOUR

Dionysiac Heroines

Κάδμου κόραι, Σεμέλα μὲν 'Ολυμπιάδων ἀγυιᾶτις,
'Ινὼ δὲ Λευκοθέα
    ποντιᾶν ὁμοθάλαμε Νηρηῖδων,
ἴτε σὺν 'Ηρακλέος ἀριστογόνῳ
    ματρὶ πὰρ Μελίαν χρυσέων ἐς ἄδυτον τριπόδων
θησαυρόν, ὃν περίαλλ' ἐτίμασε Λοξίας,
'Ισμήνιον δ' ὀνύμαξεν, ἀλαθέα μαντίων θῆκον,
ὦ παῖδες 'Αρμονίας,
    ἔνθα καὶ νυν ἐπίνομον ἡρωΐδων
στρατὸν ὁμαγερέα καλεῖ συνίμεν . . .

Daughters of Kadmos, Semele neighbor of the Olympians,
and Ino Leukothea
    who shares the sea nymphs' chambers,
come now, with Herakles' highborn mother
    to the side of Melia, into the inner sanctum,
treasury of golden tripods, which Loxias honored above all,
and named Isthmian, the seat of true oracles,
O children of Harmonia,
    where now he calls the local army
of heroines to gather.

—Pindar *Pythian* 11.1–8

THE HEROINE IN DIONYSIAC CONTEXT

The first time in extant Greek poetry that a word meaning "heroine"
appears is in the opening lines of Pindar's eleventh *Pythian* ode. Here the
Theban heroines Semele, Ino, and Alkmene are called on to honor Melia,
a local divinity. The first two are invoked as daughters of Kadmos, while
Alkmene is called "the highborn mother of Herakles." As I have argued
in Chapter 1, we may assume that the word *hērōís* had some currency
before Pindar's use of it, and that in any event the concept did not wait to
be named before having any mythic or ritual role to play. Long before the
word, the wives and daughters—and mothers—of heroes had a place in
epic. That these are indeed heroines is clear from the Pindaric passage.
Here, in a poem in which genealogy is not an end in itself but subordi-

nated to other concerns, the heroines are clearly identified as mothers and daughters of heroes. Thus they are inserted once more into the genealogical context in which we first find them in Greek literature.

Two of these three paradigmatic heroines, the daughters of Kadmos, are associated with Dionysos, and it is they, along with his wife, Ariadne, who will concern us in this chapter. In Chapter 3 we observed that Dionysos is the only male god who does not conform to the otherwise standard pattern of divine interaction with mortal women, which reduces them to erotic objects. In this chapter we examine the god's mythic and ritual connections with the three heroines most prominent in his myth, showing how the usual pattern is subverted. In fact, as I will show, Dionysos, by confounding gender distinctions and transcending mortality, calls into question the very categories of male and female, mortal and immortal. I will argue that it is this feature of Dionysos that explains the unusual role of women in his myth and cult. At the same time, a study of these three figures, Semele, Ino, and Ariadne, reveals a constant recasting of the major motifs of the myth of Dionysos. Birth and its perils, death and its transcendence—issues that dominate the myths of the god—are worked out again in the myths of the heroines surrounding him. At the same time, the prominence of these heroines in Dionysiac cult may provide a way for the worshiper to identify with the god and reenact elements of his travails.

The Dionysiac material shows a high degree of consistency in working and reworking a limited number of motifs, and correspondences can easily be shown from one version to another, as well as from one figure to another. For this reason I will avoid privileging one version of any given myth over another. Thus, for example, the motif of the hostile stepmother which occurs in the Dionysos myth shows up again in the myth of Ino, where in some versions she herself takes on the role, while in others, it is taken up by her rival. These themes are inherent in the myth of Dionysos, from which variations are then generated. If there were a larger body of evidence to draw on, we might be able to say which versions were most widely known, but I am not sure that even this would tell us which versions are the most "Dionysiac."

In these myths themes of death and immortality are paramount. In the genealogy of the Theban royal house, as presented by Pindar, the intertwining of divine and mortal elements is immediately apparent. The heroines Semele and Ino, who themselves attain immortality, are not only the daughters of Kadmos (*Kadmou korai*), but also daughters of Harmonia (*paides Harmonias*), a goddess who is herself the daughter of Aphrodite. This feature is of particular relevance to the biography of the god Dionysos, the only Olympian god born into a mortal house. Finally, in the myth of Ariadne, the third heroine to play a significant role in Dionysiac myth, once again questions of immortality and apotheosis assume great importance.

This chapter offers a case study, examining the mythic and cultic interactions of a group of heroines with a particular divinity. Its aim is to situate the heroines within the Dionysiac context. If an examination of Dionysos exclusively through his mythic and cultic relations to women allows us to see him in a new light, so much the better. Others have written eloquently on Dionysos as a confounder of categories. My account builds on these but differs in emphasizing the connection between gender ambiguity and transcendence of mortality, and in relating both of these features to the special role of women in Dionysiac myth and cult.

ORIGIN AND ICONOGRAPHY OF DIONYSOS

It is difficult to speak with confidence about the origin and identity of Dionysos.[1] Euripides' portrayal of him as simultaneously a stranger from Lydia and a native of Thebes is emblematic of this problem. Until the decipherment of Linear B in 1952, it was customary to take the myths of resistance to his cult as evidence of a historical event, and to take his foreignness at face value.[2] Since the appearance of the name Dionysos on two Mycenaean tablets from Pylos, we must assume the god's presence in Greece from a much earlier date. The constant mythic feature of resistance to his cult, rather than being the trace of a historical reality, may indeed point to the fact that Dionysos is conceived as the bringer of a new technology, viticulture, and a new product, wine.[3] The introduction of viticulture was of course a prehistoric event, of which no actual human memory is possible. Yet the uniqueness of this drink, with its inexplicable powers of intoxication, is expressed as an eternally new and miraculous development, and therefore brought by a god who is perceived as always arriving for the first time. Consequently, the myths of resistance

---

[1] Out of a vast bibliography on the god Dionysos, I have found the following works particularly helpful: H. Jeanmaire, *Dionysos: Histoire du culte de Bacchos* (Paris, 1951); E. R. Dodds, *The Greeks and the Irrational* (Berkeley, 1951), as well as his commentary on the *Bacchae* (Oxford, 1960); W. Otto, *Dionysus, Myth and Cult*, trans. Robert B. Palmer (Bloomington, 1965); M. P. Nilsson, *Geschichte der griechischen Religion* (Munich, 1967); M. Massenzio, *Cultura e crisi permanente: La "Xenia" dionisiaca* (Rome, 1970); M. Daraki, *Dionysos* (Paris, 1985). See now also T. H. Carpenter and C. A. Faraone, eds., *The Masks of Dionysos* (Ithaca, 1993).

[2] See, for example, W.K.C. Guthrie, *The Greeks and Their Gods* (London, 1955) 146.

[3] This is not to deny that there was historical resistance to Dionysiac cult, as any reader of Livy knows. The suppression of the Roman Bacchanalia of 186 B.C.E. can, however, only be understood in the context of social and political pressures in Roman society after the second Punic War. See C. Gallini, *Protesta e integrazione nella Roma antica* (Bari, 1970).

hinge on the problem of integrating the new and potentially disruptive invention into ordered society. This is the "permanent crisis" to which the title of Massenzio's book on Dionysos aptly refers.[4] It is Dionysos the newcomer who teaches humankind the proper use of his gift, the right mixture of water and wine. For only the god can drink it straight.[5] The "exoticizing" of Dionysos is simultaneously a way of expressing the foreignness of the experience of ecstatic ritual.[6]

Even if the cult of Dionysos was present in Greece from very early on, it did not have the same significance in all periods. Iconographic studies of Attic vase-painting show that Dionysos is at first a rather minor god, attaining Olympian status only in the mid-sixth century.[7] In the late fifth century, he loses his beard and mature appearance to become a beardless ephebe, or even a baby. There are also changes in the company he keeps. Early images show him in the company first of Aphrodite, and then Semele. Sometime in the late sixth century, he begins to be represented with Ariadne. This may be the expression of a growing Athenian interest in the political value of the mythic association with Dionysos through Theseus and Ariadne. While changes in the physical representation of the god make him less mature, the change of companion, from mother to wife, leads him in the other direction. We should therefore be cautious about forcing the material into a progression, from maturity to infancy, taking care instead to acknowledge the ambiguity that pervades his representation.

There are geographical differences as well as temporal ones. The bulk of myth places Dionysos in a Theban context, and his cult is especially strong all over Boiotia, as well as at Delphi in nearby Phocis.[8] But Dionysos plays a major role in Athenian religion, with a whole series of festivals dominating the Attic calendar during the months of winter and early spring. The evidence suggests that his cult, whatever its origin, was incorporated into local traditions in Thebes at an early date and soon spread to Athens, later taking on Eastern elements. Although the cult of

[4] See above, n. 1.

[5] Both literary and iconographic evidence clarify this point. Greek wine was traditionally mixed with water before drinking, and the proper mixing of wine distinguished the human symposium from the revels of satyrs and the god's solitary drinking. See J.-L. Durand, F. Frontisi-Ducroux, and F. Lissarrague, "Wine: Human and Divine," in *A City of Images: Iconography and Society in Ancient Greece*, ed. Claude Bérard et al., trans. D. Lyons (Princeton, 1989) 121–29.

[6] Guthrie (1955) 172 makes this point, although he also believes in Dionysos' actual foreignness.

[7] This section owes much to the work of T. H. Carpenter, *Dionysian Imagery in Archaic Greek Art* (Oxford, 1986).

[8] For Boiotian cults of Dionysos, see A. Schachter, *Cults of Boiotia. BICS* suppl. 38.1 (1981) 1:172–95.

Dionysos appears all over the Greek world, the examples that concern us come mostly from these two areas. This geographical limitation, moreover, helps to offset the fact that strict delineation of the historical period is impossible. By concentrating on the mainland, we will at the same time be giving our attention to cults that were certainly well established by the classical period.[9]

CROSSING THE BOUNDARIES OF IMMORTALITY AND GENDER

The figure of Dionysos presented to us by Euripides in the *Bacchae* is a nexus of contradictions. A stranger from the East, he is also a native-born Theban. An immortal god, he must nevertheless return home to prove his legitimacy and vindicate the honor of his mortal mother Semele. A male god, he is attended almost exclusively by women, and he is taunted for his effeminate appearance. Inspired by him, peaceful maenads act in extraordinary harmony with nature, in their enthusiasm bringing forth milk and honey from the ground. For those who resist his cult, however, he brings madness, loss of identity, violence, and ultimately disintegration. Without privileging the Euripidean account, we may take it as a convenient starting point for an exploration of these contradictions, particularly as they relate to gender and immortality, and the ways in which they are played out in the myth and cult of the heroines Semele, Ino, and Ariadne.

Dionysos is born into ambiguity and opposition. This god, in so many ways the exception among Greek divinities, concentrates within himself the opposing terms *mortal/immortal* and *female/male*, bringing them together in a kind of mediation. The son of a mortal mother, Semele, he has, of all the Olympians, the most intimate experience of mortality, being the only one to suffer death.[10] Dionysos is often characterized by a certain degree of sexual ambiguity. Female figures are prominent in his myths, and his cult is marked by a level of participation by women unknown for any other male divinity.

[9] Hellenistic developments in Dionysiac worship are for the most part beyond the scope of the present project. On this topic see Jeanmaire (1951) 417–82; A. Henrichs, "Changing Dionysiac Identities," in *Jewish and Christian Self-definition*, vol. 3: *Self-Definition in the Graeco-Roman World*, ed. Meyer and Sanders (London, 1982) 137–60; 213–36.

[10] See in particular Otto (1965), especially 189–201, for a discussion of the significance of Dionysos' relation to death. He also has a great deal to say on the subject of Dionysos' relations with women. Much of it is quite perceptive, although marred by Victorian attitudes. See, for example, his remarks on "the slighter importance of [female] sexual desire" (178).

His marked relation to death begins with his birth, which is in fact synonymous with the death of his mother, Semele. His nurture is then taken over either by Semele's sister Ino, or by a group of "nurses" variously identified by local tradition. His situation is precarious, and in some versions he must be hidden. Throughout his childhood he is dependent on women for protection. Even in maturity, something of the vulnerability of childhood clings to him. Glaukos, in his speech to Diomedes in *Iliad* 6.130ff. tells of the pursuit of the god and his nurses (*tithēnas*) by Lykourgos. Dionysos is terrified and leaps into the sea, where he is comforted by Thetis.[11]

Dionysos is born mortal, and the process by which he becomes immortal is far from clear. In some versions immortality is a reward for his services in bringing Hephaistos back to Olympos to release Hera from a trick throne of his invention where she has been held prisoner.[12] Elsewhere, it is the second birth from Zeus' thigh that gives him access to immortality, and that will ultimately allow him to confer it on others.[13] In any case it is striking that while the mythic tradition is unanimous that Herakles must suffer an anguished death before achieving immortality, there is no canonical myth of the death of Dionysos. The theme of his death occurs, as Burkert has observed, primarily in ritual contexts.[14] The scholia to *Iliad* 14.319 preserve a tradition by which the hero Perseus not only engages in battle with Dionysos but actually succeeds in killing the god. Pausanias (2.20.4; 2.22.1) mentions the tombs of the female companions, known as *Haliai*, who died attempting to defend him, but says nothing to indicate that the god himself was killed.

Although the god is often threatened, nowhere else is he actually murdered, outside of the Orphic tradition. Here we find the story of the infant Dionysos torn to bits by the Titans who have distracted the baby by giving him toys and a mirror. While he is looking at himself in the mirror, they attack him with knives and cook and eat him.[15] As it happens, his heart remains intact, and from it he is reconstructed by the

---

[11] I do not, as some commentators have, take the use of the word *nurses* to indicate that the god is still in his infancy, but read it rather as a generic term for his followers. See G. Privitera, *Dioniso in Omero* (Rome, 1970) 61n.18; R. Seaford, "Dionysos as Destroyer of the Household: Homer, Tragedy, and the Polis" in Carpenter and Faraone (1993) 116n.3. This passage is discussed at length in Chapter 3.

[12] This version is implied in a fragment of Alcaeus (349 Campbell). See D. L. Page, ed., *Sappho and Alcaeus* (Oxford, 1955) 258–60. See also Pausanias 1.20.3.

[13] This is implied in Diodorus' account (5.52.2), in what is perhaps a late rationalization, when he says that Zeus killed Semele before she could bear Dionysos, so that that the child would have not one but two immortal parents, and so itself be born immortal.

[14] W. Burkert, *Homo Necans* (Berkeley, 1983) 176.

[15] Clem. Al., *Protr.* 2.18 = Orph. frg. 34–35 Kern. See M. L. West, *The Orphic Poems* (Oxford, 1983) 140–75.

other gods. It is tempting to say that this is not the same Dionysos who was worshiped in civic cults throughout Greece, and yet this version accords with the Delphic tradition of a tomb of Dionysos.[16] As incongruous as this Orphic myth seems, it is consonant with the figure of the Olympian who so completely straddles the line between mortal and immortal.[17]

If we turn now to Dionysos' relations to women, we find that his participation in ambiguity is nowhere more apparent than here. From the moment of his strange double birth, he is marked by gender confusion.[18] As Segal has commented, the double birth is one of the ways in which he combines both sexes.[19] According to Apollodorus (3.4.3) he is raised as a girl by Athamas and Ino. We have alluded to the theme of gender ambiguity in Euripides' *Bacchae*. Pentheus taunts the stranger, whom he does not recognize as a god, for his feminine appearance (453ff.). Later, as Dionysos carries out his revenge on Pentheus, the first step in the beguiling of his victim is to persuade him to assume the effeminacy of dress he had earlier despised in the god. As Dodds has pointed out in his edition of the play, neither element is a Euripidean invention. Fragments of the earlier *Edonai* of Aeschylus contain similar jeers at the god's appearance. "Where does this sissy come from?" is the question addressed to the captive Dionysos.[20] The scene of cross-dressing has precedents in Dionysiac ritual, while in comedy (for example in the *Frogs* of Aristophanes) Dionysos is dressed in female garments and mocked for his effeminacy.[21] In Heschyius' lexicon the dialect form *dionus* (διονῦς) is defined as a "weakling and sissy" (*ho gunaikias kai parathēlus*).

On the other hand, the women who serve Dionysos take on certain male roles, if not male characteristics, as nurses turn into warriors, and

---

[16] Callim. frgs. 643, 517 Pfeiffer; Plut. *Isis* 365a. See O. Kern, "Dionysos," *RE* 5.1 (1905) 1019. See also Burkert (1983) 123f.; West (1983) 150–52.

[17] See Marcel Detienne, *Dionysos mis à mort* (Paris, 1977) 163–207; Albert Henrichs, "'He Has a God in Him': Human and Divine in the Modern Perception of Dionysos," in Carpenter and Faraone (1993) 26–29.

[18] See Henrichs (1982) 158–59 on role reversal in the Dionysiac material. See also M. Jameson, "The Asexuality of Dionysos," in Carpenter and Faraone (1993) 44–64, which reaches similar conclusions to my own. I prefer, however, to speak of "sexual ambiguity" rather than "asexuality."

[19] C.P. Segal, "The Menace of Dionysos: Sex Roles and Reversals in Euripides' *Bacchae*," in *Women in the Ancient World: The Arethusa Papers*, ed. Peradotto and Sullivan (Albany, 1984) 201. Segal notes (196–97) that Dionysos and women are both associated with threats to the social order.

[20] ποδαπὸς ὁ γύννις, Aristoph. *Thesm.* 136 = Aesch. frg. 61 Nauck.

[21] See Dodds (1960) xxviii ff. and 133–34 on the ritual aspects of cross-dressing, with references. See also C. Gallini, "Il travestismo rituale di Pentheo," *SMSR* 34 (1963) 211–28, who connects the scene in the *Bacchae* with the Oschophoria and other initiatory cross-dressing.

maenads into hunters. They defend the god when he is attacked by Perseus or Lykourgos. As Euripides portrays Agave in her madness, she believes herself to be a great lion-killer and asks her father to congratulate her on her masculine achievement.[22] A Macedonian name for the maenads was *Mimallones*, "because they imitate men" (*para to mimeisthai tous andras*).[23]

It is against this backgound of gender ambiguity that we must consider the unique character of Dionysos' mythic associations with female figures. He is the only male divinity among the Olympians whose relationships to mortal women are not exclusively erotic. Apollo, Poseidon, Hermes, and especially Zeus have many encounters with mortal women on whom they father numerous children with the unfailing fertility that characterizes the gods. Otherwise, heroines or mortal women figure relatively little in their myths. Himself the product of a typical union between a god and a mortal women, Dionysos does not repeat the pattern. Unlike these divinities, he has few myths uniting him with mortal women and is credited with the paternity of very few children. By the same token, women figure in his myths in many other roles, appearing as mother, nurse, opponent, and supporter.

Unlike most of the other Olympians, he has no divine consort granted to him but instead elevates the heroine Ariadne to immortality, to be his wife. His myths set him apart from the other gods by making him virtually "monogamous." The status of this union is unparalleled among the myths of amorous connections of the gods with mortals and, unlike the unions of other gods and heroines, it becomes a legitimate marriage.[24] The absence of erotic violence and the emphasis on marriage are reflected in Athenian iconography.[25] This marriage, frequently represented in vase painting, has its ritual parallel in the *hieros gamos* consummated between the god and the *Basilinna*, wife of the *Archon Basileus*, during the Athenian festival of the Anthesteria.[26]

Dionysos differs from other male divinities in yet another respect, in

---

[22] *Bacchae* 1202–15; 1233–43. See Segal (1984) 206–7.

[23] *Etym. Mag.* (587.53).

[24] Diodorus 44.61.5 refers to Ariadne as the "wedded wife" (γυναῖκα γαμετὴν) of Dionysos.

[25] See S. Kaempf-Dimitriadou, *Die Liebe der Götter in der attischen Kunst* (Berne, 1979) 12, 30–32. As C. Bérard and C. Bron note in "Bacchos au coeur de la cité. Le Thiase dionysiaque dans l'espace politique," in *L'Association dionysiaque dans les sociétés anciennes* (Rome, 1986) 22–23, one of the striking paradoxes of Dionysiac erotic imagery is the total absence of rape, pursuit, and violence. On the contrary, scenes of the god and Ariadne are represented by the "official" iconographic conventions of marriage.

[26] Richard Hamilton, *Choes and Anthesteria: Athenian Iconography and Ritual* (Ann Arbor, 1992) 53–56 has recently called into question the traditional association of the *hieros gamos* with the Anthesteria. See below.

that he is more of a son than a father. Two of the figures central to his myth are his mother Semele and his aunt and foster-mother Ino. In the matter of his birth, we may compare him to Athena, another product of Zeus' reproductive creativity. Her birth from his head effectively writes the mother out of the picture and clearly marks this goddess as "for the male in all things."[27] Dionysos is also born twice, the first time snatched from the womb of the mortal, dying mother who is thus reduced to metonymic status. She fulfills her role and then, having been no more than a womb, is removed from the scene, while he will have a second birth from his father's thigh.

In both of these myths, we see once again the common tendency in Greek myth to sidestep the issue of maternity. This tendency expresses itself, in its mildest form, in the substitution of foster motherhood for biological motherhood, as in the myth of Erichthonios. Its more radical manifestation is the fantasy of redesigning human reproduction to eliminate the mother altogether.[28] Euripides puts into the mouths of both Hippolytos and Jason wishes expressing in exaggerated form the misogyny endemic to Greek culture: "If only the gods would invent another way of having children, so that men could free themselves of this evil that is woman."[29]

Despite his second birth from his father's body, Dionysos remains his mother's son, and while partaking of her mortality, seems also to take on aspects of her feminine nature to a degree that has no parallel among the other gods. In Dionysiac myth the father's annihilating gesture toward the mother is counteracted by the son, who goes down to the depths of the Underworld to bring her back and install her in triumph in Olympos.[30] In the usual scheme of things, mothers give life to their sons. In Greek myth divine mothers and mother-substitutes also frequently try to give immortality to their sons, and inevitably fail.[31] Dionysos, however, succeeds in giving immortality to his mother, and in so doing, seems almost to reverse the natural order once more. Semele has been prevented from giving birth to her own son, yet he will give her immor-

[27] Aesch. *Eum.* 737f.: τὸ δ' ἄρσεν αἰνῶ πάντα, πλὴν γάμου τυχεῖν, / ἅπαντι θυμῷ, κάρτα δ' εἰμὶ τοῦ πατρός.

[28] On the "dream of a purely paternal heredity," see J.-P. Vernant, "Hestia-Hermès," in *Mythe et pensée chez les Grecs* (Paris, 1971) 2:133; M. Arthur, "The Dream of a World without Women," *Arethusa* 16 (1983) 97–116. See also Chapter 3, this volume.

[29] *Hipp.* 616–24, *Medea* 573–75. Clearly these utterances are not to be taken as the expression of the playwright's own sentiments, but rather as revelatory of the characters who speak them.

[30] Paus. 2.31.2, 2.37.5; Plut. *De ser. num. vind.* 566a; Diod. 4.25.4.

[31] E.g., Thetis and Achilles, Medea and her children, Demeter and Demophoön. See L. Slatkin, *The Power of Thetis* (Berkeley, 1991) and "The Wrath of Thetis" *TAPA* 116 (1986) 1–24. I plan to return to this topic in another project.

tal life. This rescue is yet another appropriation of the maternal function, this time by Dionysos, and is clearly dependent on the first appropriation, in which Zeus' thigh serves as a womb for the embryonic god. At the same time, it also fits clearly into the pattern of heroic myth, in which the son on reaching maturity returns to defend his mother (as Perseus rescued Danae). In this, Dionysos more resembles a hero than a god.

Semele is made immortal by the direct intervention of Dionysos. As we shall see, he also plays a large role in the apotheosis of both Ino and Ariadne. While Dionysos is not explicitly given credit for Ino's transformation into a goddess, it is because of her association with him that she is driven mad, leaps into the sea, and is immortalized. As for Ariadne, the sources are unanimous in making Dionysos the agent of her apotheosis. Connection with Dionysos, the mortal-born god, allows these heroines to escape the finality of death, in much the same way that he himself has escaped it.

FEMALE ROLES IN DIONYSIAC MYTH

The unusual nature of Dionysos' relations with women can also be seen from the proliferation in his myths of other female figures who are not sexual objects for the god. As we have observed, most gods have very little to do with mortal women if not for erotic purposes. Dionysiac myth, however, presents a different model of gender-relations, one that is by turns co-operative and combattive, but that is not based on the sexual domination of the female by the male. In this context women appear as the nurses and companions of the god, worshipers or resisters of his cult, and figures connected with the introduction of wine.

The nurses of the gods are usually nymphs, or other minor female divinities, or animals, like the goat Amalthea who nursed Zeus. Dionysos also has his share of nymph-nurses, but many of his nurses are mortal. They are generally collective entities, bands of women for whom a single name suffices: *Haliai* or *Lenai* or *Thyiads*.[32] Mythic collective groups of "nurses of Dionysos" are often called by the same name as the nonmythic bands of worshipers of the god. Plutarch, for instance, uses the word *Thyiads* to refer to participants in festivals of Semele and Dionysos.[33] The names differ according to local tradition, and in some cases an individual woman is named as his nurse. The Thyiads are said to

---

[32] Roscher under "Dionysos" lists the following as names for the women in Dionysos' entourage: Bacchai, Mainades, Thyiades, Lēnai; and in Macedonia, Klōdōnes and Mimallones. Athenaeus (5.198e) calls them Mimallones, Bassarai, and Lydai.

[33] Semele: *Quaest. Gr.* 12, 293d. Dionysos: *De mul. virt.* 249e–f.

take their name from one Thyia, the first priestess of Dionysos (Paus. 10.6.4). In the Theban version, the role of nurse is given to Ino, the daughter of king Kadmos, to whom we return below.

Female collectivities figure prominently in the myths of Dionysos. Some of these groups nurture and support the god, while others resist him. These collectivities, hostile and friendly alike, serve as prototypes of Dionysiac worshipers. Often they are a large, undifferentiated band like the "nurses" of the Lykourgos episode (*Iliad* 6.130ff.) or the followers in the *Bacchae*. More commonly in the myths of resistance, the collectivity consists of the three daughters of the king. At Orchomenos they are the daughters of Minyas, at Argos the daughters of Proitos, and at Thebes, the daughters of Kadmos.[34] Although the punishment differs, the crime is always the same: refusal to recognize the god and to participate in his cult. The daughters of Minyas, like the daughters of Kadmos, end up killing one of their children, in their madness, while the unmarried daughters of Proitos are eventually cured by the seer Melampos, who marries one of them and finds husbands for the others. That their cure leads directly to their marriage points up the extent to which Dionysiac cult is a cult of married women. In the words of Calame, "If young girls were not entirely excluded from the Dionysiac mysteries, the Bacchic choruses were nevertheless composed mainly of married women. . . . That Dionysos intervenes principally in the domain of married women explains the slippage in the myth of the Proitides from the sphere of Dionysos to that of Hera, and vice versa."[35]

There is another kind of Dionysiac heroine, for the most part distinct from the nurse or prototypical maenad, whom we might call the Dionysiac "culture heroine." These figures are almost exclusively connected with the myths of introduction of wine and the resistance to it.[36] Although these figures clearly belong to the sphere of Dionysos, the myths depend very little on the personal contact of the heroine with the god, and not at all on erotic contact.[37] The Attic myth of Ikarios and

---

[34] Sources for the Minyades: Plut. *Quaest. Gr.* 38, 299e–f; Ant. Lib. 10; Ovid *Met.* 4.1–40, 390–415. For the Proitides: Hes. *frg.* 131 M-W = Apollod. 2.2.2. According to Apollodorus, Hesiod says that they were driven mad for a slight against Dionysos, while Akusilaos says that Hera was the offended deity. For another group of daughters, see Semachidai in the Appendix.

[35] C. Calame, *Les Choeurs de jeunes filles en Grèce archaïque* (Rome, 1977) 242–43. Burkert (1983) 172 has a slightly different reading, based on the fact that the divine anger of the myth is attributed in some versions to Hera. As he puts it, "Thus, Dionysos' priest returns again to Hera's sphere of power, for she is the goddess of marriage." See also his comments on the traditional antagonism between the cults of Dionysos and Hera, and their complementarity (185).

[36] See Massenzio (1970) passim, for a provocative treatment of these myths.

[37] It is only in Ovid that Dionysos has an erotic encounter with Erigone: *Liber et*

Erigone, which serves as *aition* for the Aiora, a ritual incorporated into the Anthesteria, centers on Dionysos' gift of wine, and the fatal misunderstanding of that gift.[38] Ikarios is killed by his neighbors who take their intoxication to be the effect of poison. In grief his daughter Erigone hangs herself. A plague follows, and a ritual reenactment of the hanging is necessary as restitution. This festival, in which the young women of Attica swing on swings, is carried out yearly in honor of Erigone. At this time a special song called the *Alētis* (wanderer), after another name for the heroine, is sung.[39]

Another category of heroines in wine-introduction myths are descendants of Dionysos such as the daughters of Staphylos. In these myths the principal figures are given names that connect them even more transparently with the new technology. According to Plutarch (*Thes.* 20.2) the brothers Staphylos and Oinopion are the sons of Ariadne and Theseus. Elsewhere, however, as we might expect from their names, they are said to be the sons of Dionysos himself. According to Apollodorus (*Ep.* 1.9), Thoas, Staphylos, Oinopion, and Peparethos were the sons of Ariadne and Dionysos. Diodorus (5.79.1–2) states that some call Oinopion the son of Dionysos, from whom he learned wine-making (*oinopoiia*). Staphylos (Grape-Cluster) has three daughters, Molpadia, Rhoio, and Parthenos. The daughters, set to watch over the father's wine, throw themselves into the sea when pigs get in and spoil it. They are rescued by Apollo, the lover of Rhoio (Pomegranate). Molpadia appears to belong to the spheres of both Apollo and Dionysos. Her name itself suggests Apolline interest in song, and the myth clearly places her under his protection. At the same time, the anger of Staphylos against his daughters has to do with the spoiling of his wine, "a drink only recently known to men," and the form their escape takes is a leap into the sea. These two details put us unmistakably in the realm of Dionysos. The recent introduction of wine and the failure to use it properly suggest a persecution story like the myth of Erigone and Ikarios, while the daughters' sea-leap calls to mind other sea-leaps, such as that of Dionysos himself and that of Ino. But Diodorus' version of the myth obscures this connection, ending with the ultimate elision of the Dionysiac element—the ritual prohibition against wine in the cult of Hemithea.

A second group of sisters, the Oinotropoi or Oinotrophoi, have the

---

Erigonem falsa deceperit uva ("Bacchus tricked Erigone with a false bunch of grapes," *Met.* 6.125). This is one of the scenes of *caelestia crimina* which Arachne weaves in her ill-fated competition with Athena. Whether Ovid is relying on a version long since lost, or shaping the tale for his own purposes, we cannot say.

[38] Eratosthenes, *Katast.* 8 (Robert 79); Apollod. 3.14.7; Schol. *Iliad* 22.29; Hyg. *Fab.* 130; Ovid *Met.* 6.125. See Massenzio (1970) 13ff., Burkert (1983) 241–43, and Daraki (1985) 87ff.

[39] Kern, "Dionysos," *RE* 5.1 (1905), 1020. See also *RE* s.v. "*Aiora*."

suggestive names Oino, Spermo, and Elais, and the power to turn whatever they touch into the substances (wine, grain, and oil, respectively) from which they take their names. They are in fact also descendants of Dionysos, being the daughters of Anios, the son of Apollo and Rhoio, and seem to be a doubling of the daughters of Staphylos. Their myth has to do not with the introduction of wine, but with the exploitation of this and other forms of agricultural production. The young women are taken along against their will by the Greeks on the expedition against Troy, for the purpose of provisioning the army, and are rescued by Dionysos, who turns them into doves.[40]

These figures are most closely paralleled by those connected to another divinity who introduces a new technology. Demeter, associated with the introduction of agriculture, is attended by the wife and daughters of Keleos, and we know from Pausanias (1.39.2) that Metaneira, at least, received cult honors. These heroines, however, are firmly placed within the cult of a female divinity. In the myths of male divinities, only the Hyperborean Maidens who worship Apollo resemble in any way these Dionysiac heroines.[41] As we have noted, the daughters of Staphylos and Anios are also in some way connected to Apollo. Why that should be the case is not clear, although perhaps these myths express certain other affinities between the two deities who share the sanctuary at Delphi.

WOMEN IN DIONYSIAC CULT

Thus far I have traced the god's mythic connections with women. We may now consider how these connections are reflected in ritual. Here again we find that Dionysos is anomalous. What sets him apart from the other male gods is that, although he is served by male priests, a large number of rituals in his honor are performed exclusively by women. In general the strong sexual dimorphism of Greek life is also expressed in religious contexts.[42] It is customary, for example, for male divinities to be served mainly by male priests and celebrants, and female divinities to be served by priestesses.[43] Even the gods invoked in oaths are divided by sex, with men calling on male deities and women calling on female ones.

---

[40] See under Oinotrop(h)oi in Appendix.

[41] On the Hyperborean Maidens, see J. Larson, *Greek Heroine Cults* (Madison, 1995) 118–21, who stresses more their connection with Artemis.

[42] See pp. 43–44 with n.22 above.

[43] E. S. Holderman, *A Study of the Greek Priestess* (Chicago, 1913) emphasizes this phenomenon. J. A. Turner, *HIEREIAI: Acquisition of Feminine Priesthoods in Ancient Greece* (Ph.D. dissertation, University of California at Santa Barbara, 1983) affirms the general rule while exploring exceptions. See also I. Savalli, *La Donna nella società della Grecia antica* (Bologna, 1983) 93–95 and Giampiera Arrigoni, *Le Donne in Grecia* (Rome, 1985) xxi n. 11.

At times the rituals are restricted by sex as well, and for the most part, when women enact religious ritual without men, it is in honor of a female deity. For example, Demeter and Kore are frequently served by priestesses, and one of their most important festivals, the Thesmophoria, is celebrated exclusively by women. The goddess Artemis, the protector of the young, is attended by women, and her rituals are enacted by women and young people of either sex. These restrictions do not apply to all festivals of a particular god, and indeed a civic goddess such as Athena was honored by the entire city, most notably at the Panathenaia. The cults of Dionysos are by no means all restricted to women, nor is he the only god to have such cults.[44] Nor do women have a role to play in all Dionysiac cults. Nonetheless, the sheer number of Dionysiac cults calling for the exclusive participation of women is remarkable.[45] Moreover, as we shall see, these cults involve the formation of religious associations of women such as the "official" maenads of Athens, the *Gerarai* who participate in the Anthesteria, the Sixteen Women who organize the chorus of Physkoa, and the college of women who sacrifice to Semele at Erchia.

As an example of a Dionysiac cult restricted to women, let us consider the festival known at least to modern scholars as the Oreibasia, which took place during the winter months at Delphi.[46] This festival, whose name means "mountain running," comes closest to an enactment of the ecstasies of the maenads presented by Euripides. To this festival came delegations of official Maenads from many cities including Athens. Plutarch describes the rescue of a group of Thyiads who unwittingly wandered into the city of Amphissa in Phocis during a time of war, and exhausted by their frenzy, fell asleep in the marketplace. The women of Amphissa, fearing that harm would come to them, stood watch silently around them until they revived and could be given a hot dinner and safe conduct to the borders (*de mul. virt.* 249e–f).

---

[44] Cf. the cult of Ares Gynaikothoinas at Tegea (Paus. 8.48.4–5).

[45] L. R. Farnell, *Cults of the Greek States* (Oxford, 1909) 5:160 cites the cult of Dionysos at Brysiai as the only one that excluded men. On Dionysiac cult in general, he adds that "the woman-ministrant was more essential generally to this cult than to that of any other male divinity, and was never excluded as she frequently was in the others." As I indicate below, I believe that there may have been other occasions when men were excluded. See R. Seaford, *Reciprocity and Ritual: Homer and Tragedy in the Developing City-State* (Oxford, 1994).

[46] While no inscriptional source supports using this word for the activities on Parnassos, as Dodds did in his commentary on the *Bacchae*, he is not alone in extrapolating the name from Euripides. See, for example, W. Burkert, *Greek Religion* (Cambridge, Mass., 1985) 291. Henrichs, "Die Maenaden von Milet" *ZPE* 4 (1969) 223–41 explicitly addresses this issue in his discussion of third-century inscriptions from Miletos and the Maeander area, emphasizing the importance of mainland precedent in the establishment of the cult, and treating the *oreibasia* as a distinct part of that cult. He concludes that Euripides had cult realities in mind. Both authors cite Plut. *De mul. virt.* 249e–f and Paus. 10.4.3 and 10.32.7 as independent testimony to the practice, if not its name.

The mythic groups of women we have discussed above, whose madness is in itself service to the god, are thought of as prototypical maenads, the forerunners of the willing celebrants of the god in historical times. Plutarch tells us of a ritual at Orchomenos, the Agrionia, which he connects with the myth of the daughters of Minyas. It seems that the descendants of these women, known as *Oleiae* (Murderesses) are pursued by the priest of Dionysos, sword in hand. "Any one of them that he catches he may kill, and in my time the priest Zoïlus killed one of them. But this resulted in no benefit for the people of Orchomenos; but Zoïlus fell sick from some slight sore and, when the wound had festered for a long time, he died."[47] This ritual, with its parallel to Lykourgos' pursuit of Dionysos and his nurses, shows the familiar oscillation between worshiper of the god and victim of the god that we have seen in the myth of Pentheus. The element of pursuit is common to both the myth and the ritual, while the value of the group of women can be either positive or negative. In the myth of Lykourgos, the women are allies of Dionysos, whereas in the cult at Orchomenos, they are treated as antagonists.

Women's worship of Dionysos, although segregated, could also be located at the heart of the city. The Athenian festival of the Anthesteria, which occurred in the month Anthesterion in early spring, took place over several days.[48] Its name indicates a connection with flowers, and at this time children three years old were crowned with garlands. The first day of the festival saw the opening and tasting of the new wine, while on the second the citizens took part in drinking contests. At this time the dead were supposed to circulate freely in the city. All temples were consequently cordoned off, to avoid pollution, with the exception of the temple of Dionysos in the Marshes, which was opened on this day alone. On this day also, with its ill-omened connection with the dead, there took place a ritual of great importance for women, the holy marriage (*hieros gamos*) of the *Basilinna* with Dionysos.[49] Her marriage with the god, whether purely metaphorical or not, was accompanied by sacrifices performed by a group of chaste older women, the *Gerarai*.

Most of what we know about the *hieros gamos*, whose secrets were carefully guarded, comes from the oration *Against Neaira*, which gives

[47] *Quaest. Gr.* 38, 299e–300a (trans. F. C. Babbitt). That this event also had political ramifications is evident from Plutarch's comment that from then on the priesthood was made hereditary rather than elected.

[48] On the Anthesteria see Jeanmaire (1951) 48–56; Burkert (1983) 213–47; Daraki (1985) 72ff; Hamilton (1992) passim.

[49] Thus Jeanmaire (1951) 54–55, for whom it is a crucial point. Burkert, on the other hand, considers it out of the question that the marriage could have taken place on a day of ill omen. Recently Hamilton (1992) has also challenged the assumption that this event took place at the Anthesteria. If he is correct, this would not diminish the centrality of the ritual but would obviously call into question its association with death.

evidence for the secret rites (*ta arrēta hiera*), the date on which the temple was opened, and even the text of the oath of the *Gerarai* (59.74–79).[50] Aristotle (*Ath. Pol.* 3.5) is less detailed but more matter-of-fact about the hierogamic nature of the ritual: "But the king inhabited what is now called the Boukolion, near the Prytaneion (a proof of this is that even today the union and marriage of the king's wife with Dionysos takes place there)."[51]

As men excluded from women's mysteries, these writers are limited in what they can tell us, although the insinuating tone of Ps.-Demosthenes derives in part from a courtroom strategy of implanting suspicions of impropriety in the minds of his hearers. It may be argued that no evidence for the exclusion of men from anything but the *hieros gamos* itself exists and that, moreover, from this all women except the *Basilinna* were also excluded. The texts themselves suggest otherwise, showing much sketchier acquaintance with the entire ritual than we find in the case of other more clearly public rites. I would suggest as a parallel a ritual dedicated to Dionysos at Bryseai in Lakonia, where Pausanias tells us, in strikingly similar language, that "only women are allowed to see the image in the temple, for women perform the sacrificial rights by themselves in secret."[52] Similarly, Plutarch (*Quaest. Gr.* 12, 293c) says that the *Hērōis* is mostly secret. There is a *mystikos logos* known only to the Thyiads, and the public portions of the ritual allow him only to conjecture the meaning of the whole. These rituals seem to be in some way cognate with the *hieros gamos* of the Anthesteria and suggest that the *Gerarai* had their secrets too.

The bits of information we do have, despite possible voyeuristic distortion, permit us to make several observations. The *hieros gamos* of Dionysos with the *Basilinna* takes place on the most ill-omened day of the year, a day permeated by death. It is in this context that we must view the consorting of the god with the representative of all the women of Athens, a ritual that would have direct bearing on the prosperity of the city for the next year.[53] The dead are the bringers of prosperity, and this proximity to pollution is necessary for the good of the community. But

[50] This oration, once said to be the work of Demosthenes, is now usually ascribed to "Pseudo-Demosthenes." W. K. Lacey, *The Family in Classical Greece* (Ithaca, 1968) 10, questions the usefulness of this distinction.

[51] The phrase used is σύμμειξις . . . τῷ Διονύσῳ καὶ ὁ γάμος. The sexual meaning of *summeixis* here has been disputed. See P. J. Rhodes, *A Commentary on the Aristotelian Athenaion Politeia*, rev. ed. (Oxford, 1993) on this passage. Although the events leading up to it may have been public, the sacred marriage itself was apparently witnessed by no one.

[52] τὸ δὲ ἐν τῷ ναῷ [ἄγαλμα] μόναις γυναιξὶν ἔστιν ὁρᾶν· γυναῖκες γὰρ δὴ μόναι καὶ τὰ ἐς τὰς θυσίας δρῶσιν ἐν ἀπορρήτῳ (3.20.3). Trans. adapted from Jones and Ormerod. See n. 45 above.

[53] Jeanmaire (1951) 51–52. See also Daraki (1985) 78, who speaks of the queen as "Athènes devenue femme."

the union is not without its threatening side, for it is a union with Dionysos in his Underworld aspect. Here, as Jeanmaire has pointed out, is an illustration of the saying of Heraclitus, "Hades and Dionysos are one and the same."[54] If Dionysos can be equated with the king of the Underworld, then marriage with him is a kind of death. This funereal union recalls the fatal marriage that produced Dionysos himself, and it takes place in a climate of ambiguity that is by now familiar.

THREE DIONYSIAC HEROINES

As I have argued, Dionysos enjoys a special relation to death and to women. I have hinted at a kind of exchange by which the god confers on his female associates something of his own special status with regard to death. In this section I elaborate on this, examining the cases of individual heroines. At the same time I stress the homology between Dionysos and these heroines, not only at the broadest thematic level, but in the recurrence of motifs. From version to version and figure to figure, the same motifs are repeated: pregnancy and childbirth with their attendant dangers, protection of children versus persecution or even infanticide, the benevolent mother or nurse versus the hostile stepmother, the threat of death and rescue from it. These motifs are for the most part presented in pairs, which point to the contradictory nature of much of human experience. Slater, for example, has pointed out the hostility toward children that pervades Dionysiac myth.[55] A mythic tradition that acknowledges the culture's ambivalence toward children is not far from projecting that ambivalence onto women, who are themselves already seen as deeply equivocal beings. In this collection of repeating and interwoven motifs, the roles assigned to women are inconsistent. The woman is simultaneously the good mother and the bad mother, simultaneously identified with and opposed to the child. Her interests are at times the same as his, and at others split off. Slater deserves credit for this important insight into the Dionysiac material. Nonetheless, I part company with his assessment of the myths, as I see in them male projections onto women, rather than reactions to clinically explicable behaviors acted out by actual women.[56]

---

[54] ὡυτὸς δὲ Ἀίδης καὶ Διόνυσος (Heraclit. frg. 15 Diels-Kranz). See Jeanmaire (1951) 56; also Daraki (1985) 80–81.

[55] P. Slater, *The Glory of Hera: Greek Mythology and the Greek Family* (Boston, 1968) 222–24. This point is later taken up in the work of B. Simon, *Mind and Madness in Ancient Greece: The Classical Roots of Modern Psychiatry* (Ithaka, 1978) 119, 257.

[56] For a highly critical view of Slater's work, see H. Foley, "Sex and State in Ancient Greece," *Diacritics* 5.4 (1975) 31–36. A slightly more sympathetic discussion appears in M. Arthur, "Review Essay: Classics," *Signs* 2.2 (1976) 395–97.

SEMELE

The familiar outlines of the myth of Semele state the themes that will be worked out in variations in the myths of Ino and Ariadne. Her genealogy is given in *Theogony* 975ff. She is the daughter of Kadmos of Thebes and Harmonia, the daughter of Aphrodite, and her sisters are Ino, Agave, and Autonoe. She also has a brother, Polydoros, about whom little more is heard. She is listed among the heroines whom Zeus has seduced, in *Iliad* 14.323–25, where the son she bears him is called "Dionysos . . . delight of mortals" (*charma brotoisin*).

Her seduction by Zeus is followed by some kind of impiety, whether on her part or that of her sisters, and she is blasted by lightning. Keune suggests that in the earliest versions, her death may be brought on by infidelity, and he connects this with Stesichorus' account of the death of Aktaion as punishment for an attempt on Semele.[57] Apollodorus makes this into a slander on her by her sisters (3.4.3). In some versions her sisters' incredulity about the identity of the father of Semele's child leads to her destruction. In others she falls victim to the hostility of Hera who engineers her death. In the form of an old woman, she persuades Semele to ask Zeus to appear to her as he appears to his wife. The mortal woman cannot survive exposure to the god's true form and is destroyed in a flash of lightning.[58] Semele's chamber becomes a holy place, an *abaton*, a place where no one may walk (Paus. 9.12.3–4).

The tradition that Semele was made immortal is quite old, our earliest attestation being *Theogony* 942: "a mortal woman [bore him] an immortal [son], but now they are both gods" (ἀθάνατον θνητή· νῦν δ' ἀμφότεροι θεοί εἰσιν). This change of state was accompanied by a change in name, memorialized in the *Homeric Hymns*:

> καὶ σὺ μὲν οὕτω χαῖρε, Διώνυσ' εἰραφιῶτα,
> σὺν μητρὶ Σεμέλῃ ἥν περ καλέουσι Θυώνην.

> And so farewell Dionysos the in-sewn,
> with your mother Semele, whom now they call Thyone.
>
> (*Homeric Hymn* 1.20–21)

Diodorus Siculus (4.25.4) makes the connection explicitly: "For according to the myths, he brought up his mother Semele from Hades, and, sharing with her his immortality, he called her by a new name, Thyone." This name, generally connected with the verb θύειν (*thuein*, "to rage,

[57] J. B. Keune, "Semele," *RE* 2A.2 (1923) 1344.
[58] See Brelich, *Gli eroi greci* (Rome, 1958) 89 on the death by lightning as a hero's death.

rush") suggests the movement of the Thyiads.[59] It had sufficient currency as to appear side-by-side with the old name on an Attic vase from the last quarter of the sixth century.[60]

Various places were identified as the spot where Dionysos brought his mother up from the Underworld. Pausanias recounts two differing local traditions, one connected with the temple of Artemis Soter at Troizen and the other with the Alcyonian Lake (2.31.2 and 2.37.5), although he himself is sceptical about the story. "I cannot bring myself to believe even that Semele died at all, seeing that she was the wife of Zeus" (trans. Jones), but here we are bound to take his reporting of local traditions more seriously than his opinions about them. The traditions mentioned by Pauasanias point to the fact that the worship of Semele, as part of the cult of Dionysos, was by no means restricted to Thebes. We know from the Greater Demarchia that the women of Erchia in Attica sacrificed to Semele in the month of Elaphebolion, the same month in which they sacrificed to her son.

The dossier may be completed with the mention of a festival dedicated to the mother of Dionysos at Delphi. Our informant is Plutarch (*Quaest. Gr.* 12, 293d). At Delphi, he tells us, there was celebrated every eight years a series of three festivals, the second of which is called *Hērōís*, the earliest attested Greek word for "heroine."[61] Plutarch here suffers from the same disability as does the orator of the speech *Against Neaira* in his descriptions of the *hieros gamos*: this festival is limited to women, and he is not allowed to know its content, much less to participate in it. As he says, "The greater part of the Herois has a secret import (*mystikon logon*) which the Thyiads know; but from the portions that are performed in public, one might conjecture that it represents the evocation (*anagōgē*) of Semele [from the Underworld]" (trans. Babbitt).

As discussed in Chapter 2, the heroine's biography is so much a part of the hero's that it is almost impossible to separate them. It is consequently impossible to isolate the main themes of Semele's myth from those of Dionysos. The dangers of her own pregnancy and death are congruent

---

[59] For example, schol. Lycoph. 143: Θυάδος [Βάκχης παρὰ τὸ θύω τὸ ὁρμῶ ("Thyiad: Bacchant, from the verb *thuo*, to rush or be inspired")].

[60] On a hydria in Berlin by the Leagros group (Berlin 1904; *LIMC* s.v. "Semele" 22), a woman named both Semele and Thyone stands by as Dionysos mounts his chariot. See Carpenter (1986) 24. A. Kossatz-Deissmann in *LIMC* s.v. "Semele," however, regards the second inscription, usually read as "Thyone," as meaningless. I have not been able to inspect the vase. Dr. Ursula Kästner of the Berlin Antikensammlung has kindly done so and assures me that while the reading "Thyone" is suspect, the inscription is not meaningless but requires further study.

[61] For this festival, and a survey of evidence for the Thyiads, see M.-C. Villanueva Puig, "A propos des thyiades de Delphes," in *L'Association dionysiaque dans les sociétés anciennes* (Rome, 1986) 31–51.

with the dangers of his babyhood. We can nonetheless ennumerate certain recurring motifs. As the wife of Zeus, Hera makes an appearance as the wicked step-mother, who wishes to destroy both her rival and her rival's children. The death of Semele while carrying a child introduces the theme of interrupted maternity. Hera's murderous impulses toward the baby Dionysos and the efforts to protect him reflect the ambivalence toward children that, as Slater has remarked, runs through the Dionysiac material.[62] Finally, the rescue of Semele from the Underworld parallels not only the numerous rescues of Dionysos, but also the rescues that he will undertake on behalf of the other heroines.

INO

Of all the heroines associated with Dionysos, Ino has perhaps the richest tradition. As noted in Chapter 2, where she is compared to Herakles, she is one of the few heroines who can compete with male heroes in range of action. The earliest reference to her is in the *Odyssey*, where she appears to save Odysseus from drowning. Here she is identified as "Kadmos' daughter, slender-ankled Ino—Leukothea, who once was a mortal endowed with human speech, but now deep in the sea has a share of honor among the gods," (5.333–35). The general outline of her myth is as follows:[63] Entrusted with the baby Dionysos after the death of her sister Semele, Ino incurs the enmity of Hera, who is no friend to the lovers of Zeus and their children. Both Ino and her husband Athamas are driven mad by the goddess, and he kills their son Learchos. Ino at this point leaps into the sea holding her other son, Melikertes. The sea-leap changes them both: she becomes Leukothea, "the white goddess," and her son, now known as Palaimon, becomes the hero of the Isthmian games at the Isthmos of Corinth.[64]

This heroine, like the others associated with Dionysos, becomes immortal and like Semele, she acquires a new name. Dionysos is not directly responsible for her transformation into a goddess, although in one version he does save her from the anger of Athamas (Hyginus, *Fab*. 2). The sea-leap is, however, a characteristically Dionysiac manoeuvre fa-

---

[62] Slater (1968). See note 55, above.

[63] J. Fontenrose, "The Sorrows of Ino and of Procne," *TAPA* 79 (1948) 125–67 provides a detailed review of the evidence. His method, however, which involves forcing selected versions into a story-pattern, leads him to some extraordinary conclusions, such as that Ino and Semele were originally identical (147).

[64] This is substantially the version given in Apollod. 3.4.3, but see 1.9.1–2 for another version.

miliar from the *Iliad* passage discussed above.[65] In this way the apotheosis of Ino takes place as much under the sign of Dionysos as does that of Semele.[66]

Athamas marries more than once, and the many myths of Ino consequently tell of deadly rivalries between her and the other wives. There is no unanimity on the order of the wives, although usually Nephele is the first wife, Ino the second, and Themisto the third.[67] Here the theme of the wicked stepmother, which we have already seen in Hera's persecutions of Semele, surfaces again. Ino turns out to be an ambivalent figure, at times taking on the stepmother role herself, while at others, being the persecuted one. Some sense can be made of the multiplicity of versions, since it is generally the supplanting wife who tries to kill the children by the previous marriage. Thus, in the versions in which Ino is the second wife, she concocts a plot to kill Helle and Phrixos, children of the first wife, Nephele. She persuades the women to roast the seed before planting it. When famine ensues, she manufactures an oracle calling for the sacrifice of the king's son. The plot is discovered, and Ino leaps into the sea with Melikertes to escape Athamas' wrath (Hyginus *Fab.* 2). In another version, the plot of Euripides' tragedy, Ino is the prior wife and therefore the persecuted one.[68] Athamas, thinking her dead, has married Themisto. He then discovers that she is actually engaged in Bacchic orgies on Parnassos, and secretly reintroduces her into the house, perhaps as a servant. When Themisto finds out, she decides to murder Ino's sons Learchos and Melikertes, but Ino, by a trick of switching clothing, engineers matters so that Themisto kills her own children. In this way, despite being the persecuted victim, she maintains the ambivalence with which she is portrayed in other versions. Athamas kills Learchos, but "Ino, together with her younger son Melicertes, threw herself into the sea and became a goddess" (*Ino cum minore filio Melicerte in mare se deiecit et dea est facta*, Hyg. *Fab.* 4).

In Ino we have as problematic a figure of motherhood as possible. Ino's maternity in different versions is by turns threatened, interrupted, and perverted. As the foster mother of Dionysos, she takes the place of a real

---

[65] In a forthcoming piece on Arion of Methymnos, I explore the Dionysiac associations of leaping into the sea.

[66] In an unusual variation, Plutarch (*De frat. am.*, 492d) suggests that Leukothea is in fact responsible for the immortalization of Dionysos.

[67] S. Eitrem, "Leukothea," *RE* 12.2 (1912) 2293–306 reviews the evidence, commenting on the difficulties caused mythographers by the various wives of Athamas.

[68] Hyg., *Fab.* 4 gives us the hypothesis of this lost play. *Fab.* 1–5 all concern the story of Ino, offer several permutations. Other sources include schol. Lycoph. 22 and 229; Eust. 667.5 on *Iliad* 7.86; Eust. 1543.20-32 on *Od.* 5.333; Apollod. 1.9.1–2. See J. G. Frazer's notes to this last passage (Cambridge, Mass., 1921) 1:74–77.

mother and attracts Hera's enmity as if she were the real mother.[69] She destroys the children of a rival, either out of pure jealousy or in order to protect her own. Nonetheless, her conduct toward her own children is not above suspicion. Under the influence of madness, she tries to kill them or perhaps to rescue them. The *lebēs* (cauldron) in which one of them is placed could be called the ultimate projection of maternal ambivalence. Is this her attempt to resuscitate or immortalize the child killed by its father, or is she herself engaged in murder? According to Apollodorus (3.4.3), Ino throws Melikertes into a boiling cauldron before leaping with him into the sea. Another source offers an equally confusing picture: either she herself throws Learchos into the *lebēs* or she grabs Melikertes just as his father is about to throw him in (schol. Lycoph. 229). That the cauldron embodies simultaneously the threat of death and the promise of rebirth is clear from the myth of Medea, and it should undoubtedly be read as ambivalent in this context as well.[70] Finally, even the leap into the sea with her son Melikertes is ambiguous. For Ino it is an escape from Athamas, and the path to divinity. For Melikertes it seems to bring only death, albeit a heroic one. It is true that Hyginus (*Fab.* 224) counts him among mortals who become gods, but elsewhere he is clearly a hero.

In Chapter 2 we discussed the widespread diffusion of Ino's cult throughout the Greek world, mentioning the many festivals and other observances in her honor. As we noted above, her cult is dual in nature, since at times she is honored with heroic cult, and at others with divine cult. The combination of lamentation and rejoicing in her festival rejected by Xenophanes is also found in the cult of the hero Hyakinthos, whose festival is made up of two days completely different in mood, but it is not common.[71] The case of Ariadne, which we shortly have occasion to consider, appears to be the only other example.

ARIADNE

Ariadne, the only "official" wife of Dionysos, is connected by tradition and etymology with Crete and plays an important role in the myth of the

---

[69] Plutarch, who equates her with Matuta, presents her as the figure of disinterested sisterly affection, suggesting that women at her shrine pray for their sisters' children because Ino was fond of her sister and took care of her sister's son, while being unlucky with her own children (*Quaest. R.* 17, 267e; cf. *De frat. am.* 492d). See below, n.95.

[70] See L. R. Farnell, *Greek Hero Cults and Ideas of Immortality* (1921) 42–43; *contra* Fontenrose (1948) 166–67.

[71] For the Hyakinthia, see Didymos quoting the *Lakonika* of Polykrates in Athenaeus 4.139d–f. See Chapter 3, n.64.

Athenian hero Theseus.[72] Although the tradition of marriage to Dionysos is generally presumed to be older than that of marriage to Theseus, the standard narrative inverts the order of events. It runs something like this: The daughter of the Cretan king Minos, Ariadne betrays her father by helping the Athenian hero Theseus to kill her brother the Minotaur and to escape. In the most famous version, she gives him a ball of string, which allows him to find his way out of the Labyrinth, the home of the monster. Elsewhere, she simply shows him the secret of negotiating the Labyrinth, which she has learned from its maker, Daidalos, or lights the way with a crown that was, according to Hyginus, originally a gift from Dionysos.[73] He takes her with him, but for one reason or another does not manage to bring her back home to Athens. Instead, he abandons her on the island of Naxos, either from carelessness, or because he has fallen in love with Aigle (Plut. *Thes.* 29), or because Artemis or Dionysos (in a dream, according to Diodorus 5.51.4) has ordered him to do so. In our earliest account, in the *Odyssey* (11.324–25), Artemis intervenes at this point to kill her, on the orders of Dionysos (Διονύσου μαρτυρίῃσι). In most versions, however, she is rescued from her desolation by the god Dionysos, who carries her off to make her his wife and bring her to Olympos, setting her crown in the heavens.[74] Ariadne, who after all never makes it to Athens, nevertheless becomes very important in Athenian iconography of Dionysos. Numerous vases show their marriage, or present them riding in state together in a chariot. In fact the *hieros gamos* that takes place in Athens during the *Anthesteria* is sometimes seen as the representation of the marriage of Ariadne and Dionysos.[75]

[72] For general discussion of the Ariadne material, see R. Wagner,"Ariadne" *RE* 2.1 (1896) 803–11; A. M. Marini, "Il mito di Arianna nella tradizione letteraria e nell'arte figurativa," *Atene e Roma* n.s. 13 (1932) 60–97, 121–42; Johan Meerdink, *Ariadne, een Onderzoek naar de oorsponkelijke Gestalte en de Ontwikkeling der Godin* (Wageningen, [1939]); T.B.L. Webster, "The Myth of Ariadne from Homer to Catullus," *Greece and Rome* n.s. 13 (1966) 22–31. The most extended ancient treatment is Plut. *Thes.* 19–21. Others include Diod. 4.61, Apollod. *Ep.* 1.7–10, the scholia to *Od.* 11.322 and *Iliad* 18.591, and Eust. on the same passages.

[73] String: scholia to *Od.* 11.322, Apollod. *Ep.* 1.9; secret of the labyrinth: Hyg. *Fab.* 42; Diod. 4.61.4; crown: Hyg. *Astr.* 2.5. This crown is, somewhat illogically, connected with the one given Theseus by Amphitrite (Bacch. 17). See Webster (1966) 24–26 for an attempt to sort out the different versions.

[74] Eratosth. *Kat.* 5; AR. 3.1003; Arat. *Phaen.* 71; Ovid *Fasti* 3.459 and *Met.* 8.176–79.

[75] See Bérard and Bron (1986) 22–23. It has been suggested that this festival, and the mythic marriage of Dionysos and Ariadne with which it has been connected, show the effects of Athenian propaganda. While the myth of marriage to Ariadne may have been politically convenient for the Athenians, this does not mean that it was invented out of thin air. It could only be viable if it reflected something in the character of the god Dionysos as he was perceived by his worshipers.

In this myth the motif of infidelity is elaborated in several ways. If the marriage to Dionysos is prior to the union with Theseus, then the death at the hands of Artemis is a punishment for her infidelity.[76] In such a version, the theme of marriage with a god would preserve the menacing quality it so often has in Greek myth and would present a perfect parallel to the version of Semele's myth in which she is punished for infidelity with Aktaion. (Koronis is another heroine punished by her immortal lover for betraying him with a mortal.) The supplanting of Ariadne by Aigle is comparable to the replacement of Ino by Themisto, or Nephele by Ino. As Semele was abandoned by Zeus, and Ino by Athamas, so Ariadne was abandoned by Theseus. Conversely, the rescue of Ariadne by Dionysos recalls his rescue of his own mother, the *anagōgē* of Semele celebrated by the Thyiads at the festival of the *Hērōis*.

Plutarch (*Thes.* 20) gives us a very peculiar local version, attributed to one Paion the Amathusian, according to which Theseus leaves the pregnant Ariadne on the island of Cyprus and is then unable to return to her. By the time he gets back, she has died in childbirth, and he atones by setting up statuettes in her honor and instituting sacrifices to her. In the same passage Plutarch tells of a sacrifice on the second day of the month of Gorpiaios, at which a young man performs a ritual *couvade*, lying down and mimicking the cries of a woman in childbirth. Here again we find the exchange of gender roles that permeates the cult of Dionysos. At the same time the myth and the ritual both emphasize the dangers of childbirth, a theme already apparent in the myth of Semele. Plutarch also tells us that the Naxians believe that there were two Ariadnes, one the bride of Dionysos, and the other the woman abandoned by Theseus, who died on Naxos and was given honors there, "for the festival of the first Ariadne is celebrated with mirth and revels, but the sacrifices performed in honor of the second are attended with sorrow and mourning."[77]

The story of the two Ariadnes is not very convincing, nor do we need it to explain the phenomenon of a cult in which death and immortality are combined. I believe it is no coincidence that of the relatively few examples of this kind of mixed cult, two of them are in honor of heroines associated with Dionysos. This is not the only notice concerning Ariadne's death. Pausanias (2.23.8) tells us of the tomb of Ariadne in the precinct of Cretan Zeus. It seems that, like Dionysos, Ariadne may have both immortality and a place of burial.

In addition to the images set up by Theseus in honor of Ariadne, he

---

[76] Webster (1966) 23–25 reads *Odyssey* 11.321 as Dionysos' punishment of Ariadne for running off with Theseus. As support for this, he cites the passage of Hyginus mentioned above, in which she lights the way for Theseus with Dionysos' crown.

[77] Trans. B. Perrin, *Plutarch's Lives,* vol. 1 (Cambridge, 1967).

also dedicated an image of Aphrodite given to him by Ariadne and instituted a Labyrinth dance, called the crane-dance by the Delians (Plut. *Thes.* 21.1). Can this testimony be connected with other elements of the myth of Ariadne? The earliest attestation for this heroine, in the *Iliad*, connects her with dance, specifically with the χόρος (*choros*) that Daidalos made for her:

> ἐν δὲ χορὸν ποίκιλλε περικλυτὸς ἀμφιγυήεις,
> τῷ ἴκελον οἷόν ποτ' ἐνὶ Κνωσῷ εὐρείῃ
> Δαίδαλος ἤσκησεν καλλιπλοκάμῳ 'Αριάδνῃ.

> And on it, the famous smithy worked a dancing floor
> like the one that once in broad Knossos
> Daidalos fashioned for Ariadne of the beautiful hair.

> (18.590–92)

The word *choros* can be translated as "dance" or "dancing-place."[78] Although in the Homeric passage it almost certainly indicates a "dancing-place," this does not prevent us from connecting the *choros* made by Daidalos for Ariadne with the Labyrinth dance instituted by Theseus.[79] Dance is a common feature of Dionysiac worship. When Pausanias mentions the mass grave of the Haliai, women who helped Dionysos fight against Perseus, he also refers to the individual grave of Choreia (Choral Dance), one of the Haliai (2.20.4) who, according to the Argives, was given separate burial because of her high rank. Her name takes on greater meaning in light of Pausanias' explanation (10.4.3) of Homer's reference to *kallichoros Panopeus* (*Od.* 11.581). He tells us that it refers to the Thyiads' custom of stopping to dance at various places, including Panopeus, along the road from Athens to Delphi.[80] Thus, dance is a point of contact between Ariadne, the official wife of Dionysos, and the maenads and Thyiads who follow him.

As we have noted, aside from Ariadne, Dionysos has very few liaisons with mortal women, most of them found only in later sources.[81]

---

[78] Schol. T. *Iliad* 18.590 glosses χορός as τὸν πρὸς χορείαν τόπον (a place for the dance). D. Boedeker, *Aphrodite's Entry into Greek Epic* (Leyden, 1974) 43–63 discusses the *choros* and its associations with both Ariadne and Aphrodite (as well the associations between these two figures).

[79] See Calame (1977) 108 on Theseus as a "mythic *chorēgos*," and on the significance of Ariadne's alliance with him.

[80] See Boedeker (1974) 152 on the epithet *kallichoros*.

[81] In addition to Physkoa, discussed below, there are Althaia, the mother of Deianeira by Dionysos (Hyg. *Fab.* 129 and Apollod. 1.8.1); Araithyrea, mother of Phlias by Dionysos (Paus. 2.12.6); Karya, beloved of Dionysos (Servius, *Ad Verg. ecl.* 8.29); Pallene, won by the god in a wrestling match (Nonnos *Dion.* 48.90ff.). His connections with men are even more limited. See Chapter 3.

Pausanias reports that at the festival of the Heraia, there were two choral dances, "one called that of Physkoa and the other of Hippodameia. This Physkoa they say came from Elis in the Hollow, and the name of the deme where she lived was Orthia. She mated with Dionysos and bore him a son called Narkaios. . . . They also say that Narkaios and Physkoa were the first to worship Dionysos. So various honors are paid to Physkoa, especially that of the chorus, named after her and managed by the Sixteen Women" (5.16.5–7, adapted from Jones). Hippodameia is honored for founding the *Heraia* (out of gratitude to Hera for her marriage to Pelops), and Physkoa, for her role in founding the local Dionysiac cult. Thus the two choruses are founded in honor of heroines who themselves founded cults, and they are set up by a group of women, the successors of the original Sixteen Women of Elis and Pisa who made peace between their two cities. As with the Athenian Thyiads, we find in a Dionysiac context an apparently independent religious association of women.

Physkoa, who is united erotically with Dionysos, could also be considered the first mythic Thyiad at Elis.[82] In general the canonical mythic tradition distinguishes sharply between the lovers and the followers of Dionysos. That Physkoa is both lover of the god and founder of his cult suggests that the distinction is somewhat artificial. It is also tempting to make a connection between the *choros* of Ariadne and that of Physkoa.[83] This may seem to be an isolated local tradition, but there is other evidence to challenge the distinction. We have already shown that Ariadne's connection to dance brings her into the sphere of Dionysos' worshipers, the Thyiads and the Haliai. Thus Ariadne's *choros* is a point of similarity with Physkoa, the first Thyiad of Elis, while Semele is connected with Thyia and the Thyiads by means of her divine name, and Ino by her function as nurse of Dionysos.[84]

DIONYSIAC IMMORTALITY

The three heroines we have discussed in detail all transcend death in one way or another, and all of them are honored in ritual that marks this fact: Ariadne and Ino have festivals that combine mourning and rejoicing, while the mysteries of Semele seem to tell of her return from the Underworld. These heroines are all possessed of a striking doubleness, marking their mortal and divine aspects. Ariadne has two husbands to mark her

[82] R. Hanslik, "Physkoa," *RE* 20.1 (1941) 1166.

[83] See Calame (1977) 244.

[84] Webster (1966) notes that from the late fifth century, Attic painting shows Ariadne dressed as a maenad (p. 29). For Ariadne and dance, see Calame (1977) 225–26.

two aspects, a mortal one who abandons her and an immortal one who stays with her forever. Ino and Semele each have a mortal name and an immortal one.[85] Above all, these heroines have two fates: a human death and an immortal life.

As we have already had occasion to note, heroines are more likely to cross the boundary from mortal to immortal than male heroes. The heroines associated with Dionysos do this with striking consistency. Are they immune to death because they are under the protection of Dionysos, or are they drawn into his sphere because of their ability to transcend death? Throughout this discussion, I have spoken of these figures as heroines who become immortal. From the standpoint of myth, this is true, for this is the way in which the mythic narrative is shaped. There is in fact a larger historical problem that must be mentioned. Semele, Ino, and Ariadne are all local heroines whose myths are intertwined with the myth of Dionysos. They are also figures all of whom at one time or another have been considered to be goddesses in their own right. Although I reject the "faded god" theory as a general account of the origin of heroes (see the discussion in Chapter 3), we must nonetheless consider whether it has explanatory power for individual figures. A case has been made for the original divine status of all three of these heroines. Some scholars consider there to be a connection between the name Semele and a local Thracian or Semitic deity, a kind of mother goddess.[86] Similarly, Leukothea seems to be a sea goddess, and Ariadne a Cretan nature goddess whose cult was found throughout the Aegean islands, and particularly on Naxos.[87]

By talking in mythic terms, I have taken a deliberately nonhistorical approach to this problem. Nonetheless, the question can be reformulated from a historical perspective. If in fact Semele, Ino, and Ariadne were originally goddesses in other places, how did they come to be attached to the cult of Theban-born Dionysos? Dionysos himself provides a cautionary example for the difficulty of speculating on the origin of the Greek gods. Nonetheless, we can reframe the question by asking what it is about this god that could attract to his myth and cult female figures pre-

---

[85] Ovid in the *Fasti* (3.511–13) gives even Ariadne a new divine name: *tu mihi iuncta toro mihi iuncta vocabula sumes, / nam tibi mutatae Libera nomen erit* (As you have shared my bed, so you shall share my name, for in your changed state your name shall be Libera [trans. adapted from Frazer]). In so doing, he is making use of a familiar equation of the old Roman gods Liber and Libera with Dionysos and his female partner. See J. G. Frazer's commentary (Hildesheim, 1973) 3:109–10.

[86] P. Kretschmer, "Semele und Dionysos," in *Aus der Anomia, archäologische Beiträge Carl Robert dargebracht* (Berlin, 1890) 21. Larson (1995) 91 takes for granted Semele's original divinity.

[87] R. F. Willetts, *Cretan Cults and Festivals* (London, 1962) 193–97.

viously worshiped as divine in other parts of the Aegean. Allowing for
the possibility that the myths of apotheosis reflect actual syncretic activity, I think we might sketch an answer. The frequently invoked method
of incorporation of a foreign divinity into an already existing mythic
structure is to demote her or him to mortal or heroic status, and then
incorporate this figure into the myth of a local god. No other god would
so easily lend himself to this project as Dionysos, who is mired in mortality and yet transcends death.

Yet, it is this very feature of Dionysos that provides material for a
strong attack against the syncretic model. Here we must take cognizance
of the objections of Walter Otto: "The hypothesis [sc., of Semele's original divinity] does unheard-of violence to the myth as it comes down to us
in all of the sources. The myth not only presents Semele as a mortal, but
it lays the greatest emphasis on the fact that she was not a goddess and
nevertheless gave birth to a god. . . . The mortality of the mother, therefore, must have been one of the essentials of the myth of Dionysus."[88] As
evidence for her original mortality, Otto also points to the necessity of
giving Semele a new divine name, and to the heroic character of her cult
at Thebes.

In this matter I am in agreement with Otto. We have had occasion
before to comment on the shifting status of the heroines who are central
to this study. Those with the most detailed myth and widespread cult are
the ones who most often make the transition to divinity. As we observed
above, it was at one time commonly held that this mythic transition was
the trace of an earlier historical moment in which heroines were in fact
goddesses. As I have argued throughout, I believe that this possibility of
transcending heroic status is paradoxically one of the characteristics of
heroines, and that this does not in any way undermine the integrity of the
category but rather gives it its specificity. Only by insisting on the existence of heroes as a clearly marked religious category, and by recognizing
the specific place of female heroized figures within this category, can we
make sense of the phenomena.

HEROINES IN THE CULT OF DIONYSOS

In Chapter 3, I speculated that a symbolic exchange of natures takes place
between Dionysos and his heroines, in which the god partakes of femi-
ninity while transmitting to the heroines something of his immortality.
In further investigating this claim, we have seen a whole network of
correspondences between the myths of Dionysos and of the heroines

---

[88] Otto (1965) 70.

connected to him. At times the exchange of characteristics seems to operate with respect to the categories of both gender and existential status, forming a kind of chiastic pattern. Dionysos shows signs of mortality in the Orphic myths and the story of Lykourgos, while his female followers take on the male activities of hunting and war. Not only do issues of gender and immortality shape the narratives of all the figures involved, but we have also found that many of the specific motifs of Dionysiac myth are recapitulated in the myths of these heroines.

At the same time we have found that women have a far greater role to play in Dionysiac worship than in the worship of other male gods. Let us consider what relationship there might be between the high visibility of female figures in Dionysiac myth and the unusual role of women in Dionysiac cult. It seems that, in myth, Dionysos' birth from a mortal woman makes him vulnerable to death and therefore accessible to mortals, particularly to (mythic) mortal women. Attempts have been made to speculate about the benefits of Dionysiac cult for ancient Greek women. Notable among these is the work of Ross S. Kraemer, which draws on cross-cultural evidence to explain the appeal of ritual possession to marginal groups.[89] Froma Zeitlin has pointed out the caution that is necessary in reading Greek ritual in this way. The notion that maenadic or other temporary ecstatic behaviors enacted by women operated as safety valves must be examined critically. Often these festivals, while allowing women temporary freedom to act in ways that were normally forbidden, at the same time reinscribe a male fantasy of feminine nature unbound. Thus the alternative version of women's nature which the festival offers may be as socially conditioned and as much a projection as the everyday one.[90] Recognizing the importance of this critique, as well as the difficulty of assessing religious motivations in any society, much less an ancient one, I will nonetheless offer a few suggestions of my own about the possible benefits of participation in Dionysiac ritual for ancient Greek women.

Given the level of identification between god and worshiper in Dionysiac cult, and the fact that women worshiped the mother of Dionysos as well as the god himself, we might suppose that there was a promise of blessedness in the afterlife held out to the women who participated in a festival like the *Hērōis* at Delphi.[91] After all, this is the appeal of the Eleusinian mysteries, which are also closely tied to myths of victory over

---

[89] "Ecstasy and Possession: The Attraction of Women to the Cult of Dionysos," *HThR* 72 (1979) 55–80.

[90] F. I. Zeitlin, "Cultic Models of the Female: Rites of Dionysos and Demeter," *Arethusa* 15 (1982) 129–57; Seaford (1994) 258, 311.

[91] For Henrichs (1982) 139, 153–54, 160, this was a major component of Dionysiac religion for both men and women.

death. We may also find a point of comparison in the role of the mother in these two cults. Demeter is not only mother to her daughter Kore, but in some sense an earth mother, while Semele's short-lived maternity gives her special status in the cult of Dionysos.[92] A possible clue may be found in the previously mentioned conjecture of Plutarch, that the meaning of the festival of *Hērōis* has to do with Semele's return from the Underworld (*Quaest. Gr.* 12, 293d). Perhaps the ultimate promise of Dionysiac cult in one of its aspects was triumph over death for the women who followed the god. We must not assume that Greek ritual roles for women were conceived for the benefit of the participants. Nonetheless, it is tempting to think that the cults of Dionysos offered women not only a temporary loosening, however compromised, of the rigid bonds of the gender roles in which they lived out their daily lives, but also that brief respite from the constraints of mortality that all of humankind desires.

A distinctive feature of many Dionysiac cults restricted to women is the prominent part played by one of the heroines. In order to understand the significance of these rituals for female worshipers, we must take account of the "pivotal" role the heroine at times plays between the god and the worshiper. By this, I mean that the heroine is presented at a moment in her own myth which has thematic resonances with the myth of Dionysos, and which simultaneously invites the mortal female participant to recreate that moment. For example, the mysteries of the festival of *Hērōis* focus worship on the moment in which the god wins victory over death for his mother. This moment is, in its turn, a recapitulation of the god's own victory over death and attainment of immortality. At the same time the ritual may allow the worshipers themselves to hope for some mitigation of the horrors of death.

For another example, let us return to the hierogamy of the *Anthesteria*, which may have been a reenactment of the marriage of Dionysos and Ariadne, with a mortal woman standing in for the heroine. The taboos that surround this ritual point to the extreme danger associated with marriage between a mortal and a god, for which we have only to think of the union that produced Dionysos himself. The hierogamy was experienced directly only by one presumably highly privileged woman, with the assistance of the *Gerarai*, but it seems likely that the event was the focus for women's worship of Dionysos during this part of the festival. If the *Basilinna* was, in the words of Daraki, "Athènes devenue femme," she was at the same time the stand-in for all Athenian women, in her union with the god.

We know less of the particulars of cults of Ino, but according to

---

[92] Even if we discount the possibility that her name may connect her to the Thracian-Phrygian earth goddess, as maintained by Kretschmer (1890).

Conon, there were mysteries in her honor.[93] Plutarch's account of the Roman cult of Mater Matuta, whom he closely identifies with the Greek Ino-Leukothea, suggests that it allows women to identify with the foster-mother role taken on by the heroine. During the festival of Matuta, women show affection for their sisters' children.[94] Pausanias tells us of a cave at Brasiai where Ino was supposed to have nursed the infant god, and it is possible that this spot may have been the focus of cult.[95] In each of these cases, women worshiped Dionysos through the mediation of a female figure. By mediation I do not mean intercession, but a process by which the female worshiper could identify with a being more like herself than the male god, for all his sexual ambiguity, could ever be. In this way the various festivals emphasize rescue by the god (with perhaps a hint of a promise of immortality), care for the infant god, or union with the mature god.

Even if, as we have suggested, Dionysos' vulnerability and sexual ambiguity make him particularly available to women as a figure for identification, there still seems to be a two-step process, in which the heroines play a major role. Whether the prominence of heroines is the key to women's participation in Dionysiac cult, or the result, we cannot say. In either case, I would suggest, the heroine reenacts elements of Dionysos' myth in ways that are accessible to female worshipers, and this reenactment facilitates identification with the god.

[93] Henrichs (1969) shows that in Miletos, Ino was an important model for women worshiping Dionysos, and that she was invoked for the founding of thiasoi.

[94] *De frat. am.* 492d. In this and two other passages (*Quaest. R.* 16–17, 267d–e and *Camillus* 5.1–2), he stresses women's enactment of the ritual and its connection with the myth and cult of Ino-Leukothea. Extrapolation from Roman to Greek practice is hazardous, but Plutarch is himself Greek and familiar with Greek practices.

[95] Paus. 3.24.4. Schachter, *Cults of Boiotia* (*BICS* supplement 38.2 [1986]) 62–64 discusses the evidence for Boiotia and the problems of interpretation.

CHAPTER FIVE

The Goddess and Her Doubles

Λατὼ καὶ Νιόβα μάλα μὲν φίλαι ἦσαν ἔταιραι

Leto and Niobe were truly dear companions.

—Sappho (fr. 142 Lobel-Page = Campbell)

ANTAGONISM AND RECIPROCITY

When we turn our attention to relations between heroines and female divinities, we find reciprocity and exchange at the center once more. Whereas the interaction between Dionysos and his heroines involved the exchange of those very characteristics that most defined their differences—differences of gender and existential status—the interaction between heroines and goddesses emphasizes not differences but similarities. At the same time, while the relations of Dionysos with female figures are characterized by a relative absence of hostility and violence, the relations between heroines and goddesses are frequently marked by antagonism. In what follows, I suggest that these ambivalent relations are played out in myths and metaphors of doubling and exchange, as heroine and goddess compete with, and ultimately replicate, one another.

The focus of this discussion will be the goddess-heroine pair Artemis and Iphigeneia. Much has been written recently about this body of myth and its relation to Greek rituals of female initiation.[1] I have covered some of the same territory here, but my goal is rather different. As with the Dionysiac heroines, I will have something to say about the importance of Iphigeneia to worshipers, but my main purpose is to elucidate the nature of heroines and their place in religious ideology. In tracing the resonances of heroine/goddess interactions in myth and cult, I hope to add to the picture that has taken shape in previous chapters.

Starting with Iphigeneia and Artemis, I will have recourse as well to the enigmatic figure of Helen, who seems to circle about these two, a restless third term, between goddess and heroine but with ties to both.

---

[1] Most notably P. Brulé, *La Fille d'Athènes* (Paris, 1987) and K. Dowden, *Death and the Maiden* (London, 1989). See my remarks in the Introduction. It will be clear that Dowden's more historical approach with its insistence on origins is very different from my take on the material. A. Brelich's *Paides e Parthenoi* (Rome, 1969) continues to be a valuable and provocative treatment of this material.

For Helen, although most often associated with Aphrodite, at times dances in the chorus of Artemis and at others plays the double, the foil, even the mother of Iphigeneia. Before coming to grips with this material, however, it may be helpful to consider another myth that introduces in smaller compass many of the themes that we find repeated in the far more complex example of Iphigeneia and Artemis to which most of this chapter is devoted.

NIOBE AND LETO: A PRELIMINARY EXAMPLE

The myth of Niobe, as it is most often remembered, is a simple case of hybris. Incautious enough to boast of having more children than the goddess Leto, Niobe suffers immediate retribution. Leto's children, Apollo and Artemis, make short work of the children of Niobe, who becomes the emblem of inconsolable grief. What then are we to make of the Sappho fragment (142 L-P) telling us that Leto and Niobe were the best of friends? The mythic tradition surrounding Leto does little to clarify her relations with heroines, since it deals almost exclusively with the solitary vicissitudes of childbirth (most notably in the *Homeric Hymn to Apollo*). The myth of her struggles to bear Apollo and Artemis accords with her cultic significance for mortal women, as well as her genealogical connection with Artemis, another goddess associated with childbirth.[2] There are, however, no direct parallels for Leto's rivalry with Niobe. As a relatively minor goddess, she is not explicitly associated with other heroines.

We might begin by considering the stress laid by the myth on the abundance of Niobe's children.[3] This fecundity is a characteristic we might expect to find in a childbirth goddess. Instead we find that Leto's myth emphasizes the small number of her children and the difficulty with which she bears them, while Artemis has no children at all. We have discussed above the tendency in Greek myth to de-emphasize or even deny the maternity of goddesses.[4] This may be accomplished by displacement

---

[2] For the notion of Leto as hypostasis of Artemis, see Wernicke, "Artemis," *RE* 2.1 (1896) 1358–59. As W. Burkert, *Greek Religion* (Cambridge, Mass., 1985) 261 has observed, Leto also has a role in initiation. See for example Antoninus Liberalis 17, which provides an *aition* for the Cretan festival of the Ekdysia. For cults of Leto, see Wehrli, *RE* Suppl. 5 (1931) 555–65. An interesting possible echo of the Sappho fragment is found in Callimachus' *Hymn* 3.185, "which heroines have you taken as your companions?" (ποίας ἡρωίδας ἔσχες ἑταίρας;).

[3] The exact number varies. See Niobe in the Appendix.

[4] See F. Zeitlin, "The Dynamics of Misogyny: Myth and Mythmaking in the *Oresteia*,"

(as in the birth of Athena or Erichthonios) or by splitting, as I propose to be the case with Niobe. The functions associated with a goddess of child-birth have been split off, so that they are no longer found in a single figure. Leto has the travails, while Niobe has the profusion of offspring.

Since Niobe in some sense usurps the function of Leto (speaking not historically, but synchronically), it makes sense that their relationship will be seen as a hostile one. At the same time, there is an affinity, if not an identity, and it is in this way that the fragment of Sappho might be read. As in so many other narratives of mortal/immortal interaction, destruction visited on the heroic figure by a divinity is frequently pre-ceded by some kind of closeness, whether erotic or purely companion-able. Now, we can reconstruct a hypothetical narrative in which Niobe is Leto's beloved companion who falls from grace because of hybris. Such a narrative could be compared to that of Orion, once the hunting compan-ion of Artemis, who is destoyed by hybris. The poignancy of her fall would thus be heightened by contrast with the privileged position of closeness to the goddess that she once enjoyed.

The death of Niobe's children is not the end of the story, however. Pausanias reports, however sceptically, a Corinthian tradition that two of the children, Amyklas and Meliboia, survived by praying to Leto and afterward built her a temple.[5] (Meliboia was so struck with fright that she never regained her normal color and was thenceforth known as Chloris, "the pale one.") In this temple, next to the cult-image of Leto, there is a statue of a maiden said to be Chloris. If we take this local tradition into account, we see that more is involved than simply mortal hybris and divine retribution. The conflict, which has been displaced onto the second generation, is there resolved. The children of Leto avenge the slight, while Niobe's children make restitution and in so do-ing, regain divine favor. The resolution, as is customary, takes the form of cult. Meliboia-Chloris, together with her brother, founds a temple of Leto and is herself honored there. The name Chloris, which can stand by itself as the name of a divinity, is suggestive. Could this be the trace of another myth of apotheosis accompanied by name change? The sources do not allow us to go further, as they will in the case of Iphigeneia, to whom we now turn in order to delve deeper into these contradictions of antagonism and identity.

---

in *Women in the Ancient World*, ed. Peradotto and Sullivan (Albany, 1984), discussed in Chapter 3.

[5] Pausanias (2.21.10) denies that any of Niobe's children survived, quoting the verse of Homer (*Iliad* 24.609): τὼ δ' ἄρα καὶ δοιώ περ ἐόντ' ἀπὸ πάντας ὄλεσσαν, "Though they were only two, yet they destroyed them all."

IPHIGENEIA AND ARTEMIS

When we turn to the relationship between Iphigeneia and Artemis, we find once again antagonism between mortals and gods, retribution visited on the second generation, and ultimately a resolution by means of cult. Here again, the emphasis is not so much on the exchange of characteristics as on the creation and reproduction of immortality and divinity.[6]

Artemis' interactions with heroines are hard to classify. Often at her side there is a mortal hunting companion who emulates the goddess in maintaining her chastity, until some fatal event, perhaps rape or seduction by a god, puts her at odds with her protector. These heroines suffer death, sometimes preceded by metamorphosis. For example, when her companion Kallisto is seduced by Zeus, Artemis transforms her into a bear, later to be shot by her own son. In this chapter, however, our focus is on Artemis' relations with Iphigeneia, a heroine who does not fit into this pattern. Although heroines associated with Artemis usually come to grief through inappropriate crossing of the boundary of virginity, this is not the story of Iphigeneia, who is portrayed as virginal and blameless in her fate. Iphigeneia, instead, remains blocked at the moment of transition, and instead of undergoing the changes by which women's lives are usually marked, becomes a stand-in for the goddess herself.

Iphigeneia presents a particularly rich opportunity for investigation, since she combines in herself many of the characteristic heroine roles. She is, as we have noted, a figure in epic, an illustrious dead person, the daughter of a hero, and a recipient of cultic honors. She is also a sacrificed bride, the object of a miraculous rescue with overtones of transformation, a priestess, and a cult-founder. In some versions of her story, she is also grandchild of Zeus (as daughter of Helen), the wife of a hero (Achilles), and ultimately one of those rare figures who transcend the mortal/immortal distinction: she is transformed into the goddess Hekate.

---

[6] Much of the massive bibliography on Iphigeneia deals with the myth as background to a treatment of one of the dramas, extant or not, dealing with this theme. Here I cite some of the most useful works: L. Séchan, "Le Sacrifice d'Iphigénie," *REG* 44 (1931) 368–426 reconstructs the plot of Sophocles' *Iphigeneia* and analyzes the character of the protagonist of Euripides' *Iphigeneia at Aulis* in light of Aristotle's remarks in the *Poetics* (1454a32); H. P. Foley, *Ritual Irony: Poetry and Sacrifice in Euripides* (Ithaca, 1985) offers a rich analysis of the plays, giving particular attention to the ritual elements of sacrifice. On Euripides' *Iphigeneia among the Taurians*, A. Burnett, *Catastrophe Survived: Euripides' Plays of Mixed Reversal* (Oxford, 1971) is provocative; H. Lloyd-Jones, "Artemis and Iphigeneia," *JHS* 103 (1983) 87–102 is extremely thorough in his examination of the myth, with the goal of interpreting Aeschylus' *Agamemnon*.

What special claim does Iphigeneia have on our attention? For the Greeks themselves she, or her predicament, was particularly interesting, as we see from the rich literary tradition about her from cyclic epic to the tragedians. As a prominent figure in one of the central cycles of Greek myth, the story of the house of Atreus, and by extention, the fall of Troy, she is the focal point of two surviving tragedies, and the ramifications of her fate resonate through many others. These powerful works cast their shadow over any attempt to study the myth of Iphigeneia. It is impossible to escape their influence, nor would one necessarily want to do so. It is, however, important to recognize their status as secondary elaborations of much older traditions that may, paradoxically, be more accessible to us through the much later reports of local lore and ritual practice.[7] For this reason, as in the rest of this project, the reader will find greater reliance on Pausanias than on Euripides, who must nonetheless be given his due as one of the most brilliant interpreters this myth has ever known.[8]

In Chapter 3, we outlined the possibilities for relations between goddesses and heroines, noting that although these could be roughly arranged under the headings protégée, antagonist, or double, they were often sufficiently ambivalent and overlapping as to defy categorization. No other heroine illustrates this more clearly than Iphigeneia. Quite apart from historical questions about the "original" nature of the relationship between the two figures, which attempt to recover an "original" identity, the extant body of conflicting variants allows us to see Iphigeneia as ritual antagonist or victim of Artemis, as her priestess or as her double.

Throughout this discussion the relationship of Artemis to Iphigeneia will at all times be our touchstone. It is difficult, however, to discuss Iphigeneia without taking into consideration another figure of equally ambiguous status, the divinized heroine Helen. These two figures, superficially so different, are in fact tied by a network of interconnections, both thematic and genealogical. As Iphigeneia is the protégée of Artemis, so Helen is the protégée of Aphrodite.[9] In each case, it is clear that this divine protection is double-edged, bringing with it enormous risks for the mortal partner. For a woman, the moment of crisis lies in the successful transition from virginity to marriage (and ultimately to childbearing). This transition, represented ritually as a passage from the realm of Ar-

---

[7] See Chapter 1 for a more extended discussion of this problem and its methodological implications.

[8] For the long afterlife of the Iphigeneia myth, see J.-M. Gliksohn, *Iphigénie: De la Grèce antique à l'Europe des lumières* (Paris, 1985).

[9] Although C. Calame, *Les Choeurs de jeunes filles en Grèce archaïque* (Rome, 1977) 334–39 points out that Helen herself has connections with Artemis and with choruses of young girls.

temis to that of Hera, is not successfully managed by either of these two figures.[10] Iphigeneia, the *parthenos*, remains caught at this point in life, achieving marriage only in death. Helen, on the other hand, fails in marrying too often.[11] The faithful wife, under the sign of Hera, makes the transition only once, instead of circulating repeatedly, like Helen.

WHO WAS IPHIGENEIA?

By the time of Aeschylus, Iphigeneia is known as the daughter of Agamemnon and Klytemnestra, sacrificed to appease Artemis so that the Greek fleet could sail to Troy. While we might consider this version the "vulgate," competing versions challenge the most basic elements of this myth, making Iphigeneia the daughter not of Klytemnestra but of her sister Helen, and claiming that she was not really sacrificed, but rescued and made immortal by Artemis. Some have argued that Iphigeneia is really the conflation of two separate figures, a Brauronian birth-goddess, and the daughter of Agamemnon.[12] Even her name, as we shall see, is not stable.

In the *Iliad* Agamemnon has three daughters, none of whom is called Iphigeneia. They are listed by name—Chrysothemis, Laodike, and Iphianassa (9.145 = 287)—as they are offered to Achilles, who will angrily refuse them. The A scholiast comments that "he [sc., Homer] doesn't know of the sacrifice of Iphigeneia told by the later poets." The earliest reference to an (attempted) sacrifice of Agamemnon's daughter is in the Hesiodic *Catalogue of Women* (23a 17ff. M-W), where she is called Iphimede. The *Kypria* gives Agamemnon four daughters, including both Iphigeneia and Iphianassa, who appear side-by-side.[13] Later, for example in Sophocles' *Elektra*, Laodike drops out, to be replaced by Elektra.[14] Iphigeneia is already dead and there is no mention of Iphianassa.

---

[10] See Calame (1977) 43, passim.

[11] Stesichorus (frg. 46 *PMG* = 223 Campbell) says that the fecklessness of Helen and her sisters is due to Tyndareos' slight of Aphrodite, who in revenge made his daughters "twice-marriers and thrice-marriers and leavers of husbands" (διγάμους τε καὶ τριγάμους . . . καὶ λιπεσάνορας).

[12] L. R. Farnell, *Greek Hero Cults and Ideas of Immortality* (Oxford, 1921) 58, holds to this view, as does more recently M. Hollinshead, "Against Iphigeneia's Adyton in Three Mainland Temples" *AJA* 89 (1985). As I have indicated above, Chapter 2, n. 45, I reject these kinds of arguments.

[13] Schol. Eur. *El.* 157 = *Kypria* p. 27 Kinkel.

[14] Aelian (*Varia Historia* 4.26) quotes the (early sixth c.?) poet Xanthos' attempt to reconcile conflicting traditions by resorting to a false etymology. Laodike, because she did not marry, was later known as Elektra, from *a-lektron*, "without the marriage-bed" (See D. A. Campbell, *Greek Lyric III* (Cambridge, 1991) 27.

Is the Homeric Iphianassa equivalent to our Iphigeneia? Such variations in names of female figures, in which only one element of the compound changes, are not uncommon, as was noted in Chapter 2. Here the important first element *Iphi-* (strength) is preserved, and the two names are also metrically equivalent, although this is not enough to establish identity. Their equally aristocratic meanings carry a somewhat different emphasis, since the later form replaces "ruling" with "birth." Eustathius, in his commentary on *Iliad* 9.145, etymologizes the names of the three daughters, stressing their appropriateness to Agamemnon. The name Iphianassa has to do with kingly power, that is, ruling with strength (*iphi anassein*).[15] Interestingly, the name Iphimede(ia) is synonomous with Iphianassa[16] and in its longer form, it is also metrically equivalent to the other two. Since Iphimede and Iphigeneia are almost certainly the same person, it is tempting to argue for the equivalence of all three.

Turning to the form Iphigeneia, we find no agreement about either her name or her origin. The linguistic argument hinges on whether compounds ending in -*genes* can be transitive, or only intransitive, as Chantraine maintains.[17] If one accepts his reasoning, the name cannot have the active meaning "she who brings forth children in strength," but only the passive "she who is born with force." Building on Chantraine, Calame argues that the name is in any case applicable to a childbirth goddess, since "the goddess who is born 'with force' is also she who brings about robust births."[18] Although using essentially the same etymology, Wilamowitz bases his derivation of the name, which he translates as "die Gewaltgeborene" (she who is born by/with force), on an alternative tradition in which Iphigeneia is ostensibly the offspring of the rape of Helen by Theseus.[19] In this he follows an ancient tradition. Euphorion, writing in the third century B.C.E., also defines the name with reference to the force with which Theseus impregnated Helen.[20]

---

[15] ἡ δὲ Ἰφιάνασσα τῆς βασιλικῆς ἰσχύος, ἤτοι τοῦ ἴφι ἀνάσσειν. Eustath. in *Iliad* 9.145.

[16] R. Arena, "Sul nome Ἰφιγένεια," in *Studi in onore di Ferrante Rittatore Vonwiller*, II (Como, 1980) 24.

[17] Pierre Chantraine, *Dictionnaire etymologique de la langue greeque* (Paris, 1968) s.v. γίγνομαι.

[18] "La déesse qui est née 'avec force' est aussi celle qui favorise les naissances vigoreuses." Calame (1977) 292n.234.

[19] U. v. Wilamowitz, "Die beide Elektren," *Hermes* 18 (1883) 258–63.

[20] Frg. 94 von Groningen, cf. *Etym. Mag.* s.v. "Ἰφιγένεια," cited by Séchan (1931) 372. This interpretation is made less plausible by the fact that "speaking names," when applied to mortals, more often refer to a characteristic of the parent, not the child. (For example, Telemachos' name refers to his father's "far-off battle" at Troy.) For a different view, see C. Higbie, *Heroes' Names, Homeric Identities* (New York, 1995) 189. The name Iphigeneia could in fact be interpreted as referring to the birth of Helen from the rape of Leda.

In this tradition, which we find in Pausanias (2.22.7) among others, Iphigeneia is actually the product of an early illicit union between Theseus and Helen. This is the outcome in some versions of Theseus' and Peirithoös' attempt to carry off Helen as a wife for Theseus. Although unsuccessful—they are stopped by the Dioskouroi—the attempt is not as disastrous as their other endeavor, to get Persephone as a wife for the hapless Peirithoös. In most accounts Helen, who is still quite small, is rescued before anything untoward can happen. In Plutarch, for example, the emphasis on the heroine's immaturity acts as a guarantee that she returns inviolate to her father's house, to be given in lawful marriage when she is older.[21]

As we shall see below, with the marriage of Iphigeneia and Achilles, it is enough in myth to state that something did not happen, for an alternate version to arise in which it did. Thus the chastity of Penelope gives rise to another version in which she is the lover of *all* the suitors (hence the birth of the god Pan). In the same way, the child Helen is raped and becomes the mother of Iphigeneia, who is then adopted by Klytemnestra, already a married woman. Pausanias (2.22.6–7) cites Euphorion of Chalcis, Alexandros of Pleuron, and Stesichorus of Himera as authorities for this parentage of Iphigeneia. Keeping in mind the sometime divinity of Helen, this double parentage would give Iphigeneia both a mortal and a divine mother. This would provide a rare parallel to the pattern of double paternity common for heroes, according to which the divine parent withdraws, leaving the child to be raised by the mortal counterpart.[22]

The tradition of the sacrifice first appears in a fragment of Hesiod (23a 24–26 M-W), in which Agamemnon's daughter, here called Iphimede, is to be sacrificed on the altar of Artemis.[23] But no sacrifice actually occurs, and instead Iphimede is rescued by the goddess who has demanded her death:

Ἰφιμέδην μὲν σφάξαν ἐυκνή[μ]ιδες Ἀχαιοὶ
βωμῶ[ι ἔπ᾽ Ἀρτέμιδος χρυσηλακ]άτ[ου] κελαδεινῆς,

[21] οὐ καθ᾽ ὥραν (untimely); ἔτι νηπίαν οὖσαν (still being a child), Plut. *Thes.* 31.1. Discussed by Calame (1977) 282–83.

[22] Cf. Paus. 10.6.1 discussed in Chapter 2. Helen herself, as well as at least one of her brothers, fits into the more common pattern of double paternity, as children of both Zeus and of Tyndareos, but this is also rare for a heroine.

[23] That this may be a very ancient form of the name is suggested by the appearance of the form *i-pe-me-de-ja* on a tablet from Pylos (*Py Tn* 316 v.). See Pietro Scarpi, "Un teonimo miceneo e le sue implicazioni per la mitologia greca," *Bolletino dell'Istituto di Filologia greca dell'Università di Padova* 2 (1975) 230–51. He traces an elaborate chain of connections that would place Iphimedeia in the chthonic realm as a double of Hekate. His observations on the cult title Anassa may also have importance for the name Iphianassa, but he does not address this point.

ἤματ[ι τῶι ὅτε νηυσὶν ἀνέπλ]εον Ἴλιον ε[ἴσω
ποινὴ[ν τεισόμενοι καλλισ]φύρου Ἀργειώ[νη]ς,
εἴδω[λον αὐτὴν δ᾽ ἐλαφηβό]λος ἰοχέαιρα
ῥεῖα μάλ᾽ ἐξεσά[ωσε, καὶ ἀμβροσ]ίην [ἐρ]ατε[ινὴν
στάξε κατὰ κρῆ[θεν, ἵνα οἱ χ]ρὼς [ἔ]μπε[δ]ο[ς] ε[ἴη,
θῆκεν δ᾽ ἀθάνατο[ν καὶ ἀγήρ]αον ἤμα[τα πάντα.
τὴν δὴ νῦν καλέο[υσιν ἐπὶ χ]θονὶ φῦλ᾽ ἀν[θρώπων
Ἄρτεμιν εἰνοδί[ην, πρόπολον κλυ]τοῦ ἰ[ο]χ[ε]αίρ[ης.

Iphimede was sacrificed by the well-greaved Achaians
on the altar of hunt-crying Artemis of the golden bow,
on the day when they sailed their ships to Troy
to avenge the theft of beautiful-ankled Argive Helen,
But it was a phantom, for the arrow-pouring deer-slayer
easily rescued her, anointing her with lovely ambrosia
from head to foot, so that her flesh would not perish,
and made her immortal and unaging for all time.
Now the tribes of men on the earth call her
Artemis Einodia, servant of the glorious arrow-pourer.

(*Catalogue of Women* 23a 17–26 M-W)[24]

Here we confront the curious fact that the earliest surviving account of the sacrifice is also the earliest account of its not actually having taken place.[25] In other words our earliest testimony is apparently a revisionist account. We must consider the possibility that the version in which the sacrifice does not take place is the original version, the arguments of Solmsen notwithstanding.[26] By this account the theme of virgin sacrifice becomes the theme of sacrifice averted.

The tradition of the sacrifice of Iphigeneia or Iphimede is echoed by later authors. Pausanias, as we might expect, gives credit to Hesiod: "I know that Hesiod wrote in the *Catalogue of Women* that Iphigeneia did not die, but by the will of Artemis, was Hekate."[27] He is no doubt quoting

---

[24] I print here the text of R. Merkelbach and M. L. West, *Fragmenta Hesiodea* (Oxford, 1967), with their conjectures in brackets. My translation includes a few phrases added for clarification.

[25] Emily Vermeule and Suzanne Chapman, "A Protoattic Human Sacrifice?" *AJA* 75 (1971) 285–93 tentatively propose a nearly contemporary piece of visual evidence for the sacrifice of Iphigeneia.

[26] F. Solmsen, "The Sacrifice of Agamemnon's daughter in Hesiod's 'EHOEAE," *AJP* (1981) 353–58 maintains that the "real" sacrifice was the original version and was known to the epic poets. He sees the appearance of Herakles' *eidōlon* in the Nekyia and Iphigeneia's here as support for the authenticity of the Hesiodic fragment 358 M-W (placed among the testimonia dubia). I find this argument unconvincing, for it seems more likely that the other *eidōla* could have inspired a creative borrowing. See below, p. 160.

[27] Paus. 1.43.1 = Hes. frg. 23b M-W: οἶδα δὲ Ἡσίοδον ποιήσαντα ἐν καταλόγῳ γυ-

from memory the lines cited above. For him, the identifications of Iphimede with Iphigeneia and Einodia with Hekate are self-evident. The same is true for Philodemus (*Peri Euseb.* 24g), who states that "Stesichorus in his *Oresteia*, following Hesiod, said that Iphigeneia the daughter of Agamemnon was now called Hekate. . . ." This is very like unanimity, although we cannot know whether the transitions from Iphimede to Iphigeneia and from Einodia to Hekate were made first by Stesichorus or not.

None of this allows us to decide whether Iphigeneia and Iphianassa represent the same figure, but even if they do, neither real sacrifice nor the sacrifice of an *eidōlon* or animal substitute can be easily harmonized with the Homeric tradition. Not only does the sacrifice not appear in the *Iliad*, there is no hint of it in the *Odyssey*, where it might have found a place in one of the many retellings of the death of Agamemnon.[28] It is of course possible that the sacrifice of Iphigeneia was known to the poet of the *Iliad*, but excluded, along with many other details felt to be out of keeping with the heroic conception of the poem.[29]

This survey of the traditions surrounding the figure of Iphigeneia does not allow a resolution of the contradictions of her myths, but neither does it present a more fragmented picture than those of the other heroic figures we have discussed previously. In what follows we assume the essential unity of the mythic figure, while examining the variations in her myth, and their implications for the cults of Artemis. We discuss in particular the myths of rescue and ritual substitution, Iphigeneia's chthonic aspect, and her role as cult-founder.

IPHIGENEIA AND THE RITES OF PASSAGE

The many versions of the sacrifice and rescue of Iphigeneia introduce a multitude of themes, some of them mutually exclusive. The rescue itself, which is somewhat overdetermined, has three main elements, not all of which appear in every account. Artemis saves Iphigeneia by 1) replacing

---

ναικῶν ᾽Ιφιγένειαν οὐκ ἀποθανεῖν, γνώμῃ δὲ ᾽Αρτέμιδος ῾Εκάτην εἶναι (trans. Jones). For Hekate's connection with Einodia, see T. Kraus, *Hekate* (Heidelberg, 1960) 78–83; 87, although he has nothing to say about Iphigeneia. On Hekate as a goddess of transitions, see S. I. Johnston, *Hekate Soteira* (Atlanta, 1990).

[28] Some have seen a veiled reference in Agamemnon's address to Kalchas as "prophet of evils" (*manti kakōn, Iliad* 1.106 with Eustathius' commentary). See Paul Clement, "New Evidence for the Origin of the Iphigeneia Legend," *AC* 3 (1934) 394n.2 and Wolfgang Kullmann, "Die Töchter Agamemnons in der Ilias," *Gymnasium* 72 (1965) 201.

[29] This is the opinion of Séchan (1931) 379n.9, who remarks that the reference to *Iphianassa* does not prove Homer's ignorance of the sacrifice of *Iphigeneia*.

Figure 7 Sacrifice of Iphigeneia, Apulian volute krater, related to the
Ilioupersis Painter, c. 370–355 B.C.E. (British Museum BM F 159).

her with an *eidōlon*, 2) replacing her with an animal, and 3) transporting
her out of harm's way, to the very edge of the known world. The multiplicity of versions is captured in a fourth-century vase-painting in which
the young girl being led to the altar has the head of a deer superimposed
on her own (figure 7).[30] Moreover, Iphigeneia's new life includes, in different versions, priesthood, death, burial in Artemis' sanctuary, posthumous marriage, apotheosis, the assumption of Artemis' role in childbirth, and some connection with the Underworld.

These mythic sequels to Iphigeneia's rescue connect her, directly or
indirectly, with three of the most important transitions in the lives of
women—marriage, childbirth, and death. Meanwhile, the rescue itself
has affinities with Attic initiation rituals and can be shown to share elements with the structure of rites of passage, as mapped out by van Gennep.[31] Here Iphigeneia seconds the role of Artemis, the goddess who

[30] See discussion in *LIMC* s.v. "Iphigeneia" 11.

[31] A. Van Gennep, *The Rites of Passage*, trans. Vizedom and Caffee (Chicago, 1964). For
an extensive discussion of these myths in terms of the initiation of young girls, together
with sources, see Brelich (1969), 229–311, "Le Fanciulle Ateniesi." See also C. Sourvinou-
Inwood, *Studies in Girls' Transitions* (Athens, 1988) as well as Brulé (1987) esp. 177–283 and
Dowden (1989).

helps women through transitions by which she is herself untouched.[32] As we shall see, Iphigeneia's myth and cult associate her with each of these transitions in a different way, and with all of them in ways that differ from both the directness of mortal human experience and the remote involvement of the goddess.

Most versions of the rescue by Artemis include substitution by an animal, a more appropriate sacrificial victim according to normal Greek protocol. The exact species of the animal seems to depend on local tradition. In what we have called the vulgate, the animal is a deer: "But Artemis snatched her up and took her to the Taurians and made her immortal, placing a deer on the altar instead of the girl."[33] According to the *Etymologicum Magnum* (s.v. Ταυροπόλον), "They say that when the Greeks wanted to sacrifice Iphigeneia at Aulis, Artemis substituted a deer, but Phanodemos says a bear, and Nicander a bull." As we shall see, these variants are not fortuitous but are directly connected with local variations in the Attic cults of Artemis.

The bull (*tauros*) mentioned by Nicander is associated with the Tauric Artemis, to whom Iphigeneia, after her rescue, sacrificed shipwrecked strangers.[34] At Halai Araphenides, where Orestes founded a cult of Artemis Tauropolis, the "bloodthirsty" goddess preserves at least a symbolic need for human blood. Here the custom is that a sword is run lightly over a man's neck until a drop of blood falls, in commemoration of the human sacrifice once carried out by Iphigeneia (Euripides *I.T.* 1456–61).[35]

At Brauron, where Iphigeneia established a cult of Artemis, the goddess is milder, presiding over the *arkteia*, an initiation ritual for young Attic girls. Here, a version of the sacrifice is told in which Iphigeneia is substituted by a bear (*arktos*). According to the Brauronian foundation myth, the *arkteia*, "playing the bear," is in itself a kind of ritual substitution, in this case of young girl for animal, in expiation of the death of a favorite bear.[36] This initiatory service to the goddess is mentioned in the *Lysistrata* and commemorated in vase-paintings of girls engaged in races,

[32] For this articulation of Artemis' role, I am indebted to H. King, "Bound to Bleed: Artemis and Greek Women," in *Images of Women in Antiquity*, ed. Cameron and Kuhrt (1983) 109–27, discussed further below.

[33] *Kypria* in Proclus p. 19 Kinkel.

[34] Ant. Lib. 27 after Nicander; cf. Hdt. 4.103.

[35] For evidence for the cult at Aulis, see A. Schachter, *Cults of Boiotia. BICS* suppl. 38.1 (1981) 94–98.

[36] See W. Sale, "The Temple Legends of the Arkteia," *RM* 118 (1975) 265–84; T.C.W. Stinton, "Iphigeneia and the Bears of Brauron," *CQ* 26 (1976) 11–13; C. Montepaone, "L'ἀρκτεία a Brauron," *Studi storico-religiosi* III (Rome, 1979) 343–64; and S. G. Cole, "The Social Function of Rituals of Maturation: The Koureion and the Arkteia," *ZPE* 55 (1984) 233–44.

and sculptures of children holding small animals.[37] These artifacts themselves point to a softer side of the goddess's demeanor. Meanwhile, to Iphigeneia's lot falls the clothing of women who died in childbirth (Eur. *I. T.* 1464–67).[38]

Iphigeneia's connection to these traditions is somewhat oblique.[39] It is true that she and her brother are consistently associated with the foundations of these cults. Both Brauron and Halai figure in the later part of the rescue myth, which we might call the "sacral" part. Moreover, the foundation myths for both Brauron and Halai insist on the derivation of the Attic cults from the Tauric one, tracing their origin to Iphigeneia and her brother returning to Greece with the image of the Tauric Artemis. Orestes establishes a cult at Halai, and she, one at Brauron, where she serves as priestess. There she is buried and receives cultic honors at her *heroön*.[40] Nonetheless, as much as she might be an appropriate emblem of failure to leave behind the status of *parthenos*, she is nowhere explicitly connected with the *arkteia*. What we know of the role of the heroine at Brauron connects her with childbirth, but not with the presumably prepubescent bears.

What unites these myths is the theme of ritual substitution, although while the Iphigeneia myths emphasize that an animal is substituted for the girl, the foundation myths of Brauron and its cognate cult at Mounichia threaten to make the girl stand in for the animal. At Brauron the killing of an animal sacred to Artemis (bear) is followed by a plague or famine. The expiation demanded is the sacrifice of a young girl (sister of the killers), which is then replaced by the *arkteia*. At Mounichia, where things do not fit as nicely, the foundation myth tells again of the death of a bear, ensuing calamity, and the demand for the sacrifice of a daughter. The expiation, however, takes the form of a sham sacrifice, in which a man called Embaros slaughters a goat dressed to resemble his daughter. This disguised sacrifice is accepted, he is given a hereditary priesthood, and an institution similar to the *arkteia* is established.[41]

---

[37] On the Aristophanes passage, see C. Sourvinou, "Aristophanes, *Lysistrata* 641–647," *CQ* 21 (1971) 339–42, and M. Walbank, "Artemis Bear-Leader," *CQ* 31(2) (1981) 276–81. Walbank dismisses the possibility that the *arkteia* was dedicated to Athena (281). For the vase-paintings, see L. Kahil, "Quelques vases du sanctuaire d'Artémis à Brauron," *Neue Ausgrabungen in Griechenland* (*AK* suppl. 1) (Olten, 1963) 5–29, and "Autour de l'Artémis attique," *AK* 8 (1965) 20–33. The statues are to be seen in the Brauron museum.

[38] For the suggestion by Christian Wolff that in fact it was the clothing of those who survived childbirth that was dedicated, see Chapter 2, n. 27.

[39] Brelich (1969) 275. Clement (1934) 401 discusses some ancient attributions of the *arkteia* to Iphigeneia.

[40] Other cities also laid claim to her tomb. For the pretentions of Megara, sceptically recorded, see Paus. 1.43.1.

[41] Sources for Brauron: *Suda* s.v. Ἄρκτος ἡ Βραυρωνίοις, schol. Aristoph. *Lys.* 645,

In each case an animal sacred to Artemis is killed and a human sacrifice is demanded, only to be ultimately replaced by the killing of another animal. This seems to be an inversion of the myth of the sacrifice at Aulis where, at least in some versions, the maiden is sacrificed as if she were an animal. The myth of the sacrifice at Aulis can, however, be made to fit the paradigm of local Attic versions. For this we must go back to a different version of Agamemnon's hybris. We may recall that in the "vulgate" he boasts, as he kills a deer, of being a better hunter than Artemis.[42] The pattern emerges more clearly if we consider the version in which Agamemnon compounds his offense by killing a deer in a grove sacred to Artemis (Soph. *El.* 566ff.).[43] The punishment is *aploia*, the inability of the fleet to sail to Troy, whether because of a storm or a calm. The expiation demanded is the sacrifice of a daughter. Agamemnon, unlike Embaros (who becomes a byword for cleverness), takes this literally, actually putting his daughter on the altar. The goddess, however, no more literal-minded than at Brauron or Mounichia, herself places the deer on the altar and takes Iphigeneia as her priestess. This version of the sacrifice at Aulis brings it closely into line with both the Brauronian and the Mounichian traditions.[44] Paul Clement has even suggested a parallel ritual that would correspond to the Aulis version of the myth, citing evidence for a similar kind of service to Artemis Pagasitis in Thessaly, known as the *nebreia*, or "playing the deer."[45] If we compare the rescue myth of Iphigeneia with the narratives of Brauron and Mounichia, it becomes clear, as Brelich has emphasized, that the relevant motif is not virgin sacrifice, but virgin sacrifice averted.[46]

Nonetheless, ritual, if not actual, death is characteristic of the rites of

---

Anecd. Bekk. 1.444. For Mounichia: *Suda* s.v. Ἔμβαρός εἰμι; Paus. in Eust. *Iliad* 2.732. Apostol. 7.10 and *Append. prov.* 2.54, both s.v. Ἔμβαρός εἰμι. These and other sources are reproduced and discussed in Brelich (1969) 248–49. See also Montepaone (1979) for a dissenting view of the relationship between the Brauronian and Mounichian rites, as well as her "Il mito di fondatori del rituale munichio in onore di Artemis," *Recherches sur les cultes grecs et l'occident* 1 (1970) 65–76.

[42] *Kypria* in Proclus p. 19 Kinkel; Callim. *Hymn to Artemis* 263; Apollod. *Ep.* 3.21; schol. to Eur. *Or.* 658.

[43] This version is discussed by Séchan (1931) 376, who cites Hyg. *Fab.* 98 and *schol. A. Iliad* 1.108 as corroboration. Interestingly enough, the scholiast gives the animal as a goat. This may have relevance for the Mounichian version.

[44] Brulé (1987) 183–86 lays out schematically the points of similarity of the three local cults. See also Dowden (1989) 15, who remarks that "Iphigeneia must die because a deer was killed."

[45] Clement (1934) 401–9. The parallel is fascinating, but it is a leap to suggest as he does that "the legend of the sacrifice of Agamemnon's daughter grew out of the ritual of the *nebreia* in the cult of Artemis at Aulis," (408) since we have no evidence for this ritual outside of Thessaly.

[46] Brelich (1969) 257. See also Brulé (1987) 182–86, 195–97.

passage as elucidated by van Gennep. Just as Iphigeneia's death is equivocal—in most versions she does not actually die—so death may here be interpreted as a metaphor for the abandonment of a social category, to be followed by symbolic rebirth into a new one. Van Gennep notes, describing the pattern of initiation, that in some cases the initiate is considered dead and later resurrected. We may note that two other elements of Iphigeneia's myth correspond to the schema. The rescue is accompanied by transportation to a remote place at the edge of the known world, the land of the Taurians, where Iphigeneia serves the goddess in a remote temple.[47] As van Gennep remarks, frequently "the passage from one social position to another is identified with a *territorial passage.*" Iphigeneia, unable to make the life-transitions of an ordinary mortal woman, nevertheless makes extraordinary transitions of space and time, being carried to the edges of the known world, and back again. The initiates in van Gennep's examples frequently mark their passage to adulthood by a separation and a period of segregation, during which they are considered dead, followed by acquisition of a new name under which they will be incorporated into adult society.[48] As we have observed, in many versions of the myth, Iphigeneia is given a new name—Einodia, Hekate, or Orsilochia.

At this point we must take notice of a difficulty. While various features of Iphigeneia's mythic and cultic role encourage us to see her as being of marriageable age, such as the fictitious betrothal with Achilles and the association with childbirth, the bears of Brauron most probably are not. Their actual age is set by the Aristophanes passage (*Lys.* 643–45) as between seven and ten, although this is called into question by the scholiast, who speaks of the ritual as one required for all Attic girls before marriage.[49] The discussion has also been hindered by a certain vagueness about rites of puberty versus rites preceding marriage.[50] Compounding the difficulty is the fact the Iphigeneia seems to have been assimilated to the (apparently prepubescent) Attic girls who performed the *arkteia.*

Without becoming embroiled in these ultimately insoluble difficulties, I would point out that Iphigeneia is not the only figure whose age and social status are indeterminate. Calame notes that Helen is attended by a

---

[47] Van Gennep (1964); Brelich (1969) 262 has connected Iphigeneia's segregation in the land of the Taurians with the segregation of bears at Brauron.

[48] Van Gennep (1964); on ritual death, see 75; on territorial passage, 192; for examples of name change, see 83, 105, 112.

[49] Brelich (1969) 263ff. Dowden (1989) 26–31 addresses the questions, "Who were the Bears?" and "How old were the Bears?" He concludes that they were the daughters of the elite and ranged in age from about seven to eleven.

[50] See van Gennep (1964) 65 on this problem, and on the difference between physiological puberty and "social puberty."

similar ambiguity, alternating between adolescence and adulthood.[51] Helen, in her earlier adventures, is especially desirable as she is poised at the moment when she is already attractive but not yet old enough to be marriageable. In social terms Helen's ambiguity stems from her repeated unions, and therefore her repeated crossing of the boundary that is meant to be crossed only once. Iphigeneia the *parthenos*, on the other hand, remains eternally about to cross this boundary. I say more about Iphigeneia and marriage in the next section.

MARRIAGE, CHILDBIRTH, AND THE CHTHONIC IPHIGENEIA

Some have wanted to see Iphigeneia as the personification of Artemis' cruel side. The suggestion has been made, for example, that while the heroine at Brauron received offerings of clothing of the dead, Artemis received those of the living.[52] Indeed, the heroine's chthonic connections might suggest this, but the myths also present her as the bridge between bloody Tauric practice and the more acceptable Attic rituals. The truth is that Iphigeneia herself is ambiguous. As a young victim of sacrifice, she falls into the chthonic category of the angry dead.[53] But as a rescued victim, she stands for the mitigation of human sacrifice and becomes just the figure needed to negotiate the transition from actual to symbolic sacrifice. The fearsome, chthonic side of Iphigeneia is not, however, so easily elided. We have yet to take account of the transformation of the heroine into the goddess Hekate, or one of her hypostases. In order to get the fullest picture of Iphigeneia's chthonic side, we must take what might seem at first an unlikely detour through the traditions of the marriage of Iphigeneia.

Most versions of the sacrifice of Iphigeneia include the detail that she is brought to Aulis on the pretext of marriage with Achilles. If this version was in circulation at the time of the composition of the *Iliad*, then it serves to heighten the tactlessness and brutality of Agamemnon's offer to marry one of his daughters to Achilles.[54] There is no way to determine the antiquity of this detail, which already occurs in Stesichorus, but it

[51] Calame (1977) 333. He also relates this in cultic terms to the alternation between Artemis and Aphrodite, 334. See also 344n.336.

[52] Dissenting from this view are Brelich (1969) 275, and Lloyd-Jones (1983) 96, who criticizes the idea that Artemis is "altogether kindly" while Iphigeneia is "responsible for the sinister elements," remarking that these two functions cannot be so easily separated.

[53] On the *aoroi*, the "untimely dead," see S. I. Johnston, "Penelope and the Erinyes: *Odyssey* 20:61–82," *Helios* 21 (1994) 138–40.

[54] For Kullmann (1965) 201, the offer at *Iliad* 9.145ff. does in fact reflect the Aulis tradition.

could also be seen as a later ironic touch, especially given Achilles' words to the embassy in *Iliad* 9. The categorical refusal given by the hero would, over time, become the source of the persistent tradition of a marriage between the two in some sort of afterlife. As we have seen above with Theseus' abduction of Helen and the supposedly compromised chastity of Penelope, the mythic tradition tends over time to turn denials into affirmations.

The dead Achilles is a great consumer of brides, of whom Polyxene is only the best-known example.[55] Iphigeneia's chthonic connections, discussed below, as well as the echo of an old ruse, make the union logical. On the other hand, a case can be made for the opposite view, that Agamemnon's lie is actually the rationalization of an old tradition of marriage between Iphigeneia and Achilles, which has also left its traces in *Iliad* 9.145ff.[56] Furthermore, one could argue for an intrinsic connection of Iphigeneia with marriage, or rather with the failure to achieve it. For Iphigeneia remains at the threshold of a transition that is frequently equated symbolically with death.[57] Euripides makes this equation explicit at line 369 of *Iphigeneia among the Taurians*, where he has Iphigeneia refer to her sacrifice as a marriage not to Achilles but to Hades. Interestingly enough, the poet puts the two names together in the line, in a way that seems calculated to be ambiguous: *Haïdes Achilleus*.[58]

Another piece of evidence comes to us from Antoninus Liberalis, in whose version the young girl is substituted by a *tauros* and whisked off to the land of the Taurians, where she becomes the priestess of Artemis Tauropolis. "At the appropriate time, she [Artemis] brought her to the White Isles, beside Achilles, and made her immortal, giving her the name Orsilochia."[59] He then reports that she became Achilles' wife. It is important to note that when Iphigeneia is finally married to Achilles, it is a posthumous marriage. To be the bride of Achilles in the Isles of the Blessed is perhaps not so different from being the bride of Hades, a connection already made in the Euripides passage discussed above. More-

---

[55] Other posthumous brides of Achilles are Medea and Helen. There are traditions of marriage to Deidameia on Skyros and an actual marriage to Iphigeneia at Aulis (see under individual names in Appendix). See also H. Hommel, *Der Gott Achilleus* (Heidelberg, 1980) 27ff. On posthumous unions see J. Larson, *Greek Heroine Cults* (Madison, 1995) 78–79.

[56] Hommel (1980) 34.

[57] R. Seaford, "The Tragic Wedding," *JHS* 107 (1987) 108, notes that the myth of Iphigeneia combines "two kinds of substitute death," of the mythical maiden and the sacrificial animal.

[58] Ἀΐδης Ἀχιλλεύς. On the equation of death with marriage to Hades, see S. Mizera, *Unions Holy and Unholy: Fundamental Structures of Myths of Marriage in Early Greek Poetry and Tragedy.* Ph.D. dissertation, Princeton University (1984) 32, 147.

[59] ἐποίησεν αὐτὴν ἀγήρων καὶ ἀθάνατον δαίμονα καὶ ὠνόμασεν ἀντὶ [τῆς] Ἰφιγενείας Ὀρσιλοχίαν (She made her an unaging and immortal goddess and called her, instead of Iphigeneia, Orsilochia). (Ant. Lib. 27, after Nicander).

over, she may be compared to another posthumous bride of Achilles, Polyxene, whom further investigation reveals to be enmeshed in a network of chthonic connections.[60]

We know from Ammianus Marcellinus that Orsiloche is an epithet of "Diana" in the Tauric Chersonese. "For these peoples offer human victims to the gods and sacrifice strangers to Diana, whom they call Orsiloche, and affix the skulls of the slain to the walls of her temple, as a lasting memorial of their valorous deeds."[61] Interestingly enough, Ammianus goes on to locate (apparently without much accuracy) the island of Leuke, "dedicated to Achilles," in the land of the Taurians (22.8.35). Despite the bloodthirsty aspect of this goddess brought out by Ammianus, her name suggests a connection with childbirth.

The Brauronian material discussed above has already established that in Attic cult, at least, Iphigeneia shares some of Artemis' power over childbirth. The text of Antoninus Liberalis adds to this picture in two ways. For one thing, it brings together, however loosely, the motifs of marriage and childbirth in the myth of Iphigeneia.[62] As we have suggested, these two critical moments in women's lives, moments over which Artemis has some kind of jurisdiction, are significant for the myth and cult of Iphigeneia. Generally, she is a figure associated with the difficulties of making these transitions, neither of which she experiences personally in the "vulgate" tradition. Second, the account of Antoninus suggests that this role is in some way intrinsic to the Tauric Chersonnese. These accounts of a childbirth-goddess who demands human sacrifice may reflect an actual cult, however distorted the Greek view of it may have been.[63] Whatever they knew or thought they knew about the Tauric goddess encouraged them to equate her with Artemis or her heroic double, Iphigeneia.

A similar story is told of Molpadia, to whose shrine at Kastabos on the Carian Chersonnese people come for incubation cures and help in pregnancy (Diod. 5.63.2).[64] Molpadia, together with the other daughters of

---

[60] Some connection between Achilles and Hades may lurk behind the words of Agamemnon (*Iliad* 9.158), suggesting that Achilles' failure to be moved by the offer of gifts might make him hated as Hades is hated for being *ameilichos*, "implacable." For Achilles as "Gott der Toten," see Hommel (1980) passim.

[61] "Deos enim hostibus litantes humanis et immolantes advenas Dianae, quae apud eos dicitur Orsiloche, caesorum capita fani parietibus praefigebant, velut fortium perpetua monumenta facinorum" (22.8.34), trans. John C. Rolfe, Loeb Classical Library (Cambridge, Mass., 1956).

[62] See below for the way in which this connection is disrupted in the Iphigeneia material.

[63] Fritz Graf, "Das Götterbild aus dem Taurerland," *AW* 10 (1979) 34.

[64] See J. M. Cook and W. H. Plommer, *The Sanctuary of Hemithea at Kastabos* (Cambridge, 1966) for material remains of the cult, which may go back to the late sixth century. For an inscription dedicating a temple to Hemithea, see also W. Blümel, *Die Inschriften der rhodischen Peraia* (Bonn, 1991) no. 451.

Staphylos and Chrysothemis, flees from the wrath of her father and throws herself over a cliff. Apollo, the lover of one of the sisters, rescues them, and Molpadia, on her arrival in Kastabos, is given the name Hemithea, half-goddess, and honored by the local inhabitants.[65] The myth of Hemithea, which we know only from rather late texts, may have been contaminated in some way by that of Tauric Iphigeneia.[66]

The various accounts about Iphigeneia lead nevertheless to very much the same conclusion: whether she becomes Einodia or Hekate or Orsilochia, Iphigeneia becomes an aspect of Artemis.[67] In this way the goddess replicates herself. The connection with childbirth is also part of Iphigeneia's function at Brauron, where the offerings she receives clearly show her in full possession of this role. That Artemis, although herself a virgin goddess, has jurisdiction over childbirth is easily explained by her role as the *potnia thērōn*, the mistress of the animals. Her concern is for the young of all species. At the same time she has power over women undergoing childbirth, and it is power not only to help, but to harm.

Here the work of Helen King may help to conceptualize the role played by Artemis, and the way in which this role is recreated by Iphigeneia. She writes that "she [Artemis] is the goddess of transition, and assists other women to cross the boundaries which she rejects. Thus, as Lochia and Eileithyia, she assists in childbirth, although she has not given birth; as Lysizonos she 'releases the girdle' both in defloration and in labour."[68] Clearly Iphigeneia, herself having been prevented from crossing these twin boundaries, permanently arrested at the threshold of the first, takes on the role of Artemis.

Not only does Iphigeneia take on the role of Artemis, but in some sense she becomes Artemis. A consistent feature of the rescue of Iphigeneia is her apotheosis. As early as the Hesiod fragment (23a 24–26 M-W), we are told that she is made immortal (*athanaton kai agēraon ēmata panta*) and takes on the name of Artemis Einodia.[69] Later authors, as we have seen, call her Hekate or Orsilochia. I have argued above, in my discussion of Dionysiac heroines in Chapter 4, for the importance of the

[65] (Diod. 5.62). I have already commented in Chapter 4 on Molpadia's position in the spheres of both Apollo and Dionysos. It is also surprising to find a goddess of childbirth in the sphere not of Artemis, but of Apollo.

[66] Could these two quite different Chersonneses (peninsulas) have promoted conflation of the two stories? While the Tauric Chersonnese is in the vicinity of the Black Sea, Kastabos is located in an area known as the Rhodian *peraia*, i.e., the coast opposite Rhodes.

[67] Séchan (1931) 369, 371 comments on the connection between Orsilochia and the epithets of Artemis.

[68] King (1983) 122.

[69] Interestingly, something similar had happened to her aunt Phylonoe, sister of Klytemnestra, according to the Hesiodic *Catalogue of Women* (23a10–12 M-W). See N. Austin, *Helen of Troy and Her Shameless Phantom* (Ithaca, 1994) 109.

change of name as a feature of apotheosis, and it seems at least as strongly marked in the Iphigeneia material. To it we may compare the transformation of Semele into Thyone and of Ino into Leukothea. What is unusual is that Iphigeneia's divine name is not standardized but appears in so much variation, and that despite the differences, each name shows her to be an aspect of the goddess with whom she is so closely allied. For now, I wish to concentrate on the transformation to Hekate, since this connection can be traced as far back as the alternate tradition of Iphigeneia's birth to Helen.

According to Pausanias, Helen dedicated a temple to Eileithyia, on the spot where Iphigeneia was born. He follows this with the tantalizing information that beyond or next to the temple of Eileithyia was the temple of Hekate (2.22.7). Without placing too much weight on their proximity alone, one could postulate some symbolic connection between the two temples. Wilamowitz went so far as to speculate that the second temple was actually dedicated to Iphigeneia-Hekate.[70] In support of this, we must consider that temples of Hekate are rather rare, particularly on the Greek mainland.[71] This is the only one mentioned in Pausanias, who lists in addition only one altar and one statue dedicated to this goddess. Iphigeneia's association in her Black Sea exile with not only Hekate or Einodia, but also with Orsilochia encourages us to look for further ties between Hekate and Eileithyia. Artemis herself is at times known as "Locheia" or "Eulocheia." Although we cannot assume identity of these three figures, they are closely related, at times sharing epithets.[72]

Let us digress for a moment to explore other implications of the Hekate connection, which will ultimately bring us back to Polyxene and to Iphigeneia's posthumous marriage. A fragment of Callimachus tells of the Ephesian woman who, because she refused hospitality (*xenia*) to the goddess Artemis, was transformed into a dog. Although she was turned back into human form, she hanged herself in shame. The goddess once more took pity on her and, placing her own adornment around the woman, called her Hekate.[73] This strange story does call to mind the rescue of Iphigeneia by Artemis, with its accompanying change of name. In that case, as we have seen, the earliest text gives the name as Einodia, which all later sources equate with Hekate.

---

[70] Wilamowitz (1883) 257.

[71] Cults of Hekate with elaborate temple complexes become important in Asia Minor in the Imperial period. See Alfred Laumonier, *Les Cultes indigènes en Carie* (Paris, 1958).

[72] See S. Pingiatoglou, *Eileithyia* (Würzburg, 1981) 93, 111; Séchan (1931). Dowden (1989) 208n.18 discounts any etymological connection of the name Orsiloche(ia) with childbirth, but it was interpreted this way in antiquity.

[73] Callim. frg. 461 Pfeiffer. See L. R. Farnell, *The Cults of the Greek States* (Oxford, 1896) vol. 2:506

The dog was sacred to Hekate, and various ancient testimonia point to the custom of sacrificing a black puppy to the underworld goddess.[74] Euripides' *Hekabe* ends with a prophecy by Polymnestor, on whom the protagonist has just taken revenge for the murder of her son, that she will be transformed into a dog (1265). This transformation will be recorded for future generations in the name given her tomb, the *Kynos Sēma*, or "Tomb of the Dog" (1273). That Hekabe and Hekate were sometimes associated with one another in antiquity may be in part due to the similarity of the names.[75] The myth of the Ephesian woman, however, suggests another connection. Hekabe's transformation came about as a result of the revenge she exacted for a serious violation of *xenia*, the murder of her son Polydoros, who had been sent to apparent safety at the house of Polymnestor.[76]

Finally, we should take into consideration another figure of similar name, Hekale, the woman who provides hospitality to Theseus, and whom he honors with heroic cult after her death, naming a deme of Athens and a cult of Zeus after her. Hekale is honored for her *philoxenia*, and once again the chthonic overtones are heightened by a reference in the same text to Persephone, wife of Hades, euphemistically called "the wife of hospitable (*polyxeinoio*) Klymenos."[77] Among the honors paid her was the institution of *Deipna Hekaleia*, Hekale's suppers. This is suspiciously reminiscent of the *deipna* for Hekate mentioned in Aristophanes—suppers set up at the crossroads for the goddess.[78]

What is the common thread to tie these disparate figures together? If we recall that Iphigeneia among the Taurians must sacrifice any *xenoi* (here meaning "foreigners") who come her way, and that she is equated with Einodia or Hekate, a pattern emerges.[79] Clearly, Hekate, Hekabe,

[74] Euripides frg. 968 Nauck on the dog as the *agalma* of Hekate. For dog sacrifices to her, see Paus. 3.14.9.

[75] The scholion to Lykophron's *Alexandra*, 1176 sceptically relates a tradition that Hekabe, a follower of Hekate, was turned into a dog and also mentions that Hekate is followed by black dogs. A. P. Burnett, "Hekabe the Dog," *Arethusa* 27 (1994) 151–64 suggests that "for Euripides there was a close connection between the Trojan queen and the goddess who was separated from her only by a consonant."

[76] R. Meridor, "Hecuba's Revenge: Some Observations on Euripides' *Hecuba*," *AJP* 99 (1978) 28–35, stresses the equation Hecuba = κύων (dog), without insisting on other connections.

[77] *Philoxenia*: Callim. *Hek.* frg. 231 Pfeiffer = 2 Hollis; *polyxeinoio*: frg. 285 Pfeiffer = 100 Hollis; Plut. *Thes.* 14.2. See *Callimachus' Hecale*, edited with commentary by A. S. Hollis (Oxford, 1990).

[78] For the *deipna* of Hekale, see Callim. frg. 264 Pfeiffer = 83 Hollis; for those of Hekate: Aristoph. *Plut.* 594 with schol.; Plut. *Quaest. conviv.* 7.6, 708f–709a; Athen. 3.110c quoting Sophron; Soph. fr. 668 Nauck. See Karl Meuli, "Griechische Opfergebräuche," in *Phyllobolia*, Festscrift Von der Mühll (Basel, 1946) 189–200; Kraus (1960) 88–91.

[79] The word *xenos* or *xeinos* brings together concepts that might seem unrelated—

and Hekale are in some way connected, as figures associated with the enforcement of *xenia*, the correct behavior of hosts and guests. How do we account for the apparently "negative" *xenia* practiced by Iphigeneia (Hekate)? It may help in this connection to consider that Hekate as a chthonic goddess is also a "welcomer" of the dead, like Hades, who is known as the "All-receiver" or "Welcomer."[80] When we take into account the names of Hekabe's children, Polyxene (Many-guests) and Polydoros (Many-gifts), one of whom is sacrificed to be the bride of Achilles and the other of whom has been murdered, provoking Hekabe's gruesome revenge, her chthonic connection seems even stronger. Neither of these names would be out of place as an epithet for an underworld goddess like Hekate. "Polyxene" would point to her welcoming of the dead, while "Polydora" would suggest the gifts of prosperity that chthonic deities provide to the living.

In this complex of associations, Iphigeneia is important not only as an aspect of Hekate, but as an analogue to Polyxene. The mirrored fates of these two figures serve as brackets to the Trojan War, in that the sacrifice of Iphigeneia allows the hostilities to go forward, while the sacrifice of Polyxene appeases the spirit of Achilles and allows the hostilities to end.[81] The similarity goes even further, since Polyxene is, like Iphigeneia, a posthumous wife of Achilles. In the myth of Polyxene, the equation "marriage to Achilles = sacrifice," which was only implicit in the myth of Iphigeneia, is made explicit.

As Hekate or Einodia, Iphigeneia is the infernal double of Artemis, while as the bride of Achilles—or Hades—she becomes the double of the daughter of the Hekabe-Hekate figure. So far, we may be working with a series of folk etymologies that create connections based primarily on sound associations. There are, however, several other elements that may be pieces of the same puzzle. A passage in Pausanias (3.19.9–10) recounts Helen's death by hanging, at the hands of her supposed friend Polyxo, and in the section that follows, Helen's marriage to Achilles on the White Island (Leuke), which was sacred to him, and her anger against Stesichorus.[82] This Polyxo has a similarly chthonic name, which also reminds us of another bride of Achilles. No explicit connection is made,

---

"stranger," "foreigner," "guest," and "friend." The institution of *xenia* (guest-friendship) turns strangers or foreigners into friends through the practice of hospitality. The sacrifice of *xenoi* suggests the otherness of the Taurians.

[80] Hades is called *polydegmōn* (*Hom. Hymn* 2 [Demeter] 17), *polydektēs* (*Hom. Hymn* 2.9), *polyxenōtaton* (Aesch. *Suppl.* 157), *klymenos* (Paus. 2.35.9), etc. See Hommel (1980) 31–32, on epithets of Hades and their implications for Polyxene.

[81] Burkert, *Homo Necans* (Berkeley, 1983) 67.

[82] On hanging in connection with Artemis, see Brelich (1969) 443–44n.2, King (1983) 118ff.

but the proximity of the two passages calls to mind the myth of Polyxene.[83]

What does it mean for a mortal heroine to assume the identity of a presumably preexisting goddess? Pausanias (1.43.1) uses the word *einai*, "to be," instead of a verb of becoming, as we might expect. These confusions cannot be resolved in myth. Here we are in the synchronic world of cult, in which such identifications are not required to fit into any linear narrative, and the identity of two divinities may easily overlap.

This identity, or at least a certain amount of confusion, is reflected in Pausanias' musings about the relationship between Artemis and Iphigeneia. At Hermione the goddess herself is known as Artemis Iphigeneia (2.35.1). But at Aigeira in Achaia, Pausanias suggests that Iphigeneia was the original goddess: "There is a temple of Artemis, with an image in the modern style of workmanship. The priestess is a maiden, who holds the office until she reaches the age to marry. There stands here too an ancient image, which the folk of Aigeira say is Iphigeneia the daughter of Agamemnon. If they are correct, it is plain that the temple must have been built originally for Iphigeneia."[84] The maiden priestess is also an interesting detail with many resonances in the Iphigeneia material.

We have seen how thoroughly Iphigeneia is enmeshed in a network of chthonic associations. Given this, what do we make of the myths of her marriage? And what is the connection with childbirth? For it should be obvious that the generally self-evident connection between the two is problematized in the myths of Iphigeneia. Marriage in Greek society, as in most others, is assumed to include the bearing of children. (Hence the word for "bride," *numphē*, is traditionally extended to a woman who has not yet born a son.) Nonetheless, they are not the same, and Iphigeneia's myth emphasizes that fact. Just as the sacrifice at Aulis threatens real death rather than ritual death for the young girl or woman on the threshold of this transition, the cults of the Chersonnese, with their bloodily ambiguous goddess, as well as the cleaned-up Attic version, serve to remind us that natural events like childbirth are dangerous, and that one needs the aid of a powerful and not necessarily gentle deity to help one

---

[83] The implications of these connections are explored by M. Suzuki, *Metamorphoses of Helen* (Ithaca, 1989) 6ff.: "The substitution of sacrificial victims motivates the metamorphoses of Helen into other female figures."

[84] δηλός ἐστιν ἐξ ἀρχῆς Ἰφιγενείᾳ ποιηθεὶς ὁ ναός (7.26.5), trans. Jones. Scholars such as Farnell have debated whether such cases are the result of back formations from split-off divine epithets, or manifestations of faded gods. For a discussion of the theoretical problems involved, see Chapter 2. Either way, the system read synchronically shows us an exchange of identity and name between the two figures. We shall probably never unravel the origin, divine or human, of Iphigeneia, nor am I willing to subscribe to Farnell's two-Iphigeneia theory (1921) 58, which is no more satisfying than the two-Ariadne theory of the Naxians.

along. In making these remarks, I do not mean to suggest that Iphigeneia alone stands for these darker outcomes, in counterdistinction to Artemis, but that she, as a heroine, and therefore closer to death and to human events, has a special role to play in the cults of Artemis.

Artemis' connection with transitions in women's lives has been discussed above. Here I would suggest that Iphigeneia functions as a kind of halfway figure, much as the Dionysiac heroines discussed in Chapter 4. She experiences marriage only posthumously (and only in some versions), and childbirth she does not experience at all. Death, that most remote of experiences for a divinity, is hers only in the versions that do not allow her rescue and apotheosis, but virtually all these versions associate her with death for mortals. (It is perhaps because of its potential for bringing death to woman that she is associated with childbirth at all.) Nonetheless, she comes much closer to all of these intrinsically human experiences of marriage, childbirth, and death than a virgin goddess ever could. Artemis is the far-shooter, whose arrows bring death to women, but from a distance.[85] Unlike Dionysos, she has no hint of mortality about her. While his transcendence of mortality forms an important part of his myth, Artemis is never subject to death but is only a dealer of death to others. That aspect is instead split off and projected onto her double Iphigeneia, who attracts to herself all the chthonic elements also associated with Artemis' other alter ego, Hekate. At the same time Iphigeneia herself transcends death in apotheosized form, whatever name she assumes. Dionysos and his heroines are of different sexes, but their myths do everything possible to mitigate this as well as the other major difference between them. Artemis and her heroine are of the same sex, which serves to throw into higher relief the difference in their relations to mortality.

EIDŌLON AND APOTHEOSIS: REVISIONIST STRATEGIES

The rescue of Iphigeneia, whether or not it represents the "original" form of the myth, requires a certain suspension, if not of belief, then at least of the narrative. It depends for its dramatic value on the audience's holding a set of "false beliefs" which can then be corrected. These beliefs are as follows: 1) Agamemnon sacrificed his daughter, 2) Iphigeneia was sacrificed to Artemis, and 3) Iphigeneia died on the altar at Aulis. To each of these beliefs, the myth provides an answer: 1) ritual substitution, 2) the eidōlon, and 3) apotheosis. It might perhaps seem to us, having read the Oresteia, not to mention the Poetics, that these "prior" beliefs make a

---

[85] See Chapter 3, n. 105 and following. The Artemis of Euripides' Hippolytos (1437–38), however, displays a marked unwillingness to witness death.

better story. From a ritual standpoint, however, the "revisions" are infinitely more satisfying, because of what they tell us about the contract between mortals and immortals. We have already discussed the first of these, ritual substitution, above in Chapter 3. In this section, we turn to the *eidōlon* and to apotheosis. As we shall see, these two elements bring together Iphigeneia with that other deeply ambiguous figure, Helen.

The *eidōlon* of Iphigeneia's rescue (Hes. frg. 23a M-W) seems to be the signpost of revisionist mythmaking, and a highly self-conscious one at that.[86] Let us consider several similar occurrences of the word in archaic poetry. In *Odyssey* 11, Odysseus sees Herakles in the Underworld, but it is really only his *eidōlon*, because the actual Herakles had gone to Olympos:

> Τὸν δὲ μέτ' εἰσενόησα βίην Ἡρακληείην,
> εἴδωλον· αὐτὸς δὲ μετ' ἀθανάτοισι θεοῖσι
> τέρπεται ἐν θαλίῃς καὶ ἔχει καλλίσφυρον Ἥβην
> παῖδα Διὸς μεγάλοιο καὶ Ἥρης χρυσοπεδίλου.

> And after him I saw the powerful Herakles,
> or rather, his phantom; he himself among the immortal gods
> enjoys the feast and has as his wife lovely-ankled Hebe,
> child of great Zeus and golden-sandled Hera.

> (*Odyssey* 11.601–4)

Critics have long pointed to the clumsiness with which this "crude" interpolation attempts to reconcile two conflicting versions of Herakles' fate, one mortal-heroic, and the other divine.[87] No matter how transparent the attempt, there is something significant in the choice of manoeuvre.

No discussion of the *eidōlon* as a narrative device in myth is complete without a consideration of Helen's *eidōlon* and the Palinode of Stesichorus.[88] Here we are in the unusual situation of having not only a fragment of the poem, but also a legend about how it came to be composed.

---

[86] For the "eidōlon-technique" as a way for the poet to introduce an alternate version, see Mark Griffith, "Contest and Contradiction in Early Greek Poetry," in *Cabinet of the Muses*, ed. M. Griffith and D. J. Mastronarde (Atlanta: 1990) 197–99.

[87] See the comments by Alfred Heubeck, ed., *Omero. Odissea* ([Milan], 1983) on this passage and also the discussion in Chapter 1.

[88] See Thaddeus Zielinski, "De Helenae Simulacro," *Eos* 30 (1927) 54–58, Vittore Pisani, "Elena e l'ΕΙΔΩΛΟΝ," *Revista di Filologia e di Istruzione classica* (n.s. 6) 56 (1928) 476–99; C. M. Bowra, "The Two Palinodes of Stesichorus," *Classical Review* 77 (1963) 245–52; J. A. Davison, "De Helena Stesichori," *QUCC* 2 (1966) 80–90. More recently, the similarities between the two *eidōlon* myths have been discussed by Solmsen (1981) 353–58; M. L. West, *Hesiodic Catalogue of Women* (Oxford, 1985) 134–35; and Griffith (1990) 198–99. See now N. Austin, *Helen of Troy and her Shameless Phantom* (Ithaca, 1994).

Stesichorus' poem about the Trojan War aroused the anger of Helen, who blinded him for telling lies about her behavior. As Pausanias (3.19.13) tells us, Leonymos of Kroton sailed to the island of Leuke, and there he saw heroes of the Trojan War, as well as Helen, who ordered him to sail to Himera and tell Stesichorus that his blindness was caused by her anger. Consequently he wrote the palinode and regained his sight. The three lines we have make no mention of an *eidōlon*, but they do make the point, with anaphora, that Helen never went to Troy:

> οὐκ ἔστ' ἔτυμος λόγος οὗτος,
> οὐδ' ἔβας ἐν νηυσὶν εὐσέλμοις
> οὐδ' ἵκεο πέργαμα Τροίας . . .

> It is not true, that story—
> you did not go in the well-benched ships
> you did not reach the towers of Troy . . .

(192 PMG = Plato Phaedrus 243a)

We know about the *eidōlon* from Plato, who refers in the *Republic* (9.586c) to "the phantom of Helen which Stesichorus says was fought over by those in Troy, in ignorance of the truth."[89] Here, there is no question about the revisionist nature of the poet's enterprise, and the whole apparatus of surrounding lore shows that this is how the poem was read in antiquity. (It is not necessary to believe in the literal truth of the poet's blindness to acknowledge the point.) Stesichorus is in a tight spot and needs a way to reconcile two irreconcilable versions of Helen's myth. Here again the *eidōlon* comes in handy, to pretty up an otherwise nasty story.[90] As Gregory Nagy has pointed out, Stesichorus, in telling his version of the story of Helen, offers a challenge to Homeric poetics.[91]

The myth of the woman with a phantom double is ancient and has Vedic parallels.[92] At the same time, scholars have noticed Vedic parallels for the figure of Helen.[93] The only one to connect the *eidōlon* with Vedic

---

[89] τὸ τῆς Ἑλένης εἴδωλον ὑπὸ τὴν ἐν Τροίᾳ Στησίχορός φησι γενέσθαι περιμάχητον ἀγνοίᾳ τοῦ ἀληθοῦς (*Republic* 586c). See also Aristid. *Or.* 2.234; Tzetzes *ad Lycoph.* 113.

[90] As Davison (1966) 86, points out, the manoeuvre also serves Stesichorus' purpose in showing himself "poetam esse meliorem Hesiodo, Homero feliciorem"—"a better poet than Hesiod, a luckier one than Homer."

[91] For Stesichorus' version as a *poetic* alternative to the Homeric poetics of Helen, see Gregory Nagy, *Pindar's Homer* (Baltimore, 1990), esp. 419–23.

[92] Occurrences of the motif in Indic and other literatures have been studied by Wendy Doniger in an unpublished paper that she has kindly allowed me to see. In her examples the phantom is usually a way to avoid a sexual encounter, as with Helen, or Hera and Ixion. For Helen and Ixion, see also F. I. Zeitlin, "Travesties of Gender and Genre in Aristophanes' *Thesmophoriazousae*," in Foley (1981) 201ff.

[93] For Helen's Vedic antecedents, see G. Nagy, "Sappho's Phaon and the White Rock of

precedents is Skutsch, who is unfortunately led to conclude thereby that there were two Helens.[94] Here it seems more fruitful, rather than looking for a one-to-one correspondence between the various figures, to see their traits as recurring in different combinations in the Greek material. Thus the *eidōlon*, even if not specifically associated with a Vedic "equivalent" of Helen, was apparently circulating in the same mythic milieu. If the *eidōlon* were inherited along with the figure of Helen, then the motif should have been known in some form before Stesichorus wrote his Palinode. It, like the sacrifice of Iphigeneia, may well have had pre-Homeric currency without being incorporated into the epic.[95] Perhaps the Homeric poems or poets knew a great deal more than they were willing to tell.[96]

Another fragment of Stesichorus (193 *PMG* = Campbell) refers to two palinodes, in one of which, "he blames Homer for saying that Helen went to Troy, instead of her *eidōlon*, and in the other, he blames Hesiod." Given this, it comes as something of a surprise to read ancient testimony to the effect that "Hesiod was the first to tell of Helen's phantom."[97] The editors of the Hesiodic corpus treat this fragment with suspicion and remark that it would make more sense to attribute the distinction to Stesichorus. Whereas Solmsen sees the occurrence of the *eidōlon* motif in the Iphigeneia fragment and in the Nekyia as bolstering the claim of this "dubious" fragment, I submit that the emphasis of doubt should fall not on the word *Hēsiodos* or *eidōlon* but on *Helenēs*.[98] In other words, "Hesiod was the first to tell of *Iphigeneia*'s phantom." For if Hesiod was first with an *eidōlon* story, it is far more likely to be the one we have about the sacrifice of Iphigeneia at Aulis (23 M-W). He may well have been the first to tell of an *eidōlon* in the rescue of Iphigeneia (though perhaps not the

---

Leukas" *HSCP* 77 (1973) 165; D. Boedeker, *Aphrodite's Entry into Greek Epic* (Leiden, 1974) 61–63; L. Clader, *Helen* (1976) 52–54; and Ann Sutor, "Aphrodite/ Paris/ Helen: A Vedic Myth in the *Iliad*." *TAPA* 117 (1987) 51–58. Most recently S. W. Jamison, "Draupadī on the Walls of Troy: *Iliad* 3 from an Indic Perspective," *CA* 13 (1994) 5–16 argues for traces of Indo-European marriage law in the *Teichoskopia*.

[94] O. Skutsch, "Helen, Her Name and Nature," *JHS* 107 (1987) 189. He speculates that Saranyu, the mother of the Asvins, is in fact cognate with Helen, which suggests to him the existence of two Helens.

[95] Séchan (1931) 379–80 n. 9.

[96] Stesichorus' priority with the myth of Helen's *eidōlon* is thrown into crisis by the idea of an Indo-European precedent. Nonetheless, there is no good evidence for the story in any earlier Greek author. He may well have been the first to challenge the prevalent Homeric version. The motif could have been preserved before Stesichorus by extra-literary means, such as vase-painting, but this is pure speculation.

[97] πρῶτος Ἡσίοδος περὶ τῆς Ἑλένης τὸ εἴδωλον παρήγαγε (*Paraphrasis Lycoph*. 822). Merkelbach and West assign this to the Fragmenta Dubia (358).

[98] Austin (1994) 109–10 has reached a similar conclusion.

first to tell of the rescue altogether), while the testimony about Stesichorus would make no sense if Hesiod had already told of Helen's *eidōlon*. Moreover, the confusion could have been enhanced by the fact that
Stesichorus in his *Oresteia* seems to have told of Iphigeneia's rescue.[99] It
seems that the two stories produced their own confusion even in
antiquity.[100]

So Helen never went to Troy, Herakles is not really dead, but immortal, and Iphigeneia was not really sacrificed by her father. A common
thread to all these myths, and one that has not received sufficient attention, is the theme of apotheosis.[101] It is explicit in the Herakles passage in
the *Odyssey*, as it is in the Iphimede passage from the *Catalogue of Women*,
where immortality is part of the rescue effected by the goddess. The
divinity of Helen is not made explicit in connection with her *eidōlon* but
recurs in many versions of the myth and lurks beneath the surface of the
surrounding myth of Stesichorus' composition of the palinode.[102]

At this point it may be helpful to summarize the common elements
and points of contact between the myths of these two figures. To begin
with, Helen may be the mother of Iphigeneia. (This could be a way of
spelling out the necessary logical relation given their importance in starting and continuing the Trojan War.) Iphigeneia the virgin is made to die
for Helen the adulterous wife. If Helen is the *casus belli*, without
Iphigeneia the Trojan War could not have taken place.[103] There is also a
tradition that Helen was to be sacrificed in Sparta to avert a plague, but at

---

[99] Philod. *Peri Euseb.* 24g.

[100] Here, for example, is Trimalchio's account of the Trojan War: "You see, there were
these two brothers, Ganymede and Diomedes. Now, they had this sister called Helen, see.
Well, Agamemnon eloped with her and Diana left a deer as a fill-in for Helen. Now this
poet called Homer describes the battle between the Trojans and the people of a place called
Paros, which is where Paris came from. Well, as you'd expect, Agamemnon won and gave
his daughter Iphigeneia to Achilles in marriage. And that's why Ajax went mad. . . ."
Petronius, *Satyricon* 59, trans. W. Arrowsmith.

[101] Of course, not all appearances of an *eidōlon* have to do with apotheosis. When Apollo
uses an *eidōlon* to deceive the Achaeans while rescuing Aineias (*Iliad* 5.449), it is only a
temporary diversion. It does save him, but he will have to wait nearly a millenium for his
apotheosis in Vergil's *Aeneid*. In fact, the *Homeric Hymn to Aphrodite* explicitly refuses him
immortality. See Chapter 3.

[102] Zeitlin (1981) 201 remarks that "the case of Stesichorus has been referred to the
violation of the cultic norms of Sparta where Helen was indeed worshiped in a cult role as a
goddess. The palinode, in its creation of the *eidōlon*, therefore unequivocally confirmed her
divine status." See Clader (1976) for the evidence for Helen's divinity. Cf. Isoc. *Praise of
Helen* 217d. Usually Helen does not require an explicit apotheosis, but one is furnished in
Eur. *Or.* 1684–90.

[103] In the same way, Iphigeneia and Polyxene balance each other as virgins sacrificed at
the beginning and the end of the Trojan War. Not only that, but in each case, the sacrifice is
equated with marriage to Achilles.

the last minute an eagle picked up the knife and dropped it on a heifer, thus putting an end to maiden sacrifices.[104] For both Iphigeneia and Helen, there is an apparent revision of the well-known version of the myth in which an *eidōlon* is used to resolve a contradiction. They are each rescued by being transported east, far beyond the boundaries of the Greek world, and they are again rescued in the other direction. These similarities were not lost on Euripides, and indeed he seems to have emphasized them. It is impossible to say how much was his own invention, but it is likely that when writing the *Iphigeneia among the Taurians*, presumably soon after the success of the *Helen*, he imitated the rescue plot of the earlier play, making each heroine carry away a cult image in her flight.[105] Then, each of them is said to be the bride of Achilles in the afterlife. Finally, both Helen and Iphigeneia belong to that small category of heroines who become goddesses.

THE *AGALMA* OF THE GODDESS AND THE *EIDŌLON* OF HER PRIESTESS: DOUBLING AND EXCHANGE

As we have seen, the *eidōlon* in the myths of Helen and Iphigeneia can be seen as the sign of apotheosis, a mark of special favor conferred on a mortal by a god. As I have argued throughout, however, the relationship of mortal and immortal is not one-sided, but reciprocal. Reciprocity of a mortal to a god may take the form of cult-foundation. It is the sign of this reciprocity, the ἄγαλμα (*agalma*, pl. *agalmata*), that I now wish to examine.[106] In its narrow sense, the *agalma* is the image of the goddess with which a cult may be founded. It is in this sense that the concept has direct relevance to Iphigeneia. Taken in its broader sense, however, it has wide-ranging implications for the mythic role of women and brings us back to Helen.

Women may themselves be *agalmata*. In Aeschylus' *Agamemnon* Iphigeneia is the *agalma* of the house.[107] The language of the *Agamemnon* also connects Helen very clearly to the world of *agalmata* as well as *ei-*

---

[104] Ps.-Plut. *Hist. Parall.* 314c.

[105] See Mizera (1984) 132ff. for the resonances of these two myths as used by Euripides. Already in Herodotus, we find both Helen's sojourn in Egypt (2.113–17) and Iphigeneia's Tauric episode (4.103). Both passages contain the theme of killing strangers, although in the Egyptian episode, Proteus stresses his unwillingness to kill a stranger, even one so impious as Paris.

[106] Mizera (1984) 135–36, has remarked on the symmetry of the *eidōlon* and the *agalma*, which she places in relation to the image of Hera in the aetiology of the *Tonaia*.

[107] *Ag.* 208; See J.-P. Vernant, "Le Mariage en Grèce antique," *PP* 28 (1973) 56 for women as *agalmata*. Also J. Redfield, "Notes on the Greek Wedding," *Arethusa* 15 (1982) 186.

dōla.[108] *Agalmata* may be gifts exchanged among mortals, but the word can also refer to gifts given to the gods, dedications. Women may themselves be the givers of these gifts to the gods. The word is doubly ambiguous, because it may mean any object dedicated to a god, but since dedications often take the form of a statue of the divinity being honored, *agalma* comes to mean "image" or "statue."[109]

In his essay "The Mythical Idea of Value in Greece," Louis Gernet discusses *agalmata* as the embodiment of "value," as precious objects that attract a kind of religious awe.[110] He mentions in passing the importance of the role of woman as agent of transmission of a talisman or precious object."[111] His comment about women as agents of transmission needs to be supplemented by anthropological accounts of the role of women as themselves *objects* of exchange.[112] We have only to look briefly at the *Iliad* to see how pervasive this is.[113] Lévi-Strauss's model of marriage based on an exchange of women among groups of men describes the system functioning smoothly. As long as marriage works, women are merely the objects of exchange. What is striking about Gernet's examples is how often they point to situations in which the ordinary relations of marriage have failed. He discusses the seduction of Atreus' wife by Thyestes and the bribing of Eriphyle, but most telling for us is a story about the tripod of the Seven Sages. This tripod, made by Hephaistos, was among the *ktēmata* (goods, property) stolen by Paris from the house of Menelaus when he abducted Helen. She, according to Diogenes Laertius (I.32), threw it into the sea, for she said it would be a cause of strife (*perimachētos*). Although later the tripod would circulate peacefully from one sage to another until it had come full-circle, Helen sees in it a cause of strife. Like the tripod, she herself will be fought over, as her abduction will soon provoke the Trojan War, and like the tripod she herself will come full-circle, passed from hand to hand until she is returned to Men-

---

[108] See J.-P. Vernant, "Figuration de l'invisible et catégorie psychologique du double: Le Colossos," in *Mythe et Pensée chez les Grecs* (Paris, 1981 [1965]) 2:70–71.

[109] See A. A. Donohue, *Xoana and the Origins of Greek Sculpture* (Atlanta, 1988) and S.R.F. Price, *Rituals and Power, the Roman Imperial Cult in Asia Minor* (Cambridge, 1984) 176–78.

[110] In *The Anthropology of Ancient Greece*, trans. J. Hamilton and B. Nagy (Baltimore, 1981) 73–111.

[111] Gernet (1981) 109n.91.

[112] See Claude Lévi-Strauss, *Elementary Structures of Kinship* (Boston, 1969 [1949]). For a feminist critique of the supposed universality of his model, see Gayle Rubin, "The Traffic in Women," in R. Reiter, *Toward an Anthropology of Women* (New York and London, 1975) 157–210.

[113] The first few books of the *Iliad* could be read as a textbook on the value of women in an elaborate economy based on tangibles (like cattle) and intangibles (like *kleos*). I plan to return to this topic as part of another project on the economics of gender in ancient Greece.

elaos. In the normal course of things, women do not circulate ad infinitum, but are exchanged once and remain fixed.[114] It is only by circulating outside the marriage arrangement that they become agents of transmission of these highly charged objects. Not only in Diogenes Laertius' account, but also in the *Iliad*, Helen is equated with movable *agalmata*. Paris is repeatedly called upon to end the war by returning to Menelaos both Helen and the goods (*ktēmata*) stolen along with her.[115]

Unlike Helen, the unfaithful wife who circulates repeatedly, Iphigeneia participates in a different dynamic of exchange. The sacrifice at Aulis, whether completed or not, becomes an exchange in which she is given up to get Helen back. For her the *agalma* is an object of worship transported to honor the gods, in a way that mirrors her own transportation away from and then back to Greece, where she will serve Artemis as priestess and cult-founder. As we have already noted, it is customary for female deities to be served by priestesses. For this there is historical as well as mythic evidence.[116] Heroines are frequently named as the founders of cult. We have touched already on the mythic significance of the first person to complete a specific action, and the frequency with which these first actions are connected with heroic figures. Although women are severely limited in their public roles, we have some historical evidence for women as founders of cults. In myth, meanwhile, examples are plentiful. Transport of Artemis' *agalma* is hardly without precedent and needs to be placed in the larger context of cult-founding by heroines in general (see the Appendix to this chapter).[117]

The transport of a cult-image (*xoanon*, *bretas*, or *agalma*) occurs frequently to indicate the founding of a cult-site. A specific image may be associated with a heroine. In his *Life of Theseus*, Plutarch tells of several dedications made by the hero, of objects closely associated with Ariadne. After her death in childbirth on Cyprus, Theseus dedicates two statuettes in her honor (*Thes.* 20.6), and in the temple of Apollo at Delos, an image of Aphrodite that he had received from her (21.1). The abduction of a woman may be compensated with an image, as in the story told by Pausanias (3.16.3), in which the Dioskouroi take away a young girl, leaving pictures of themselves behind. In one version of the *eidōlon* story of Helen, Paris is either tricked or bought off with a picture of her (schol. Aristid. *Or.* 1.128 = Stesich. 192 *PMG*).

---

[114] See Redfield (1982) 192.

[115] *Iliad* 3.70: Ἑλένη καὶ κτήμασι πᾶσι; also lines 72, 91, 282, 285, 458, etc.

[116] For discussion and bibliography, see Chapter 4.

[117] While Pausanias is the richest source for heroines as cult-founders, as even a glance at the Appendix to this chapter will show, he is not the only author to attribute this role to them. See C. Dewald, "Women and Culture in Herodotus' Histories," in Foley (1981) 110–12, 122 on female cult-founders in Herodotus.

Figure 8 Rape of Kassandra, Attic calyx krater attributed to the
Altamura Painter, c. 465 B.C.E. (Boston MFA 59.178). William Francis
Warden Fund. Courtesy Museum of Fine Arts, Boston.

The movement of a goddess from one place to another is frequently
depicted as illicit or violent. The Palladion, perhaps the most famous
example of a "kidnapped" goddess, was tied to the fate of Troy.[118] Its
theft by Odysseus and Diomedes is told in the *Kypria*, but Plutarch tells
of efforts to obtain it by magic.[119] These efforts may be equated with
rape and seduction, but the equation is made even more explicit by the
tradition of the rape of Kassandra at the altar of the Palladion. In this
version the homology of stealing the cult-image and abducting the
priestess becomes clear. This theme was apparently a popular one, since

[118] Dion. Hal. 1.68; Vergil *Aen.* 2.165f; Ovid *Met.* 13.380f.
[119] *Ilias Parva* p. 43 Kinkel; Plut. *Quaest. R.* 61, 278f. C. A. Faraone, *Talismans and Trojan
Horses* (Oxford, 1992) 136–40 argues that *evocatio* is not, in fact, a Greek practice.

Pausanias lists no less than four depictions of it in his descriptions of works of art, and many surviving vases show the scene as well (see figure 8).[120] The very origin of this image in a rivalry between a goddess and a heroine makes the myth even more appropriate to our purposes: Athena accidentally kills Pallas during play and in remorse makes the Palladion, an image of the dead heroine. This suggests an identity between the goddess and the heroine, of a kind that is by now familiar to us. Elsewhere, the image is directly assimilated to Athena, as we see from the tradition that the virgin image raises its eyes to avoid seeing the rape.[121]

The Samian festival called the *Tonaea* is said to originate in an attempted abduction of an image of Hera. The rape of the image is carried out in retaliation for the flight of Hera's priestess Admete and suggests an equation between carrying off the priestess and carrying off the goddess.[122] Pausanias reports two episodes of divine images carried off, both of which are presented as seduction or rape of the priestess. The priestess Kleo is captured with an image (*xoanon*) of Thetis, for whom a cult is established by Leandris the wife of Anaxandros. Pausanias also relates sceptically the story that a Cretan priestess of Artemis was persuaded to run away with a Lakonian called Knageus, after whom the goddess was henceforth known.[123] In this way the natural waywardness of women becomes associated with female divinities as well. The goddess becomes a movable piece of goods, and therefore somewhat unreliable.[124] There is a great similarity between a young woman who can be transported by a goddess or carried off by a young man, and the goddess, who can for all intents and purposes be picked up and abducted. Even a virgin goddess like the one represented by the Palladion may be abducted. These myths point to a certain anxiety about the permanence of the goddess's stay among mortals, or her loyalty to a particular city. If the young woman who is carried off is a priestess with her *agalma*, then a double abduction is accomplished.

[120] Paus. 1.15.2: Stoa Poikile; 5.11.6: throne of Zeus; 5.19.5: Kypselos chest; 10.26.3 and 31.2: Polygnotos' Nekyia. For other vases, see *LIMC* s.v. "Aias" II 16–111.

[121] Lycoph. 361f.; Callim. *frg.* 35 Pfeiffer. Herodotus assumes that Palladion = image of Pallas, i.e., Athena (4.189). See the article by L. Ziehen and G. Lippold, "Palladium," *RE* 18.2 (1949) 171–201.

[122] The account is in Menodotos (*FGrH* 541 F 1 = Athen. 15.671e–73b). See Mizera (1984) 17–20.

[123] Paus. 3.14.4; 3.18.4. This second passage has been discussed above in the context of a discussion of gods who bear the names of heroes; see Chapter 3.

[124] On the mobility of both *bretas* and *xoanon*, see Vernant (1981), vol. 2:66. One of his examples, Hera Lygodesma (Athen. 15.672ff.), emphasizes the possibility of seduction, as does Pausanias 3.18.4. Faraone (1992) 136–39 has interesting comments on the practice of binding statues.

Let us now turn to the tradition that makes of Iphigeneia not the immortal double of Artemis but her mortal servant, her priestess and cult-founder. That a heroine may be the priestess of a goddess is sometimes used as a rationalizing explanation of burial in a temple.[125] While Iphigeneia is said to be buried at Brauron, this seems far too limited an explanation of this dynamic interaction. Nonetheless, although the myths insist on the identity of Iphigeneia and Artemis, they also insist on Iphigeneia's role as a mortal servant of Artemis.

The role of Iphigeneia as cult-founder is marked by her transportation of an image of the goddess Artemis from the Black Sea to Attica, where its symbolic importance can be seen from the fact that several cult-sites claim to have this original cult-image. Pausanias devotes a great deal of space to evaluating the various claims, citing first (1.33.1ff.) the Brauronian claim to have the original Tauric image but then coyly remarking, "There is indeed an old wooden image of Artemis here, but who in my opinion have the one taken from the foreigners I will set forth in another place" (trans. Jones). That place turns out to be his discussion of the Limnaion in Sparta (3.16.7ff.), where he lists his reasons for supporting the Spartan over the Athenian claim.

This *agalma* traces a journey that is the reverse of Iphigeneia's rescue, accompanied by Iphigeneia herself, the *agalma* of Agamemnon's house. In the version of the Iphigeneia material known to us from Euripides' *Iphigeneia among the Taurians*, what is particularly striking is the double movement of the myth, as first Artemis transports Iphigeneia to the Taurians, and then Iphigeneia carries the goddess back to Greece. As Burnett has perceptively remarked, "Someone saw that the solution here was to rescue the goddess as well as her priestess."[126] In her discussion of the myth, Burnett suggests that the arrival of Orestes, the rescue and return of Iphigeneia, and the capture of the statue of Artemis are all the invention of Euripides. This possibility is denied by Brelich, who argues that the number of cult-sites all over Attica that claim to have the original image shows instead that the myth is very old. For mythographers there would be no incentive to multiply the claims, but rather to simplify them.[127]

---

[125] Farnell (1921) chap. 2 and passim; F. Pfister, *Reliquienkult* (Geissen, 1909–12). See Chap. 3 above.

[126] Burnett (1971) 75.

[127] Brelich (1969) 243–45. In this connection, he quotes the remark of Aelius Lampridius (*Hist. Aug. Elagabalus* 7.6): *Orestem. . .non unum simulacrum Dianae nec uno in loco posuisse, sed multa in multis* (Orestes did not put one image of Diana in one place, but many images in many places.)

Iphigeneia, having returned from her Tauric exile, brings Artemis out of exile as well, and leaving behind the "barbaric" practice of human sacrifice, makes her "Greek" again. In the process she becomes identified with the goddess herself and acquires her own cult at Brauron, while in a sense also "creating" the goddess Artemis in her new home, the cult site at Brauron. In effect the goddess and the heroine "reproduce" one another through reciprocal actions of apotheosis and cult-founding. The *eidōlon* and the *agalma* are the outward forms of these reciprocal actions. Among the many ways of resolving the ambiguity of the divine-mortal relation, or of imaging that relationship, this one might be called reflexive: the mortal-heroic figure is made immortal, while simultaneously recreating and reduplicating the divine figure by the establishment of a cult. For while Artemis is in some sense always Artemis, Artemis Tauropolis is not exactly the same as Artemis Brauronia.[128]

Perhaps the myths betray on some level the knowledge that the gods are indebted to their worshipers for their form and even their very existence. After all, that the gods are dependent on the honor and sacrifices of mortals, and that their raison d'être, if not their actual survival, depends on the continued existence of the human race, is implicit in the *Homeric Hymn to Demeter*:

καί νύ κε πάμπαν ὄλεσσε γένος μερόπων ἀνθρώπων
λιμοῦ ὑπ᾽ ἀργαλέης, γεράων τ᾽ ἐρικυδέα τιμήν
καὶ θυσιῶν ἤμερσεν Ὀλύμπια δώματ᾽ ἔχοντας,
εἰ μὴ Ζεὺς ἐνόησεν ἑῷ τ᾽ ἐφράσσατο θυμῷ.

She would have destroyed the whole mortal race
by cruel famine and stolen the glorious honor of gifts
and sacrifices from those having homes on Olympos,
if Zeus had not seen and pondered their plight in his heart.

(2.310–13[129])

What has often been interpreted as a usurpation of the cult of an older divinity by a newer one may in fact be instead a recognition of the existential fragility of the gods. Only the gods can confer immortality on mortals, but it is equally true that only mortals can confer cult on the gods. Apotheosis and cult-foundation break down the barriers between mortals and immortals, as goddesses turn heroines into goddesses, and heroines provide the worship without which divinity is worthless.

---

[128] See J. Rudhardt, *Notions fondamentales de la pensée religieuse* (Geneva, 1958) 85–106, on the limits to polytheism and the anthropomorphic conception of the gods.

[129] Trans. H. Foley, *The Homeric Hymn to Demeter* (Princeton, 1994).

APPENDIX TO CHAPTER FIVE:
MYTHIC FEMALE CULT-FOUNDERS

ABIA nurse of Herakles' son Glenos, sets up temple to Herakles (Paus. 4.30.1).

ADMETE (daughter of Eurystheus) has role in foundation of the Tonaia (Athen. 15.672).

AITHRA founds temple of Athena Apaturia and establishes tradition of dedication of girdles by young girls before marriage (Paus. 2.33.1).

AMAZONS dedicate an *agalma* of Ephesian Artemis (Paus. 4.31.8); found sanctuary of Ephesian Artemis (Paus. 7.2.7 citing Pindar).

ARIADNE gives "Daedalic" image of Aphrodite to Theseus, which he dedicates to Delian Apollo (Paus. 9.40.3; Plut. *Thes.* 21).

CHLORIS (with Amyklas) founds temple to Leto, according to the Argives (Paus. 2.21.10).

DANAIDS dedicate stone image of Aphrodite at Lerna (Paus. 2.37.2); bring the Thesmophoria with them to Egypt and teach it to the Pelasgian women (Hdt. 2.171); dedicate a temple to Athena on Rhodes (Hdt. 2.182).

DIOMEDE dedicates statue of Athena Anemotis (of the winds) (Paus. 4.35.8).

Two EGYPTIAN women captives found the mysteries in Libya and Greece (Hdt. 2.54).

ELEKTRA (daughter of Agamemnon) brings scepter of Zeus to Phocis (Paus. 9.40.12).

Women of ELIS found sanctuary of Athena Meter (Mother) (Paus. 5.3.2).

EURYDIKE (wife of Akrisios) founds temple of Argive Hera (Paus. 3.13.8).

HARMONIA dedicates three images (*xoana*) of Aphrodite under the aspects of Ourania, Pandemos, and Apostrophia (Paus. 9.16.3).

HELEN founds temple of Eileithyia (Paus. 2.22.6).

HIPPODAMEIA institutes the Heraea at Olympia (Paus. 5.16.4).

HYPERBOREAN MAIDENS found cults and have cults associated with them (Hdt. 4.33; 4.35.1).

HYPERMNESTRA dedicates a *xoanon* of Aphrodite Nikephoros at Argive Heraion (Paus. 2.19.6); founds temple of Artemis Peitho (Persuasion) (Paus. 2.21.1).

IPHIGENEIA brings *xoanon* of Tauric Artemis to Brauron (Paus. 1.33.1).

Priestess of KNAGIAN ARTEMIS brings image of the goddess from Crete, named for Knagios with whom the priestess ran away (Paus. 3.18.4).

LAODIKE dedicates robe to Athena Alea (Paus. 8.5.3); temple of Aphrodite called Paphian (Paus. 8.53.7).

LEANDRIS sets up a temple of Thetis in response to a vision, when Kleo, priestess of Thetis, is captured with image of the goddess (Paus. 3.14.4).

MEDEA dedicates a temple to Aphrodite in Corinth in thanks for curing her of her love for Jason, or for curing him of his love for her rival Thetis (Plut. *De Herodot. malig.* 871b).

MESSENE establishes Eleusinian mysteries at Andania (Paus. 4.1.5, 8–9), founds precinct of Zeus at Ithome with her husband (Paus. 4.3.9).

METANEIRA, together with her daughters, has a role in founding the cult of Demeter at Eleusis (Hom. *Hymn* to Demeter).

NIKAGORA (historical figure) founds cult of Asklepios in Sikyon (Paus. 2.10.3).

PELARGE revives rites of the Kabeiroi (Paus. 9.25.7–8).

PHAIDRA brings two Cretan *xoana* of Eileithyia to Athens (Paus. 1.18.5), temple of Aphrodite Kataskopia named for her spying on Hippolytos there (Paus. 2.32.3).

PHYSKOA first to honor Dionysos in Elis, receives chorus in her honor (Paus. 5.16.6–7).

PROKNE dedicates image of Athena at Daulis brought from Athens (Paus. 10.4.9–10).

Conclusion

I HAVE endeavored here to present a more complex view of the role of heroines in Greek myth and cult than is usually acknowledged. Reliance on a stereotyped notion of the purely passive heroine has resulted in certain distortions, not least an underestimation of the function of heroic figures in divine cult. By making room for the heroine within the category of heroic beings, we necessarily change our view of that category. While heroines do not generally initiate action but rather react to others, they can nevertheless be seen to have unique powers, related to their ability to transcend death. Acting in sympathy with gods, they mediate symbolically between the remoteness of divinity and the direct experience of mortals.

As we have seen, many apparently essential elements of the heroine's identity are subject to variation and change. As in the case of Semele, Ino, and Iphigeneia, even their names may be changed in the course of their myths. This is not the case with male heroes, few of whom ever acquire new names. Not only the name, but the nature, of heroines is radically transformable. Heroines, to a far greater extent than heroes, are subject to metamorphosis, taking on the shape of animals at the will of the gods. I have argued that female mythic figures are much more likely to be metamorphosed than male ones. While it may be asking too much to seek a unified explanation for this phenomenon, it may be related to the actual physical transformations of menarche, defloration, childbirth, and menopause which occur during the female life cycle, or to men's projections about these transformations. A figure like Iphigeneia, who resists the physical transformations of metamorphosis, avoids becoming a bear like Kallisto. The substitution that structures the rescue myths becomes her experience of transformation. Iphigeneia experiences not metamorphosis but ritual substitution and is thereby saved for the biggest transformation of all—apotheosis. This is certainly the ultimate metamorphosis of which a mortal is capable. And yet it seems to be the radical indeterminacy of the heroine's existence that gives her the flexibility needed to transcend the divide between mortals and immortals.

We have seen how heroines may play a mediating role in cult, between the god they serve and the worshiper who serves that god. For the Dionysiac heroines, that role has its basis in a sympathy between mortal and immortal, and in the exchange of qualities. It is the very similarities between heroines and goddesses that serve to heighten the rivalry and antagonism between them. As noted in Chapter 3, divinities come into conflict with heroic figures who most closely resemble them. Antagonist pairs are frequently, although not always, of the same sex. In the case of Dionysos, however, something different occurs. The double difference between Dionysos and the heroines, of gender and existential status, allows for the possibility of a defusing exchange.

With heroines and goddesses, the gender difference is eliminated, exposing all too clearly the mortal/immortal split. This emphasis on mortality comes into focus when we notice that while Dionysos is rarely responsible for the death of any of the figures connected with him, Artemis is a frequent cause of death for heroines. At the same time, the case of Artemis and Iphigeneia shows that where there is hostility, there may also be identity and reciprocity. This observation leads to a modification of the idea of ritual antagonism, with particular application to female figures, both heroic and divine.

The examples chosen are not in every way typical—Dionysos is anomalous among gods as Iphigeneia is among heroines. Nonetheless they point to a central feature of Greek cosmology. Each member in the system, and each class of members, is absolutely dependent on the others for knowledge of its place. Thus mortals and immortals need one another for self-definition, and heroines and heroes, as the intermediate category, are necessary to both because they allow a working out of the tensions and ambiguities inherent in a system of anthropomorphic divinities worshiped by a society that glorified the works of human beings. The Greeks knew how much their gods depended on them and told their myths to prove it.

A Catalogue of Heroines

THIS CATALOGUE lists all major and most minor heroines found in ancient sources. The references are not intended to be exhaustive but include the earliest mentions as well as those of particular interest. A few of these entries represent figures who are not strictly speaking heroines, but rather naiads, nymphs, or minor divinities who have entered heroic genealogies or who share a name with one or more heroines. I have also noted heroine-names used as divine epithets. All of these items are marked with an asterisk. I have included a few bibliographic references for some heroines who receive little treatment in the text. In general, however, see the index for further discussion and bibliography.

ABIA nurse of Herakles' son Glenos. Because she founded a temple to Herakles, the city of Abia in Messenia was named in her honor (Paus. 4.30.1).

ABROTE. See Habrote.

ACHAIIA the first of the Hyperborean Maidens, according to Olen the Lycian (Paus. 5.7.8), but see Opis.

ADIANTE daughter of Danaos and Herse, marries Daiphron (Apollod. 2.1.5).

ADITE daughter of Danaos and Pieria, marries Menalkes (Apollod. 2.1.5).

ADMETE
    1) daughter of Okeanos and Tethys (Hes. *Theog.* 349), a companion of Kore (*Hom. Hymn* 2.421).
    2) daughter of Amphidamas, wife of Eurystheus, mother of Admete (3) on marble relief in the Villa Albani, Rome (*LIMC* s.v. "Admete" 1). But see Antimache.
    3) daughter of Eurystheus, priestess of Hera and cult founder, she has a role in the foundation myth of the Tonaia, a festival on Samos (Athen. 15.672). For the festival see Paus. 7.4.4; 8.23.5.

ADRASTE servant of Helen (*Od.* 4.123 with schol.).

ADRASTINE. See Aigiale(ia).

AEDON daughter of Pandareos and Harmothoe of Miletos, wife of Zethos, mother of Itylos (Itys). She accidentally kills him instead of the son of her rival Niobe and is transformed into a nightingale (*Od.* 19.518 with schol.). In the Attic version, she is the daughter of Pandion, wife of Tereus, whose rape of her sister Philomele the women avenge with the murder of her son. In another version her husband is Polytechnos, and their marital strife is the result of her boast of a happier marital life than Hera and Zeus (Ant. Lib. 11 after Boios). See Philomele, Prokne.

AEROPE(IA)

1) (Crete) daughter of Katreus, sister of Klymene, Apemosyne, and Althaimenes, mother of Agamemnon and Menelaos by Pleisthenes (Hes. *Cat.* 195.3; Apollod. 3.2.2), or Atreus (Eur. *Or.* 18, 1009; *Helen* 390; schol. A. *Iliad* 1.7), whom she betrays to his brother Thyestes (Apollod. *Ep.* 2.10ff.). She is caught in bed with a slave, and her father gives her to Nauplios to throw into the sea, but he instead marries her to Atreus or Pleisthenes, or the drowning is punishment for adultery with Thyestes (Soph. *Aias* 1297 with scholia citing Eur. *Kressai*).

2) daughter of Kepheus, bears Aeropos to Ares and dies in childbirth (Paus. 8.44.6–8).

AGAMEDE daughter of Augeias, wife of Mulios, expert in herbs (*Iliad* 11.739–41). Mother of Belos, Diktys, and Aktor by Poseidon (Hyg. *Fab.* 157). The witch Perimede in Theocritus 2.16 and Propertius 2.4.8 appears to be inspired by her.

AGANIPPE

1) See Eurydike (6).

2) *spring on Helicon, daughter of the Termessus (Paus. 9.29.5).

AGAVE

1) daughter of Danaos and Europe (4), wife of Lykos (Apollod. 2.1.5).

2) (Thebes) daughter of Kadmos and Harmonia, sister of Semele, Ino, Autonoe, and Polydoros (Hes. *Theog.* 976). She appears as wife of Echion and mother of Pentheus in Aeschylus' fragmentary *Pentheus*, as well as in the *Bacchae* of Euripides. Dionysos punishes her with madness when she refuses to accept his divinity. In her delusion she kills her son and is exiled for the crime.

3) *Nereid (*Iliad* 18.42; Hes. *Theog.* 247).

4) Amazon (Hyg. *Fab.* 163).

AGLAIA

1) *one of the Graces, married to Hephaistos (Hes. *Theog.* 945).

2) daughter of Mantineus, wife of Abas, mother of Akrisios and Proitos (Apollod. 2.2.1).

3) wife of Amythaon, mother of Bias and Melampous (Diod. 4.68.3), but see Eidomene.

4) wife of Charopos, mother of Nireus of Syme (*Iliad* 2.671; Diod. 5.53.2).

5) daughter of Thespios, mother of Antiades by Herakles (Apollod. 2.7.8).

AGLAONIKE daughter of Hegetor, uses skill in astronomy to appear to be a witch (Plut. *Praec. coniug.* 48, 145c; *De def. orac.* 13, 417a), daughter of Hegemon (schol. AR. 4.59).

AGLAUROS or AGRAULOS

1) daughter of Aktaios; first king of Attika; wife of Kekrops; mother of Erysichthon, Aglauros (2), Herse, Pandrosos (Eur. *Ion* 496).

2) daughter of Kekrops and Aglauros (1), sister of Herse and Pandrosos. She disobeys Athena's command not to look in the basket containing the baby Erichthonios, sees a snake, and in terror leaps off the Akropolis with sister Herse (Eur. *Ion* 21ff.; Apollod. 3.14.6; Hyg. *Fab.* 166). Her temenos: Paus. 1.18.2. Mother of Alkippe (2), who is said to be the daughter of Ares (Paus.

1.21.4); mother of Keryx. She sacrifices herself for the city (Demosth. 19.303 with schol.), sanctuary on the Akropolis (Hdt. 8.53), called upon in oath of ephebes (Plut. *Alcib.* 15.4), eponym of the deme Agryle. See Herse, Pandrosos.

3) *epithet of Athena (*Suda* s.v. Ἄγλαυρος).

AGRIOPE. See Eurydike (1).

AIGIALE(IA) daughter of Adrastos, wife of Diomedes, also called Adrastine (*Iliad* 5.412–15). Her mother is Amphithea (Apollod. 1.9.13). Her infidelity to Diomedes (schol. BV. *Iliad* 5.412; Lycoph. 610) was, according to Mimnermos, Aphrodite's revenge for the wound he inflicted on her (*PLG* II 33 Bergk = schol. Lycoph. 610).

AIGINA daughter of Asopos and Metope, sister of Thebe (Hdt. 5.80) and Nemea, Harpina, and Korkyra (Paus. 5.22.6). Other sisters include Salamis, Euboia, Sinope, Thespia, and Tanagra, all of them carried off by Olympian gods (Corinna, *PMG* 654 col. iii–iv, "The Daughters of Asopos"; see also schol. Pindar *Ol.* 6.144; Apollod. 3.12.6; Diod. 4.72.1). Aigina is the mother of Aiakos by Zeus (Tzetzes ad Lycoph. 176 = Hes. *Cat.* 205), who came to her as an eagle (Athen. 13.566d) or fire (Ovid *Met.* 6.113).

AIGLE

1) Hesperid (Serv. *in Verg. Aen.* 4.484).

2) See Koronis (1).

3) daughter of Panopeios, beloved of Theseus for whom he deserts Ariadne (Hes. frg. 298; Plut. *Thes.* 20; Athen. 13.556f.).

AIGLEIS. See Lytaia.

AINARETE daughter of Deimachos, wife of Aiolos (Hes. *Cat.* 10a restored). Also spelled Enarete (Apollod. 1.7.3). Known by other names; see Amphithea (2).

AISCHREIS daughter of Thespios, mother of Leukones by Herakles (Apollod. 2.7.8).

AITHILLA daughter of Laomedon, sister of Priam, Astyoche (4), Medesikaste (2). She has a role in the foundation of Skione (Conon *Narr.* 13; Tzetzes ad Lycoph. 921).

AITHOUSA

1) (Boiotia) daughter of Poseidon, mother of Eleuther by Apollo (Paus. 9.20.1).

2) See Thoösa (2).

AITHRA

1) daughter of Pittheus, wife of Aigeus, mother of Theseus by Aigeus or Poseidon (Plut. *Thes.* 6), who rapes her while she was carrying out a sacrifice to Athena which the goddess had commanded in a dream. Because of this she founds the sanctuary of Athena Apatouria (Deceiver) in Troizen (Paus. 2.33.1). Bellerophon also tries unsuccessfully to marry her (Paus. 2.31.9). As a companion of Helen, she is captured by the Dioskouroi (Apollod. 3.10.7–8), later taken to Troy (*Iliad* 3.144; Plut. *Thes.* 34), and finally rescued by her grandsons Akamas and Demophon (Apollod. *Ep.* 5.22).

2) wife of Phalanthos, founder of Tarentum (Paus. 10.10.7–8).

AKAKALLIS
1) (Arcadia) daughter of Minos; mother, by Hermes, of Kydon founder of Kydonia (Paus. 8.53.4).
2) (Crete) *nymph, bears sons to Apollo (Paus. 10.16.5).

AKIDOUSA (Boiotia) wife of Skamandros, eponym of spring, mother of three daughters honored as the "Maidens" (Plut. *Quaest. Gr.* 41, 301b).

AKRAIA
1) (Argolid) daughter of Asterion. With her sisters Euboia and Prosymna, she nurses Hera, gives her name to a hill opposite the sanctuary of Argive Hera (Paus. 2.17.1).
2) *epithet of Aphrodite, Artemis, Athena, Hera (Hesych. s.v. Ἀκρέα, Ἀκρία).

AKTAIA daughter of Danaos and Pieria, marries Periphas (Apollod. 2.1.5).

ALALKOMENIA (Boiotia) daughter of Ogygus, eponym of Alalkomenai, honored with her sisters as the Praxidikai (Paus. 9.33.5), connected with Athena's epithet *Alalkomeneis*.

ALEXANDRA. See Kassandra.

ALEXIDA daughter of Amphiaraos. Her descendants have power to avert epileptic attacks (Plut. *Quaest. Gr.* 23, 296f.).

ALKAIA. See Chlidanope.

ALKANDRE wife of Polybos of Thebes in Egypt, gives Helen a silver basket (*Od.* 4.126).

ALKATHOE daughter of Minyas, sister of Leukippe and Arsinoe (2) (Plut. *Quaest. Gr.* 38, 299e) or Arsippe (Ant. Lib.10 after Nicander and Corinna).

ALKESTIS daughter of Pelias, wife of Admetos (*Iliad* 2.714; Hes. *Cat.* 37), her mother is Anaxibia (3) or Phylomache (Apollod. 1.9.10). She dies in place of her husband and is rescued by Herakles (Eur. *Alk.*; Apollod. 1.9.15).

ALKIDAMEIA mother of Bounos by Hermes (Paus. 2.3.10).

ALKIDIKE daughter of Aleus, wife of Salmoneus, mother of Tyro (Apollod. 1.9.8; Diod. 4.68.2).

ALKIMEDE mother of Jason, daughter of Klymene (5), granddaughter of Minyas or else the daughter of Phylakos (schol. AR. 1.230–33). Possibly also mother of Hippolyte (5) (schol. AR. 1.287). For other versions see Polymele (1).

ALKIPPE
1) one of the seven daughters of Alkyoneus, who leap into the sea on the death of their father and are transformed into birds (Eust. 776.35; *Suda* s.v. Ἀλκυονίδες ἡμέραι).
2) daughter of Ares and Agraulos, raped by Halirrhotios, a son of Apollo (Apollod. 3.14.2; Paus. 1.21.4), for which Ares kills Halirrhotios (Eur. *El.* 1258–63).
3) servant of Helen (*Od.* 4.124).

4) *Titan, daughter of Krios and Eurybie, sister of Astraios, Pallas, and Perses (Hes. *Theog.* 375).

5) daughter of Oinomaus, wife of Euenos, mother of Marpessa (Plut. *Parall.* 40, 315e). Possible confusion with Alkippe (2) since in Plutarch, Euenos is the son of Ares.

ALKIS. See Androkleia.

ALKMENE daughter of Elektryon and Lysidike (1) (Plut. *Thes.* 7), wife of Amphitryon, mother of Herakles by A. or Zeus (*Iliad* 14.323–24; *Od.* 11.266), who comes to her in the likeness of her husband (Pindar *Nem.* 10.15f.). In some versions she bears two sons, Herakles and Iphikles, conceived by two fathers in a single night (Pindar *Pyth.* 9.84ff.; *Shield* 48ff.). She is also the mother of Laonome (2). She is married posthumously to Rhadamanthys. She has a heroon in Thebes and a tomb in Megara (Paus. 1.41.1). The Thebans, however, say she has no tomb but was turned into a stone upon her death (Paus. 9.16.7). She has cults in Boiotia, Attica, Megara (Plut. *De gen. Soc.* 577e), an altar in Athens (Paus. 1.19.3). Animal sacrifices to her are specified on the calendar of Thorikos in Attica (*SEG* 26.136.37). According to Asios, she is the daughter of Amphiaraos and Eriphyle (Paus. 5.17.7). Elsewhere her mother is Anaxo (2) (Apollod. 2.4.5) or Eurydike (11) (Diod. 4.9.1).

ALKYONE

1) (Boiotia or Argolid) one of the Pleiades, the seven daughters of Atlas and Pleione (Hes. *Cat.* 169). With her sister Taygete, depicted on the throne at Amyklai, being carried off by Poseidon and Zeus (Paus. 3.18.10). Mother of Hyperes and Anthas, Boiotian kings, by Poseidon (Paus. 2.30.8). See Pleione.

2) daughter of Aiolos and Ainarete, wife of Keyx, the whole family changed to birds because of their hybris (Hes. *Cat.* 10a; Apollod. 1.7.4). Fragments survive of a *Wedding of Keyx*, which was ascribed in antiquity to Hesiod (Hes. frgs. 263–69).

3) daughter of Sthenelos and Nikippe (1), sister of Medousa (2) and Eurystheus (Apollod. 2.4.5).

4) See Kleopatra (2).

5) (Corinth) daughter of Agemon, wife of Anthedon (Athen. 7.296b; 15.696f.).

ALOPE (Eleusis) daughter of Kerkyon, mother by Poseidon of Hippothoön. Tomb mentioned by Pausanias (1.39.3).

ALPHESIBOIA

1) See Arsinoe (3).

2) wife of Phoinix, mother of Adonis (Hes. *Cat.* 139 = Apollod. 3.14.4).

ALTHAIA daughter of Thestios and Eurythemis(te), sister of Leda and Hypermestra, and in some traditions also Melanippe (3), wife of Oineus of Kalydon, mother of Meleager, Deianeira, Ankaios. Deianeira was said to be the daughter of Dionysos (Hyg. *Fab.* 129; Apollod. 1.8.1), and Meleager, the son of Ares (Apollod. 1.8.1). When her brothers are accidently killed by her son, in her anger she curses him or burns the firebrand to which his survival is linked

(*Iliad* 9.529; Hes. *Cat.* 25; Bacchyl. 5.142; Aesch. *Choe.* 602ff.; Apollod. 1.8.2). She commits suicide (Apollod. 1.8.3).

AMPHINOME

1) *Nereid (*Iliad* 18.44).
2) See Polymele (1).
3) daughter of Pelias, married to Andraimon (Diod. 4.53.2).

AMPHISSA daughter of Makar, beloved of Apollo, eponym of Amphissa in Ozolian Lokris, tomb (Paus. 10.38.4–5).

AMPHITHEA

1) wife of Autolykos, mother of Antikleia (*Od.* 11.85, 19.416).
2) wife of Aiolos, mother of incestuous pair Makareus and Kanake (Eur. *Aiolos* frg. 14–42 Nauck). Elsewhere called Ainarete, etc.
3) wife of Lykourgos, mother of Archemoros who becomes the hero Opheltes. See Eurydike (7).
4) daughter of Pronax, sister of Lykourgos, wife of Adrastos, mother of Argeia, Deipyle, Aigialeia, Aigialeus, and Kyanippos (Apollod. 1.9.13; Athen. 12.528d). Perhaps confused with or same as (3).

AMYMONE daughter of Danaos, eponym of spring and river (Paus. 2.37.1), mother of Nauplios by Poseidon (Paus. 2.38.2). Her mother is Europe (4); she marries Enkelados (Apollod. 2.1.5).

ANAXANDRA. See Lathria.

ANAXIBIA

1) sister of Agamemnon and Menelaos, mother of Pylades by Strophios (Paus. 2.29.4), but see Astyoche(ia) (3).
2) daughter of Kratieus, wife of Nestor (Hes. *Cat.* 35.14, restored), mother of Peisidike (2), Polykaste (2), and six sons (Apollod. 1.9.9) or she is the daughter of Bias, wife of Pelias (Hes. frg. 37.19, restored), mother of Akastos, Peisidike, Pelopeia (1), Hippothoe, and Alkestis (Apollod. 1.9.10). But see Phylomache.
3) daughter of Danaos, marries Archelaus (Apollod. 2.1.5).

ANAXIROE (Elis) daughter of Koronos, wife of Epeios, mother of Hyrmina (Paus. 5.1.5).

ANAXO

1) Troizenian heroine carried off by Theseus (Athen. 13.557b), listed among his wives by Plutarch (*Thes.* 29).
2) daughter of Alkaios, brother of Amphitryon, wife of Elektryon, mother of Alkmene and nine sons. Her mother is Laonome, Hipponome, Astydameia, or Lysidike (Apollod. 2.4.5). See Alkmene, Eurydike (11).

ANCHINOE daughter of Neilos (Nile), wife of Belos, mother of Danaos and Aigyptos (Apollod. 2.1.4).

ANDANIA eponym of the city by this name (Paus. 4.33.6).

ANDROKLEIA (Boiotia) daughter of Antipoinos; together with sister Alkis, sacrifices herself for Thebes (Paus. 9.17.1).

ANDROMACHE daughter of Priam, wife of Hector, mother of Astyanax (*Iliad* passim). Sappho describes her wedding to Hector (frg. 44 Lobel-Page). She is later the wife of Neoptolemos (Pyrrhos) by whom she has Molossos, Pielos, and Pergamos. Later she marries Helenos, with whom she founds Buthroton, and by whom she is the mother of Kestrinos. She has a heroon in Pergamon (Paus. 1.11.1–2).

ANDROMEDA daughter of Kepheus and Kassiepeia (Hes. *Cat.* 135). Because her mother angers the Nereids by boasting of her own beauty, she is condemned to be sacrificed to a sea monster. Perseus rescues her and by him she is the mother of Perses, Alkaios, Sthenelos, Heleios, Mestor, Elektryon, Gorgophone (Apollod. 2.4.3–5; Hyg. *Fab.* 64). Perses was considered to be the ancestor of the Persians (Hdt. 7.61; 150).

ANTEIA. See Stheneboia.

ANTHEIA daughter of Thespios, mother of a son by Herakles (Apollod. 2.7.8).

ANTHEIS. See Lytaia.

ANTHELIA daughter of Danaos and the naiad Polyxo, marries Kisseus (Apollod. 2.1.5).

ANTHIPPE daughter of Thespios, mother of Hippodromos by Herakles (Apollod. 2.7.8).

ANTIANEIRA. See Laothoe (6).

ANTIBIA. See Nikippe (1).

ANTIGONE
1) daughter of Eurytion of Phthia, first wife of Peleus, mother of Polydora (3), hangs herself because of machinations of her rival Astydameia (Apollod. 3.13.1ff.). Pindar (*Nem.* 4.57) calls her Hippolyte.

2) daughter of Oidipous; in earlier versions, her mother is Eurygane(ia) (Pherec. in schol. Eur. *Phoin.* 53), later Iokaste. Sophocles' play is the first extant account of her death for burying her brother. In other versions she does not die but marries Haimon and bears a son, Maion (cf. *Iliad* 4.394 where she is not named). The place where she buries Polyneikes is known as the "dragging" (*surma*) of Antigone (Paus. 9.25.2).

3) daughter of Laomedon, sister of Priam, dared to compete with Hera and was changed to a stork (Ovid *Met.* 6.93–95).

4) daughter of Pheres of Thessaly, mother of the Argonaut Asterion (Hyg. *Fab.* 14).

5) mother of Tlepolemos by Phylas, according to some, but Homer makes him the son of Herakles and Astyocheia, and Pindar has Astydameia as his mother (*Iliad* 2.658; schol. Pindar *Ol.* 7.42). See Astyocheia (1), Astydameia (1).

ANTIKLEIA
1) daughter of Autolykos, wife of Laertes, mother of Odysseus and Ktimene (*Od.* 11.85).

2) daughter of Diokles, wife of Machaon, mother of Nicomachus and Gorgasos, healers (Paus. 4.30.2).

3) mother of Periphates by Hephaistos (Apollod. 3.16.1).

4) See Philonoe.

ANTIMACHE daughter of Amphidamas, sister of Melanion, wife of Eurystheus (Apollod. 3.9.2). But see Admete (2).

ANTINOE

1) (Arcadia) daughter of Kepheus, founder of new Ptolis (Paus. 8.8.4), her tomb at Mantineia (Paus. 8.9.5).

2) (Arcadia) daughter of Pelias, according to the painter Mikon. She has a tomb in Arcadia, together with her sister Asteropeia (Paus. 8.11.3).

ANTIOCHE Amazon (Hyg. *Fab*. 163).

ANTIOPE

1) (Boiotia) daughter of Asopos, mother of Amphion and Zethus by Zeus (*Od*. 11.260ff.) or daughter of Nykteus and Polyxo (2) (Apollod. 3.10.1), wife of Epopeus who is killed by her brother. She is held as a slave by Lykos and Dirke until her sons return to release her. She is driven mad by Dionysos and then healed by Phokos, who marries her. Their grave in Tithorea (Paus. 9.17.4; 10.32.10). Euripides' *Antiope* survives in fragments (Page [1970] 60–71; frgs. 179–227 Nauck).

2) Amazon, daughter of Ares and Otrere, sister of Hippolyte, mother of Hippolytos by Theseus. Sometimes called Hippolyte, Glauke, or Melanippe. Her monument in Athens (Paus. 2.1.1). See Glauke (3), Hippolyte (1), Melanippe (2).

3) daughter of Thespios, mother of Alopios by Herakles (Apollod. 2.7.8).

APEMOSYNE daughter of Katreus of Crete, sister of Aerope, Klymene, and Althaimenes. She is raped by Hermes and killed by her brother as a result (Apollod. 3.2.1–2).

ARACHNE (Colophon) daughter of Idmon. Antagonist of Athena, who turns her into a spider (Ovid *Met*. 6.5–145). See Weinberg (1956); *LIMC* s.v. "Arachne."

ARAITHYREA (Corinth) daughter of Aras, sister of Aoris. She and her brother were known as hunters and warriors. She is the eponym of Araithyrea (the place-name is mentioned at *Iliad* 2.571). Mother of Phlias by Dionysos (Paus. 2.12.6). The Phliasians look toward their graves and call on Aras and his children at the libations before the mysteries of Demeter (Paus. 2.12.5).

ARCHIPPE. See Nikippe (1).

ARENE daughter of Oibalos and Gorgophone, sister of Tyndareos and Ikaros, wife and half-sister of Aphareus, mother of Idas, Lynkeus, and Peisos (Apollod. 3.10.3; Paus. 4.2.4). She and her husband and children are initiated into the rites of the Great Goddesses (Paus. 4.2.4–6); she is the eponym of a Messenian city and a spring (Paus. 5.5.6). Called Laokoösa by Peisandros (*FGrH* 1.16, frg. 2). Theocritus (22.206) says that the mother of Idas and Lynkeus is Polydora.

ARETE daughter of Rhexenor, wife of Alkinoös (*Od.* 7.66ff.), also his sister (Hes. *Cat.* 222; schol. *Od.* 7.54), mother of Nausikaä.

ARGE. See Hyperborean Maidens.

ARGEIA

1) daughter of Okeanos, sister and wife of Inachos, mother of Phoroneus and Io (Hyg. *Fab.* 143, 145).

2) daughter of Adrastos and Amphithea, sister of Deipyle and Aigialeia (Apollod. 1.9.13), wife of Polyneikes (schol. T. *Iliad* 23.679 = Hes. *Cat.* 192; schol. A. *Iliad* 4.376; Apollod. 3.6.1).

3) daughter of Autesion, wife of Aristodemos, mother of Prokles and Eurysthenes (Apollod. 2.8.2; Hdt. 6.52).

ARGELE daughter of Thespios, mother of Kleolaos by Herakles (Apollod. 2.7.8).

ARGIOPE

1) *nymph, mother of Thamyris by Philammon (Apollod. 1.3.3; Paus. 4.33.3).

2) See Eurydike (1).

3) daughter of Teuthras, wife of Telephos (Diod. 4.33.12).

4) daughter of Neilos, wife of Agenor, mother of Kadmos (Pherec. *FGrH* 3 F 21; Hyg. *Fab.* 6).

ARGYPHIA mother of Lynkeus and Protius by Aigyptos (Apollod. 2.1.5).

ARIADNE daughter of Minos and Pasiphae, sister of Phaidra (*Od.* 11.321). She aids Theseus in fight against the Minotaur (schol. AB. *Iliad* 18.590; Apollod. *Ep.* 1.9; Hyg. *Fab.* 42) and is carried off by him (depicted on the François Vase, Flor. Mus. Arch. 4209, Kleitias, c. 570). In some versions she is already married to Dionysos. Either she is killed by Artemis on his orders (*Od.* 11.324–25) or abandoned by Theseus for another woman (Plut. *Thes.* 29) and rescued by Dionysos. The Athenian hero Keramos is said to be their son (Paus. 1.3.1) as is Oinopion (schol. Arat. *Phaen.* 640), and sometimes Demophon, but see Phaidra, Iope. Beloved of Glaukos, who lay with her after Theseus' desertion (Athen. 7.296bc). In some versions she is deified, but Argos claims to have her tomb (Paus. 2.23.8). Role in cult of Aphrodite (Paus. 9.40.4), her own cult first hinted at in *Iliad* 18.591; more clearly in Plut. *Thes.* 20. Her chorus on the shield of Achilles (*Iliad* 18.590).

ARISTAICHME daughter of Hyllos and perhaps Iole, sister of Euaichme (Hes. frg. 251a).

ARISTODEME daughter of Priam (Apollod. 3.12.5).

ARISTOMACHE daughter of Priam, wife of Kritolaos (Stesich. frg. 208 *PMG* = Paus. 10.26.1); painted by Polygnotos (Paus. 10.26.1).

ARKADIA wife of Nyktimos; see Phylonome.

ARNE

1) (Boiotia) daughter of Aiolos, eponym of the city Arne, which was later called Chaironeia (Paus. 9.40.5).

2) See Melanippe (1).

ARSINOE

1) (Messenia) daughter of Leukippos, sister of Hilaira and Phoibe, who were stolen by Dioskouroi. The mother of Asklepios by Apollo, she is the eponym of a spring in Messene (Paus. 4.31.6) and has a sanctuary (*hieron*) in Sparta (Paus. 3.12.8). The mother of Asklepios is called Koronis in the Thessalian version of myth (Paus. 2.26.7). See Koronis (1).

2) one of Minyades, sister of Leukippe and Alkathoe (Plut. *Quaest. Gr.* 38.299e).

3) daughter of Phegeus, cast-off wife of Alkmaion (Apollod. 3.7.5) also called Alphesiboia (Paus. 8.24.8).

4) Orestes' nurse (Pindar *Pyth.* 11.17). See Laodameia (4).

5) young woman who scorns the love of Arkeophon, thus arousing the anger of Aphrodite, who turns her to stone (Ant. Lib. 39 after Hermesianax).

ARSIPPE. See Alkathoe.

ASIA wife of Prometheus, perhaps the eponym of the continent (Hdt. 4.45).

ASOPIS daughter of Thespios, mother of Mentor by Herakles (Apollod. 2.7.8).

ASPALIS (Phthia) daughter of Argaios and Melite, hangs herself to escape a tyrant, whom her brother Astygites, dressed in her clothes, then kills. Her body disappears, a statue next to that of Artemis is called Aspalis Ameilete Hekaerge. Origin of the Aiora (Ant. Lib. 13 after Nikandros), which is usually associated with Erigone (1).

ASTERIA

1) daughter of Danaos, marries Chaitos (Apollod. 2.1.5).

2) mother of Herakles by Zeus, according to Eudoxos of Knidos (Athen. 9.392d).

ASTERODEIA (Elis) daughter of Deion (Hes. *Cat.* 58) and Diomede (Apollod. 1.9.4), wife of Endymion, elsewhere his wife is Hyperippe, daughter of Arkas, or Chromia, daughter of Itonos (Paus. 5.1.4).

ASTERODIA. See Periboia (1).

ASTEROPE

1) daughter of Atlas and Pleione (Hes. *Cat.* 169).

2) *Nymph, daughter of Kebren, sister of Oinone, wife of Aisakos (Apollod. 3.12.5, 3.12.6).

ASTEROPEIA. See Antinoe (2).

ASTYDAMEIA

1) daughter of Amyntor (Pindar *Ol.* 7.42 and schol.), mother by Herakles of Tlepolemos (Pindar *Ol.* 7.23ff.) or Ktesippos (Apollod. 2.7.8). In *Iliad* 2.658, Tlepolemos' mother is Astyoche(ia) (1). In other authors, daughter of Phylas or Ormenos (Hes. *Cat.* 232). Also called Astygeneia. See also Antigone (5).

2) wife of Akastos, rival of Antigone (1) (Apollod. 3.13.3).

3) daughter of Pelops and Hippodameia, sister of Lysidike (1) and Nikippe (1) (Hes. *Cat.* 190), also Pittheus and Thyestes. Wife of Alkaios, mother of Amphitryon and Anaxo (Apollod. 2.4.5).

4) See Hippolyte (4). But see Hipponome, Laonome (1), Lysidike (1) for other versions.

5) daughter of Phorbas, mother of Kaukon by Poseidon (Zenodotos in Athen. 10.412a).

ASTYGENEIA. See Astyoche(ia) (1).

ASTYKRATEIA

1) sister of Manto (1), daughter of Polyidos. Her tomb in Megara by entrance to the sanctuary of Dionysos (Paus. 1.43.5).

2) daughter of Amphion and Niobe (Apollod. 3.5.6).

ASTYMEDOUSA daughter of Sthenelos and Nikippe (1), third wife of Oidipous after Iokaste. She accuses his sons of sexual misconduct, which provokes his curse on them (schol. A. *Iliad* 4.376; schol. Eur. *Phoin.* 53 = Pherec. *FGrH* 3 F 95). Also called Medousa (Apollod. 2.4.5).

ASTYNOME. See Chryseis.

ASTYOCHE(IA)

1) daughter of Phylas, mother of Tlepolemos by Herakles (*Iliad* 2.658; Apollod. 2.7.6,8). Also called Astydameia (1), Astygeneia. Her father is also said to be Amyntor or Ormenos (schol. Pindar *Ol.* 7.42). See also Antigone (5).

2) daughter of Aktor, mother of Askalaphos and Ialmenos by Ares (*Iliad* 2.513; Paus. 9.37.7).

3) daughter of Atreus (or Pleisthenes) and Aerope, sister of Agamemnon and Menelaos, wife of Strophios, mother of Pylades (Hyg. *Fab.* 117), but see Anaxibia (1).

4) daughter of Laomedon, wife of Telephos, mother of Eurypylos, sister of Aithilla, Priam, Medesikaste (2) (Apollod. *Ep.* 6.15c; schol. Lycoph. 921). Priam sent her a golden vine so that she would send her son to defend Troy, where he died (*Od.* 11.521). Fragments have survived, apparently from Sophocles' *Eurypylos*, in which she laments her son.

5) daughter of Amphion and Niobe (Apollod. 3.5.6).

6) daughter of Simoeis, wife of Erichthonios, mother of Tros (Apollod. 3.12.2; schol. Lycoph. 29).

ATALANTE (Arcadia), daughter of Iasos and Klymene, raised by a bear. Takes part in voyage of Argo, Kalydonian boar-hunt (depicted on temple of Athena Alea at Tegea—Paus. 8.45.6). She kills the centaurs Rhoikos and Hylaios, who tried to rape her (Apollod. 3.9.2), defeats Peleus at wrestling at the funeral games of Pelias (Apollod. 3.9.2; earliest evidence: a fragmentary *dinos*, Athens Nat. Mus. Akr. 590, c. 570–60). She refuses all suitors, challenging them to a footrace (Theog. 1287–93). She marries Melanion, after he defeats her by distracting her with golden apples. They are turned into lions for defiling temple of Zeus (Apollod. 3.9.2; Callim. *Hymn* 3.221ff.; Hyg. *Fab.* 185), depicted on Kypselos chest (Paus. 5.19.2). Elsewhere the offended god is Kybele. She is the mother of Parthenopeus by Melanion or Ares (Apollod. 3.9.2). According to Hesiod, her father is Schoineus, while Euripides calls him Mainalos and her suitor, Hippomenes (Apollod. 3.9.2 = Hes. *Cat.* 72; schol. T. *Iliad* 23.683 = Hes. *Cat.* 74; Hes. *Cat.* 76). Pausanias mentions a spring in Lakonia made by Atalante (3.24.2), and her *dromoi* in Arcadia (8.35.10).

ATLANTIDES. See Pleiades, Pleione.

AUGE Tegean heroine, daughter of Aleos and Neaira (3) (Apollod. 3.9.1), wife of Teuthras, beloved of Herakles (Paus. 10.28.8), to whom she bears Telephos (Hes. *Cat.* 165 restored; Apollod. 2.7.4). Her angry father exposes the child and sends her to Nauplios, to be drowned (Paus. 8.48.7). In Apollodorus' version she is to be sold, but Nauplios gives her to Teuthras, who marries her (2.7.4; 3.9.1). Her tomb at Pergamos (Paus. 8.4.9). She is a priestess of Athena, who also sometimes bears the epithet Auge. The goddess Eileithyia at Tegea is called Auge *en gonasi* (Paus. 8.48.7).

AUTOLYTE. See Theano (2).

AUTOMATE (Achaia) daughter of Danaos, wife of Busiris (Apollod. 2.1.5). See Skaia.

AUTOMEDOUSA daughter of Alkathoös, mother of Iolaos by Iphikles (Apollod. 2.4.2).

AUTONOE
   1) daughter of Danaos and Polyxo, marries Eurylochos (Apollod. 2.1.5).
   2) *Nereid (Apollod. 1.2.7).
   3) daughter of Kadmos and Harmonia; sister of Semele, Ino, Agave, Polydoros; wife of Aristaios; mother of Aktaion (Hes. *Theog.* 977; Hes. *Cat.* 217a). Her grave in Megarid (Paus. 1.44.5).
   4) daughter of Pireus, mother of Palaimon by Herakles (Apollod. 2.7.8).
   5) attendant of Penelope (*Od.* 18.182).

AUXESIA with Damia, honored by the Epidaurians by order of the Pythia, their images then stolen by the Aiginetans (Hdt. 5.82–87; Paus. 2.30.4). In Troizen supposed to be maidens who died by stoning, honored with a festival called the Lithobolia (Paus. 2.32.2).

BASILE an Attic heroine, though possibly a misreading for "Iasile." A priestess of Basile seems to be mentioned in an inscription from the Agora (Agora inv. I 4138; *SEG* 19.78.10). See Basilis (2).

BASILIS
   1) daughter of Laomedon (schol. Neot. Soph. *Aias* 1302).
   2) *an epithet of various goddesses, also Basile or Basileia.

BATEIA daughter of Teukros, marries Dardanos, mother of Ilos and Erichthonios (Apollod. 3.12.1).

BAUBO wife of Dysaules, mother of Mise. Connected with the cult of Demeter and in particular with ritual obscenity (Orph. frg. 52 Kern; Hesych. s.v., who cites Empedokles). She is mentioned on an inscription from Naxos (*SEG* 16.478). See Olender (1990). See also Iambe.

BAUKIS (Latin spelling, Baucis) a poor Phrygian woman who, together with her husband Philemon, hosts the gods (Ovid *Met.* 8.626–724 is the only extant version of this apparently Greek story).

BOLBE mother of Olynthos by Herakles, and eponym of Lake Bolbe (Athen. 8.334e).

BOUDEIA

1) wife of Klymenos, mother of Erginos, connected with the invention of the plow (schol. *Iliad* 16.572). Also called Bouzyge, daughter of Lykos (schol. AR. 1.185).

2) *Thessalian epithet of Athena (Lycoph. 359 with schol.).

BOURA (Achaia) daughter of Ion and Helice, city named for her (Paus. 7.25.8).

BRISEIS captive given to Achilles as booty, taken by Agamemnon. The name means either "of Brisa" on Lesbos, or daughter of Briseus. The A scholia to *Iliad* 1.392 give her the proper name Hippodameia (4). She is depicted by Polygnotos in the Lesche at Delphi (Paus. 10.25.4).

BRYKE daughter of Danaos and Polyxo, marries Chthonios (Apollod. 2.1.5).

CASSANDRA. See Kassandra.

CHALKIOPE

1) daughter of Rhexenor, second wife of Aigeus (Apollod. 3.15.6; Tzetzes ad Lycoph. 494; schol. Eur. *Medea* 673 gives her father as Chalkodon).

2) daughter of Aietes of Kolchis and Idyia, sister of Medea, wife of Phrixos (schol. AR. 2.1122). But see Iophossa.

3) daughter of Eurypylos of Kos, mother of Thettalos by Herakles (Apollod. 2.7.8). Her temple on the island of Kos (Callim. *Hymn* 4.160–61).

CHALKIS. See Kombe.

CHARIKLO

1) *Naiad, daughter of Apollo, Okeanos, or Perseus, wife of Cheiron, mother of Endeis (Pind. *Pyth.* 4.103; schol. Pind. *Pyth.* 4.181). Elsewhere, Endeis is daughter of Skiron and Chariklo (Plut. *Thes.* 10.3).

2) *Nymph, companion of Athena in Boiotia, mother of Teiresias by Eueres (Callim. *Hymn* 5.57ff.; Apollod. 3.6.7).

CHARILA (or Charilla) a young girl who is humiliated when the king of Delphi refuses her food. She hangs herself and a famine ensues, which ends with the institution of the festival *Charila* in her honor (Plut. *Quaest. Gr.* 12.293d–f).

CHIONE

1) daughter of Boreas and Oreithyia, mother of Eumolpos by Poseidon, throws him into the sea to escape discovery, Poseidon saves him (Paus. 1.38.2).

2) daughter of Daidalion, bears simultaneously Autolykos, son of Hermes, and Philammon, son of Apollo. Brags of her beauty and is killed by Artemis (Eur. *Autolykos* frgs. 282–84 Nauck; Hyg. *Fab.* 200, 201; Ovid *Met.* 11.291–345). See Leukonoe (1).

CHLIDANOPE wife of Hypseus, mother of Kyrene and Alkaia (Pin. *Pyth.* 9.13ff. with scholia).

CHLORIS

1) *a goddess of vegetation (Ovid *Fasti* 5.195ff.).

2) daughter of Amphion and Niobe, the only one saved by Artemis because she prayed to Leto. Telesilla calls her Meliboia (cited in Apollod. 3.5.6). Pausanias says that Meliboia was her original name and that she was later called Chloris because she turned pale from fright. The temple to Leto built by her and Amyklas (Paus. 2.21.9). Wife of Neleus, mother of Nestor, Chromios, Periklymenos, and Pero (*Od.* 11.218, 287; Hes. *Cat.* 33a restored). A winner of the footrace at the Heraia at Olympia (Paus. 5.16.4). Her friendship with Thyia depicted by Polygnotos (Paus. 10.29.5). Peisandros (*FGrH* 1.181) says that the mother of Periklymenos is a daughter of Teiresias. See also Polymede (2).

3) wife of Ampyx, mother of Mopsos (schol. AR. 1.65; Hyg. *Fab.* 14).

CHOIRA. See Marpessa (2).

CHOREIA maenad, killed by Perseus in battle with Dionysos, buried in Argos (Paus. 2.20.4).

CHROMIA daughter of Itonos, wife of Endymion. See Asterodeia (Paus. 5.1.4).

CHRYSANTHIS tells Demeter of the rape of Kore (Paus. 1.14.2). She is represented on a relief found near Lerna, together with the goddess and her husband (or father?) Mysios and two daughters (*IG* IV.664). For Mysios as founder of a temple of Demeter, see Paus. 7.27.9.

CHRYSE daughter of Almos, sister of Chrysogeneia, mother of Phlegyas by Ares (Paus. 9.36.1).

CHRYSEIS
1) "woman from Chryse" or daughter of Chryses (*Iliad* 1.111, etc.). She is also called Astymone (schol. A. *Iliad* 1.392). In later tradition she is the mother of Chryses the younger by Agamemnon, although she claims that Apollo is the father (Hyg. *Fab.* 121).

2) daughter of Thespios, mother of Onesippos by Herakles (Apollod. 2.7.8).

CHRYSIPPE daughter of Danaos and Memphis, marries Chrysippos (Apollod. 2.1.5).

CHRYSOGENEIA daughter of Almos, sister of Chryse (Paus. 9.36.1), mother of Chryses by Poseidon (Paus. 9.36.4).

CHRYSORTHE (Aigialea) daughter of Orthopolis, mother of Koronos by Apollo (Paus. 2.5.8).

CHRYSOTHEMIS
1) mother by Apollo of Parthenos, died and made a star (Hyg. *Astr.* 2.25). Or mother of Parthenos, Molpadia, and Rhoio by Staphylos (Diod. 5.62.1).

2) daughter of Agamemnon and Klytemnestra (*Iliad* 9.145, 287), sister of Laodike, Iphianassa (Homer); Elektra (Soph.); and Iphigeneia (Eur.).

CHTHONIA
1) daughter of Phoroneus, sister of Klymenos, with whom she founds a temple to Demeter at Hermion. In another version she is the daughter of Kolontas, who refuses to receive the goddess, despite his daughter's disapproval. Demeter punishes him but takes Chthonia to Hermione where she founds a

temple. Her name becomes both an epithet of Demeter and the name of a festival in honor of the goddess (Paus. 2.35.4–5).

2) (Attica) daughter of Erechtheus and Praxithea, sister of Kreousa and Pro-kris (1) (Eur. *Erechtheus* frg. 357 Nauck). In other versions she is one of four or six sisters. See Praxithea (1), Oreithyia (2), Pandora (5).

CHTHONOPHYLE daughter of Sikyon, mother of Polybos by Hermes; wife of Phlias, mother of Androdamas (Paus. 2.6.6).

CLYTEMNESTRA. See Klytemnestra.

DAEIRA mother of Immarados by Eumolpos, buried in the Eleusinion under the Akropolis (Clem. Al. *Protr.* 3.39).

DAMIA. See Auxesia.

DANAE daughter of Akrisios and Eurydike (6) or Aganippe (Hyg. *Fab.* 63), be-loved of Zeus, mother of Perseus (*Iliad* 14.319–20), despite father's efforts to keep her from bearing a child (Apollod. 2.4.1). Zeus' appearance to her in the form of showers of gold (Soph. *Ant.* 944ff.). When he discovers she is preg-nant, Akrisios has her put to sea. In a poem by Simonides, she speaks to her baby son of the dangers they face from the waves, and prays for rescue (543 *PMG* = Dio. Hal. *Comp.* 26). Later she is persecuted by Polydektes, who wishes to marry her, and rescued by her son (Apollod. 2.4.3). Her *thalamos* at Argos (Paus. 2.23.7).

DANAIDS the fifty daughters of Danaos who, married against their will to their cousins, the fifty sons of Aigyptos, murder their husbands on their wedding night on the orders of their father (Aesch. *Suppl.*; Apollod. 2.1.5). Only one disobeyed (see Hypermestra). Athena and Hermes purified them, and their father married them to the victors of an athletic contest (Pindar *Pyth.* 9.112ff.; Apollod. 2.1.5). Their punishment in the Underworld was to carry water in sieves (Plato *Rep.* 363d; Horace *Odes* 3.11.25).

DAPHNE

1) daughter of Ladon and Ge, beloved of Apollo, who turns into a tree to escape his advances (Ovid *Met.* 1.452–567). Pausanias says that according to the Arcadians and Eleans, she was courted by Leukippos, son of Oinomaos, dressed as a woman. Apollo's jealousy leads to his exposure and death (Paus. 8.20.1–4). She is also equated with Pasiphae, the mistress of an oracle at Thalamai. See Pasiphae (2), Kassandra.

2) see Manto (1).

DAPHNIS *Nymph, first prophetess at Delphi (Paus. 10.5.5).

DEIANEIRA daughter of Oineus and Althaia, sister of Meleager and Gorge, wife of Herakles (Hes. *Cat.* 25), or daughter of Althaia and Dionysos (Apollod. 1.8.1). According to Pausanias, her grave in Herakleia at the foot of Mt. Oita, not in Argos (2.23.5). Mother of Makaria (Paus. 1.32.6), Hyllos, Ktesippos, Glenos, and Oneites (Apollod. 2.7.8). According to Apollodorus, she drove a chariot and went to war (1.8.1). In another version, she is the daughter of Dexamenes, promised to Herakles, stolen by Centaur Eurytion, won back by Herakles (Hyg. *Fab.* 31).

DEIDAMEIA

1) descendant of Aiolos (Hes. *Cat.* 10a).

2) daughter of Lykomedes of Skyros, mother of Neoptolemos by Achilles (*Kypria* in Proclus p. 19 Kinkel; schol. Lycoph. 182; Apollod. 3.13.8), later married Helenos (Apollod. *Ep.* 6.13).

3) daughter of Bellerophon, mother of Sarpedon by Zeus or Evandros, called Laodameia in *Iliad* 6.197.

DEINOME Trojan captive mentioned in the *Little Iliad*, depicted by Polygnotos (Paus. 10.26.2).

DEIOPE wife of Musaios, mother of Triptolemos (Arist. *mir.* 131) or of Eumolpos (Phot. s.v. Εὐμολπίδαι) or daughter of Triptolemos and mother of Eumolpos (Istrus in schol. Soph. *O.C.* 1053; cf. Paus. 1.14.2).

DEIPYLE daughter of Adrastos and Amphithea; sister of Argeia, Aigialeia, Aigialeus, and Kyanippos (Apollod. 1.9.13); wife of Tydeus; mother of Diomedes (Apollod. 1.8.5; Hyg. *Fab.* 97). Or mother is Eurynome (Hyg. *Fab.* 69).

DEMO

1) daughter of Keleos, king of Eleusis, and Metaneira, sister of Kallidike, Kleisidike, and Kallithoe (*Hom. Hymn* 2.109). Her brother is Demophoön (*Hom. Hymn* 2.234). See Kallidike (1).

2) *name of Cumaian sibyl (Paus. 10.12.8f), short for Demophile.

3) *short form of Demeter (*Suda*; *Etym. Mag.* 264.8), Demonassa.

DEMODIKE

1) second wife of Athamas, stepmother of Phrixos, or wife of Kretheus, aunt of Phrixos, whom she accuses of rape when he spurns her advances (Pind. *Pyth.* 4.162, 288 with schol.). Phrixos is saved by the ram with the golden fleece (Hyg. *Astr.* 2.20), but see Helle. See also Ino, Nephele, Themisto.

2) daughter of Agenor (Hes. *Cat.* 22) and Epikaste, mother of Evanos, Molos, Pylos, and Thestios by Ares (Apollod. 1.7.7). Her name varies: Demonike in Apollodorus, Demodoke elsewhere (schol. B. *Iliad* 14.200 citing Hesiod).

DEMODOKE. See Demodike (2).

DEMO(A)NASSA

1) daughter of Amphiaraos and Eriphyle, sister of Amphilochos, mother of Tisamenos by Thersandros. After her death Tisamenos made a hero-shrine for her (Paus. 3.15.8; 9.5.15). Appears on the Kypselos chest (Paus. 5.17.7).

2) wife of Poias and mother of Philoktetes (Hyg. *Fab.* 97, 102).

3) mother of Aigialos by Adrastos (Hyg. *Fab.* 71).

DEMONIKE. See Demodike (2).

DEXITHEA daughter of Phorbas, mother of Romulus by Aineias, in a divergent tradition (Plut. *Rom.* 2.2).

DIA

1) *female counterpart to Zeus, or his daughter. Sometimes associated with Ganymeda or Hebe (Strabo 8.6.24). See Ganymeda.

2) daughter of Eioneus, wife of Ixion, who killed his father-in-law. Mother of Peirithoös, with Zeus usually named as father (*Iliad* 14.317f.).

3) daughter of Lykaon, mother of Dryops by Apollo (schol. Lycoph. 480; schol. AR. 1.1218). But see Polydora (2).

DIOGENEIA
1) daughter of Keleos (Paus. 1.38.3). See Saisara.

2) daughter of Kephisos, wife of Phrasimos, mother of Praxithea (1) (Apollod. 3.15.1).

DIOMEDE(IA)
1) daughter of Xuthos, wife of Deion(eus), mother of Asterodia, Ainetos, Aktor, Kephalos, and Phylakos (Hes. *Cat.* 10a; Apollod. 1.9.4).

2) captive from Lesbos, concubine of Achilles (*Iliad* 9.665), shown in painting by Polygnotos at Delphi (Paus. 10.25.4).

3) daughter of Lapithes, wife of Amyklas, mother of Kynortes and Hyakinthos (Hes. *Cat.* 17 restored; Apollod. 3.10.3).

DIOMENEIA daughter of Arkas. Portrait-statue of her in agora of Mantineia (Paus. 8.9.9).

DIOXIPPE
1) daughter of Danaos and Pieria, marries Aigyptos (Apollod. 2.1.5).

2) Amazon (Hyg. *Fab.* 163).

DIRKE daughter of Ismenos, helps rescue Dionysos, married to Lykos (Eur. *Herak.* 27), she persecutes Antiope, whose sons have her killed by a bull, when they rescue their mother. Her bones are thrown into the fountain of Ares in Thebes, and a river is named after her (Eur. *Bacch.* 520f.; Paus. 9.25.3). Secret rites were enacted at her tomb (Plut. *De gen. Socr.* 578b). See Antiope (1).

DORIOS Danaid, marries Kerketes (Apollod. 2.1.5).

DRYOPE daughter of Dryopos, bears Amphissos to Apollo while married to Andraimon. Stolen away by nymphs. Amphissos builds a sanctuary to the nymphs. (Ant. Lib. 32 after Nikandros). Ovid (*Met.* 9.324) has a different version, in which she is turned into a tree.

DYME possible eponym of city in Achaia (Paus. 7.17.6).

ECHEMELA. See Iphiloche.

E(E)RIBOIA
1) daughter of Eurymachos (schol. B. *Iliad* 5.385), granddaughter of Hermes, stepmother of the Aloades (*Iliad* 5.389f.).

2) See Periboia (5).

EIDOMENE daughter of Abas; sister of Akrisios, Proitos, Kanethos; wife of Amythaon; mother of Melampous (Apollod. 2.2.2). But see also Aglaia (3).

EIDOTHEA
1) daughter of Proteus (*Od.* 4.366).

2) daughter of Okeanos (Hyg. *Fab.* 182).

3) sister of Kadmos, second wife of Phineus, persecutes first wife Kleopatra (1) and her children (schol. Soph. *Ant.* 992). In some versions the second wife is Idaia (Apollod. 3.15.2–4; Diod. 4.43.4) or Eurytia (schol. *Od.* 12.69).

4) *Nymph, mother of Kerambos by Euseiros (Ant. Lib. 22).

5) daughter of Eurytos, king of the Carians, mother of the twins Kaunos and Byblis by Miletos (Ant. Lib. 30).

EIRENE daughter of Poseidon and Melantheia, eponym of Eirene, later called Kalaureia, an island off the coast of the Argolid (Plut. *Quaest. Gr.* 19, 295e).

ELACHEIA daughter of Thespios, mother of Bouleus by Herakles (Apollod. 2.7.8).

ELAIS. See Oinotrop(h)oi.

ELATE sister of the Aloades, mourned her brothers, changed to a fir tree (Liban. *Narr.* 34 = App. *Narr.* 10).

ELEKTRA

1) *daughter of Okeanos and Tethys. Mother of Iris and the Harpies by Thaumas (Hes. *Theog.* 266,349), companion of Kore (*Hom. Hymn.* 2.418).

2) daughter of Danaos and Polyxo, marries Peristhenes (Apollod. 2.1.5).

3) *daughter of Atlas and Pleione, one of the seven Pleiades (schol. Pindar *Nem.* 2.16 = Hes. *Cat.* 169, 177; Apollod. 3.10.1), but see Hesione (3). Mother by Zeus of Iasion, Dardanos, Harmonia (Diod. 5.48.2; Dion. Hal. 1.61, AR. 1.916 = Hellanicus *FGrH* 4 F 23). Later connected with Palladion and with Korythos. On Rhodes = Alektrona, daughter of Helios (Hellan. *FGrH* 4 F 23). See Elektryone (2), Pleione.

4) sister of Kadmos, one of Theban gates named for her (Paus. 9.8.4).

5) daughter of Klytemnestra and Agamemnon (Hes. *Cat.* 23a). Originally called Laodike, later Elektra (false etymology from *a-lektron*, "without the bed") because she long remained unmarried (Xanthos in Aelian *Varia Historia* 4.26). After the murder of her mother, married to Pylades, mother of Strophios and Medon. Location of grave at Mykene (Paus. 2.16.7). See Laodike (2).

6) handmaiden of Helen in Polygnotos' depiction of the fall of Troy (Paus. 10.25.4).

ELEKTRYONE

1) patronymic of Alkmene (*Shield* 16).

2) identified with Alektrona on Rhodes, daughter of Helios and Rhodos, who receives heroic honors on the island of Rhodes (Diod. 5.56.5; schol. Pindar *Ol.* 7.24). An inscription from Ialysos (Rhodes) gives rules for her cult (Sokolowski [1969] no.136). See Elektra (3).

ELEPHANTIS mother of Hypermestra (1) and Gorgophone (2), by Danaos (Apollod. 2.1.5).

ENARETE. See Ainarete.

ENDEIS daughter of Skiron, wife of Aiakos, mother of Peleus and Telemon (Pindar *Nem.* 5.12f.). Her mother is Chariklo (Plut. *Thes.* 10.3).

EONE daughter of Thespios, mother of Amestrios by Herakles (Apollod. 2.7.8).

EPHYRE daughter of Okeanos, eponym of city later called Corinth (Paus. 2.1.1). According to Eumelos, daughter of Okeanos and Tethys, wife of Epimetheus; otherwise, daughter of Epimetheus (schol. AR. 4.1212) or of Myrmex.

EPIKASTE
1) in *Od.* 11.271, mother and wife of Oidipous. See Iokaste (2).
2) daughter of Kalydon and Aiolia, sister of Amythaon, wife of Agenor, mother of Demonike and Porthaon (Apollod. 1.7.7).
3) daughter of Augeias, mother of Thestalos by Herakles (Apollod. 2.7.8).
4) See Polykaste (2).
5) See Iokaste (1).

EPILAIS daughter of Thespios, mother of Astyanax by Herakles (Apollod. 2.7.8).

EPIONE wife of Asklepios, daughter of Herakles, mother of Machaon (also called Xanthe in schol. AD. *Iliad* 4.195) and Podaleirios, and of the goddesses Iaso, Akeso, Panakeia, and Aigle and Hygieia (*Suda*, s.v.). Statue of her at Epidauros (Paus. 2.27.5).

ERATO
1) daughter of Danaos and Polyxo, marries Bromios (Apollod. 2.1.5).
2) daughter of Thespios, mother of Dynastes by Herakles (Apollod. 2.7.8).

ERIBOIA. See Periboia (5).

ERIGONE
1) daughter of Ikarios, connected with myth of Dionysos and the origin of the Aiora (schol. AB. *Iliad* 22.29 citing Eratosthenes; Apollod. 3.14.7; Hyg. *Fab.* 130). For the *Alētis*, a song sung in her honor at the festival (Athen. 14.618e). See Maira (3).
2) daughter of Aigisthos and Klytemnestra, rescued from Orestes by Artemis, becomes a priestess (Hyg. *Fab.* 122), mentioned in Paus. 2.18.7 as mother of Orestes' son Penthilos.

ERIOPIS daughter of Jason and Medea, sister of Medeus, according to Kinaithon of Lakedaimon (Paus. 2.3.9).

ERIPHYLE daughter of Talaos and Lysimache (Apollod. 1.9.13) or Lysianassa (Paus. 2.6.6), sister of Adrastos and Pronax, wife of Amphiaraos, whom she betrays for a necklace (*Od.* 11.326; 15.247; Pindar *Nem.* 9.16). Later killed by her son Alkmaion (Apollod. 3.7.5). Her necklace (Paus. 9.41.2–3). Mother of Eurydike (9) and Demonassa, depicted together on Kypselos chest (Paus. 5.17.7). According to Asios, also mother of Alkmene (Paus. 5.17.8). In Diodoros' version she also accepts a robe in exchange for the life of Alkmaion (4.66.3).

ERYTHEIA
1) daughter of Geryon, mother of Norax by Hermes (Paus. 10.17.5).
2) daughter of Nux, one of the Hesperides (Hes. frg. 360 = Serv. *in Verg. Aen.* 4.484). Also Erytheis (AR. 4.1427).

ETHODAIA. See Neaira (5).

ETIOKLYMENE. See Klymene (5).

EUADNE
1) daughter of Poseidon and Pitane, mother of Iamos by Apollo. She hides the pregnancy, snakes help her give birth and feed the child honey (Pind. *Ol.* 6.28ff. with scholia; Paus. 6.2.5).

2) daughter of Iphis, throws herself on pyre of her husband Kapaneus (Eur. *Suppl.* 980ff.; Apollod. 3.7.1).

3) daughter of Strymon and Neaira (2), wife of Argos (Apollod. 2.1.2).

EUAICHME

1) (Megara) daughter of Megareus, second wife of Alkathoös (Paus. 1.43.4). See Pyrgo, Iphinoe (2).

2) daughter of Hyllos, wife of Polykaon (Hes. frg. 251; Paus. 4.2.1).

EUBOIA

1) daughter of Asterion, sister of Akraia and Prosymna (Paus. 2.17.1–2).

2) daughter of Thespios, mother of Olympos by Herakles (Apollod. 2.7.8).

3) daughter of Larymnos, mother of Glaukos by Polybos (Athen. 12.296b).

EUBOTE daughter of Thespios, mother of Eurypylos by Herakles (Apollod. 2.7.8).

EUBOULE. See Leo korai.

EUIPPE

1) (Boiotia) daughter of Leukon, sister of Peisidike (4) and Hyperippe (3), wife of Andreus, mother of Eteokles by him or by river Kephisos (Hes. *Cat.* 70.10; Paus. 9.34.9).

2) daughter of Danaos and the naiad Polyxo, marries Imbros (Apollod. 2.1.5).

EUKLEIA

1) *an epithet of Artemis, as well as a goddess in her own right.

2) the daughter of Herakles and Myrto (sister of Patroklos), honored by the Boiotians and Lokrians with an altar and statue in the agora, and sacrifices before marriage by both sexes (Plut. *Arist.* 20.6).

EUPHEME nurse of the Muses (Paus. 9.29.5–6), mother of Krotos by Pan (Hyg. *Astr.* 2.27; Hyg. *Fab.* 224).

EUROPE(IA)

1) *Nymph, daughter of Okeanos and Tethys (Hes. *Theog.* 357).

2) *Boiotian earth-goddess hidden in a cave by Zeus (Paus. 9.19.1), daughter of Tityos, mother of Euphemos, wife of Boiotian Zeus (Philostr. *Ep.* 47 p. 248K).

3) daughter of Phoinix (schol. Eur. *Phoin.* 5) or Agenor and Telephassa, carried off by Zeus in shape of a bull, sought by her brother Kadmos. By Zeus mother of Minos, Rhadamanthys, and Sarpedon; later marries Asterion (schol. A. *Iliad* 12.292, citing Hesiod and Bacchylides; Hes. *Cat.* 140, 141). Praxilla says that she is the mother by Zeus of Karneios, who was raised by Apollo and Leto (Paus. 3.13.5).

4) mother of Automate, Amymone, Agave (1), and Skaia by Danaos (Apollod. 2.1.5).

5) *epithet of Demeter in Lebadeia (Paus. 9.39.4).

EURYALE

1) *Gorgon (Hes. *Theog.* 276; Pind. *Pyth.* 12.20; Apollod. 2.4.2).

2) mother of Orion (Erat. *Katast. Ep.* 32; Hyg. *Astr.* 2.34) by Poseidon (Hes. *Cat.* 148; Pherec. in Apollod. 1.4.3).

EURYANASSA wife of Minyas, mother of Klymene (5) (schol. *Od.* 11.326).

EURYBIA daughter of Thespios, mother of Polylaos by Herakles (Apollod. 2.7.8).

EURYDIKE

1) wife of Orpheus. Chased by Aristaios (Verg. *Georg.* 4.453ff.), she is bitten by a snake and dies. Orpheus wins permission from Persephone to bring her back from the Underworld but fails to meet the condition that he not look back at her and loses her forever (Plat. *Symp.* 179d, Eur. *Alk.* 357 unnamed; first named in Moschos, *Epit. Bion.* 124; also called Argiope or Agriope, Athen. 13.597b).

2) daughter of Adrastos, wife of Ilos, mother of Laomedon (schol. T. *Iliad* 20.236; Apollod. 3.12.3).

3) wife of Nestor, daughter of Klymenos (*Od.* 3.451f.), but see Anaxibia (2).

4) wife of Aineias (Paus. 10.26.1 after the *Kypria*).

5) wife of Kreon king of Thebes (Soph. *Ant.* 1183ff.), also called Henioche (schol. Soph. *Ant.* 1180 citing Hesiod; *Shield* 83).

6) daughter of Lakedaimon, wife of Akrisios, mother of Danae (Apollod. 2.2.2), also called Aganippe (Hyg. *Fab.* 63). Her mother is Sparte (Apollod. 3.10.3). Founder of a temple to Hera in Lakonia (Paus. 3.13.8).

7) wife of Lykourgos king of Nemea (Apollod. 1.9.14), also called Amphithea (3). Mother of Opheltes or Archemoros who was killed by a snake and had games established in his honor (Simon. frg. 553 *PMG* = Athen. 9.396e, restored, Apollod. 3.6.4).

8) daughter of Danaos and Polyxo, marries Dryas (Apollod. 2.1.5).

9) daughter of Amphiaraos and Eriphyle, depicted on Kypselos chest (Paus. 5.17.7).

10) daughter of Aktor, wife of Peleus and mother of Polydora (3) (Staphylos in schol. A. *Iliad* 16.175). See Polydora (3) for other versions.

EURYGANE(IA) in the cyclic *Oidipodeia*, second wife of Oidipous and mother of Antigone, Ismene, Polyneikes, and Eteokles (Pherec. in schol. Eur. *Phoin.* 13, 53, 1760; Paus. 9.5.11). See Iokaste (2), Astymedousa.

EURYKLEIA daughter of Ops, Odysseus' nurse (*Od.* 1.429, etc.).

EURYKYDA Elean heroine, daughter of Endymion, mother of Eleios by Poseidon (Paus. 5.1.4; 5.1.8).

EURYMEDE. See Eurynome (2).

EURYMEDOUSA attendant of Nausikaa (*Od.* 7.8).

EURYNOME

1) *daughter of Okeanos and Tethys (*Iliad* 18.398; Hes. *Theog.* 358), mother of the Graces by Zeus, sanctuary with festival near Phigalia, local people believe E. to be an epithet of Artemis (Paus. 8.41.4–6).

2) daughter of Nisos, wife of Glaukos, mother of Bellerophon by Poseidon (Hes. *Cat.* 43a.70 restored), also called Eurymede (Apollod. 1.9.3).

3) attendant of Penelope (*Od.* 17.495).

4) See Kleophyle.

5) See Deipyle.

6) See Leukothoe.

EURYPYLE daughter of Thespios, mother of Archedikos by Herakles (Apollod. 2.7.8).

EURYTE. See Sterope (4).

EURYTELE daughter of Thespios, mother of Leukippos by Herakles (Apollod. 2.7.8).

EURYTHEMIS(TE) daughter of Porthaon, sister of Stratonike (1) and Sterope (4) (Hes. *Cat.* 26), wife of Thestios, mother of Leda, Althaia, and Hypermestra (2) (Hes. *Cat.* 23). Pherecydes calls her Laophonte (schol. AR. 1.146).

EUXIPPE. See Molpia.

EXOLE daughter of Thespios, mother of Erythras by Herakles (Apollod. 2.7.8).

GALATEIA

1) *Nereid, daughter of Nereus and Doris (*Iliad* 18.45; Hes. *Theog.* 250), loved by Polyphemos (Theocr. 6,11).

2) daughter of Eurytios, wife of Lampros, mother of a daughter transformed by Leto into a man (Ant. Lib. 17 after Nikandros).

3) *name of statue created by Pygmalion and brought to life. See Ovid *Met.* 10.243–97 for the story. The use of this name is not ancient and may have begun with Rousseau, *Pygmalion. Scène lyrique* (1775).

GALINTHIAS daughter of Proitos, helps Alkmene in childbirth and is changed into a weasel by Hera. She serves in Hekate's temple and receives sacrifices before the festival of Herakles in Thebes (Ant. Lib. 29 after Nicander; Ovid *Met.* 9.273–323). See Historis.

GANYMEDA sometimes equivalent to Hebe, possibly a heroine, but worshiped as a goddess in Phlias (Paus. 2.12.4; 2.13.3). See Dia (1).

GLAUKE

1) *Homeric epithet of the sea, then name for Nereid, Nymph (*Iliad* 18.39).

2) daughter of Kreon, bride of Jason, poisoned by Medea, throws herself in the spring known from then on by her name (Paus. 2.3.6). Also called Kreousa (3) (schol. Eur. *Med.* 19, 404, and hypothesis).

3) Amazon, wife of Theseus, mother of Hippolytos (Apollod. *Ep.* 5.2; Hyg. *Fab.* 163). Other versions give her other names. See Hippolyte (1), Melanippe (2), Antiope (2).

4) daughter of Kychreos, mother of Telemon by Aktaios (Pherec. cited in Apollod. 3.12.6).

5) daughter of Danaos and a hamadryad, wife of Alkes (Apollod. 2.1.5).

GLAUKIA daughter of Skamandros, mother of a second Skamandros by Deimachos (Plut. *Quaest. Gr.* 41, 301a–b).

GLAUKIPPE daughter of Danaos and Polyxo, marries Potamon (Apollod. 2.1.5).

GORGE

1) daughter of Oineus and Althaia, sister of Meleager and Deianeira, wife of Andraimon (Apollod. 1.8.1). Mother of Tydeus by her own father (Apollod. 1.8.5). Buried with Andraimon in Amphissa (Paus. 10.38.5). See Periboia (6).

2) wife of Korinthos, mother of Megareus. Leaps into Eschatiotis, then called Gorgopis after her (Hesych. s.v. Γοργῶπις; Aesch. Ag. 302).

3) daughter of Danaos and a hamadryad, wife of Hippothoös (Apollod. 2.1.5).

GORGO mother of six sons by Aigyptos (Apollod. 2.1.5).

GORGOPHONE

1) daughter of Perseus, wife of Perieres and mother of Aphareus and Leukippos (Paus. 4.2.4), then wife of Oibalos, and mother of Tyndareos (Paus. 3.1.4) and Arene (Paus. 4.2.4). First woman to remarry (Paus. 2.21.7). Elsewhere, Perieres is the father of Tyndareos and Ikarios as well.

2) daughter of Danaos and Elephantis, wife of Proteus (Apollod. 2.1.5).

3) *epithet of Athena "Gorgon-slayer" (Eur. Ion 1478).

HABROTE daughter of Onchestos, wife of Nisos of Megara, garment worn in her honor by Megarian women (Plut. Quaest. Gr. 16, 295a–b). Also Habrite or Abrote.

HALIAI women who came from the Aegean Islands to help Dionysos when he was attacked by Perseus, and whose tomb is in Argos (Paus. 2.22.1).

HARMONIA

1) daughter of Ares and Aphrodite, wife of Kadmos, mother of Ino, Semele, Agave, Autonoe, Polydoros (Hes. Theog. 937, 975). On Samothrace she is the daughter of Zeus and Elektra (3) (= Elektryone [2]), stolen by Kadmos and sought by her mother, like Kore (schol. Eur. Phoin. 7, Ephorus). A tomb of Kadmos and Harmonia in Illyria (Athen. 11.462b citing Phylarkos). Her thalamos (bedchamber) in Thebes (Paus. 9.12.3); tomb (Strabo 1.2.39 citing Callimachus).

2) *daughter of Zeus, mother of the Muses, a goddess (Aesch. Prom. 551).

HARPALYKE

1) daughter of Thracian king Harpalykos, raised as a hunter. Ritual games by shepherds at her grave (Verg. Aen. 1.317; Hyg. Fab. 193, 252).

2) daughter of Klymenos, mother of Presbon by her own father (schol. T. Iliad 14.291; Hyg. Fab. 206). Elsewhere her father is Periklymenos (schol. V. Iliad 14.291).

3) a virgin who commits suicide for love of Iphikles, singing contest held in her honor (Athen. 14.619e).

HARPINA (Elis) mother of Oinomaus, who named a city after her (Paus. 6.21.8).

HEKABE daughter of Dymas, Kisseus, or the river god Sangarios, second wife of Priam, mother of 19 children (or 20: schol. Iliad 10.252 = Simon. frg. 559 PMG), including Hektor, Paris, Polyxene, Polydoros. She leads the embassy to Athena at Iliad 6.269ff. After taking her revenge on Polymestor for the murder of Polydoros, she is transformed into a dog (Eur. Hek. 1259–73; Apollod. Ep. 5.23), possible connection with Hekate (Tzetzes ad Lycoph. 1176).

According to Stesichorus, she was taken to Lycia by Apollo (frg. 193 *PMG* = Paus. 10.27.1). Her tomb near the Hellespont was known as the *Kynos Sēma*, or "tomb of the dog" (Eur. *Hek.* 1273). See Ilione for another version.

HEKAERGE
1) *epithet of Artemis (Callim. *Hymn* 4.292), Ktesylla (Ant. Lib. 1 after Nicander).
2) See the Hyperborean Maidens.

HEKALE eponym of the Attic deme, an old woman who gives hospitality to Theseus while he is engaged in his labors. When he returns to find her dead, he establishes a cult in her honor. Also called Hekaline (Callim. *Hekale* frg. 230–377 Pfeiffer or Hollis passim; Plut. *Thes.* 14.2 = Philochoros *FGrH* 328 F 109). According to a doubtful source (Mnaseas = *Testamenta Dubia* 17 Hollis), she is the mother of Boulias or Bounas.

HEKAMEDE daughter of Arsinous of Tenedos, captive of Nestor, mixer of potions (*Iliad* 11.624; 14.6).

HELEN (or Helene) daughter of Leda and Zeus, in the form of a swan. Helen was supposed to have been born from an egg that was on view in Sparta (Paus. 3.16.1; see Athen. 2.57f. for egg lore). Elsewhere her parents are Zeus and Nemesis (*Kypria* p. 24 Kinkel; Athen. 8.334c), who gave her to Leda to raise (Paus. 1.33.7), or Leda and Tyndareos. Sister of Kastor and Polydeukes (*Iliad* 3.237–38), Phylonoe, Timandra, Klytemnestra (Hes. *Cat.* 176). When men come from all over Greece to woo her, Tyndareos makes them swear to come to the aid of the successful suitor. When Paris steals her from Menelaos, the suitors sail against Troy (schol. A *Iliad* 2.339 citing Stesichorus). In some versions Paris and Helen are blown off course to Egypt (Hdt. 2.133–37), and Helen never goes to Troy (Stesich. 192 *PMG* = Plat. *Phaedr.* 243a), while the Trojan War is fought over a phantom (Plat. *Rep.* 586c). After the death of Paris, she is married to Deiphobos, despite the rivalry of Idomeneus (Ibycus and Simonides in schol. T *Iliad* 13.516). Menelaos, overcome by her beauty, is unable to kill her after the fall of Troy (Aristoph. *Lys.* 155–56), and their married life resumes (see *Od.* 4). There is a tradition that she was abducted as a young girl by Theseus but rescued by her brothers, the Dioskouroi (Apollod. 3.10.7). According to the dominant tradition, her only child is Hermione, daughter of Menelaos (*Od.* 4.12–14), but other traditions include among her children Iphigeneia by Theseus (Paus. 2.22.7), Nikostratos by Menelaos (Hes. *Cat.* 175 = Laur. schol. Soph. *El.* 539), and Korythos or Helenos by Paris (schol. *Od.* 4.11). In one version she is hanged to avenge the men killed in the Trojan War, which gives rise to a tree-cult (Paus. 3.19.10; Theocr. *Idyll* 18.48 for another tree-connection). Or she becomes the wife of Achilles on the isle of Leuke, the "White Island" (Paus. 3.19.13). She and Menelaos were buried at Therapne in Lakonia (Paus. 3.15.2), where they were worshiped as gods (Isocr. *Praise of Helen* 217d; cf. Alc. frg. 7 *PMG*). The Homeric tradition has M. going to the Isles of the Blessed.

HELIADES the five daughters of Helios, sisters of Phaethon, who mourn him and are turned into poplars who weep amber tears (Eur. *Hipp.* 735–41; Hyg. *Fab.*

154; Athen. 13.568e). For other daughters of Helios, see Lampetie and Phaethousa.

HELIKE
1) daughter of Selinos of Aigaleia, marries Ion, who names a city for her (Paus. 7.1.1–4). But elsewhere Pausanias connects the city name with Helicon (7.24.5–6).
2) mother of Merope (2) by Oinopion (Erat. *Kat.* 32).

HELIKONIS daughter of Thespios, mother of Phalias by Herakles (Apollod. 2.7.8).

HELLE daughter of Athamas and Nephele, sister of Phrixos. Their mother sends them to Kolchis on the ram with the golden fleece to save them from her rival Ino. Helle falls into the sea, which takes her name, i.e., Hellespont (Pindar frg. 29, 179; Aesch. *Pers.* 68). But see Demodike (1).

HEMITHEA
1) See Molpadia.
2) daughter of Kyknos and Prokleia, sister of Tennes, with whom she is put to sea in a chest after stepmother Philonome charges Tennes with making advances (Apollod. *Ep.* 3.24; Paus. 10.14.2–3).

HENIOCHE
1) *epithet of Hera at Lebadeia (Paus. 9.39.5).
2) See Eurydike (5).
3) daughter of Kreon, sister of Pyrrha. They sacrifice themselves to save their city and are honored with statues at the Ismenion in Thebes (Paus. 9.10.3).
4) daughter of Pittheus, wife of Kanethos, mother of Skiron or Sinis (Plut. *Thes.* 25.4–5).

HEPHAISTINE mother of four sons by Aigyptos (Apollod. 2.1.5).

HERKYNA (Lebadeia) a companion of Kore. She has a temple on the banks of the river of the same name (Paus. 9.39.2–3). It is unclear whether she received divine or heroic cult there.

HERMIONE
1) daughter of Helen and Menelaos (Hes. *Cat.* 175, 204), married to Neoptolemos (*Od.* 4.4ff.; Apollod. *Ep.* 6.14). In some versions she marries Orestes after he kills Neoptolemos, and Tisamenos is their son (Paus. 1.33.8; 2.18.6). Marriage to Diomedes (schol. Pindar *Nem.* 10.12a). Rival of Andromache (Eur. *Andr.*). An image of her dedicated by the Spartans at Delphi (Paus. 10.16.4).
2) *Syracusan name for Persephone (Stesich. frg. S104 Campbell with note).

HERO the female protagonist of a tale of star-crossed love. Her lover Leandros drowns while swimming the Hellespont to meet her. The story is told by Musaios in the 5th c. C.E. and in Ovid's *Heroides*, but fragments exist from the 1st c. C.E. of a poem on this theme, which may be Hellenistic. See Page (1970) 3:512–15.

HEROPHILE early Sibyl, who calls herself wife, sister, or daughter of Apollo. Her tomb in the Troad, where she is said to be the daughter of the shepherd Theodoros and a nymph (Paus. 10.12.1–7).

HERSE

1) one of the three Aglaurides, with Aglauros and Pandrosos. They are daughters of Kekrops in some versions (Paus. 1.2.6; Apollod. 3.14.2). Mother of Kephalos by Hermes (Apollod. 3.14.3). According to Alc. (frg. 57 *PMG*) she is daughter of Zeus and Selene. Connection with the festival of the Arrephoria, sometimes called Hersephoria. See Aglauros (2), Pandrosos.

2) mother of Hippodike and Adiante by Danaos (Apollod. 2.1.5).

HESIONE

1) *Okeanid, wife of Prometheus (Aesch. *Prom.* 560).

2) See Klymene (4).

3) wife of Atlas, mother of Elektra, ancestor of Trojan royal house (schol. Eur. *Phoin.* 1129).

4) daughter of Laomedon. When Poseidon sends a sea monster because of her father's hybris, she is set out to appease it and is rescued by Herakles (*Iliad* 20.144; 5.638; Soph. *Aias* 1301ff.; Apollod. 2.5.9). When Laomedon refuses him a reward, Herakles sacks the city and gives her to Telamon, by whom she is the mother of Teucer (Apollod. 3.12.7). She ransoms her brother Podarkes with a veil, hence his new name Priam (Apollod. 2.6.4; Tzetzes ad Lycoph. 34; Hyg. *Fab.* 89).

HESYCHEIA daughter of Thespios, mother of Oistrobles by Herakles (Apollod. 2.7.8).

HILAIRA daughter of Leukippos, together with her sister Phoibe, carried off by the Dioskouroi. She is the mother of Anogon by Kastor (Apollod. 3.11.2). According to the *Kypria*, she and her sister Phoibe are daughters of Apollo (Paus. 3.16.1). At their temple in Lakonia, they were served by young priestesses also called Leukippides (Paus. 3.16.1). See Phoibe (2).

HIPPE

1) See Hippolyte (1).

2) daughter of Cheiron, mother of Melanippe by Aiolos or Apollo. Changed into a constellation (Hyg. *Astr.* 2.18; Eur. *Melanippe*, frgs. 480–88 Nauck). In Eur. originally called Okyrrhoe (4). Also called Hippo.

3) See Molpia.

HIPPO

1) *Okeanid (Hes. *Theog.* 351).

2) Amazon (Callim. *Hymn* 3.239, 266), apparently the same as Hippolyte (2).

3) See Hippe (2).

4) nurse of Dionysos, also known as Hipta (Orph. *Hymn* 49).

5) See Molpia.

6) daughter of Thespios, mother of Kapylos by Herakles (Apollod. 2.7.8).

HIPPODAMEIA

1) daughter of Oinomaos and Sterope, wife of Pelops, mother of Atreus and Thyestes, Astydameia (3), Lysidike (1), and Nikippe (1). Her father challenges and kills her suitors (Hes. frg. 259a = Paus. 6.21.10), until Pelops wins by trickery (Apollod. *Ep.* 2.3–9; Hyg. *Fab.* 84) or the help of Poseidon (Pind. *Ol.* 1). H. inaugurated the Heraia as a thank-offering to Hera for her marriage (Paus. 5.16.4). Buried in the Altis at Olympia, sanctuary called Hippodameion, where women pay her honors (Paus. 5.16.6; 6.20.7).

2) daughter of Adrastos, wife of Peirithoös, mother of Polypoites (*Iliad* 2.740). Her marriage is the occasion for the war between the Lapiths and Centaurs (Apollod. *Ep.* 1.21; Hyg. *Fab.* 33; frequently represented in art).

3) wife of Amyntor, mother of Phoinix (schol. *Iliad* 9.448).

4) See Briseis.

5) one of Penelope's maids (*Od.* 18.182).

6) wife of Autonoös, mother of Erodios, Anthos, Schoineus, Akanthos, Akanthis (Ant. Lib. 7 after Boios).

7) daughter of Danaos and a hamadryad, marries Istros (Apollod. 2.1.5), but see also Kleodameia.

8) eldest daughter of Anchises (*Iliad* 13.429).

HIPPODIKE daughter of Danaos and Herse, marries Idas (Apollod. 2.1.5).

HIPPOKRATE daughter of Thespios, mother of Hippozygos by Herakles (Apollod. 2.7.8).

HIPPOLYTE

1) Amazon, daughter of Ares (schol. A. *Iliad* 3.189) and Otrere (Hyg. *Fab.* 30, 163), carried off by Theseus, also called Antiope, Hippe (*Hes. Cat.* 147 = Athen. 13.557), Glauke, or Melanippe (Apollod. *Ep.* 1.16). According to Apollodorus she is the mother of Hippolytos (Apollod. *Ep.* 5.2), but see Antiope (2).

2) queen of the Amazons, killed by Herakles for her belt (Eur. *Herak.* 407ff.; Apollod. 2.5.9). There is some confusion between (1) and (2), and it is not clear which is meant to be buried at Megara (Paus. 1.41.7).

3) daughter of Dexamenos, rescued from centaur by Herakles (Diod. 4.33), but see Deianeira.

4) daughter of Kretheus, wife of Akastos, also called Astydameia (Pindar *Nem.* 4.57, 5.23ff.; schol. AR. 1.224).

5) sister of Jason? See Alkimede.

6) See Antigone (1).

HIPPOMEDOUSA daughter of Danaos and a hamadryad, marries Alkemenor (Apollod. 2.1.5).

HIPPONOME daughter of Menoikeus, wife of Alkaios, mother of Anaxo (2) and Amphitryon (Apollod. 2.4.5). But see Astydameia (4), Laonome (1), Lysidike (1).

HIPPOTHOE

1) *Nereid (Hes. *Theog.* 251; Apollod. 1.2.7).

2) one of the daughters of Pelias, whom Medea tricks into killing their father (Apollod. 1.9.10; Hyg. *Fab.* 24).

3) daughter of Mestor and Lysidike, mother of Taphios by Poseidon (Apollod. 2.4.5).

4) Amazon (Hyg. *Fab.* 163).

5) daughter of Pelias and Anaxibia (Apollod. 1.9.10). See Anaxibia (2).

HISTORIS (Boiotia) daughter of Teiresias, helps Alkmene in childbirth (Paus. 9.11.3). See Galinthias.

HYADES. See Hyakinthides.

HYAKINTHIDES the daughters of Erechtheus and Praxithea (1) sacrificed to save Athens in time of war, also called Hyades. There are as many as six: Chthonia (2), Kreousa (2), Prokris (1), Oreithyia (2), Pandora (5), Protogeneia (2). The name Hyakinthides can also refer to the daughters of Hyakinthos—Antheis, Aigleis, Lytaia, and Orthaia—sacrificed by the Athenians to avert a plague (Apollod. 3.15.8). See also under individual names. See also Koronis (2).

HYLLIS daughter of Hyllus son of Herakles, mother of Zeuxippos by Apollo (Ibycus frg. 282a.41 *PMG*).

HYPERA sister of Anthos, who searches for her brother. They are eponyms of Anthedonia and Hypereia (Plut. *Quaest. Gr.* 19.295e–f; but Athen. 1.31c has Hyperos).

HYPERBOREAN MAIDENS young women sent by the Hyperboreans to bring offerings to Apollo at Delos. According to the Delians, the maidens, called Hyperoche and Laodike, died there and the boys and girls of Delos cut off a lock of hair in mourning for them (Hdt. 4.33). Clement places their tomb in the Artemision at Delos (*Protr.* 3.39). Herodotus also suggests some connection with Eileithyia, the goddess of childbirth. He mentions an earlier pair of Hyperborean Maidens, Opis and Arge, on whose tomb ashes from sacrifices are scattered (Hdt. 4.33–35). Pausanias calls them Opis and Hekaerge (Paus. 5.7.8), and Callimachus has three: Hekaerge, Opis, and Loxo, which perhaps indicates "partner of Loxias," i.e., Apollo (*Hymn* 4.292).

HYPERIPPE

1) Elean heroine, wife of Endymion; see Asterodeia.

2) daughter of Danaos and Krino, marries Hippokorystes (Apollod. 2.1.5).

3) (Boiotia) daughter of Leukon, sister of Euippe and Peisidike (Hes. *Cat.* 70 restored).

4) daughter of Munichos and Lelante (Ant. Lib. 14 after Nicander). See Lelante.

HYPERMESTRA (or Hypermnestra)

1) Danaid, the only one who disobeys her father's order to kill her husband (Pindar *Nem.* 10.6). Wife of Lynkeus, mother of Abas. In thanks for the goddess' defense against a charge of impiety by her father, she dedicates an image of Aphrodite Nikephoros (Paus. 2.19.6) as well as a temple to Artemis Peitho (Paus. 2.21.1). Her tomb is in Argos (Paus. 2.21.2). According to Apollodorus, her mother is Elephantis (2.1.5).

2) (Argos) daughter of Thestios and Eurythemis(te), wife of Oikles, mother of Amphiaraos, buried near Hypermestra (1) (Paus. 2.21.2), or daughter of Thespios, mother of Iphianeira (2), Polyboia, and Amphiaraos (Diod. 4.68.5–6).

3) See Mestra.

HYPEROCHE. See Hyperborean Maidens.

HYPSIPYLE(IA)

1) daughter of Thoas of Lemnos. The Lemnian women slight Aphrodite and are punished with a horrible smell. When their husbands abandon them for Thracian women, the Lemnian women kill their fathers and husbands and rule the island. Hypsipyle alone spares her father. When the Argonauts stop on Lemnos, they sleep with the women. She is the mother of Euneos and Thoas or Nebrophonos by Jason (Iliad 7.469; AR. 1.620; Apollod. 1.9.17). Later, she is the nurse of Opheltes (Archemoros), son of Lykourgos and Eurydike. While she directs the Seven against Thebes to a spring, Opheltes dies of a snakebite, and the Nemean games are founded in his honor (Apollod. 3.6.4). Extensive fragments survive of Euripides' Hypsipyle (Bond [1963]; Page [1970] 76–109).

2) See Iphthime.

HYRIE (Aitolia) daughter of Amphinomos, mother of Kyknos, transformed into a sea of this name at her son's death (Ovid Met. 7.371–81). In Ant. Lib. 12 (after Nicander), the name is given as Thyrie, and the son's father is Apollo, who changes them both to swans.

HYRMINA (Elis) daughter of Epeios and Anaxiroe (Paus. 5.1.6), mother of Aktor by Phorbas. Her son names a city for her (Paus. 5.1.11). The city mentioned in Iliad 2.616.

HYRNETHO daughter of Temenos, wife of Deiphontes, sister of Kerunos and Phalkes. Eponym of the tribe Hyrnethioi in Argos. Mother of Antimenes, Xanthippos, Argeus, and Orsobia. She is accidentally killed by her brothers, who build a heroon for her (Paus. 2.23.3; 2.28.37). See Larson (1995) 141–43.

IAMBE servant in the house of Keleos who cheers Demeter with her jokes (Hom. Hymn 2.195, 202). A personification of the practise of aischrologia (ritual obscenity) connected with the Eleusinian mysteries, she appears in a late-third-century Hymn to Demeter attributed to Philikos (in Page [1970] 407). See Baubo.

IANTHE

1) *Okeanid (Hes. Theog. 349), companion of Persephone (Hom. Hymn 2.418).

2) See Iphis (2).

IDAIA daughter of Dardanos, second wife of Phineus, antagonist of first wife, Kleopatra (1). In some versions the second wife is Eidothea (Apollod. 3.15.2–4). See Kleopatra (1), Eidothea (3).

IDYIA. See Neaira (4).

ILIONE oldest daughter of Priam, wife of Polymestor, saves her brother Polydoros, tricking Polymestor into killing Deipylos, their son, instead. She kills Polymestor, then herself (Hyg. *Fab.* 109, 240, 243). But see Hekabe for another version.

INO daughter of Kadmos and Harmonia, sister of Semele, Agave, Autonoe, and Polydoros (Hes. *Theog.* 975ff.; *Od.* 5.333ff.). Wife of Athamas, mother of Learchos and Melikertes. Other versions tell of her rivalry with Athamas' first wife, Nephele, and attempts to kill her children (Apollod. 1.9.1). Elsewhere she is the supplanted wife, persecuted by Themisto (Hyg. *Fab.* 4 is apparently based on Euripides' *Ino*, of which a few fragments survive. See Nauck, *Tragicorum Graecorum Fragmenta* [2] 482ff.). Driven mad by Hera for nursing Dionysos, Athamas kills Learchos, and she leaps into the sea with Melikertes (Alc. frg. 50 *PMG*; Apollod. 3.4.3) and becomes the goddess Leukothea (*Od.* 5.333ff.). Her cult is both heroic and divine (Xenophanes in Arist. *Rhet.* 1440b5; Paus. 4.34.4). As Ino she is associated with divination at Limera (Paus. 3.23.8), and near Thalamai in Lakonia (Paus. 3.26.1, but see also Kassandra and Pasiphae). In Crete she has a festival called the Inacheia. At Megara, where they claim to have been the first to call her Leukothea, there is a yearly sacrifice to her (Paus. 1.42.7). As Leukothea she is honored in Miletos by games (Conon *Narr.* 33), in Colchis with a temple founded by Phrixos near his own oracle (Strabo 11.2.17), and with festivals and month-names in many Greek cities.

IO daughter of Inachos and Melia, priestess of Hera, loved by Zeus. She is changed into a cow, either by him to hide her from Hera, or by Hera in revenge (Aesch. *Suppl.* 291ff.). She is watched over by Argos, until Hermes kills the monster and she wanders to Egypt where she gets back human form and gives birth to Epaphos (Aesch. *Prom.* 851). She marries Telegonos, is identified with Isis (Apollod. 2.1.3). Sometimes her father is said to be Iasos (Paus. 2.16.1) or Peiren (Hes. *Cat.* 124 = Apollod. 2.1.3). As Io Kallithyessa, she is said to be the first priestess of Athena (Hesych. s.v. Ἰὼ Καλλιθύεσσα). This may be a mistake, since every other tradition connects Io with Hera. Elsewhere Kallithyia, a possible doublet of Io, is the first priestess of Argive Hera. See Kallithyia.

IODAMA daughter of Itonos, sister of Athena, who kills her during weapon play (Simonides *FGrH* 9 F 1) or priestess of Itonian Athena, turned to stone at sight of the goddess with the gorgoneion, honored daily with fire (Paus. 9.34.1; schol. Lycoph. 355). Or she is the daughter of Tithonos, mother of Thebe by Zeus (schol. Lycoph. 1206).

IOKASTE

1) (Boiotia) mother of Agamedes and Trophonios by Zeus or Apollo. She is in some traditions called Epikaste and is said to be the wife of Agamedes and mother of Trophonios (schol. Aristoph. *Clouds* 508).

2) daughter of Menoikeus, sister of Kreon, wife of Laios and mother of Oidipous (*Od.* F 11.271, where called Epikaste). Mother by Oidipous of Antigone, Ismene, Polyneikes, Eteokles. In Sophocles' *O.T.*, she kills herself upon

discovering her incestuous union. In Stesichorus' fragmentary *Thebiad* or *Seven against Thebes* (frg. 222a *PMG*), she lives long enough to try to make peace between her warring sons. Elsewhere, she is mother of Phrastor and Laonytos (Pherec. *FGrH* 3 F 95), while the children named above are the product of another marriage. See Eurygane(ia), Astymedousa.

IOLE(IA) daughter of Eurytos in Oichalia, beloved of Herakles, at his death given to his son Hyllos (Hes. *Cat.* 26; Soph. *Trach.*).

IOPE daughter of Iphikles, mother of Demophon by Theseus, according to Stesichorus (frg. 193.23–24 *PMG*), but elsewhere his mother is Ariadne. Plutarch lists her among Theseus' wives (*Thes.* 29).

IOPHOSSA wife of Phrixos, mother of Argos, Phrontis, Melas, and Kytisoros (schol. AR. 2.1122, citing the Great Ehoiai). But see Chalkiope (2).

IPHIANASSA

1) daughter of Proitos and Stheneboia (or Anteia, *Iliad* 6.160) together with sisters Lysippe and Iphinoe slights Dionysos, according to Hesiod, or Hera as cited in Akousilaos, and is driven mad (Apollod. 2.2.2. = Hes. *Cat.* 131). Marries Melampous, after he cures her of madness (Pherec. *FGrH* 3 F 114). See Iphinoe (2), Iphianeira (1).

2) daughter of Agamemnon and Klytemnestra (*Iliad* 9.144f., etc.). In the *Kypria* (p. 27 Kinkel = schol. Laur. in Soph. *El.* 157), both she and Iphigeneia appear. Elsewhere they are perhaps the same. See Iphigeneia.

3) mother of Aitolos by Endymion (Apollod. 1.7.6).

IPHIANEIRA

1) daughter of Megapenthes, mother of Antiphates, Manto, Bias, Pronoe, by Melampous. Same story as Iphianassa (1) (Diod. 4.68.4). But see Iphianassa (1).

2) daughter of Oikles and Hypermestra (2), sister of Amphiaraos (Hes. *Cat.* 25), sister also of Polyboia (Diod. 4.68.5).

IPHIGENEIA daughter of Agamemnon and Klytemnestra. She is brought to Aulis on the pretext of marriage to Achilles and instead sacrificed to Artemis (Pindar *Pyth.* 11.21ff.; Aesch. *Ag.* 150ff., 1415ff., etc.) or rescued by the goddess (Hes. *Cat.* 23a under name Iphimede). Some sources equate her with the goddess Hekate (Hes. *Cat.* 23b = Paus. 1.43.1; Stesich. frg. 215 *PMG* = Philod. *Peri Euseb.* p. 24). Associated with worship of Artemis in the Tauric Chersonnese (Hdt. 4.103). Priestess of Artemis, shares sanctuary at Brauron, associated with childbirth (Eur *I. T.*). According to others, she is the daughter of Helen and Theseus (Stesich. frg. 14 *PMG* in Paus. 2.22.6; schol. Lycoph. 102, 143, etc.), given to Klytemnestra to raise. Apparently the same as Iphimede (1), and perhaps Iphianassa (2). There is a tradition that the "marriage" at Aulis was actually consummated and resulted in the birth of Neoptolemos (schol. BT. *Iliad* 19.326 = Douris of Samos *FGrH* 76 F 88; schol. Lycoph. 183 and 325). See also Iphis (1).

IPHILOCHE daughter of Alektor and wife of Menelaos' son Megapenthes. Also called Echemela (*Od.* 4.10, named only in the scholia).

IPHIMEDE(IA)

1) daughter of Agamemnon and Klytemnestra (Hes. *Cat*. 23), sacrificed to Artemis, made immortal. Honored by Carians (Paus. 10.28.8). See Iphigeneia.

2) daughter of Triopas, wife of Aloeos, mother of Otos and Ephialtes, who were known as the Aloiades but whose father was really Poseidon (*Od*. 11.305; Hes. *Cat*. 19 = schol. AR. 1.482; Pindar *Pyth*. 4.89).

IPHIMEDOUSA daughter of Danaos and a hamadryad, marries Euchenor (Apollod. 2.1.5).

IPHINOE

1) daughter of Nisos, wife of Megareus (Paus. 1.39.6).

2) daughter of Alkathous (her mother is either his first wife, Pyrgo, or his second, Euaichme), to whom Megarian girls sacrifice their hair before marriage (Paus. 1.43.4).

3) daughter of Proitos, with her sisters Iphianassa and Lysippe (Hes. *Cat*. 129), driven mad for offending either Hera or Dionysos. The seer Melampous undertakes a cure, but she dies in the attempt (Apollod. 2.2.2). A fourth-century inscription records that her tomb was set up in the agora of Sikyon (*SEG* 15.195). See Iphianassa (1).

IPHINOME Amazon (Hyg. *Fab*. 163).

IPHIS

1) mother of Neoptolemos by Achilles, also called Iphigeneia in one source (Lycoph. 323ff. with scholia).

2) daughter of Lygdos and Telethousa, raised as a boy, betrothed to Ianthe, Iphis changes her sex so they can marry (Ovid *Met*. 9.666–797).

3) daughter of Thespios, mother of Keleustanor by Herakles (Apollod. 2.7.8).

IPHTHIME daughter of Ikarios, sister of Penelope, wife of Eumelos of Pherai (*Od*. 4.797). According to the scholia (schol. *Od*. 4.797), also called Meda, Laodameia, Hypsipyle, or Laodike (schol. *Od*. 1.277).

ISMENE

1) (Thebes) daughter of Oidipous and either Iokaste or Eurygane(ia) (Pherec. in schol. Eur. *Phoin*. 53). Connected with the town and spring of the same name; the hero Ismenos, son of Amphion and Niobe; the Ismenion; and the oracle of Apollo Ismenios (Paus. 9.10.2–6). A Corinthian amphora (Louvre E640, c. 560) shows her being killed by Tydeus because of her union with Periklymenos.

2) *a nymph, daughter of Asopos, mother of Iasos by Argos (Apollod. 2.1.3), brought into the Theban genealogy by confusion with (1).

KABYE (or Kambyse) (Elis) daughter of Opous, wife of Lokros, mother of Opous by Zeus (mentioned unnamed in Pindar *Ol*. 9.57ff.; Plut. *Quaest. Gr*. 15.294e).

KAINIS daughter of Elatos of Thessaly, raped by Poseidon. When he offers her a favor, she asks to become a man, and therefore invulnerable to rape. She is henceforth known as Kaineus (Hes. *Cat.* 87; Ovid *Met.* 12.189–209). Ovid describes a later metamorphosis into a bird (12.459–97).

KALAMETIS daughter of Thespios, mother of Astybies by Herakles (Apollod. 2.7.8).

KALCHINIA daughter of Leukippos, bears son Peratos to Poseidon (Paus. 2.5.7).

KALIADNE *river nymph, mother of twelve of the sons of Aigyptos (Apollod. 2.1.5).

KALLIDIKE
1) daughter of Keleos, king of Eleusis, and Metaneira. Her sisters are Kleisidike, Demo, and Kallithoe (*Hom. Hymn* 2.109). Her brother is Demophoön (*Hom. Hymn* 2.234). But see also Saisara. The tombs of the daughters of Keleos were honored (Clem. Al. *Protr.* 3.39).
2) Thesprotian queen, married to Odysseus, mother of Polypoites (*Telegony* p. 57 Kinkel; Apollod. *Ep.* 7.35).
3) daughter of Danaos and Krino, marries Pandion (Apollod. 2.1.5).

KALLIPATEIRA woman who invades the Olympic games, also called Pherenike (Paus. 5.6.7; 6.7.2), possibly historical figure.

KALLIRHOE
1) *Okeanid, companion of Kore (*Hom. Hymn* 2.419).
2) daughter of Acheloös, wife of Alkmaion (Apollod. 3.7.5), mother of Akarnan and Amphoteros. Her desire to have the necklace of Eriphyle, which he had given to his first wife Alphesiboia, leads to Alkmaion's death (Paus. 8.24.9–10).
3) daughter of Skamandros, wife of Tros, mother of Assarakos, Ilos, Ganymede, Kleopatra (3) (Apollod. 3.12.2; schol. Lycoph. 29; schol. T. *Iliad* 20.231 citing Hellanicus).
4) Kalydonian maiden beloved of Dionysos' priest (Paus. 7.21.1, perhaps after Nicander).
5) Trojan maiden in Milesian tale (Ps.-Aesch. *Ep.* 10).
6) mother of Geryon by Chrysaor (Stesich. frg. S10–11 Campbell).

KALLISTO daughter of Lykaon, companion of Artemis. Seduced by Zeus, transformed into bear by Artemis (Hes. *Cat.* 163 = Erat. *Kat.* 1; Eur. *Hel.* 375ff.). Mother of Arkas, ancestor of the Arkadians. In other versions, transformed by Hera, shot by Artemis or Arkas (Apollod. 3.8.2 with different genealogies). Her grave at Trikolonoi near Megalopolis in temple of Artemis Kalliste (Paus. 8.35.8). Cult title of Artemis in Athens (Paus. 1.29.2) and in Arkadia (Paus. 8.35.8). Her statue on the Akropolis (Paus. 1.25.1); painted by Polygnotos (Paus. 10.31.10). See also Ktimene (1).

KALLITHOE
1) daughter of Keleos, king of Eleusis, and Metaneira. Sister of Kallidike, Kleisidike, and Demo (*Hom. Hymn* 2.109) and Demophoön (*Hom. Hymn* 2.234). See Kallidike (1).
2) See Kallithyia, Io.

KALLITHYESSA. See Kallithyia, Io.

KALLITHYIA daughter of Peiras, who founded the Argive Heraion, priestess of Hera (Plut. frg. 158; Arist. Or. 45.3). Also called Kallithoe (Phoronis frg. 4 Kinkel). Perhaps to be identified with Kallithyessa, first priestess of Athena (Hesych. s.v. Ἰὼ Καλλιθύεσσα). See Io.

KALYKE

1) daughter of Aiolos and Ainarete (Apollod. 1.7.3), mother of Endymion by Aethlios or Zeus (Apollod. 1.7.5; Hes. Cat. 245), mother of Polykaste by Aethlios (Hes. Cat. 10a).

2) daughter of Hekaton, mother of Kyknos by Poseidon, also known as Skamandrodike, etc. (schol. Pindar Ol. 2.147; Hyg. Fab. 157).

3) commits suicide for love of Euathlos, jumping from the white rock of Leukas. Her story was recounted in a poem entitled Kalyke, attributed by some to Stesichorus (Athen. 14.619d–e).

KAMEIRO daughter of Pandareos. After the death of their parents (perhaps for impiety), she and her sister Klytie are raised by Aphrodite, Hera, Artemis, and Athena, but stolen by the Harpies to be given to the Erinyes before they can be married (Od. 20.66–78). Depicted in the Lesche at Delphi by Polygnotos, who is the source for their names (Paus. 10.30.1–3).

KANAKE daughter of Aiolos and Ainarete, bears five children to Poseidon (Apollod. 1.7.3–4), committs incest with her brother Makareus (Od. 10.5ff.; Aristoph. Clouds 1371 and schol. Tzetzes; Frogs 849; Hyg. Fab. 242).

KARME daughter of Eubolos and Demeter; by Zeus, mother of Britomartis (Paus. 2.30.3; Diod. 5.76.3). Elsewhere her parents are Phoinix and Kassiepeia (Ant. Lib. 40).

KARYA daughter of Dion, beloved of Dionysos, rivalry with sisters Lyko and Orphe, transformed into a nut tree, aetiology for Artemis Karyatis (Serv. in Verg. Ecl. 8.29).

KASANDRA. See Philonoe.

KASSANDRA daughter of Priam and Hekabe, twin sister of Helenos, betrothed to Othryoneus (Iliad 13.366), then Koroibos. Apollo gives her gift of prophecy (Iliad 24.699) but curses her when she refuses to sleep with him, with the result that no one believes her prophecies (Aesch. Ag. 1203f.; Apollod. 3.12.5; Hyg. Fab. 93; for a different version: schol. Iliad 7.44). Raped by Aias at fall of Troy (Alcaeus frg. 298 Campbell). Killed by Klytemnestra and Aigisthos (Od. 11.421). Her grave and sanctuary are in Lakonia, where she is equated with Alexandra (Paus. 3.19.6; 3.26.4). Her tomb is at Amyklai, along with tomb of infant sons Teledamos and Pelops (Paus. 2.16.6). A votive relief dedicated to Alexandra (SEG 23.281) dates to about the first century B.C.E. She is possibly the possessor of an oracle at Thalamai under the cult-title Pasiphae (Plut. Agis 9), but see also Pasiphae (2), Ino.

KASSIEPEIA (or Kassiopeia)

1) daughter of Arabos, wife of Phoinix, mother of Kilix, Phineus, Dorykles, mother of Atumnos by Zeus (Hes. Cat. 138 = schol. AR. 2.178). See Karme.

2) wife of Kepheus, mother of Andromeda (Ps. Erat. 16; Hyg. Astr. 2.10).

KASSIPHONE daughter of Odysseus and Kirke, sister of Telegonos, married to her half-brother Telemachos, whom she kills because he kills her mother (Lycoph. 808 and schol. 798, 805, 808, 811).

KASTALIA *Nymph, daughter of Acheloös, eponym of spring (Paus. 10.8.9–10). Wife of Delphos (schol. Eur. Or. 1094).

KASTIANEIRA wife of Priam, mother of Gorgythion (Iliad 8.302).

KEKROPIDS the daughters of Kekrops, usually Aglauros, Herse, and Pandrosos, but sometimes also Prokris. See under individual names.

KELAINO
1) See Melantho (1).
2) daughter of Atlas and Pleione (Hes. Cat. 169 = schol. Pindar Nem. 2.17), one of seven sisters known as the Pleiades, mother of Lykas by Poseidon (Apollod. 3.10.1). See Pleione.
3) daughter of Danaos and Krino, marries Hyperbios (Apollod. 2.1.5).

KELOUSA mother of Asopos by Poseidon (Paus. 2.12.4).

KERDO wife of Phoroneus, her tomb in Corinth (Paus. 2.21.1).

KEREBIA mother of Diktys and Polydektes by Poseidon (schol. Lycoph. 838).

KERTHE daughter of Thespios, mother of Iobes by Herakles (Apollod. 2.7.8).

KILISSA. See Laodameia (4).

KIRKE *daughter of Helios and Perse(is), sister of Aietes, Pasiphae, Perses (Od. 10.139).

KLEISIDIKE daughter of Keleos, king of Eleusis, and Metaneira, sister of Kallidike, Demo, and Kallithoe (Hom. Hymn 2.109). Sister of Demophoön (Hom. Hymn 2.234). See Kallidike.

KLEISITHYRA. See Meda (1).

KLEITE
1) daughter of Merops and Perkote. Her tears become a spring of the same name (AR. 1.976; Parthen. 28).
2) daughter of Danaos and Memphis, marries Kleitos (Apollod. 2.1.5).

KLEITO daughter of Evenor and Leukippe in Plato's myth of Atlantis (Crito 113c).

KLEO. See Leandris.

KLEOBOIA
1) brings the mysteries of Demeter from Paros to Thasos, depicted by Polygnotos (Paus. 10.28.3).
2) wife of Phobios in Miletos, conceives an illicit passion for Antheus (Parthen. 14).

KLEOCHAREIA. See Sparte.

KLEODAMEIA daughter of Danaos and a hamadryad, marries Diocorystes (correction for Hippodameia at Apollod. 2.1.5, but possibly Phylodameia as in Paus. 4.30.2).

KLEODIKE Trojan captive perhaps invented by Polygnotos (Paus. 10.26.2).

KLEODORA
1) daughter of Danaos and Polyxo, marries Lixos (Apollod. 2.1.5).
2) See Polydora (3).

KLEODOXA daughter of Amphion and Niobe (Apollod. 3.5.6). See Niobe.

KLEOLEIA (or Kleola[a]) daughter of Dias, wife of Pleisthenes (Tzetzes *Exeg.*, Ul. p. 68.19 Hermann; cf. Hes. *Cat.* 194). Elsewhere, she is the wife of Atreus, mother of Pleisthenes (schol. Eur. *Or.* 4). The exact form of the name is uncertain. See West (1985) 110–12.

KLEOPATRA
1) daughter of Boreas and Oreithyia, wife of Phineus, rival of Idaia or Eidothea, Phineus' second wife, who persecutes her and her children (schol. *Od.* 12.69; Soph. *Ant.* 966; Apollod. 3.15.2–4).
2) daughter of Idas and Marpessa, known as Alkyone from the cry made by her mother when carried off by Apollo (*Iliad* 9.556). Wife of Meleager, urges him to return to battle although angry with his mother (*Iliad* 9.590ff.).
3) daughter of Tros and Kallirrhoe (Apollod. 3.12.2).
4) with Periboia (3), the first of the Lokrian maidens sent as expiation for the impiety of Aias (Apollod. *Ep.* 6.20–21).
5) daughter of Danaos and a hamadryad, marries Agenor (Apollod. 2.1.5).
6) daughter of Danaos and Polyxo, marries Hermos (Apollod. 2.1.5).

KLEOPHYLE wife of Lykourgos, mother of Ankaios, Epochos, Amphidamas, and Iasos. She is also called Eurynome (Apollod. 3.9.2).

KLESO. See Tauropolis.

KLYMENE
1) See Ktimene (2).
2) Trojan captive in Polygotos' painting (Paus. 10.26.1, citing Stesichorus' *Iliou Persis*), presumably same as Helen's attendant (*Iliad* 3.144). See Physadeia.
3) *Nymph (*Iliad* 18.47).
4) daughter of Katreus, sister of Aerope, Apemosyne, Althaimenes, wife of Nauplios, mother of Palamedes, Oiax, and Nausimedon, also called Philyra (*Nostoi* p. 52. Kinkel) or Hesione (2) (Apollod. 2.1.5 = Hes. frg. 297).
5) daughter of Minyas and Euryanassa, wife of Phylax, mother of Iphikles, mother of Phaethon by Helios (*Od.* 11.326 and scholia; Eust. 1688.65), mother of Alkippe, called Etioklymene by Stesichorus (frg. 238 *PMG* = schol. AR. 1.230–33, where her mother is also said to be Klytodora). In the *Nostoi* she is mother of Iphikles by Kephalos (Paus. 10.29.6). According to Apollodorus, she is the wife of Iasos or of Schoineus and the mother of Atalante (3.9.2).
6) Amazon (Hyg. *Fab.* 163). See Periklymene.
7) mother of Homer, according to the inhabitants of the island of Ios (Paus. 10.24.2). But see Polykaste (2), Themisto (2).
8) See Alkimede.
9) See Rhode (1).

KLYTEMNESTRA (or Klytaimestra) daughter of Tyndareos (*Od.* 24.199), and Leda (Aesch. *Ag.* 914), sister of Helen, Timandra, Phylonoe, and the Dioskouroi. In some versions she was first married to Tantalos (Paus. 2.22.3), before marriage to Agamemnon, by whom she is the mother of Orestes and various daughters: Iphimede and Elektra (Hes. *Cat.* 23); Chrysothemis, Laodike, and Iphianassa (*Iliad* 9.145, 287). Elsewhere, Iphigeneia is included (possibly = Iphimede or Iphianassa). Her adultery with Aigisthos and the murder of Agamemnon (*Od.* 3.195, 264; 4.512, etc.; Hes. *Cat.* 176). Motives for her faithlessness: Aphrodite's curse on Tyndareos (Stesich. frg. 223 *PMG* = schol. Eur. *Or.* 249), Agamemnon's murder of her first husband (Eur. *I.A.* 1150), or his sacrifice of Iphigeneia (Pindar *Pyth.* 11).

KLYTIE

1) *Okeanid (Hes. *Theog.* 352).

2) beloved of Helios, rival of Leukothoe, changed into a heliotrope (Ovid *Met.* 4.206–70). See Leukothoe.

3) See Kameiro.

KLYTIPPE daughter of Thespios, mother of Eurykapus by Herakles (Apollod. 2.7.8).

KLYTODORA wife of Minyas, mother of Presbon, Periklymene, and Etioklymene (schol. AR. 1.230). See Klymene (5).

KOMAITHO

1) daughter of Pterelaos king of the Teleboans, she betrays her father and country for love of Amphitryon, who kills her (Apollod. 2.4.7).

2) (Patrai) priestess of Artemis Triklaria. Her sexual union with Melanippos pollutes temple, and they are sacrificed to end plague (Paus. 7.19.1–10). See Redfield (1990).

KOMBE daughter of Asopos, the river god, also called Chalkis, eponym of city in Euboia (Eust. 279.8; Diod. 4.72), wife of Sakos, mother of the Euboian Korybantes, flees husband to Athens. Another version, transformed into a "Chalkis" bird (Ovid *Met.* 7.383).

KORKYNE nurse of Ariadne, her tomb in Naxos (Plut. *Thes.* 20.5).

KORONIDES. See Menippe (3).

KORONIS

1) daughter of the Lapith Phlegyas, beloved of Apollo, pregnant by him with Asklepios (*Hom. Hymn* 16.2), she marries Ischys. Apollo is informed by a crow (Hes. *Cat.* 60 = schol. Pindar *Pyth.* 3.48). Apollo or Artemis kills her, but Asklepios is rescued by Hermes. Elsewhere called Arsinoe (1) (Paus. 2.26.7); Aigle (Isyllos *Paian* E 46 Powell). Honored in the Asklepion at Titane (Paus. 2.11.7). See Arsinoe (1).

2) One of the Hyades (Hes. frg. 291).

KREOUSA

1) *Naiad, daughter of Okeanos and Gaia, mother of Hypseus and Stilbe by Peneios (Pindar *Pyth.* 9.16 with schol. to l.27; Diod. 4.69.1).

2) (Attica) daughter of Erechtheus and Praxithea, mother of Ion by Xuthos or Apollo (Eur. *Ion*; Strabo 8.7.1). According to Euripides, her sisters are Pro-

kris and Chthonia, but some accounts have four or six sisters. See Oreithyia (2) and Pandora (5).

3) daughter of Kreon of Thebes, intended wife of Jason, killed by her rival Medea (schol. Eur. *Medea.* 19,404, and hypothesis). Nameless in Euripides, she is called Glauke elsewhere. See Glauke (2).

4) daughter of Priam and Hekabe, wife of Aineias, mother of Ascanius (Vergil and Livy). Depicted in Delphi among the captive Trojan women (Paus. 10.26.1).

KRINO

1) daughter of Antenor, painted by Polygnotos (Paus. 10.27.4).

2) mother of Kallidike (3), Oime, Kelaino (3), and Hyperippe (2) by Danaos (Apollod. 2.1.5).

KTIMENE

1) sister of Odysseus, daughter of Antikleia (*Od.* 15.363ff.). Sometimes considered wife of Eurylochos (schol. *Od.* 10.441). According to Athenaios, called Phake (Lentil) or Kallisto (4.158c–d).

2) daughter of Phegeus, seduced by Hesiod, who is then killed by her brothers, said to be the mother of Stesichorus. Also called Klymene (Tzetzes *Vit. Hes.* 18; Plut. *Sept. sap. conviv.* 19.162d–f; *Cert. Hom. et Hes.* 214ff.).

KYDIPPE

1) mother of Kleobis and Biton (Hdt. 1.31; Paus. 2.20.3), named (Hyg. *Fab.* 254).

2) daughter of Keyx, wife of Akontios (Callim. *Aitia* frg. 67–75 Pfeiffer).

3) daughter of Ochimos and Rhodo or Rhode, later called Kyrbia, eponym of Kyrbe. She is the mother of Lindos, Ielusos, and Kameiros, by her paternal uncle Kerkaphos (schol. Pindar *Ol.* 7.131, 132, 135). Or mother is the nymph Hegetoria (Diod. 5.56–57). Plutarch tells the story of her illicit romance with her uncle (*Quaest. Gr.* 27, 297c–d).

KYRBIA. See Kydippe (3).

KYRENE *Nymph, beloved of Apollo, mother of Aristaios, eponym of N. African colony (Pindar *Pyth.* 9 with scholia quoting Hes. = frg. 215).

LABDA (Corinth) daughter of Amphion, one of the Bacchiades. Because of her lameness, rejected by nobles, marries Eetion. Mother of Kypselos, who tries to rule Corinth (Hdt. 5.92).

LAKAINA "Spartan woman," used alone always means Helen.

LAMACHE a Lemnian woman, mother of Leukophanes (ancestor of Battos) by the Argonaut Euphemos (schol. Pindar *Pyth.* 4.455).

LAMIA daughter of Poseidon, mother of the first Sibyl by Zeus (Paus. 10.12.1), mother of Skylla (Stesich. frg. 220 *PMG* = schol. AR. 4.825–31; Plut. *De def. orac.* 398c).

LAMPSAKE eponym of Lampsakos, first honored as heroine, then given divine honors (Plut. *De mul. virt.* 255e; Polyaen. 8.37).

LANASSA daughter of Kleodaios, granddaughter of Hyllus, wife of Neoptolemos (Plut. *Pyrrhus* 1.2).

LAODAMEIA
   1) daughter of Bellerophon, mother of Sarpedon by Zeus, she is killed by Artemis (*Iliad* 6.196ff.; Apollod. 3.1.1).
   2) daughter of Akastos, wife of Protesilaos (Eur. *Protesilaos*). But according to the *Kypria*, his wife was Polydora (4), daughter of Meleager (Paus. 4.2.7).
   3) daughter of Amyklas king of Lakedaimon, wife of Arkas, mother of Triphylos, Tegean hero (Paus. 10.9.5). See Leaneira.
   4) Orestes' nurse, according to Stesichorus. Called Kilissa by Aeschylus (Stesich. frg. 218 *PMG* = schol. Aesch. *Choe*. 733) and Arsinoe by Pindar (Paus. 11.17).
   5) daughter of Alkmaion, wife of Peleus, mother of Polydora (3) (*Iliad* 16.175). But see Polymele (3), Polydora (3).
   6) See Iphthime.

LAODIKE
   1) daughter of Priam and Hekabe, wife of Helikaon (*Iliad* 3.122; 6.252). Elsewhere wife of Akamas (Parthen. 16), or Telephos (Hyg. *Fab*. 101), or Demophon, by whom she is mother of Mounychos (Plut. *Thes*. 34), or swallowed by the earth at the fall of Troy (Apollod. *Ep*. 5.23; Lycoph. 316 with schol. to 447).
   2) daughter of Agamemnon and Klytemnestra, with Chryothemis and Iphianassa (*Iliad* 9.145, 287). See Elektra (5).
   3) descendant of Agapenor of Paphos, sent peplos to Athena Alea in Tegea, founded temple of Aphrodite (Paus. 8.5.2f.; 8.53.7).
   4) See Hyperborean Maidens.
   5) daughter of Kinyras, wife of Elatos, mother of Stymphalos and Pereus (Apollod. 3.9.1).
   6) daughter of Aloeus, wife of Aiolos, mother of Salmoneus and Kretheus (schol. *Od*. 11.273).
   7) See Iphthime.
   8) daughter of Kyknos (schol. B *Iliad* 1.138).
   9) daughter of Iphis, mother of Kapaneus (schol. Eur. *Phoin*. 180).

LAOKOÖSA. See Arene.

LAOMACHE Amazon (Hyg. *Fab*. 163).

LAONIKE wife of Lebados founder of Lebadeia (Paus. 9.39.1).

LAONOME
   1) daughter of Guneos, wife of Alkaios, mother of Amphitryon (Paus. 8.14.2). Also mother of Anaxo. Elsewhere the mother is Astydameia (4), Lysidike (1), or Hipponome (Apollod. 2.4.5).
   2) daughter of Amphitryon and Alkmene, sister of Herakles and wife of Euphemos (schol. Pindar *Pyth*. 4.79; Tzetzes ad Lycoph. 886). She is the granddaughter of Laonome (1).

LAOPHONTE
   1) daughter of Pleuron and Xanthippe, sister of Agenor, Sterope, and Stratonike (Apollod. 1.7.7).
   2) See Eurythemis(te).

LAOTHOE

1) daughter of Thespios, mother of Antiphos by Herakles (Apollod. 2.7.8).

2) beloved of Apollo, mother of Thestor, grandmother of Kalchas (Pherec. schol. AR. 1.139).

3) daughter of Altes, wife of Priam, mother of Kykaon and Polydoros (*Iliad* 21.85, 22.48).

4) wife of Porthaon, mother of Sterope, Stratonike, Eurythemiste (Hes. *Cat.* 26).

5) wife of the Trojan Klytios (Tzetzes ad *Hom.* 437f.6).

6) daughter of Manetos, mother by Hermes of the Argonauts Erytos and Echion (Orph. *Arg.* 135f.). Elsewhere, their mother is Antianeira (AR. 1.56).

LARISA daughter of Pelargos, eponym of three cities (Paus. 2.24.1).

LARYMNA (Boiotia) daughter of Kynos, eponym of Boiotian city (Paus. 9.23.7).

LATHRIA daughter of Thersandros, she and her twin sister Anaxandra marry the twin sons of Aristodemos, become foremothers of the Spartan kings. Their tomb is near the sanctuary of Lykourgos in Sparta (Paus. 3.16.6).

LEANDRIS wife of Anaxandros, who establishes a cult of Thetis, when her priestess Kleo is captured with an image (*xoanon*) of the goddess (Paus. 3.14.4).

LEANEIRA daughter of Amyklas, mother of Elatos and Aphidas by Arkas. Other versions give the mother as either Meganeira (for Metaneira?), daughter of Kroko, or the nymph Chrysopeleia (Apollod. 3.9.1). See also Laodameia (3).

LEDA daughter of Thestios and Eurythemis(te), wife of Tyndareos. Mother of Timandra, Klytemnestra, Phylonoe (Hes. *Cat.* 23), Kastor, Polydeukes, and Helen (schol. Eur. *Or.* 457). There are differing traditions about the fathers of these children, but according to Apollodoros, Polydeukes and Helen are the children of Zeus, who came to Leda as a swan, while Kastor and Klytemnestra are the children of Tyndareos (3.10.7). The *Homeric Hymns* call them the Tyndaridai, sons of Zeus (*Hom. Hymn* 17, 33), although at *Od.* 11.298ff. they are both sons of Tyndareos. According to Plutarch, Leda is also known as Mnesinoe (*De Pyth. Orac.* 401b).

LEIMONE (Athens) daughter of Hippomenes, walled up with a horse as punishment for a sexual transgression (Aeschines *In Timarchos 182;* Ovid *Ibis* 333, 457). Called Leimonis by Callimachus (frg. 94 Pfeiffer).

LEIPEPHILE(NE) daughter of Iolaus, wife of Phylas, mother of Hippotes and Thero. Through Thero, the grandmother of Chairon, eponym of Chaironeia (Paus. 9.40.6 = Hes. frg. 252).

LEIS (Troizen) daughter of Oros, mother of Althepos by Poseidon (Paus. 2.30.5).

LELANTE wife of Mounichos, king of the Molossians, mother of Alkandros, Megaletor, Philaios, and Hyperippe, changed to a bird (Ant. Lib. 14).

LEMNIAN women. See Hypsipyle(ia).

LEO KORAI (or Leoides) Phasithea (alternate forms: Phrasithea, Praxithea), Theope, and Euboule, the daughters of Leos, eponymous hero of one of the Athenian tribes. He allows them to be sacrificed to end a plague or famine in obedience to an oracle (Paus. 1.5.2). The Leokoreion, a shrine in the Athenian agora, may commemorate them (schol. Dem. 54.7; schol. Thuc. 1.20; Hesych. s.v. Λεοκόριον, Aelian *Varia Historia* 12.28), although it is possible that the heroines are back-formations derived from the name of the shrine. Sources are collected in Wycherley (1957) 108ff.

LEPREA (Elis) daughter of Pyrgeus, founds Lepreus (Paus. 5.5.5).

LETHAIA wife of Olenos, both changed into stone columns after she challenges a goddess to a beauty contest (Ovid *Met.* 10.68–71).

LEUKIPPE
1) playmate of Persephone (*Hom. Hymn* 2.418).
2) one of the daughters of Minyas, together with her sisters Alkathoe and Arsinoe (Plut. *Quaest. Gr.* 38, 299e) or Arsippe (Ant. Lib. 10), she offends either Hera or Dionysos and is driven to kill her son Hippasos. Ovid calls her Leuconoe (*Met.* 4.168).
3) wife of Thestios, mother of Iphikles the Argonaut (Hyg. *Fab.* 14; Bacchyl. 5.128).
4) wife of Laomedon, mother of Priam (Pherec. I 95 *FHG* frg. 99; schol. Lycoph. 18), also called Strymo or Plakia (Apollod. 3.12.3). (In Hyg. *Fab.* 250, she is the mother of Laomedon.)
5) daughter of Thestor (Hyg. *Fab.* 190). But see also Zeuxippe (3).
6) wife of Euenor and mother of Kleito in Plato's myth of Atlantis (*Crito* 113c).

LEUKIPPIDES daughters of Leukippos stolen by the Dioskouroi. At their sanctuary in Lakonia, young girls also known as Leukippides serve as priestesses (Paus. 3.16.1). See Hilaira, Phoibe (2).

LEUKONOE
1) daughter of Phosphoros, mother of Philammon by Apollo (Hyg. *Fab.* 161). Elsewhere his mother is Philonis or Chione (2).
2) See Leukippe (2).

LEUKOPHRYNE (various spellings) Clement considers her a separate figure buried in the temple of Artemis in Magnesia (Clem. Al. *Protr.* 3.39), but elsewhere the name appears as an epithet of the goddess (*Etym. Mag.* 565.16; 599.36).

LEUKOTHEA. See Ino.

LEUKOTHEAI *the Nereids (Alc. frg. 4a Campbell).

LEUKOTHOE daughter of Orchamos, king of Persia, and Eurynome, beloved of Apollo and mother of Thersanor. Her rival Klytie betrays her to her father, who buries her alive. Apollo turns her into a frankincense bush (Hes. frg. 351; Ovid *Met.* 4.190ff.; Hyg. *Fab.* 14).

LEUKTRIDES the daughters of Leuktros, who are raped by Spartans and curse Sparta before committing suicide. Their tomb at Leuktra was known as the *mnēma tōn parthenōn* (tomb of the maidens) and was later the site of a military disaster for Sparta. The same story is told of the daughters of Skedasos. Diodoros includes both groups in his version (Diod. 15.54.2–3; Xen. *Hell.* 6.4.7). See Molpia.

LIBYE daughter of Epaphos and Memphis, mother of Agenor and Belos by Poseidon. Mother of Lelex by Poseidon (Paus. 1.44.3). Eponym of Libya (Hdt. 4.45; Apollod. 2.1.4).

LOKRIAN MAIDENS young women sent to Troy to expiate the crime of Aias. See Kleopatra (4), Periboia (3).

LOXO Hyperborean, sister of Hekaerge and Opis, connection with cult of Apollo at Delos, sacrifice of hair at marriage (Callim. *Hymn* 4.292), perhaps indicates "partner of Loxias."

LYKO. See Karya.

LYSE daughter of Thespios, mother of Eumedes by Herakles (Apollod. 2.7.8).

LYSIANASSA
1) *Nereid (Apollod. 1.2.7).
2) daughter of Polybos, wife of Talaos (Paus. 2.6.6). See Lysimache (1) for another version.
3) daughter of Epaphos, mother of Bousiris by Poseidon (Apollod. 2.5.2).

LYSIDIKE
1) daughter of Pelops and Hippodameia, sister of Astydameia and Nikippe (1) (Hes. *Cat.* 190), marries one of Perseus' sons, bears either a) Hippothoe to Mestor and Taphios to Poseidon (Apollod. 2.4.5), b) Amphitryon to Alkaios (Paus. 8.14.2), or c) Alkmene to Elektryon (Plut. *Thes.* 7). See Astydameia (3), Hipponome, and Laonome (1) for alternate versions of b).
2) one of the companions of Theseus and Ariadne on the François vase (Flor. Mus. Arch. 4209).
3) daughter of the Lapith Koronos, wife of Telemonian Aias, mother of Philios (Tzetzes ad Lycoph. 53).
4) daughter of Thespios, mother of Teles by Herakles (Apollod. 2.7.8).

LYSIMACHE
1) daughter of Abas, wife of Argive king Talaos (Paus. 2.6.6 calls her Lysianassa). Mother of Adrastos, Parthenopaios, Eriphyle, etc. (Apollod. 1.9.13).
2) daughter of Priam (Apollod. 3.12.5).

LYSIPPE
1) daughter of Proitos and Stheneboia (mother called Anteia in *Iliad* 6.160). With sisters Iphianassa and Iphinoe, struck mad for impiety, cured by Melampos, marries his brother Bias (Apollod. 2.2.2 = Hes. *Cat.* 131).
2) daughter of Thespios, mother of Erasippos by Herakles (Apollod. 2.7.8).

LYTAIA one of Hyakinthides, sacrificed with her sisters Antheis, Aigleis, and Orthaia in Athens (Apollod. 3.15.8).

MAIA one of the seven Pleiades, the daughters of Pleione and Atlas (Apollod. 3.10.1). See Pleione.

MAIRA
1) *Nereid (*Iliad* 18.48).

2) (Argos) daughter of Proitos and Anteia, companion of Artemis, who kills her because she bears a son Lokros to Zeus (*Od.* 11.326 and Pherec. in schol. A).

3) (Arcadia) daughter of Atlas, wife of Tegeates son of Lykaon, buried with him in Tegea (Paus. 8.48.6), or in town in Arcadia called Maira (Paus. 8.12.7). Together they sacrifice to Apollo and Artemis (Paus. 8.53.3). Dancing place (*choros*) of Maira (Paus. 8.8.1).

4) *a dog belonging to the heroine Erigone (1).

MAKARIA daughter of Herakles and Deianeira, she sacrifices herself for victory over Eurysthenes, spring named for her near Marathon (Eur. *Herakleidai*; Paus. 1.32.6).

MAKRIS daughter of Aristaios, nurse of Dionysos (AR. 4.1131ff.). But see Nysa.

MANTO

1) daughter of Tereisias (schol. AR. 1.308; at Diod. 4.66.5 called Daphne), mother of Mopsos by Rhakios or Apollo, of Amphilochis and Teisiphone by Alkmaion (Paus. 9.33.2—one version). Founds oracle of Apollo in Asia Minor. Chair in Ismenion in Thebes (Paus. 9.10.3). Gives command to found Phaselis (Athen. 7.298a).

2) daughter of Polyidos (Hes. *Cat.* 136), sister of Astykrateia, grave at Megara (Paus. 1.43.5).

3) daughter of Melampous. See Iphianeira (1).

MARPESSA

1) daughter of Aitolian river-god Evenos and Alkippe. Carried off by Idas, then Apollo. Idas wins her from Apollo by force, or Marpessa chooses Idas herself (schol. BT *Iliad* 9.557 citing Simonides = frg. 563 *PMG*; Bacchyl. 19; Apollod. 1.7.9; Paus. 5.18.3). Mother of Kleopatra (*Iliad* 9.556; Apollod. 1.8.2). Kills herself on the death of her husband (Paus. 4.2.7).

2) pseudo-historical figure, leads Tegean women vs. Spartans. Connected with stele of Ares Gynaikothoinas, her weapons in temple of Athena Alea (Paus. 8.48.4–5). Also called Choira, Perimede (Deinias *FGrH* 306 F 4).

MARSE daughter of Thespios, mother of Boukolos by Herakles (Apollod. 2.7.8).

MEDA

1) wife of Idomeneus, seduced and murdered by Leukos, together with her daughter Kleisithyra (Apollod. *Ep.* 6.10).

2) See Iphthime.

3) daughter of Phylas, wife of Herakles, mother of Antiochos, eponym of Attic phyle Antiochis (Paus. 1.5.2; 10.10.1).

MEDEA (or Medeia) daughter of Aietes and Idyia or Neaira (4), and granddaughter of Helios (Hes. *Theog.* 961). Elsewhere Hekate is her mother and Kirke her sister (Diod. 4.45.3). When Jason comes to steal the golden fleece from her father, she goes with him, aiding him by murders of her brother Absyrtos and of Jason's enemy Pelias. She is often described as a witch, with the knowledge of poisons, and potions to rejuvenate and to cause fertility. Later abandoned by Jason for the daughter of Kreon, king of Corinth (see Glauke [2]; Kreousa [3]), she takes revenge by killing the king and his daughter, followed by her own children (variously named, see Paus. 2.3.6–11). She goes to Athens, where she is wife of Aigeus. In some versions her children are killed by the Corinthians (schol. Eur. *Medea* 264). In Thessaly she is connected with the worship of Hekate, in Corinth with Hera and Aphrodite (Plut. *De Herodot. malig.* 871b). Cult of her children in Corinth at the temple of Hera Akraia (Paus. 2.3.7–8; Eur. *Medea* 1378ff.). A number of alternate traditions surround her: that she ruled in Corinth with Jason (Simon. frg. 545 = schol. Eur. *Medea* 19), that she rejuvenated Jason (Simon. frg. 548 *PMG* = Hypothesis Eur. *Medea*), and that she was married to Achilles in the Elysian fields (schol. AR. 4.814–5 citing Ibycus and Simonides; Apollod. *Ep.* 5.5).

MEDESIKASTE

1) daughter of Priam, betrothed to Imbrios (*Iliad* 13.173). Among the Trojan captives in Polygnotos' painting (Paus. 10.25.9).

2) daughter of Laomedon, sister of Priam (Apollod. *Ep.* 6.15c). With her sisters Aithilla and Astyoche (4), sets the Greek fleet on fire (schol. Lycoph. 921). See Aithilla.

MEDOUSA

1) daughter of Priam (Stesich. frg. 204 *PMG* = Paus. 10.26.9; Apollod. 3.12.5).

2) See Astymedousa.

3) daughter of Pelias (Hyg. *Fab.* 24).

4) daughter of Orsilochos, wife of Polybos (Pherec. in schol. Soph. *O.T.* 775).

5) *Gorgon, mortal sister of Stheno and Euryale, who are immortal (Apollod. 2.4.2).

6) wife of Pisidos, claims greater beauty than Athena, who sends Perseus to kill her (schol. Lycoph. 838).

MEGAKLO daughter of Makar, king of Lesbos (Arnob. 4.24).

MEGAMEDE daughter of Arneus, wife of Thespios, and mother of the fifty daughters with whom Herakles had fifty sons (Apollod. 2.4.10). According to Diodoros (4.29.2) the daughters are by various unnamed mothers. See daughters of Thespios.

MEGARA daughter of Kreon of Thebes, wife of Herakles (*Od.* 11.269; Pindar *Isth.* 4.64), mother of the children he kills; in some versions she is killed by him as well (Eur. *Herak.*). Their children: Therimachos, Deikoön, and Kreontides (schol. *Od.* 9.269; Apollod. 2.7.8). A fourth son, Deion, is mentioned by Deinias (schol. Pindar *Isth.* 4.104). A memorial to them in Thebes (Paus. 9.11.2).

MEKIONIKE mother of Euphemos by Poseidon (Hes. frg. 253 = schol. Pindar *Pyth.* 4.36).

MELAINA. See Melantho (1).

MELANIPPE

1) daughter of Aiolos and Hippe (2), or Okyr(r)hoe and Apollo (Eur. frg. 482 Nauck), mother of Aiolos and Boiotos by Poseidon. She is the protagonist of two plays by Euripides (frgs. 480–514 Nauck). In the first, *Melanippe De-*

smōtis (*Captive*), she is sent into exile at the home of the king of Metapontos, where her sons are born and exposed. Reared by shepherds, they overcome a plot against them by the queen, Theano, who commits suicide. They are restored to their mother, who marries the king. Diodoros calls her Arne (4.67). In the second play, *Melanippe the Wise*, the children are apparently exposed closer to home and discovered by Melanippe's father, who is reconciled to them by divine intervention.

2) Amazon, daughter of Ares, sister of Antiope (AR. 2.966) carried off by Herakles, also called Antiope or Hippolyte (Apollod. *Ep.* 1.16). See Antiope (2), Hippolyte (1).

3) daughter of Oineus and Althaia (Ant. Lib. 2 after Nicander).

MELANTHO
1) daughter of Deukalion, Poseidon mates with her in the form of a dolphin, she bears Delphos (schol. Aesch. *Eum.* 2; Tzetzes ad Lycoph. 208; Ovid *Met.* 6.120). According to Pausanias (10.6.3–4) Delphos' mother is also said to be Melaina, daughter of Kephisos; or Kelaino, daughter of Hyamos; or Thyia, daughter of Kastalios. See Thyia (1).

2) daughter of Dolios, one of the faithless maids in Odysseus' house (*Od.* 18.321).

MELIA. See Io.

MELIBOIA
1) See Chloris (2).
2) wife of Theseus and mother of Aias (Istros quoted in Athen. 13.557a).

MELINE daughter of Thespios, mother of Laomedon by Herakles (Apollod. 2.7.8).

MELITE
1) *Okeanid, companion of Persephone (*Hom. Hymn* 2.419).
2) *Nereid (*Iliad* 18.42; Hes. *Theog.* 247).
3) *Naiad, mother of Hyllos by Herakles (AR. 4.538).
4) eponymous heroine of the Attic deme Melite, daughter of Myrmex, beloved of Herakles who was there initiated into the lesser mysteries (Harpocration. *FHG* frg. 74 = Hes. *Cat.* 225). Or daughter of Hoples (schol. Eur. *Medea* 673; Athen. 13.556f.). But see Meta.

MEMPHIS mother of Kleite (2), Sthenele, and Chrysippe by Danaos (Apollod. 2.1.5).

MENIPPE
1) *Nereid (schol. AR. 4.58 = Hes. frg. 260).
2) daughter of Thamyris, mother of Orpheus (Tzetzes *Chil.* 1 [12] 309).
3) daughter of Orion, with her sister Metioche instructed in weaving by Athena. They sacrifice themselves to end plague in Boiotia and are honored with a sanctuary as the Koronides (Ant. Lib. 25 after Nicander and Corinna). Ovid (*Met.* 13.692–99) says that from their ashes arose two young men, known as the Coroni after their mothers, who would perpetuate the race.

MENIPPIS daughter of Thespios, mother of Entelides by Herakles (Apollod. 2.7.8).

MEROPE

1) daughter of Atlas (Hes. *Cat.* 169 = schol. Pindar *Nem.* 2.17), she and her six sisters take the name Pleiades from their mother Pleione (Apollod. 3.10.1), wife of Sisyphos, mother of Glaukos (Apollod. 1.9.3). See Pleione.

2) daughter of Oinopion and Helike, pursued by Orion (Erat. *Kat.* 32).

3) daughter of Arkadian Kypselos, wife of Kresphontes, then Polyphontes, mother of Aipytos (Apollod. 2.8.5).

4) See Periboia (4).

5) a daughter of Erechtheus and mother of Daidalos, according to the sole testimony of Kleidemos (Plut. *Thes.* 19.5 = Kleidemos *FGrH* 323 F 17).

MESSENE (Argos) daughter of Triopas, wife of Polykaon (Paus. 4.1.1), eponym of Messenia, together with Polykaon, establishes a cult of Zeus on Ithome (Paus. 4.3.9), brings Eleusinian mysteries to Andania (4.1.5, 8–9). Honored as a heroine at the founding of Messenia, her temple and statue (Paus. 4.31.11). Pausanias relates that the mythical king Glaukos was the first person to grant her heroic honors (4.3.9).

MESTRA daughter of Erysichthon, granddaughter of Helios (Hes. *Cat.* 43), has the gift of transformation (schol. Lycoph. 1393; Callim. *Hymn* 6 for story of Erysichthon). Also known as daughter of Aithon. Wife of Glaukos, mother of Eurypalos by Poseidon. Also called Hypermestra (Ant. Lib. 17 after Nicander).

META daughter of Hoples, first wife of Aigeus before Chalkiope and Medea (Apollod. 3.15.6). But see Melite.

METANEIRA

1) wife of king Keleos of Eleusis, mother of Kallidike, Kleidike, Demo, Kallithoe, and Demophoön, connection with cult of Demeter (*Hom. Hymn* 2.161). Her sanctuary on road between Eleusis and Megara (Paus. 1.39.1).

2) See Leaneira.

METIOCHE

1) Trojan captive, perhaps invented by Polygnotos (Paus. 10.26.2).

2) See Menippe (3).

MIDEIA

1) *Nymph, mother of Aspledon by Poseidon (Paus. 9.38.9ff.).

2) mother of Likymnios by Electryon (Pindar *Ol.* 7.29).

MILETIA. See Molpia.

MILYE daughter of Zeus or Ares, sister and wife of Solymos. They are both eponyms of the people called Solymoi or Milyai (Steph. Byz. s.v. Μιλύαι).

MINYADES the daughters of Minyas: Alkathoe, Leukippe (2) (or Leukonoe [2]), and Arsinoe (2) (or Arsippe). Pausanias (2.25.9) mentions "chambers" (*thalamoi*) of the daughters of Minyas, which may have been a cult-site. See under individual names.

MISE. See Baubo.

MNESINOE. See Leda.

MNESTRA Danaid, marries Aigios (Apollod. 2.1.5).

MOLI(O)NE wife of Aktor, mother of the twins Kteatos and Eurytos, known either as the Molionidai or the Aktoriones. Their father often given as Poseidon (Hes. *Cat.* 17 = schol. A. *Iliad* 11.750), born in a silver egg (Ibycus frg. 285 *PMG* = Athen. 2.57f–58a).

MOLPADIA

1) daughter of Staphylos and Chrysothemis, together with sisters Rhoio and Parthenos, leaps off cliff for letting pigs spoil father's wine, Apollo saves them. She becomes Hemithea, goddess of childbearing women in Kastabos. Offerings to her of hydromel, no wine, no pigs (Diod. 5.62–63).

2) Amazon who kills Antiope (Plut. *Thes.* 27). She is killed by Theseus and has a tomb in Athens (Paus. 1.2.1).

MOLPIA (Boiotia) daughter of Skedasos, raped by Spartans, together with her sister Hippo. They cursed Sparta before killing themselves. Epaminondas made sacrifice to S. and his daughters before the battle of Leuktra, at which Sparta suffered a serious defeat (Paus. 9.13.5–6; 9.14.3; Plut. *Amat. Narr.* 774d). Plutarch gives their names as Hippe and Miletia or Theano and Euxippe (773c). See Leuktrides.

MOTHONE daughter of Oineus, eponym of Mothone in Messenia, according to the inhabitants. Pausanias prefers to believe that the city takes its name from a rock (Paus. 4.35.1).

MYKENE daughter of Inachos and Melia (schol. *Od.* 2.120), wife of Arestor, eponym of Mykenai (Paus. 2.16.4f. citing the *Great Ehoiai*). Mentioned in *Od.* 2.120 with Tyro and Alkmene as exemplary heroines.

MYR(R)HINE

1) eponym of Lemnian city Myrrina, daughter of Kretheus, wife of Thoas (schol. AR. 1.601) or Amazon (Dion. Chalc. frg. 2 = *FHG* 4.393).

2) daughter of Teukros, wife of Dardanos. She is called "swift Myrina" in the *Iliad*, and her grave mound in the Troad is known as "Bateia" (*Iliad* 2.814; Strabo 12.8.6).

MYRMEX (or Myrmix) (Attika) beloved and antagonist of Athena, transformed into an ant, the origin of the Mymidons (Serv. *in Verg. Aen.* 4.402). Mother of Melite (4).

MYRTO

1) daughter of Menoitios, sister of Patroklos, mother of Eukleia by Herakles (Plut. *Arist.* 20.6).

2) woman who gave her name to the Sea of Myrto, according to the antiquarians of Euboia (Paus. 8.14.12).

NAUSIKAA daughter of Alkinoös and Arete, king and queen of the Phaiakians (*Od.* 6.17; Apollod. *Ep.* 7.25; Hyg. *Fab.* 125). A later tradition has her marry Telemachos (Eust. 1796.42 citing Aristotle and Hellanicus).

NEAIRA

1) *beloved of Helios, mother of Lampetie and Phaethousa (*Od.* 12.133).

2) wife of Strymon, mother of Euadne (Apollod. 2.1.2).

3) (Arkadia) daughter of Pereus, wife of Aleos, mother of Auge (Apollod. 3.9.1). Or wife of Autolykos (Paus. 8.4.6).

4) wife of Aietes, also called Idyia (schol. AR. 3.242).

5) daughter of Amphion and Niobe, also called Ethodaia (Apollod. 3.5.6).

NELO Danaid, marries Menemachos (Apollod. 2.1.5).

NEMEA daughter of Asopos, eponym of Nemea in the Argolid (Paus. 2.15.3).

NEPHELE

1) wife of Athamas, mother of Phrixos and Helle, rival of Ino (Apollod. 1.9.1; Hyg. *Fab.* 1–3) or Themisto. See Ino.

2) image made by Zeus to deflect Ixion from his attempt on Hera, by him, mother of the Centaur (Pind. *Pyth.* 2.36ff.; Diod. 4.12, 4.69).

NESO

1) *Nereid (Hes. *Theog.* 261).

2) daughter of Teukros, king of the Troad, wife of Dardanos, mother of Sybilla, Bateia, Erichthonios, and Ilos (Lycoph. 1465 with schol.; Arrian *FGrH* 156 F 95).

NIKAGORA historical figure from Sikyon, wife of Echetimos, founder of the cult of Asklepios in Sikyon, brought god in form of a snake to Epidauros (Paus. 2.10.3).

NIKE daughter of Thespios, mother of Nikodromos by Herakles (Apollod. 2.7.8).

NIKIPPE

1) daughter of Pelops and Hippodameia, sister of Asydameia and Lysidike (Hes. *Cat.* 190), wife of Sthenelos (Hes. *Cat.* 191), mother of Alkyone (3), Medousa (2) (or Astymedousa), and Eurystheus (Apollod. 2.4.5). Also called Antibia (schol. *Iliad* 19.119) or Archippe (Tzetzes *Chil.* ii.172, 192).

2) daughter of Thespios, mother of Antimachos by Herakles (Apollod. 2.7.8).

3) priestess of Demeter in Thessaly (Callim. *Hymn* 6.42).

NIOBE daughter of Tantalos, wife of Amphion (schol. BT. *Iliad* 24.602 cites alternate fathers and husbands), originally a companion of Leto (Sappho frg. 142 Lobel-Page), she boasts of having more children than the goddess. The exact number of children varies, with ten sons and daughters according to Hesiod, six of each according to Homer (Apollod. 3.5.6; list of names: schol. Eur. *Phoin.* 159). Apollo and Artemis kill all, or all but one son and one daughter, and Niobe turns to stone from grief (*Iliad* 24.599–620; Apollod. 3.5.6). Pausanias tells of the children's tomb at Thebes (9.16.7) and the temple to Leto erected by the survivors (2.21.9). See Chloris (2).

NONAKRIS wife of Lykaon, eponym of the Arcadian town (Paus. 8.17.6).

NYKTIMENE daughter of king Epopeus of Lesbos, seduced by her father, gives birth in the wild, is changed to an owl by Athena (Hyg. *Fab.* 204, 253; Ovid *Met.* 2.589–95).

NYSA daughter of Aristaios (Diod. 3.70.1), nurse of Dionysos (Terp. frg. 8 in

Lydus *Mens.* 4.51). Cult in Athens (*CIA* III 320, 351). On a vase by Sophilos (*dinos*, Athens, Nat. Mus. Akr. 587, c. 580), there is a group of women labeled *Nysai*, but this is most likely a misspelling for *Musai* (see Carpenter [1986] 9). See also Makris.

OGYGIA daughter of Amphion and Niobe (Apollod. 3.5.6).

OICHALIA wife of Melanaos, eponym of Oichalia in Messenia (Paus. 4.2.2).

OIME daughter of Danaos and Krino, marries Arbelos (Apollod. 2.1.5).

OINO. See Oinotrop(h)oi.

OINOE eponym of Oinoe, one of the four cities of the Marathonian Tetrapolis (Paus. 1.33.8).

OINONE
1) *Nymph, daughter of Kebren, sister of Asterope (2). The first wife of Paris, she fails to prevent him from going after Helen, refuses to heal his wounds, later repents but finds him dead and hangs herself (Apollod. 3.12.6; Conon *Narr.* 23; Parthen. 4).
2) daughter of Oineus (Tzetzes ad Lycoph. 57).

OINOTROP(H)OI Oino, Spermo, and Elais, daughters of Anios and Rhoio, and thus descendants of Dionysos and Apollo. They have the ability to turn whatever they touch into wine, grain, or oil (hence their names) and for this reason, the Atreides carried them off to provision the army at Troy (schol. *Od.* 6.164 citing Simonides). They prayed to Dionysos, who changed them to doves (Lycoph. 570ff.; Ovid *Met.* 13.650–74).

OKYALE Amazon (Hyg. *Fab.* 163).

OKYPETE daughter of Danaos and Pieria, marries Lampos (Apollod. 2.1.5).

OKYR(R)HOE
1) *Okeanid (Hes. *Theog.* 360).
2) companion of Persephone (*Hom. Hymn* 2.420). Perhaps same as (1).
3) daughter of the river god Imbrasos and Chesias. Raped by Apollo (AR. in Athen. 7.283e; Aelian *Historia animalium* 15.23, unnamed).
4) daughter of Cheiron, mother of Melanippe by Apollo, transformed by the gods into a horse because she prophesied to mortals (Eur. frg. 482; Ovid *Met.* 2.635–75; Erat. Kat. 18; Hyg. *Astr.* 2.18). Also called Hippe (2) or Hippo.

OLYMPOUSA daughter of Thespios, mother of Halokrates by Herakles (Apollod. 2.7.8).

OMPHALE daughter of Iardanos, ruler of Lydia after the death of her husband Tmolos (Apollod. 2.6.3). Herakles serves her for three years as punishment. Their son Agelaos, founder of a Lydian dynasty (Apollod. 2.7.8). Elsewhere, their son is Lamos (Diod. 4.31.8; Ovid *Her.* 9.53ff.).

OPIS. See Hyperborean Maidens.

OREIA daughter of Thespios, mother of Laomenes by Herakles (Apollod. 2.7.8).

OREITHYIA

1) *Nereid (*Iliad* 18.48).

2) (Attika) daughter of Erechtheus and Praxithea, carried off by Boreas. Mother of Kleopatra (1), and Chione (1), and the winged brothers Kalais and Zetes (Apollod. 3.15.1–2; AR. 1.212 with scholion citing Simonides and Pherecydes; Plato, *Phaidr.* 229bc). During the Persian Wars, the Athenians sacrificed to Boreas and Oreithyia at Chalcis (Hdt. 7.189). For her sisters, see Pandora (5).

ORPHE. See Karya.

ORTHAIA. See Lytaia.

ORSILOCHE(IA) name of Iphigeneia when made immortal (Ant. Lib. 27 after Nicander). According to Ammianus Marcellinus (22.8.34), an epithet of Artemis in the Tauric Chersonese.

ORSOBIA (Corinth) daughter of Deiphontes and Hyrnetho, who together with her father and brothers sets up a shrine to their sister Hyrnetho after she is killed. Wife of Pamphylos (Paus. 2.28.6). See Hyrnetho.

OTRERE Amazon, mother by Ares of Hippolyte (2) (Hyg. *Fab.* 30) and of Penthesileia. Or she is the daughter of Ares and Armenia (schol. A. *Iliad* 3.189). She built the temple of Diana (Artemis) of Ephesos (Hyg. *Fab.* 223, 225). See also Antiope (1), Melanippe (2).

PALLAS daughter of Triton, inadvertently killed by Athena, who made the Palladium in memory of her (Apollod. 3.12.3; schol. Lycoph. 355 and 519).

PALLENE

1) one of the daughters of Alkyoneus. See Alkippe (1).

2) daughter of Sithon and the nymph Mendeis, marries Kleitos despite father's opposition (theme of contest between suitors). (Parthen. 6; Conon 10). Wife of Dionysos (Nonnus *Dion.* 48.90ff.).

PAMMEROPE daughter of Keleos (Paus. 1.38.3). See Saisara.

PANDAREOS, DAUGHTERS OF. See Kameiro.

PANDORA

1) *epithet of Gaia (Philostr. *Apoll.* 6.39).

2) *goddess connected with Hekate (Orph. *Arg.* 980).

3) woman created and given to men as revenge for the theft of fire by Prometheus (Hes. *Theog.* 570–616; Hes. *WD* 81; Paus. 1.24.7; Apollod. 1.7.2).

4) daughter or wife of Deukalion, bore Graikos to Zeus (Hes. *Cat.* 2 = schol. AR. 3.1086; Hes. *Cat.* 5 = Lydus *de Mens* 1.13).

5) daughter of Erechtheus, who sacrifices herself together with her sister Protogeneia, known as the Hyakinthides or the Parthenoi (Phanodemos *FGrH* 325 F 4). Phanodemos lists four other daughters: Oreithyia, Prokris, Kreousa, and Chthonia. See Hyakinthides, Praxithea.

PANDROSOS

1) daughter of Kekrops and Aglauros (1), sister of Herse and Aglauros (2). Of the three sisters, she is the only one who obeys the injunction not to look in

the basket entrusted to them by Athena (Paus. 1.2.6; Apollod. 3.14.6). She had a shrine, the Pandroseion, on the Akropolis in Athens and an apparent role in the festival of the Arrephoria (Paus. 1.27.2). A drinking-song credits her for victory over the Persians (Athen. 15.694d). The name is also an epithet of Athena (schol. Aristoph. *Lys.* 439). See Aglauros, Herse (1).

PANOPE(IA)
  1) *Nereid (*Iliad* 18.45; Hes. *Theog.* 250).
  2) daughter of Thespios, mother of Threpsippas by Herakles (Apollod. 2.7.8).

PANTHALIS servant of Helen, in the painting by Polygnotos of the fall of Troy (Paus. 10.25.4).

PARIA mother of sons of Minos (Apollod. 3.1.2).

PARTHENIA sister of Phorbas and Periergos (Athen. 6.262f.).

PARTHENOPE daughter of Stymphalos, mother of Eueres by Herakles (Apollod. 2.7.8).

PARTHENOS sister of Molpadia and Rhoio. Her honors and sanctuary in Boubastos (Diod. 5.62). See Molpadia (1) and Rhoio (1).

PASIPHAE
  1) daughter of Helios and Perseis (AR. 3.999); mother of, among others, Androgeos, Ariadne, Phaidra (Apollod. 3.1.2); wife of Minos; mother of the Minotaur (Apollod. 3.15.8).
  2) the possessor of an oracle at Thalamai in Lakonia, identified by Plutarch (*Agis* 9) as either (a) the daughter of Atlas, mother of Ammon by Zeus, or (b) the daughter of Priam, usually called Kassandra, given name Pasiphae "because she declared her oracles to all," or (c) the daughter of Amyklas, called Daphne, who fled Apollo and became a tree with oracular powers. (For other references to the oracle, see Paus. 10.7.8; 8.20.2ff.; Parthen. 15). See also Daphne, Ino, Kassandra, Manto (1).

PATRO daughter of Thespios, mother of Archemachos by Herakles (Apollod. 2.7.8).

PEIRENE
  1) daughter of Acheloös, mother of Leches and Kenchrias by Poseidon (Paus. 2.2.3), or daughter of Asopos (Diod. 4.72), wife of Sisyphos (schol. Eur. *Medea* 69), eponym of spring (Paus. 2.5.1). Or transformed into a spring because of her tears over Kenchrias when he is killed accidentally by Artemis (Paus. 2.3.2). According to the *Great Ehoiai*, daughter of Oibalos (Paus. 2.2.3).
  2) Danaid, marries Agaptolemos (Apollod. 2.1.5).

PEISIDIKE
  1) daughter of Aiolos and Ainarete, wife of Myrmidon, mother of Antiphos and Aktor (Hes. *Cat.* 10a.33, 100; Apollod. 1.7.3–4).
  2) daughter of Nestor and Anaxibia (2), sister of Polykaste (Hes. *Cat.* 35, 36 restored; Apollod. 1.9.9) or she is the daughter of Pelias and Anaxibia (2) or Phylomache; her sisters are Polykaste, Pelopeia, Hippothoe, and Alkestis (Apollod. 1.9.10) or Medousa in place of Polykaste (Hyg. *Fab.* 24).

3) daughter of Lepethymnos in Methymna, betrayed town for love of Achilles, who had her stoned (Parthen. 21).

4) (Boiotia) daughter of Leukon, sister of Euippe and Hyperippe (Hes. *Cat.* 70.10 restored).

PEISIS Trojan captive, depicted by Polygnotos in the Lesche at Delphi (Paus. 10.26.2).

PELARGE (Boiotia) daughter of Potneios, together with husband Isthmiades revives cult of Kabeiroi, receives cultic honors (Paus. 9.25.7–8).

PELOPEIA

1) daughter of Pelias and Anaxibia (2) or Phylomache (Apollod. 1.9.10; Hyg. *Fab.* 24; AR. 1.326), mother by Ares of Kyknos (Apollod. 2.7.7).

2) daughter of Amphion and Niobe (Apollod. 3.5.6).

3) daughter of Thyestes who, acting on an oracle, begets Aigisthos by her, to be the avenger of the murder of Thyestes' other children (Apollod. *Ep.* 2.14; Hyg. *Fab.* 87, 88; schol. Eur. *Or.* 14).

PENELOPE daughter of Ikarios and Periboia, sister of Thoas, Damasippos, Imeusimos, Aletes, and Perileos (Apollod. 3.10.6; her mother is called Asterodia by Pherecydes, Polykaste daughter of Lygaios by Strabo 10.2.24). In the *Odyssey* she is sister of Iphthime, wife of Odysseus, and mother of Telemachos. Often connected with Arkadia, in some traditions she is mother of Pan by Hermes or Apollo (Pindar frg. 90; Hdt. 2.145, etc.) or by the suitors (with a possible pun on *pan* = "all," Lycoph. 772). Her grave in Mantineia (Paus. 8.12.6). In the *Telegony* she marries Telegonos, Odysseus' son by Kirke (Apollod. *Ep.* 37; *Telegony* p. 58 Kinkel).

PENTHESILEIA (Amazon) daughter of Otrere (schol. A. *Iliad* 3.189), fights with Trojans at end of war, killed by Achilles. His love for her told in the *Aithiopis* (p. 33 Kinkel; also Tzetzes ad Lycoph. 997, 999; Hyg. *Fab.* 112; Apollod. *Ep.* 5.1).

PERIBOIA

1) *Naiad, wife of Ikarios, mother of Penelope and five sons. Also called Asterodia (Strabo 10.2.24). See Polykaste (1), Penelope.

2) daughter of Eurymedon, mother of Nausithoös by Poseidon (*Od.* 7.57).

3) with Kleopatra (4), first of Lokrian maidens sent as expiation to Troy (Apollod. *Ep.* 6.20–21).

4) wife of Polybos of Corinth, foster-mother of Oidipous (Apollod. 3.5.7; Hyg. *Fab.* 66–67). In Sophocles and elsewhere called Merope.

5) daughter of Alkathoös of Megara, wife of Telemon, mother of Aias (schol. A. *Iliad* 16.14; Paus. 1.42.2). According to Plutarch, she is raped by Telemon, cast out by her father, and then rescued by Telemon (*Parall.* 27.312b). As a young girl, she is sent as tribute to Crete, Minos attempts to rape her during the voyage, and she is defended by Theseus (Bacchyl. *Ode* 17.8–16; Paus. 1.42,2; 1.17.3). Bacchylides and others (Paus. 1.6.45; Soph. *Aias* 569) call her E(e)riboia. She is depicted (as Epiboia) on the François vase (Flor. Mus. Arch. 4209). A Phereboia is listed among Theseus' wives (Pherec. in Athen. 13.557b). See *LIMC* s.v. "Eriboia."

6) daughter of Hipponous, second wife of Oineus, mother of Tydeus. According to Hesiod, she was sent to Oineus to be killed when her father discovered that she had been seduced by Hippostratos. But see Gorge (1).

PERIGUNE daughter of Sinis (killed by Theseus), mother by him of Melanippos. Theseus gave her to Deioneus, by whom she is the mother of Nisos of Megara (Plut. *Thes.* 8; Athen. 13.557a).

PERIKLYMENE daughter of Minyas and Klytodora, wife of Pheres, mother of Admetos (schol. AR. 1.230; Hyg. *Fab.* 14). Elsewhere called Klymene (schol. Eur. *Alk.* 16) or Etioklymene (Stesich. frg. 54). Or Etioklymene is her sister and the mother of Iphikles or Jason (schol. AR. 1.230). See Klymene (5).

PERIMEDE
1) daughter of Aiolos and Ainarete, sister of Amphitryon, mother of Hippodamas and Orestes by Acheloös, wife of Likymnios (Apollod. 1.7.3).
2) See Marpessa (2).
3) See Polymele.
4) See Agamede.

PERIMELE daughter of Admetos, wife of Argos, mother of Magnes (Ant. Lib. 23 = Hes. frg. 256; schol. Eur. *Alk.* 264).

PERIOPIS. See Polymele (4).

PERKOTE. See Kleite (1).

PERO
1) mother of Asopos by Poseidon (Apollod. 3.12.6 with other versions).
2) daughter of Neleus and Chloris (*Od.* 11.287; Hes. *Cat.* 37), wife of Bias, mother of the Argonauts Laodikos, Areios, Talaos.
3) See Xanthippe (2).

PERSE(IS) *daughter of Okeanos and Tethys, wife of Helios, mother of Aietes, Kirke, Pasiphae, Perses (*Od.* 10.139).

PHAIDRA daughter of Minos and Pasiphae (*Od.* 11.321), sister of Ariadne and Deukalion, second wife of Theseus, mother of Demophon and Akamas. Her love for Hippolytos brings about a rape accusation and suicide (Eur. *Hipp.*; Plut. *Thes.* 28; Diod. 4.62). Brought cult-images of Eileithyia from Crete (Paus. 1.18.5), founded temple of Aphrodite Kataskopia or the temple was renamed for her spying there on Hippolytos (Paus. 2.32.3). Her tomb at Troizen (Paus. 2.32.4). See Ariadne, Iope.

PHAKE. See Ktimene (1).

PHARTIS Danaid, marries Eurydamas (Apollod. 2.1.5). Possible corruption of Phainarete or Phare.

PHASITHEA. See Leo korai.

PHEMONOE first Pythia at Delphi, inventor of the hexameter (Paus. 10.5.7; Strabo 9.3.5). Daughter of Apollo (Pliny *NH* 10.3.7).

PHENO (Athens) daughter of Klytios, wife of Laomedon, mother of Zeuxippe (2) (Paus. 2.6.5).

PHEREBOIA. See Periboia (5).

PHERENIKE. See Kallipateira.

PHIALO daughter of Alkimedon, mother of Aichmagoras by Herakles, who rescues them when they are exposed by her father (Paus. 8.12.2–4).

PHILODAMEIA. See Kleodameia, Phylodameia.

PHILOMELE in Attic version of myth, daughter of Pandion and Zeuxippe, sister of Prokne, wife of Tereus. The sisters kill Itys to punish his father Tereus for the rape of Philomele and are changed into birds (*Od.* 19.518 with schol.; Sappho frg. 135 Lobel-Page; Soph. *Tereus* frgs. 523–38 Nauck; Apollod. 3.14.8; Hyg. *Fab.* 45). See Aedon, Prokne.

PHILONIS daughter of Deion, mother of Philammon by Apollo, and Autolykos by Hermes (Hes. *Cat.* 64). See Leukonoe (1), Chione (2).

PHILONOE daughter of Lydian king Iobates, betrothed to Bellerophon (Apollod. 2.3.2), also called Antikleia (4) (schol. Pindar *Ol.* 13.82), Kasandra (schol. A. *Iliad* 6.155). Also spelled Phylonoe.

PHILONOME daughter of Kragasos, second wife of Kyknos of Kolonai, accuses Kyknos' son by first marriage Tennes of sexual advances, and he is exiled. When Kyknos discovers the truth, he buries Philonome alive. (Paus. 10.14.2; Apollod. *Ep.* 3.24).

PHILYRA
    1) Okeanid, mother of Cheiron by Kronos (*Titan.* 8. Allen = schol. AR. 1.554).
    2) See Klymene (4).

PHOIBE
    1) *Titan, daughter of Ouranos and Gaia, mother of Leto, Asteria, Hekate by Koios (Hes. *Theog.* 136, 404).
    2) daughter of Leukippos, with her sister Hilaira, carried off by the Dioskouroi (Apollod. 3.10.3). Mother of Mnesilaos by Polydeukes (Apollod. 3.11.2). See Hilaira.

PHRASITHEA. See Leo korai.

PHRONIME (Crete) daughter of Etearchos, mother of Battos, founder of Kyrene (Hdt. 4.154f.).

PHTHIA
    1) daughter of Amphion and Niobe (Apollod. 3.5.6).
    2) girl from Aigion, visited by Zeus in the form of a pigeon (Athen. 9.395a citing Autokrates in his history of Achaia).

PHYLEIS daughter of Thespios, mother of Tigasis by Herakles (Apollod. 2.7.8).

PHYLO servant of Helen (*Od.* 4.125, 133).

PHYLODAMEIA Danaid, mother of Phares (Paus. 7.22.5). See Kleodameia.

PHYLOMACHE daughter of Amphion, wife of Pelias, mother of Akastos, Peisidike, Pelopeia, Hippothoe, and Alkestis, but see Anaxibia (2) (Apollod. 1.9.10).

PHYLOMEDOUSA wife of Areithoös, mother of Menestheus (*Iliad* 7.10).

PHYLONOE
1) daughter of Leda and Tyndareos, made immortal by Artemis (Hes. *Cat.* 23a.10–12; Apollod. 3.10.6), honored in Lakonia (Athenagoras 1).
2) See Philonoe.

PHYLONOME daughter of Nyktimos and Arkadia, a companion of Artemis. Seduced by Ares, mother of twins Lykastos and Parrhasios, rulers of Arkadia (Plut. *Parall.* 36, 314e).

PHYSADEIA
1) daughter of Danaos, eponym of spring in Argos (Callim. *H.* 5.47).
2) sister of Peirithoös stolen by the Dioskouroi with Aithra (Hyg. *Fab.* 79); also called Klymene (2).

PHYSKOA beloved of Dionysos, mother by him of Narkaios, with whom she founds the cult of Dionysos in Elis. She is honored at Olympia with a chorus (Paus. 5.16.6–7). Her name is perhaps connected with the city of Physkos where a similar chorus was set up in honor of Dionysos (see no. 181 in Sokolowski [1969] 318–19).

PIERIA
1) *Naiad, mother of six of the Danaids (Apollod. 2.1.5).
2) wife of Oxylos, mother of Aitolos and Laios. Aitolos received hero cult in Elis (Paus. 5.4.4).

PITANE mother of Euadne by Poseidon (Pindar *Ol.* 6.46ff. with scholia).

PLAKIA. See Leukippe (4).

PLATAIA (Boiotia) wife or fictive wife of Zeus, *aition* of festival of the Daidala, her heroon at Plataia (Paus. 9.3.1–9).

PLEIADES the daughters of Atlas and Pleione. They are sometimes called the Peleiades, "doves" (Simon. frg. 555 *PMG*; Athen. 11.489e–491d). See Pleione.

PLEIONE Okeanid, wife of Atlas, mother of the Pleiades (schol. Pindar *Nem.* 2.17; Apollod. 3.10.1; Hyg. *Astr.* 2.21). Apollodoros lists the Pleiades as Alkyone, Merope, Kelaino, Elektra, Sterope, Taygete, and Maia, also referring to them as the Atlantides (see also Hes. *WD* 382). See also Hesione (3).

PODARKE daughter of Danaos and Pieria, marries Oineus (Apollod. 2.1.5).

POLYBOIA
1) sister of Hyakinthos, carried to heaven with him (Paus. 3.19.4). Hesychius (s.v. Πολύβοια) calls her a goddess identified with Artemis or Kore.
2) daughter of Oikles and Hypermestra (2), sister of Iphianeira (2) and Amphiaraos (Diod. 4.68).

POLYDAMNA wife of Thon, an Egyptian woman who gives Helen healing drugs (*Od.* 4.228).

POLYDORA
1) *Okeanid (Hes. *Theog.* 354).

2) Danaid, mother of Dryops by Spercheios (Ant. Lib. 32 after Nicander). But see Dia (3).

3) daughter of Peleus and Polymele (3), half-sister of Achilles, wife of Boros, mother of Menesthios by him or by the god Spercheios (*Iliad* 16.173ff.; Hes. *Cat.* 213). Also called Kleodora (Zenodotus cited in schol. T. *Iliad* 16.175). Elsewhere she is the daughter of Peleus and Antigone (1) (Apollod. 3.13.1) or Eurydike (10) or Laodameia (5) (schol. AT. *Iliad* 16.175). Elsewhere (3.13.4) Apollodorus has Polydora the daughter of Perieres as wife of Peleus, but this may be a confusion with Polymele (3).

4) daughter of Meleager and Kleopatra (2), wife of Protesilaos (Paus. 4.2.7 after the *Kypria*), elsewhere called Laodameia.

5) Amazon (Hyg. *Fab.* 163).

6) See Arene.

POLYKASTE

1) (Akarnania) daughter of Lygaios, wife of Ikarios, mother of Penelope (Strabo 10.2.24), but see Periboia (1).

2) daughter of Nestor and Eurydike (3) or Anaxibia (2), bathes Telemachos (*Od.* 3.464f.). Bears him a son, Perseptolis (Hes. *Cat.* 221). Later tradition makes her Homer's mother, also called Epikaste (*Cert. Hom. et Hes.* 39). But see Klymene (7), Themisto (2).

3) daughter of Aethlios and Kalyke, wife of Elektor (Hes. *Cat.* 10a).

POLYKRITE (Naxos) saves her city by seducing Diognotos, the enemy leader, accidently killed, buried with Diognotos, receives yearly sacrifice (Polyaen. 8.36; Parthen. 9).

POLYMEDE

1) See Polymele (1).

2) wife of Neleus, mother of Nestor (Tzetzes *Alleg. Iliad* 1.96). But see Chloris (2).

POLYMELE

1) daughter of Autolykos, wife of Aison, mother of Jason, also called Polymede (Apollod. 1.9.16), Alkimede, Polypheme (Hes. *Cat.* 38 = schol. *Iliad* 12.69), Perimede, Amphinome (Diod. 4.50.1 where she commits heroic suicide when threatened by Pelias). Her mother is Neaira (Paus. 8.4.6). See Alkimede.

2) daughter of Phylas, mother of Eudoros by Hermes, wife of Echekles (*Iliad* 16.180).

3) daughter of Aktor, wife of Peleus before Thetis, mother of Polydora (3). (Pherec. in schol. *Iliad* 16.175).

4) daughter of Peleus, wife of Menoitios, mother of Patroklos, although some say his mother is Sthenele or Periopis (Apollod. 3.13.8).

POLYPHEME. See Polymele (1).

POLYPHONTE daughter of Hipponoös and Thrassa, granddaughter of Ares, companion of Artemis. She offends Aphrodite, who causes her to mate with a bear, by whom she has two monstrous sons, Agrios and Oreios. They are all transformed into birds (Ant. Lib. 21 after Boios).

POLYXENE daughter of Priam and Hekabe, sacrificed on Achilles' tomb by his son Neoptolemos. Sometimes Achilles is said to have been in love with her (schol. Lycoph. 323). The episode is not in Homer but appears in art (Tyrrhenian neck-amphora, *LIMC* s.v. "Polyxene" 26; also *Iliou Persis* p. 50 Kinkel; Ibycus frg. 307 *PMG*; Eur. *Hekabe*; Apollod. *Ep.* 5.23). Sophocles wrote a *Polyxene*, now lost.

POLYXO
1) *Naiad, wife of Danaos, mother of several of the Danaids (Apollod. 2.1.5).
2) wife of Nykteus, mother of Antiope (1) (Apollod. 3.10.1).
3) Argive, companion of Helen, wife of Tlepolemos. Later hangs her in revenge for the death of her husband in Trojan War (Paus. 3.19.9), giving rise to the cult of Helen Dendritis.
4) nurse of Hypsipyle (AR. 1.668).

PRAXITHEA
1) (Attika) daughter of Kephisos, wife of Erechtheus, mother of Prokris, Chthonia, and Kreousa (Eur. *Erechtheus* frgs. passim: Chthonia and two unnamed sisters); also Oreithyia, Kekrops, Pandoros, and Metion (Apollod. 3.15.1), Pandora (5), and Protogeneia. One or more of her daughters is sacrificed to save city (Eur. *Erechtheus* frgs. 349–70 Nauck; Phanod. *FGrH* 325 F 4). Elsewhere she is the daughter of Phrasimos and Diogeneia (2) (Apollod. 3.15.1).
2) *Naiad, wife of Erichthonios, mother of Pandion (Apollod. 3.14.6), some confusion with (1).
3) See Leo korai.
4) daughter of Thespios, mother of Nephos by Herakles (Apollod. 2.7.8).
5) possibly daughter of Keleos and Metaneira, discovers Demeter putting Demophoön in the fire and cries out (Apollod. 1.5.1).

PROITIDES daughters of Proitos and Sthenboia (or Anteia) driven mad for impiety. See Lysippe (1), Iphianassa (1), Iphinoe (3).

PROKLEIA daughter of Klytios, sister of Kaletor, wife of Kyknos of Kolonai, mother of Tennes and Hemithea (Paus. 10.14.2).

PROKNE daughter of Pandion and Zeuxippe, sister of Philomele, wife of Tereus. The sisters kill Prokne's son Itys in revenge for Tereus' rape of Philomele and are tranformed into birds. At Daulis in Phokis, there was a sanctuary of Athena with a statue brought by Prokne (Paus. 10.4.9). See Philomele for sources. See Aedon for another version of the myth.

PROKRIS
1) (Attika) daughter of Erechtheus and Praxithea, sister of Kreousa and Chthonia (Eur. *Erechtheus* frg. 357 Nauck, where she is unnamed). In other versions she is one of four (Apollod. 3.15.1) or six sisters (Phanod. *FGrH* 325 F 4). See Oreithyia and Pandora (5). Companion of Artemis, wife of Kephalos, who accidently kills her (*Od.* 11.321; Pherec. in schol. *Od.* 11.321; Ovid *Met.* 7.690–862). Cures Minos of a curse (Apollod. 3.15.1), same story with a happy ending (Ant. Lib. 41). Daughter of Kekrops (schol. AR. 1.211) or Pan-

dion (Hyg. *Fab*. 189, 241). Sacrifices to her are recorded on the calendar of Thorikos in Attica (*SEG* 26.136.15ff.).

2) daughter of Thespios, mother of Antileon and Hippeus by Herakles (Apollod. 2.7.8).

PROMNE wife of Buphagos. Together they nurse and bury Iphikles (Paus. 8.14.9).

PRONOE daughter of Melampous (Hes. *Cat*. 136) and Iphianeira. Sister of Antiphates, Manto, Bias (Diod. 4.68.4). See Iphianeira (1).

PROSYMNA daughter of the river Asterion, sister of Euboia and Akraia, nurses of Hera, gives name to the land below the Argive Heraion (Paus. 2.17.1–2).

PROTOGENEIA

1) (Elis) daughter of Deukalion, mother by Zeus of Aethlios, first ruler of Elis (Paus. 5.1.3).

2) daughter of Erechtheus; see Pandora (5).

PSAMATHE(IA)

1) daughter of Krotopos, mother of Linos by Apollo (Paus. 1.43.7).

2) *Nereid, mother of Phokos by Aiakos (Hes. *Theog*. 260, 1004).

PSOTHIS daughter of Eryx of Sicania, mother of Echephron and Promachos by Herakles, eponym of Psothis. In other traditions, Psothis is either the son of Arrhon or the daughter of Xanthos (Paus. 8.24.1–2).

PYLARGE daughter of Danaos and Pieria, marries Idmon (Apollod. 2.1.5).

PYRGO first wife of Alkathous, tomb in Megara (Paus. 1.43.4). See Iphinoe (2), Euaichme (1).

PYRIPPE daughter of Thespios, mother of Patroklos by Herakles (Apollod. 2.7.8).

PYRRHA

1) daughter of Epimetheus and Pandora (4), wife of Deukalion, mother of Melantho (1), etc. Elsewhere, the daughter of Deukalion, beloved of Zeus, mother of Prometheus (Hes. *Cat*. 2 = schol. AR. 3.1086; cf. Hes. *Cat*. 4).

2) name of Achilles when disguised as a girl on Skyros (Hyg. *Fab*. 96; Sidon. c. 9.141). Cf. name of Achilles' son Neoptolemos = Pyrrhos.

3) See Henioche.

RHADINE lover of Leontichos, their tomb on Samos honored by star-crossed lovers (Paus. 7.5.13). Fragments survive from a poem called the *Rhadine*, with a doubtful attribution to Stesichoros (Strabo 8.3.20).

RHODE

1) eponym of the island Rhodos, daughter of Poseidon and Aphrodite (Pindar *Ol*. 7.71) or Amphitrite (Apollod. 1.4.5) or of Asopos (schol. *Od*. 17.208). Bore Helios seven sons, or Phaethon, Lampetie, Aigle, Phaethousa (schol. *Od*. etc.). Elsewhere their mother is Klymene. Cult honors on Rhodes.

2) daughter of Danaos and a hamadryad, marries Hippolytos (Apollod. 2.1.5).

3) mother of Kydippe by Ochimos. Also called Rhodo. See Kydippe (3).

RHODIA daughter of Danaos and a hamadryad, marries Chalkodon (Apollod. 2.1.5).

RHOIO

1) daughter of Staphylos and Chrysothemis, sister of Molpadia and Parthenos, pregnant with Anios by Apollo, put to sea by her father, rescued by Apollo (Diod. 5.62–63). Elsewhere she and Anios are the parents of the Oinotrop(h)oi and she is the daughter of Apollo and Chrysothemis. See Oinotrop(h)oi and Chrysothemis (1), Molpadia (1).

2) daughter of Skamandros, mother of Tithonos (schol. Lycoph. 18).

SAISARA daughter of Keleos, along with her sisters Pammerope and Diogeneia, an attendant of Demeter and Kore (Paus. 1.38.3 citing Pamphos and Homer). The people of the Athenian deme of Skambonidai say she is the wife of Krokon, a local hero (Paus. 1.38.2).

SEMACHIDAI the daughters of Semachos, the eponymous hero of the Attic deme Semachidai, receive Dionysos. An order of priestesses of Dionysos descends from them. Or the deme is Epakria (Steph. Byz. s.v. Σημαχίδαι).

SEMELE daughter of Kadmos and Harmonia, sister of Ino and Agave (Hes. *Theog.* 975ff.), mother of Dionysos by Zeus (*Iliad* 14.323ff.). Hera disguised tells her to ask Zeus to appear to her as he appears to his wife (Apollod. 3.4.3; Ovid *Met.* 3.275ff.; Hyg. *Fab.* 167, 179). Struck by lightning (Pindar *Ol.* 2.25f.), made immortal (Hes. *Theog.* 942; Apollod. 3.5.3; Diod. 4.25), receives new name, Thyone (*Hom. Hymn* 1.20–21; Sappho frg. 17 Lobel-Page). Also courted by Aktaion, whom Artemis destroyed, in one version, to keep him away from her (Stesich. frg. 236 *PMG* = Paus. 9.2.3). Places where she is honored include her *thalamos* (bedchamber) (Paus. 9.12.3) and tomb (Paus. 9.16.7), and the spot in Troizen where Dionysos was said to have brought her up from Hades (Paus. 2.31.2). She is honored by a festival at Delphi, the *Hērōis*, celebrating her return from the underworld (Plut. *Quaest. Gr.* 12, 293c–d), and sacrifices to her are specified on several Attic calendars.

SIDE

1) wife of Orion, punished by Hera for claiming to rival her beauty (Apollod. 1.4.3).

2) eponym of Phoinician Sidon, wife of Belos, mother of Danaos and Aigyptos (Joh. Antioch. *FHG* 4.544). Also the name of other heroines considered to be eponyms of Side in Pamphylia, Side in Lakonia, and Sidai in Boiotia.

SIDERO second wife of Salmoneus, she persecutes her stepdaughter Tyro until she is killed by Tyro's sons Pelias and Neleus (Soph. *Tyro*, especially frgs. 597, 598; Apollod. 1.9.8).

SKAIA (Achaia) daughter of Danaos. She and sister Automate marry Archandros and Architeles, the two sons of Achaeus (Paus. 7.1.6). In another version she and her three sisters, all daughters of Europe (4), marry four brothers, sons of Aigyptos and an unnamed mother of "royal blood." Her husband is Daiphron (Apollod. 2.1.5).

SKAMANDRODIKE. See Kalyke (2).

SKEDASOS, DAUGHTERS OF. See Molpia, Leuktrides.

SPARTE daughter of Eurotas and Kleochareia, wife of Lakedaimon, mother of Eurydike (6) and Amyklas (Paus. 3.1.2; Apollod. 3.10.3). Eponym of Sparta, her portrait statue is at Amyklai (Paus. 2.16.4).

SPERMO. See Oinotrop(h)oi.

STEROPE
1) one of the Pleiades, the seven daughters of Atlas and Pleione, wife of Oinomaos (Apollod. 3.10.1), mother of Hippodameia. Or mother of Oinomaos by Ares (Erat. *Kat.* 23), or of Euenos by Ares (Plut. *Parall.* 40.315e). See Alkippe (5), Pleione.
2) daughter of Kepheus, king of Tegea (Apollod. 2.7.3).
3) daughter of Akastos, stepchild of Astydameia (Apollod. 3.13.3).
4) daughter of Porthaon, sister of Eurythemiste and Stratonike (Hes. *Cat.* 26), mother of the Sirens by Acheloös (Apollod. 1.7.10). Apollodorus gives her mother as Euryte.
5) daughter of Pleuron and Xanthippe, sister of Agenor, Laophonte, and Stratonike (3) (Apollod. 1.7.7).

STHENEBOIA wife of Proitos (Hes. *Cat.* 129, 131 = Apollod. 2.2.2), mother of Lysippe, Iphinoe, and Iphianassa. Elsewhere called Anteia (*Iliad* 6.160). She falls in love with Bellerophon, accuses him of rape, and kills herself.

STHENELE
1) daughter of Danaos and Memphis, marries Sthenelos (Apollod. 2.1.5).
2) See Polymele (4).

STILBE. See Kreousa (1).

STRATONIKE
1) daughter of Parthaon; sister of Eurythemiste, Sterope (4); wife of Melaneus; mother of Eurytos (Hes. *Cat.* 26; schol. Soph. *Trach.* 266).
2) mother of Poimandros, carried off by Achilles (Plut. *Quaest. Gr.* 37, 299c).
3) daughter of Pleuron and Xanthippe, sister of Agenor, Sterope, and Laophonte (Apollod. 1.7.7).
4) daughter of Thespios, mother of Atromos by Herakles (Apollod. 2.7.8).

STRYMO mother of Priam according to Hellanicus (schol. A. *Iliad* 3.250). See Zeuxippe (3), Leukippe (4).

STYGNE daughter of Danaos and Polyxo, marries Polyctor (Apollod. 2.1.5).

SYBILLA. See Neso (2).

TANAGRA daughter of Aiolos (or Asopos according to Corinna), wife of Poimandros, eponym of the city of Tanagra. In old age called Graia (Paus. 9.20.1–2).

TAUROPOLIS
1) *epithet of Artemis.

2) daughter of Kleson, who together with her sister Kleso finds and buries the body of Ino, according to the Megarians (Paus. 1.42.7).

TAYGETE one of the Pleiades, the seven daughters of Atlas and Pleione, mother of Lakedaimon by Zeus (Apollod. 3.10.3; Paus. 3.1.2). See Pleione.

TEISIPHONE daughter of Manto and Alkmaion (Paus. 9.33.2). See Manto (1).

TEKMESSA concubine of Aias (unnamed at *Iliad* 1.138); in Sophocles, daughter of Phrygian king Teleutas, legitimate wife of Aias, mother of Eurysakes.

TELEPHASSA wife of Agenor, mother of Europe, Kadmos, Kilix, Phoinix (Apollod. 3.1.1), but some say Europe's father was Phoinix (schol. Eur. *Phoin.* 5).

TERPSIKRATE daughter of Thespios, mother of Euryopes by Herakles (Apollod. 2.7.8).

THEANO
    1) daughter of Kisseus, wife of Antenor, priestess of Athena (*Iliad* 6.298), mother of Glaukos and Eurymachos, all depicted by Polygnotos (Paus. 10.27.3).
    2) wife of the king of Metapontos in Euripides' *Melanippe Desmōtis*, also called Autolyte (Diod. 4.67). See Melanippe (1).
    3) daughter of Danaos and Polyxo, marries Phantes (Apollod. 2.1.5).
    4) See Molpia.

THEBE
    1) daughter of Asopos and Metope (Pindar *Ol.* 6.84), sister of Aigina (Hdt. 5.80), eponym of Thebe in Cilicia.
    2) daughter of Zeus and Iodama (schol. Lycoph. 1206).

THEMISTO
    1) daughter of Hypseus (Pindar *Pyth.* 9.13; Athen. 13.560d), third wife of Athamas, mother of Ptous (Paus. 9.23.6), also Leukon, Erythios, and Schoineus (Apollod. 1.9.2). She supplants Ino (Hyg. *Fab.* 1, 4, which preserves the plot of Euripides' *Ino*) or Nephele. Elsewhere, she is mother of Sphingios and Orchomenos. See Ino.
    2) name of Homer's mother, according to the Cypriots (Paus. 10.24.3). But see Klymene (7), Polykaste (2).
    3) *Nereid (Hes. *Theog.* 261).

THEMISTONOE daughter of Keyx of Trachis, wife of Kyknos (*Shield* 356).

THEOPE. See Leo korai.

THEOPHANE daughter of Bisaltes. Poseidon changes her into a ewe and in the form of a ram fathers upon her the ram with the golden fleece (Hyg. *Fab.* 188; Ovid *Met.* 6.117).

THERAIPHONE (Elis) daughter of Dexamenes, sister of Theronike. She and her sister marry the sons of Aktor (Paus. 5.3.3).

THERAPNE daughter of Lelex, eponym of Therapnai near Sparta (Paus. 3.19.9).

THERO
    1) said by some to be Ares' nurse (Paus. 3.19.7).

2) daughter of Phylas and Leipephile(ne), mother of Chairon by Apollo (Paus. 9.40.5–6, citing the *Great Ehoiai*).

THERONIKE. See Theraiphone.

THESEIS Amazon (Hyg. *Fab*. 163).

THESPIA daughter of Asopos, eponym of Thespiai (Paus. 9.26.6).

THESPIOS (or THESTIOS), DAUGHTERS OF the fifty daughters of Thespios or Thestios and Megamede, with whom Herakles lay in one night, or five nights (Herodorus in Athen. 13.556f.) or fifty (Paus.9.27.6; Apollod. 2.4.10; Diod. 4.29; named with their offspring at Apollod. 2.7.8).

THISBE daughter of Asopos, eponym of Thisbe (Paus. 9.32.3), beloved of Pyramos (Nonnus *Dion*. 6.344ff.).

THOÖSA
1) *daughter of Phorkys, mother of Polyphemos by Poseidon (*Od*. 1.71).
2) daughter of Poseidon, mother of Linos by Apollo (*Cert. Hom. et Hes*. 46), although this is perhaps a misreading for Aithousa. Elsewhere his mother is the nymph Psamathe (Paus. 1.43.7) or one of the Muses: Ourania (Hes. frg. 305; schol. T *Iliad* 18.570 citing Hesiod), Kalliope (Apollod. 1.3.2), or Terpsichore (*Suda* s.v. Λίνος).

THRONIE daughter of Belos, mother of Arabos by Hermes (Hes. *Cat*. 137 = Strabo 1.2.34).

THYIA
1) daughter of Kastalios, mother of Delphos by Apollo, but see Melantho (1). First priestess of Dionysos, and the first to celebrate his rites. Female worshipers sometimes called Thyiades in her honor (Paus. 10.6.4). According to Pausanias, she is beloved of Poseidon and appears in Polygnotos' painting in Delphi next to her friend Chloris (Paus. 10.29.5).
2) daughter of Kephisos, eponym of Thyia, near Delphi, where there is a shrine at which sacrifices are made to her (Hdt. 7.178).

THYONE. See Semele.

THYRIE. See Hyrie.

TIMANDRA daughter of Tyndareus and Leda, sister of Klytemnestra and Phylonoe, sister or half-sister of Helen, wife of Echimos (Hes. *Cat*. 23; Paus. 8.5.1; Apollod. 3.10.6). Because of Aphrodite's curse on Tyndareos that his daughters would be faithless (Stesich. frg. 223 *PMG* = schol. Eur. *Or*. 249), she left Echemos, by whom she was the mother of Euandros, for Phyleus (Hes. *Cat*. 176), by whom she had Meges (Eust. 305.15). See Klytemnestra, Helen.

TIPHYSE daughter of Thespios, mother of Lynkaios by Herakles (Apollod. 2.7.8).

TOXIKRATE daughter of Thespios, mother of Lykourgos by Herakles (Apollod. 2.7.8).

TRITEIA (Achaia) eponym of the city of Triteia, daughter of Triton, priestess of Athena, mother of Melanippos by Ares (Paus. 7.22.8).

TRYGON (Arcadia) nurse of Asklepios, her tomb in his sanctuary (Paus. 8.25.11).

TYRIA mother of Kleitos, Sthenelos, and Chrysippos by Aigyptos (Apollod. 2.1.5).

TYRO daughter of Salmoneus and Alkidike, mother by Poseidon of Pelias and Neleus, wife of Kretheus by whom she is the mother of Aeson, Pheres, Amythaon (*Od.* 11.235–59; Hes. *Cat.* 30–32). She is persecuted by her stepmother Sidero and rescued by her sons Pelias and Neleus (Apollod. 1.9.8–9). At *Od.* 2.120 she is listed with Mykene and Alkmene as a paragon of heroines. See Sidero.

XANTHE
    1) wife of Asklepios, mother of Machaon (Hes. *Cat.* 53, 58) but his mother is also said to be Epione (schol. AD. *Iliad* 4.195).
    2) Amazon (Hyg. *Fab.* 163).

XANTHIPPE
    1) daughter of Doris, wife of Pleuron, mother of Agenor, Sterope, Stratonike, and Laophonte (Apollod. 1.7.7).
    2) woman who feeds her imprisoned father with her own milk (Hyg. *Fab.* 254). Also called Pero (Val. Max. 4.5, ext.1).

XANTHIS daughter of Thespios, mother of Homolippos by Herakles (Apollod. 2.7.8).

XENODIKE
    1) daughter of Minos (Apollod. 3.1.2).
    2) Trojan captive in painting by Polygnotos (Paus. 10.26.1).

XENODOKE daughter of Syleus, killed with father by Herakles (Apollod. 2.6.3).

XENOKLEIA Pythia who refused oracle to Herakles when he was polluted by the death of Iphitos (Paus. 10.13.8).

ZEUXIPPE
    1) daughter of Eridanos (Hyg. *Fab.* 14), wife of Pandion, mother of Butes, Erechtheus, Philomele, Prokne (Apollod. 3.14.8).
    2) daughter of Lamedon and Pheno, married to Sikyon (Paus. 2.6.5).
    3) mother of Priam (Alc. frg. 71 *PMG* = schol. A. *Iliad* 3.250). See Strymo, Leukippe (4).
    4) daughter of Hippokoön, wife of Antiphates, mother of Oikles and Amphalkes (Diod. 4.68.5).

Abert, Hermann. "Linos." *RE* 13.1 (1926) 715–17.

Adams, Douglas Q. "῞Ηρως and ῞Ηρα." *Glotta* 65 (1987) 171–78.

Agard, W. R. "Boreas at Athens." *CJ* 61 (1966) 241–46.

Albini, Umberto. "L'*Ifigenia in Tauride* e la fine del mito." *PP* 38 (1983) 105–12.

Allen, Thomas W. *Homeri Opera*. Vol. 5: *Hymni. Cyclus Fragmenta*. Oxford: Clarendon Press, 1912.

Antonaccio, Carla M. *An Archaeology of Ancestors: Tomb Cult and Hero Cult in Early Greece*. Lanham, Md.: Rowman and Littlefield, 1995.

Arena, R. "Sul nome 'Ιφιγένεια." In *Studi in onore di Ferrante Rittatore Vonwiller*. Como: Scuola Archaeologica Comense, 1980, 21–28.

Arrigoni, Giampiera. *Le Donne in Grecia*. Rome: Laterza, 1985.

Arrowsmith, William, trans. *Petronius' "Satyricon."* New York: New American Library, 1959.

Arthur (Katz), Marylin B. "Review Essay: Classics." *Signs* 2.2 (1976) 382–403.

———. "The Dream of a World without Women." *Arethusa* 16 (1983) 97–116.

———. "Early Greece: The Origins of the Western Attitude toward Women." In Peradotto and Sullivan (1984) 7–58.

Austin, Colin, ed. *Nova Fragmenta Euripidea*. Berlin: De Gruyter, 1968.

Austin, Norman. *Helen of Troy and Her Shameless Phantom*. Ithaca: Cornell University Press, 1994.

Babbitt, F. C., ed. and trans. *Plutarch's "Moralia."* Vols 1–5 (Loeb Classical Library) London: Heinemann, 1927–1931.

Barrett, W. S. *Euripides. Hippolytos*. Edition and commentary. Oxford: Clarendon Press, 1964.

Beard, Mary, and John North, eds. *Pagan Priests: Religion and Power in the Ancient World*. Ithaca: Cornell University Press, 1990.

Bérard, Claude, et al. *A City of Images: Iconography and Society in Ancient Greece*. Trans. Deborah Lyons. Princeton: Princeton University Press, 1989.

Bérard, Claude, and Christiane Bron. "Bacchos au coeur de la cité: Le Thiase dionysiaque dans l'espace politique." In *L'Association dionysiaque dans les sociétés anciennes*. Rome: Ecole Française de Rome, 1986: 13–27.

Bergren, Ann. "Helen's Web: Time and Tableau in the *Iliad*." *Helios* 7 (1980) 19–34.

———. "Language and the Female in Early Greek Thought." *Arethusa* 16 (1983) 69–95.

Bethe, Erich. "Dioskuren" *RE* 5.1 (1905) 1087–1123.

Blümel, W. *Die Inschriften der rhodischen Peraia*. Bonn: Habelt, 1991.

Boardman, John. *Athenian Black Figure Vases*. London: Thames and Hudson, 1974.

———. *Athenian Red Figure Vases: The Archaic Period*. London: Thames and Hudson, 1975.

Boedeker, Deborah. *Aphrodite's Entry into Greek Epic*. Leiden: Brill, 1974.

—. "Hero Cult and Politics in Herodotus: The Bones of Orestes." In *Cultural Poetics in Archaic Greece*, ed. Carol Dougherty and Leslie Kurke. Cambridge: Cambridge University Press, 1993, 164–77.

Bond, G. W. *Euripides. Hypsipyle*. Oxford: Oxford University Press, 1963.

Borges, Jorge Luiz. *Other Inquisitions*. Trans. Ruth L. C. Simms. New York: Simon and Schuster, 1968.

Boswell, John. "Concepts, Experience, and Sexuality." In *differences* 2 (1990) 67–87.

Bowra, C. M. "The Two Palinodes of Stesichorus." *CR* n.s. 13 (1963) 245–52.

Brelich, Angelo. *Gli eroi greci: un problema storico-religioso*. Rome: Ateneo, 1958.

—. *Heros: il culto greco degli eroi e il problema degli esseri semi-divini*. Rome: Ateneo, 1958b.

—. *Paides e parthenoi*. Rome: Ateneo, 1969.

Bremmer, Jan. "Plutarch and the Naming of Greek Women." *AJP* 102 (1981) 425–26.

—. *Interpretations of Greek Mythology*. London: Croon Helm, 1987.

Brown, Peter. *The Cult of the Saints*. Chicago: University of Chicago, 1981.

Bruit Zaidman, Louise, and Pauline Schmitt Pantel. *Religion in the Ancient Greek City*. Ed. and trans. P. Cartledge. Cambridge: Cambridge University Press, 1992 [Paris, 1989].

Brulé, Pierre. *La Fille d'Athènes: La Religion des filles à Athènes à l'époque classique*. Centre de Recherches d'Histoire Ancienne. Paris: Les Belles Lettres, 1987.

Burkert, Walter. "Greek Tragedy and Sacrificial Ritual." *GRBS* 7 (1966) 87–121.

—. "Kekropidensage und Arrhephoria: Vom Initiationsritus zum Panathenenfest." *Hermes* 94 (1966) 1–25.

—. "Apellai und Apollon." *RM* 118 (1975) 1–21.

—. *Structure and History in Greek Mythology and Ritual*. Berkeley: University of California, 1979.

—. *Homo Necans: The Anthropology of Ancient Greek Sacrificial Ritual and Myth*. Trans. Peter Bing. Berkeley: University of California, 1983 [Berlin, 1972].

—. *Greek Religion*. Trans. John Raffan. Cambridge, Mass.: Harvard University Press, 1985 [Stuttgart, 1977].

—. "Oriental and Greek Mythology: The Meeting of Parallels." In Bremmer (1987) 10–40.

Burn, Lucilla. "Vase-Painting in Fifth-Century Athens." In *Looking at Greek Vases*, ed. Tom Rasmussen and Nigel Spivey. Cambridge: Cambridge University Press, 1991, 118–30.

Burnett, Anne Pippin. *Catastrophe Survived: Euripides' Plays of Mixed Reversal*. Oxford: Clarendon Press, 1971.

—. "Hekabe the Dog." *Arethusa* 27 (1994) 151–64.

Calame, Claude. *Les Choeurs de jeunes filles en Grèce archaïque*. Rome: Ateneo e Bizzari, 1977.

Campbell, David A., ed. and trans. *Greek Lyric I: Sappho and Alcaeus* (Loeb Classical Library). Cambridge, Mass.: Harvard University Press, 1982.

—. ed. and trans. *Greek Lyric III: Stesichoros, Ibycus, Simonides, and Others*

(Loeb Classical Library). Cambridge, Mass.: Harvard University Press, 1991.

―――. ed. and trans. *Greek Lyric IV: Bacchylides, Corinna, and Others* (Loeb Classical Library). Cambridge, Mass.: Harvard University Press, 1992.

Carpenter, Thomas H. *Dionysian Imagery in Archaic Greek Art: Its Development in Black-Figure Vase Painting.* Oxford: Clarendon Press, 1986.

Carpenter, Thomas H., and Christopher A. Faraone, eds. *The Masks of Dionysus.* Ithaca: Cornell University Press, 1993.

Carson, Ann. "Putting Her in Her Place: Women, Dirt, and Desire." In Halperin, Winkler, and Zeitlin (1990) 135–69.

Cassolà, Filippo. *Inni omerici.* Edition and commentary. [Milano]: Fondazione Lorenzo Valla, 1975.

Castriota, David. *Myth, Ethos, and Actuality: Official Art in Fifth-century B.C. Athens.* Madison: University of Wisconsin, 1992.

Catling, Hector W., and Helen Cavanagh. "Two Inscribed Bronzes from the Menelaion, Sparta." *Kadmos* 15.2 (1976) 145–57.

Chadwick, John. "Who Were the Dorians?" *PP* 31 (1976) 103–17.

Chadwick, John, and Lydia Baumbach. "The Mycenaean Greek Vocabulary." *Glotta* 41 (1963) 157–271.

Chantraine, Pierre. *La Formation des noms en grec ancien.* Paris: Klincksieck, 1968 [1933].

―――. *Dictionnaire etymologique de la langue grecque: Histoire des mots.* 5 vols. Paris: Klincksieck, 1968–80.

Chirassi Colombo, Ileana. "Heros Achilleus—Theos Apollon." In *Il Mito Greco,* ed. Bruno Gentili and Giuseppe Paione. Rome: Ateneo e Bizarri, 1977, 231–69.

―――. "Paides e Gynaikes: note per una tassonomia del comportamento rituale nella cultura attica." *QUCC* 30 (1979) 25–58.

Clader, Linda Lee. *Helen: The Evolution from Divine to Heroic in Greek Epic Tradition.* Leiden: Brill, 1976.

Clay, Jenny Strauss. *The Wrath of Athena.* Princeton: Princeton University Press, 1983.

―――. *The Politics of Olympus: Form and Meaning in the Major Homeric Hymns.* Princeton: Princeton Unversity Press, 1989.

Clement, Paul. "New Evidence for the Origin of the Iphigeneia Legend." *AC* 3 (1934) 393–409.

Cohen, David. *Law, Sexuality, and Society: The Enforcement of Morals in Classical Athens.* Cambridge: Cambridge University Press, 1991.

Coldstream, J. N. "Hero-Cults in the Age of Homer." *JHS* 96 (1976) 8–17.

―――. *Geometric Greece.* London: Ernest Benn, 1977.

Cole, Susan Guettel. "The Social Function of Rituals of Maturation: The Koureion and the Arkteia." *ZPE* 55 (1984) 233–44.

―――. "*Gunaiki ou Themis*: Gender Difference in the Greek *Leges Sacrae.*" In *Documenting Gender: Women and Men in Non-Literary Classical Texts,* ed. D. Konstan. *Helios* 19 (special issue, 1992) 104–22.

Cook, J. M. "The Cult of Agamemnon at Mycenae." In *Geras Antoniou Keramopoullou.* Athens: Typographeion Myrtide, 1953, 112–18.

Cook, J. M., and W. H. Plommer. *The Sanctuary of Hemithea at Kastabos*. Cambridge: Cambridge University Press, 1966.

Daraki, Maria. *Dionysos*. Paris: Arthaud, 1985.

Daremberg, Charles, and Edmond Saglio. *Dictionnaire des Antiquités grecques et romaines*. Paris: Hachette, 1877–1919.

Daux, Georges. "La Grande Démarchie: Un Nouveau calendrier sacrificiel d'Attique (Erchia)." *BCH* 87 (1963) 603–34.

———. "Chronique des fouilles, 1967: Péloponnèse." *BCH* 92 (1968) 773–834.

———. "Le Calendrier de Thorikos au musée J. Paul Getty." *AC* 52 (1983) 150–74.

———. "Sacrifices à Thorikos." *Getty Museum Journal* 17 (1984) 145–52.

Davison, J. A. "De Helena Stesichori." *QUCC* 2 (1966) 80–90.

Davreux, Juliette. *La Légende de la prophétesse Cassandre d'après les textes et les monuments*. Paris: Droz; Liège: Faculté de philosophie et lettres, 1942.

de Beauvoir, Simone. *The Second Sex*. Trans. and ed. H. M. Parshley. New York: Vintage, 1974 [Paris 1949].

Delcourt, Marie. *Légendes et cultes de héros en Grèce*. Paris: Presses Universitaires de France, 1942.

———. *Pyrrhos et Pyrrha: Recherches sur les valeurs du feu dans les légendes helléniques*. Paris: Belles Lettres, 1965.

Demand, Nancy H. *Thebes in the Fifth Century: Herakles Resurgent*. London: Routledge and Kegan Paul, 1982.

de Polignac, François. *La Naissance de la cité grecque*. Paris: La Découverte, 1984.

Detienne, Marcel. *Dionysos mis à mort*. Paris: Gallimard, 1977.

———. [résumé of seminar]. *Annuaire, Ecole pratique des Hautes Etudes, section des sciences religieuses* 94 (1985–86) 371–80.

Dewald, Carolyn. "Women and Culture in Herodotus' Histories." In Foley (1981) 91–125.

Diels, Hermann. *Die Fragmente der Vorsokratiker*. Tenth edition. 3 vols. Ed. W. Kranz. Berlin: Weidmann, 1960.

Dietrich, B. C. "The Dorian Hyacinthia: A Survival from the Bronze Age." *Kadmos* 14 (1975) 133–42.

Dimock, George E. "The Name of Odysseus." In *Essays on the Odyssey: Selected Modern Criticism*. Bloomington: Indiana University Press (1963), 54–72.

———. *The Unity of the Odyssey*. Amherst: University of Massachusetts Press, 1989.

Dodds, E. R. *The Greeks and the Irrational*. Berkeley: University of California, 1951.

———. *Euripides: Bacchae*. Edition and commentary. Second edition. Oxford: Clarendon Press, 1960.

Donohue, A. A. *XOANA and the Origins of Greek Sculpture* (American Classical Studies 15). Atlanta: Scholars Press, 1988.

Dougherty, Carol. *The Poetics of Colonization: From City to Text in Archaic Greece*. New York: Oxford University Press, 1993.

Dowden, Ken. *Death and the Maiden: Girls' Initiation Rites in Greek Mythology*. London: Routledge, 1989.

Dumézil, Georges. *The Stakes of the Warrior*. Trans. David Weeks. Ed. Jan Puhvel. Berkeley: University of California, 1983 [Paris, 1971].

Dunn, Francis M. "Fearful Symmetry: The Two Tombs of Hippolytus." *Materiali e discussioni per l'analisi dei testi classici* 28 (1992) 103–11.

———. "Euripides and the Rites of Hera Akraia." *GRBS* 35 (1994) 103–15.

Dupont, Florence. "Se reproduire ou se métamorphoser." *Topique: Revue Freudienne* 9–10 (1971) 139–60.

Durand, J.-L., F. Frontisi-Ducroux, and F. Lissarrague. "Wine: Human and Divine." In Bérard et al. (1989) 121–29.

Eisner, Robert. "Euripides' Use of Myth." *Arethusa* 12 (1979) 153–74.

Eitrem, S. "Leukothea." *RE* 12.2 (1912) 2293–306.

———. "Hyakinthos." *RE* 9.1 (1914) 4–16.

Faraone, Christopher A. *Talismans and Trojan Horses: Guardian Statues in Ancient Greek Myth and Ritual*. Oxford: Oxford University Press, 1992.

Farnell, Lewis Richard. *The Cults of the Greek States*. 5 vols. Oxford: Clarendon Press, 1896–1909.

———. *Greek Hero Cults and Ideas of Immortality*. Oxford: Clarendon Press, 1921.

Ferguson, William Scott. "The Attic Orgeones." *HThR* 37 (1944) 61–140.

Fick, August. *Die Griechischen Personennamen nach ihrer Bildung erklärt und systematisch geordnet*. Göttingen: Vandenhoeck und Ruprecht, 1894.

Finley, M. I. *The World of Odysseus*. Second rev. ed. New York: Viking Press, 1978.

Fitzgerald, Robert, trans. Homer. "*Odyssey*." Garden City, N.Y.: Anchor Doubleday, 1963.

———. trans. Homer. "*Iliad*." Garden City, N.Y.: Anchor Doubleday, 1974.

Foley, Helene P., ed. "Sex and State in Ancient Greece." *Diacritics* 5.4 (1975) 31–36.

———. ed. *Reflections of Women in Antiquity*. New York: Gordon and Breach, 1981.

———. *Ritual Irony: Poetry and Sacrifice in Euripides*. Ithaca: Cornell University Press, 1985.

———. *The Homeric Hymn to Demeter*. Princeton: Princeton University Press, 1994.

Fontenrose, Joseph. "The Sorrows of Ino and of Procne." *TAPA* 79 (1948) 125–67.

———. *Python: A Study of the Delphic Myth and Its Origins*. Berkeley: University of California, 1959.

———. *The Delphic Oracle*. Berkeley: University of California Press, 1978.

———. *Orion: The Myth of the Hunter and the Huntress*. Berkeley: University of California, 1981.

Forbes Irving, P.M.C. *Metamorphosis in Greek Myths*. Oxford: Clarendon Press, 1990.

Foucart, P. *Le Culte des héros chez les Grecs* (Mémoires de l'Institut National de France 42). Paris: Académie des inscriptions et belles-lettres, 1922, 1–166.

Frazer, James George, ed. *Apollodorus: The Library* (Loeb Classical Library). 2 vols. Cambridge, Mass.: Harvard University Press, 1921.

———. *Ovid's Fasti*, edition, translation, and commentary. 5 vols. Hildesheim: Olm, 1973 [London, 1929].

Friedländer, P. "Ganymedes." *RE* 7.1 (1912) 737–49.

Frontisi-Ducroux, F., and F. Lissarrague. "From Ambiguity to Ambivalence: A Dionysiac Excursion through the 'Anakrontic' vases." Trans. R. Lamberton. In Halperin, Winkler, and Zeitlin (1990) 211–56.

Furley, William D. *Studies in the Use of Fire in Ancient Greek Religion*. New York: Arno Press, 1981.

Fuss, Diana. *Essentially Speaking: Feminism, Nature, and Difference*. New York: Routledge, 1989.

Gaisford, Thomas, ed. *Paroemiographi Graeci*. Osnabrück: Biblio Verlag, 1972 [1836].

Galinsky, G. Karl. *The Herakles Theme*. Totowa, N.J.: Rowman and Littlefield, 1972.

Gallini, Clara. "Il travestismo rituale di Penteo." *SMSR* 34 (1963) 211–28.

———. *Protesta e integrazione nella Roma antica*. Bari: Laterza, 1970.

Gennep, Arnold van. *The Rites of Passage*. Trans. Monika Vizedom and Gabrielle Caffee. Chicago: University of Chicago Press, 1964 [Paris, 1909].

Gérard-Rousseau, Monique. *Les Mentions religieuses dans les tablettes mycéniennes*. Rome: Ateneo, 1968.

Gernet, Louis. *The Anthropology of Ancient Greece*. Trans. John Hamilton, S.J. and Blaise Nagy. Baltimore: Johns Hopkins, 1981 [Paris, 1968].

Gernet, Louis, and André Boulanger. *Le génie grec dans la religion*. Paris: Albin Michel, 1970 [1932].

Gilbert, Sandra M., and Susan Gubar. *The Madwoman in the Attic: The Woman-Writer and the Nineteenth-Century Literary Imagination*. New Haven: Yale University Press, 1979.

Gilligan, Carol. *In a Different Voice: Psychological Theory and Women's Development*. Cambridge, Mass.: Harvard University Press, 1982.

———. "Woman's Place in Man's Life-cycle." In *Feminism and Methodology*, ed. Sandra Harding. Bloomington: Indiana University Press, 1987, 57–73.

Gliksohn, Jean-Michel. *Iphigénie: De la Grèce antique à l'Europe des lumières*. Paris: Presses Universitaires de France, 1985.

Gould, J. "Law, Custom and Myth: Aspects of the Social Position of Women in Classical Athens." *JHS* 100 (1980) 38–59.

Gould, Stephen Jay. *Hen's Teeth and Horses' Toes*. New York: Norton, 1983.

Graf, F. "Das Götterbilt aus dem Taurerland." *AW* 10.4 (1979) 33–41.

Graham, A. John. "Religion, Women and Greek Colonization." In *Religione e città nel mondo antico* (Atti del Centro Richerche e Documentazione sull'Antichità Classica II, 1980–81), Rome (1984) 293–314.

Griffith, Mark. "Contest and Contradiction in Early Greek Poetry." In *Cabinet of the Muses: Essays on Classical and Comparative Literature in Honor of Thomas G. Rosenmeyer*, ed. M. Griffith and D. J. Mastronarde. Atlanta: Scholars Press, 1990, 185–207.

Groningen, B. A. von. *Euphorion*. Amsterdam: Hakkert, 1977.

Gruppe, Otto. "Herakles." *RE* Suppl. 3 (1918) 910–1121.

Gulick, C. B., ed. and trans. *Athenaeus: The Deipnosophists*. 7 vols. (Loeb Classical Library) Cambridge, Mass.: Harvard University Press, 1927–61.

Gunning, J. "Iodama." *RE* 9.1 (1914) 1839–41.

Guthrie, W.K.C. *The Greeks and Their Gods*. Boston: Beacon, 1955.

Habicht, Christian. *Pausanias' Guide to Ancient Greece*. Berkeley: University of California Press, 1985.

Hack, R. K. "Homer and the Cult of Heroes." *TAPA* 60 (1929) 57–74.

Hadzisteliou Price, Theodora. "Hero-Cult and Homer." *Historia* 22 (1973) 129–44.

———. *Kourotrophos: Cults and Representations of the Greek Nursing Deities*. Leiden: Brill, 1978.

———. "Hero Cult in the 'Age of Homer' and Earlier." In *Arktouros: Hellenic Studies Presented to Bernard M. W. Knox*, ed. G. Bowersock, W. Burkert, and M. Putnam. Berlin: de Gruyter, 1979, 219–28.

Halperin, David M. *One Hundred Years of Homosexuality and Other Essays on Greek Love*. New York: Routledge, 1990.

Halperin, David M., John J. Winkler, and Froma I. Zeitlin, eds. *Before Sexuality: The Construction of Erotic Experience in the Ancient Greek World*. Princeton: Princeton University Press, 1990.

Hamilton, Richard. *Choes and Anthesteria: Athenian Iconography and Ritual*. Ann Arbor: University of Michigan Press, 1992.

Hanslik, R. "Physkoa." *RE* 20.1 (1941) 1165–66.

Harrison, Jane. *Themis: A Study of the Social Origins of Greek Religion*. Cambridge: Cambridge University Press, 1927.

Häußler, Reinhard. "λίνος ante Αἴνον?" *RM* 117 (1974) 1–14.

Haviaris, Stratis. *The Heroic Age*. New York: Penguin, 1985.

Henderson, Jeffrey. "The Cologne Epode and the Conventions of Early Greek Erotic Poetry." *Arethusa* 9 (1976) 159–79.

Henrichs, Albert. "Die Maenaden von Milet." *ZPE* 4 (1969) 223–41.

———. "Human Sacrifice in Greek Religion: Three Case Studies." In *Le Sacrifice dans l'antiquité*, ed. O. Reverdin and J. Rudhardt (*Entretiens sur l'antiquité classique* 27). Geneva: Foundation Hardt, 1981, 195–242.

———. "Changing Dionysiac Identities." In *Jewish and Christian Self-Definition*. Vol. 3: *Self-Definition in the Graeco-Roman World*, ed. Ben R. Meyer and E. P. Sander. London: SCM Press, 1982, 137–60, 213–36 (notes).

———. "He Has a God in Him": Human and Divine in the Modern Perception of Dionysos." In Carpenter and Faraone (1993) 13–43.

Heubeck, Alfred, ed. *Omero. Odissea*. Vol. 3. [Verona]: Fondazione Lorenzo Valla, 1983.

Hewitt, Joseph William. "Major Restrictions on Access to Greek Temples." *TAPA* 40 (1909) 83–91.

Higbie, Carolyn. *Heroes' Names, Homeric Identities*. New York: Garland, 1995.

Hild, J. A. "Herois." In *Dictionnaire des antiquités*, ed. C. Daremberg and E. Saglio. Vol. 3.1, 139.

Holderman, Elisabeth Sinclair. *A Study of the Greek Priestess*. Chicago: University of Chicago Press, 1913.

Hollinshead, Mary B. "Legend, Cult, and Architecture at Three Sanctuaries of Artemis." Ph.D. dissertation, Bryn Mawr College, 1979.

———. "Against Iphigeneia's Adyton in Three Mainland Temples." *AJA* 89 (1985) 419–40.

Hollis, A. S., ed. *Callimachus. Hecale*. Edition with commentary. Oxford: Clarendon Press, 1990.

Hommel, Hildebrecht. *Der Gott Achilleus.* Heidelberg: Carl Winter, 1980.

Householder, Fred W., and Gregory Nagy. *Greek: A Survey of Recent Work.* The Hague: Mouton, 1972.

Hubbard, Thomas K. "The 'Cooking' of Pelops: Pindar and the Process of Mythological Revisionism." *Helios* 14 (1987) 3–21.

Hulton, A. O. "Euripides and the Iphigeneia Legend." *Mnemosyne* 15 (1962) 364–68.

Huston, Nancy. "The Matrix of War: Mothers and Heroes." In *The Female Body in Western Culture,* ed. Susan Rubin Suleiman. Cambridge, Mass.: Harvard University Press, 1985, 119–36.

Jacoby, Felix, ed. *Die Fragmente der griechischen Historiker.* Berlin: Weidmann, 1923–54. Leiden: Brill, 1957–64.

Jameson, Michael. "The Asexuality of Dionysos." In Carpenter and Faraone (1993) 44–64.

Jamison, Stephanie W. "Draupadī on the Walls of Troy: *Iliad* 3 from an Indic Perspective." *CA* 13 (1994) 5–16.

Janko, Richard. *The Iliad: A Commentary.* Vol. 4: books 13–16. General ed. G. S. Kirk. Cambridge: Cambridge University Press, 1992.

Jeanmaire, Henri. *Dionysos: Histoire du culte de Bacchus.* Paris: Payot, 1951.

Jenkins, I. D. "The Ambiguity of Greek Textiles." *Arethusa* 18 (1985) 109–32.

Johnston, Sarah Iles. *Hekate Soteira: A Study of Hekate's Roles in the Chaldean Oracles and Related Literature.* Atlanta: Scholars Press, 1990.

———. "Penelope and the Erinyes: *Odyssey* 20:61–82." *Helios* 21 (1994) 137–59.

Jones, W.H.S., ed. and trans. Vol. 2 with H. A. Ormerod. *Pausanias' Description of Greece.* 5 vols. (Loeb Classical Library) Cambridge, Mass.: Harvard University Press, 1918–35.

Just, Roger. *Women in Athenian Law and Life.* London: Routledge, 1989.

Kaempf-Dimitriadou, Sophia. *Die Liebe der Götter in der attischen Kunst der 5 Jahrhunderts v. Chr.* (*AK* suppl. 11) Berne: Francke, 1979.

Kahil, L. G. "Quelques vases du sanctuaire d'Artémis à Brauron." In *Neue Ausgrabungen in Griechenland* (*AK* suppl. 1). Olten: Urs Graf, 1963, 5–29.

———. "Autour de l'Artémis attique." *AK* 8 (1965) 20–33.

———. "L'Artémis de Brauron: Rites et mystère." *AK* 20 (1977) 86–98.

———. "La Déesse Artémis, mythologie et iconographie." In *Greece and Rome in the Classical World* (Acta 11 International Congress of Classical Archaeology). London, 1979, 73–87.

Kahn, Charles. *The Art and Thought of Heraclitus.* Edition with translation and commentary. Cambridge: Cambridge University Press, 1979.

Kaibel, Georg, ed. *Comicorum Graecorum Fragmenta.* Second edition. Vol. 1. Berlin: Weidmann, 1958 [1899].

Kamerbeek, J. C. "On the Conception of θεομάχος with Relation to Greek Tragedy." *Mnemosyne* 4th s. 1 (1948) 271–83.

Katz, Marylin Arthur. *Penelope's Renown: Meaning and Indeterminacy in the Odyssey.* Princeton: Princeton University Press, 1991.

Kauffmann, G. "Arachne." *RE* 2.1 (1896) 367–68.

Kearns, Emily. *The Heroes of Attica* (*BICS* suppl. 57) 1989.

Kern, Otto. "Dionysos." *RE* 5.1 (1905) 1010–45.

————. ed., *Orphicorum Fragmenta*. Berlin: Weidmann, 1922.

Keune, J. B. "Semele." *RE* 2A.2 (1923) 1341–45.

King, Helen. "Bound to Bleed: Artemis and Greek Women." In *Images of Women in Antiquity*, ed. Averil Cameron and Amélie Kuhrt. Detroit: Wayne State University Press, 1983, 109–27.

Kinkel, Gottfried. *Epicorum Graecorum Fragmenta*. Leipzig: Teubner, 1877.

Kirk, G. S. *Myth: Its Meaning and Functions in Ancient and Other Cultures*. London: Cambridge University, 1970.

————. *The Iliad: A Commentary*. Vol. 1: Books 1–4. Cambridge: Cambridge University Press, 1985.

Knox, B.M.W. "The *Medea* of Euripides." *YCS* 25 (1977) 193–25.

Koch, Theodor, ed. *Comicorum Atticorum Fragmenta*. 3 vols. Leipzig: Teubner, 1880–88.

Kraemer, Ross S. "Ecstacy and Possession: The Attraction of Women to the Cult of Dionysos." *HThR* 72 (1979) 55–80.

Kraus, Theodor. *Hekate: Studien zu Wesen und Bild der Göttin in Kleinasein und Griechenland*. Heidelberg: Winter, 1960.

Kretschmer, Paul. "Semele und Dionysos." In *Aus der Anomia, Archäeologische Beiträge Carl Robert Dargebracht*. Berlin: Weidmann, 1890, 17–29.

Kullmann, Wolfgang. "Die Töchter Agamemnons in der Ilias." *Gymnasium* 72 (1965) 200–203.

————. "Gods and Men in the *Iliad* and *Odyssey*." *HSCP* 89 (1985) 1–23.

Lacey, W. K. *The Family in Classical Greece*. Ithaca: Cornell University Press, 1968.

Lamberton, Robert. *Hesiod*. New Haven: Yale University Press, 1988.

Larson, Jennifer. *Greek Heroine Cults*. Madison: University of Wisconsin Press, 1995.

Lattimore, Richmond, and David Grene, eds. *Euripides I*. Chicago: University of Chicago Press, 1955.

Laumonier, Alfred. *Les Cultes indigènes en Carie*. Paris: De Boccard, 1958.

Leaf, Walter. *The Iliad*. Edition and commentary. Second ed. Amsterdam: Hakkert, 1971 [London, 1900–1902].

Lefkowitz, Mary R. *The Lives of the Greek Poets*. London: Duckworth, 1981.

Leutsch, E. L., and F. G. Schneidewin, ed. *Corpus Paroemiographicum Graecorum*. 2 vols. Hildesheim: Olms, 1958 [Gottingen, 1839–51].

Lévi-Straus, Claude. *Elementary Structures of Kinship*. Trans. J. H. Bell, J. R. von Sturmer, and R. Needham; ed. R. Needham. Boston: Beacon, 1969 [Paris, 1967].

Lexicon Iconographicum Mythologicae Classicae, Zurich: Artemis, 1981–.

Linders, Tullia. *Studies in the Treasure Records of Artemis Brauronia Found in Athens* (Skrifter Utgivna av Svenska Institutet I, Athen 4.19). Stockholm: Swedish Institute, 1972.

Linders, Tullia, and G. Nordquist, eds. *Gifts to the Gods* (Proceedings of the Uppsala Symposium 1985). Uppsala: Boreas, 1987.

Lloyd-Jones, Hugh. "Artemis and Iphigeneia." *JHS* 103 (1983) 87–102.

Lobel, Edgar, and Denys Page. *Poetarum Lesbiorum Fragmenta*. Oxford: Clarendon Press, 1955.

Loraux, Nicole. "Le Lit, la guerre." *L'Homme* 21.1 (1981) 37–67. Trans. as Chapter 1 of Loraux (1995) 23–43.

———. "Herakles: The Super-Male and the Feminine." Trans. R. Lamberton. In Halperin, Winkler, and Zeitlin (1990) 21–52. Rept. in Loraux (1995) 116–39.

———. *The Children of Athena: Athenian Ideas about Citizenship and the Division between the Sexes*. Trans. Caroline Levine (Princeton, 1993 [Paris, 1984]).

———. *The Experiences of Tiresias: The Feminine and the Greek Man*. Trans. Paula Wissing. Princeton: Princeton University Press, 1995.

Lyons, Deborah. *Configurations of the Feminine in Greek Myth and Cult*. Ph.D. dissertation, Princeton University, 1989.

———. "Manto and *Manteia*: Prophecy in the Myths and Cults of Heroines." In *Sibille e linguaggi oracolari* (Atti del Convegno Internazionale, 20–24 September, 1996, at Macerata and Norcia), ed. Ileana Chirassi Colombo and Tullio Seppilli, with Giorgio Bonamente. Pisa: Giardini, forthcoming.

McLeod, Glenda. *Virtue and Venom: Catalogues of Women from Antiquity to the Renaissance*. Ann Arbor: University of Michigan Press, 1991.

Marini, A. M. "Il mito di Arianna nella tradizione letteraria e nell'arte figurativa." *Atene e Roma* n.s. 13 (1932) 60–97, 121–42.

Martin, Richard P. *The Language of Heroes: Speech and Performance in the Iliad*. Ithaca: Cornell University Press, 1989.

Martin, Roland. *Recherches sur l'agora grecque: Études d'histoire et d'architecture urbaines*. Paris: Boccard, 1951.

Massenzio, Marcello. *Cultura e crisi permanente: La "Xenia" dionisiaca*. Rome: Ateneo, 1970.

Meerdink, Johan. *Ariadne: Een Onderzoek naar de oorspronkelijke Gestalte en de Ontwikkeling der Godin*. Wageningen: Veenman en Zonen, [1939].

Meridor, Ra'anana. "Hecuba's Revenge: Some Observations on Euripides' *Hecuba*." *AJP* 99 (1978) 28–35.

Merkelbach, R., and M. L. West, eds. *Fragmenta Hesiodea*. Oxford: Clarendon Press, 1967.

Meuli, Karl. "Griechische Opferbräuche." In *Phyllobolia für Peter von der Mühll*. Basel: Schwabe, 1946, 185–288.

Mikalson, Jon D. *The Sacred and Civil Calendar of the Athenian Year*. Princeton: Princeton University Press, 1975.

———. "Erechtheus and the Panathenaia." *AJP* 97 (1976) 141–53.

Mills, S. P. "The Sorrows of Medea." *CP* 75 (1980) 289–96.

Mizera, Suzanne M. *Unions Holy and Unholy: Fundamental Structures of Myths of Marriage in Early Greek Poetry and Tragedy*. Ph.D. dissertation, Princeton University, 1984.

Moi, Toril. *Sexual/Textual Politics: Feminist Literary Theory*. London: Routledge, 1985.

Monaco, Giusto. "La Nuova Elena." In *Letterature Comparate: Problemi e Metodo, Studi in Onore di E. Paratore*. Bologna: Pàtron, 1981, 143–51.

Mondi, Robert. "Greek Mythic Thought in the Light of the Near East." In *Approaches to Greek Myth*, ed. L. Edmunds. Baltimore: Johns Hopkins University Press, 1990, 142–98.

Monsacré, Hélène. *Les Larmes d'Achille*. Paris: Albin Michel, 1984.

Montepaone, Claudia. "'L' 'ἀρχτεία' à Brauron." In *Studi Storico-religiosi*. Rome: Scuola di Perfezionamento in Studi Storico-religiosi dell'Università L'Aquila III, 1979, 343–64.

———. "Il mito di fondatore del rituale munichio in onore di Artemis." *Recherches sur les cultes grec et l'occident* 1 (1979b) 65–76.

Most, G. W. "Sappho Fr. 16.6–7 L-P." *CQ* 31 (1981) 11–17.

Muller, Carl, and Theodore Muller, eds. *Fragmenta Historicorum Graecorum*. Paris: Firmin Didot, 1841–51.

Nagy, Gregory. "Phaethon, Sappho's Phaon, and the White Rock of Leukas." *HSCP* 77 (1973) 137–77.

———. *The Best of the Achaeans: Concepts of the Hero in Archaic Greek Poetry*. Baltimore: Johns Hopkins, 1979.

———. "On the Death of Sarpedon." In *Approaches to Homer*, ed. C. A. Rubino and C. W. Shelmerdine. Austin: University of Texas, 1983, 189–217.

———. "Theognis and Megara: A Poet's Vision of His City." In *Theognis of Megara: Poetry and the Polis*, cd. Thomas J. Figueira and G. Nagy (Baltimore: Johns Hopkins University Press, 1985) 22–81.

———. "Pindar's *Olympian* 1 and the Aetiology of the Olympic Games." *TAPA* 116 (1986) 71–88.

———. *Greek Mythology and Poetics*. Ithaca: Cornell, 1990a.

———. *Pindar's Homer: The Lyric Possession of an Epic Past*. Baltimore: Johns Hopkins University Press, 1990b.

———. "Mythological Exemplum in Homer." In *Innovations in Antiquity*, ed. R. Hexter and D. Selden. New York: Routledge, 1992, 311–31.

Nauck, A., ed. *Tragicorum Graecorum Fragmenta*. Second edition with supplement by B. Snell. Hildesheim: Olm, 1964.

Nilsson, Martin P. *Geschichte der griechischen Religion*. 3d ed. Munich: Beck, 1967.

Nock, A. D. "The Cult of Heroes." *HThR* 37 (1944) 141–70.

O'Brien, Joan V. *The Transformation of Hera: A Study of Ritual, Hero, and the Goddess in the "Iliad."* Lanham, Md.: Rowman and Littlefield, 1993.

Oldfather, C. H. *Diodorus Siculus*. Vols. 1–3 (Loeb Classical Library). Cambridge, Mass.: Harvard University Press, 1933–39.

Olender, Maurice. "Aspects of Baubo: Ancient Texts and Contexts." Trans. R. Lamberton. In Halperin, Winkler, and Zeitlin (1990) 83–113.

Ortner, Sherry B. "Is Female to Male as Nature Is to Culture?" In *Woman, Culture, and Society*. Michelle Zimbalist Rosaldo and Louise Lamphere, eds. Stanford: Stanford University Press, 1974, 67–87.

Otto, Walter. *Dionysos, Myth and Cult*. Trans. Robert B. Palmer. Bloomington, Ind.: 1965 [Frankfurt, 1933].

Page, D. L. *Sappho and Alcaeus*. Oxford: Clarendon Press, 1955.

———. *Poetae Melici Graeci*. Oxford: Clarendon Press, 1962.

———. *Select Papyri, V.3: Literary Papyri (poetry)* (Loeb Classical Library). Cambridge, Mass.: Harvard University Press, 1970 [1941].

Parke, H. W. *Festivals of the Athenians*. Ithaca: Cornell University Press, 1977.

Parke, H. W., and D.E.W. Wormell. *The Delphic Oracle*. 2 vols. Oxford: Blackwell, 1956.

Parker, Robert. *Miasma: Pollution and Purification in Early Greek Religion.* Oxford: Clarendon Press, 1983.

———. "Myths of Early Athens." In Bremmer (1987) 187–214.

Pease, Stanley Arthur. "Some Aspects of Invisibility." *HSCP* 53 (1942) 1–36.

Peek, Werner. "Die Penelope der Ionerinnen." *Athenische Mitteilungen* 80 (1965) 160–69.

Pembroke, S. "Women in Charge: The Functions of Alternatives in Early Greek Tradition and the Ancient Idea of Matriarchy." *Journal of the Warburg and Courtauld Institutes* 30 (1967) 1–35.

Peradotto, John, and J. P. Sullivan, eds. *Women in the Ancient World: The Arethusa Papers.* Albany: SUNY Press, 1984.

Perrin, Bernadotte, trans. *Plutarch's Lives.* Vol. 1 (Loeb Classical Library). Cambridge: Harvard University Press, 1967 [1914].

Pfeiffer, Rudolph, ed. *Callimachus.* Edition with commentary. 2 vols. Oxford: Clarendon Press, 1949.

Pfister, Friedrich. *Der Reliquienkult im Altertum.* 2 vols. Giessen: Töpelmann, 1909–12.

———. "Theoxenia." *RE* A10 (1934) 2256–58.

Pingiatoglu, Semeli. *Eileithyia.* Würzburg: Königshausen and Neumann, 1981.

Pipili, Maria. *Laconian Iconography of the Sixth Century, B.C.* Oxford: Oxford University Committee for Archaeology, 1987.

Pisani, Vittore. "Elena e L'ΕΙΔΩΛΟΝ." *Rivista di Filologia e di Istruzione Classica* 56 (1928) 476–99.

Platnauer, M. *Euripides: Helen.* Edition and commentary. Oxford: Clarendon Press, 1967.

Pötscher, Walter. "Hera und Heros." *RM* 104 (1961) 302–55.

———. "Der Name der Göttin Hera." *RM* 108 (1965) 317–20.

———. "Der Name des Herakles." *Emerita* 39 (1971) 169–84.

Powell, J. U. *Collectanea Alexandrina.* Oxford: Clarendon Press, 1925.

Price, S.R.F. *Rituals and Power: The Roman Imperial Cult in Asia Minor.* Cambridge: Cambridge University Press, 1984.

Privitera, G. Aurelio. *Dioniso in Omero e nella poesia greca arcaica.* Rome: Ateneo, 1970.

Puhvel, Jaan. "Eleuther and Oinoatis: Dionysiac Data from Mycenaean Greece." In *Mycenaean Studies*, ed. Emmett L. Bennett Jr. Madison: University of Wisconsin Press, 1964, 161–70.

Quinn, G. M. *The Sacrificial Calendar of the Marathonian Tetrapolis.* Ph.D. dissertation, Harvard University, 1972.

Raglan, Fitz Roy Richard Somerset, Lord. *The Hero: A Study in Tradition, Myth and Drama.* Westport, Ct.: Greenwood Press, 1975 [1956].

Rank, Otto. *The Myth of the Birth of the Hero.* Trans. F. Robbins and Smith Ely Jelliffe. New York: Robert Brunner, 1952.

Rasmussen, Tom, and Nigel Spivey, eds. *Looking at Greek Vases.* Cambridge: Cambridge University Press, 1991.

Redfield, James. "Notes on the Greek Wedding." *Arethusa* 15 (1982) 181–201.

———. "From Sex to Politics: The Rites of Artemis Triklaria and Dionysos Aisymnētēs at Patras." In Halperin, Winkler, and Zeitlin (1990) 114–34.

Rhodes, P. J. *A Commentary on the Aristotelian "Athenaion Politeia."* Rev. ed. Oxford: Clarendon Press, 1993.

Rhodes, R. F., and J. J. Dobbins. "The Sanctuary of Artemis Brauronia on the Athenian Akropolis." *Hesperia* 48 (1979) 325–41.

Rice, David G., and John E. Stambaugh, eds. *Sources for the Study of Greek Religion.* Missoula: Scholars Press, 1979.

Richardson, Rufus B. "A Sacrificial Calendar from the Epakria." *AJA* 1st ser. 10 (1895) 209–26.

Robert, Carl. *Eratosthenis Catasterismorum Reliquae.* Berlin: Weidmann, 1908.

Robertson, Martin. "Adopting an Approach I." In Rasmussen and Spivey (1991) 1–12.

Rohde, Erwin. *Psyche: The Cult of Souls and Belief in Immortality among the Greeks.* Trans. W. B. Hollis. London: Routledge and Kegan Paul, 1950 [Freiburg, 1898].

Rolfe, John C., ed. and trans. *Ammianus Marcellinus.* 3 vols. (Loeb Classical Library) Cambridge, Mass.: Harvard University Press, 1956.

Roscher, W. H., ed. *Ausführliches Lexicon der griechischen und römischen Mythologie.* Hildesheim: Olms, 1965 [Leipzig, 1884–1921].

Rose, H. J. "The Bride of Hades." *CP* 20 (1925) 238–42.

Rouse, W.H.D. *Greek Votive Offerings: An Essay in the History of Greek Religion.* Hildesheim: Olms, 1976 [Cambridge, 1902].

Rubin, Gayle. "The Traffic in Women: Notes on the 'Political Economy' of Sex." In *Toward an Anthropology of Women,* ed. Rayna R. Reiter. New York: Monthly Review Press, 1975, 157–210.

Rudhardt, Jean. *Notions fondamentales de la pensée religieuse et actes constitutifs du culte dans la Grèce classique.* Geneva: Droz, 1958.

Salapata, Georgia. "Pausanias 3.19.6: The Sanctuary of Alexandra at Amyklai" [abstract of talk delivered at 1990 annual meeting of the AIA]. *AJA* 95 (1991) 331.

Sale, William. "The Story of Callisto in Hesiod." *RM* 105 (1962) 122–41.

———. "Callisto and the Virginity of Artemis." *RM* 108 (1965) 11–35.

———. "The Temple-legends of the Arkteia." *RM* 118 (1975) 265–84.

Sansone, David. "The Sacrifice-Motif in Euripides' *IT*." *TAPA* 105 (1975) 283–95.

Savalli, Ivana. *La donna nella società della Grecia antica.* Bologna: Pàtron, 1983.

Scafuro, Adele. "Discourses of Sexual Violation in Mythic Accounts and Dramatic Versions of 'the Girl's Tragedy.'" *differences* 2.1 (1990) 126–59.

Scarpi, Pietro. "Un teonimo miceneo e le sue implicazioni per la mitologia greca." *Bollettino dell'Istituto di Filologia greca dell'Università di Padova* 2 (1975) 230–51.

Schachter, A. "A Boiotian Cult Type." *BICS* 14 (1967) 1–16.

———. *Cults of Boiotia* (*BICS* suppl. 38.1–4) 1981–94.

Schaps, David M. "The Woman Least Mentioned: Etiquette and Women's Names." *CQ* 27 (1977) 323–30.

———. *Economic Rights of Women in Ancient Greece.* Edinburgh: Edinburgh University Press, 1979.

Schauenburg, K. "Herakles unter Göttern." *Gymnasium* 70 (1963) 113–33.

Schefold, Karl. *Myth and Legend in Early Greek Art*. Trans. Audrey Hicks. New York: Abrams, [1966].

Seaford, Richard. "The Tragic Wedding." *JHS* 107 (1987) 106–30.

———. "Dionysos as Destroyer of the Household: Homer, Tragedy, and the Polis." In Carpenter and Faraone (1993) 115–45.

———. *Reciprocity and Ritual: Homer and Tragedy in the Developing City-State*. Oxford: Clarendon Press, 1994.

Sealey, Raphael. *Women and Law in Classical Greece*. Chapel Hill: Unversity of North Carolina Press, 1990.

Séchan, Louis. "Le Sacrifice d'Iphigénie." *REG* 44 (1931) 368–426.

Segal, Charles P. "The *Homeric Hymn to Aphrodite*: A Structuralist Approach." *CW* 67 (1974) 205–12.

———. "The Menace of Dionysos: Sex Roles and Reversals in Euripides' *Bacchae*." In Peradotto and Sullivan (1984) 195–212.

Segal, Robert A., ed. *In Quest of the Hero*. Princeton: Princeton University Press, 1990.

Sergent, Bernard. *Homosexuality in Greek Myth*. Trans. Arthur Goldhammer. Boston: Beacon, 1986 [Paris, 1984].

Shapiro, H. A. "Heros Theos: The Death and Apotheosis of Herakles." *CW* 77 (1983) 7–18.

———. "Old and New Heroes: Narrative, Composition, and Subject in Attic Black-Figure." *CA* 9 (1990) 114–48 + plates.

Siegal, H. "Self-Delusion and the Volte-Face of Iphigeneia in Euripides' *Iphigeneia at Aulis*." *Hermes* 108 (1980) 300–321.

Simon, Bennett. *Mind and Madness in Classical Greece: The Classical Roots of Modern Psychiatry*. Ithaca: Cornell, 1978.

Simon, Erika. *Festivals of Attica: An Archaeological Commentary*. Madison: University of Wisconsin Press, 1983.

Simpson, R. Hope, and J. F. Lazenby. *The Catalogue of the Ships in Homer's Iliad*. Oxford: Clarendon Press, 1970.

Skutsch, Otto. "Helen, Her Name and Nature." *JHS* 107 (1987) 188–93.

Slater, Philip E. *The Glory of Hera: Greek Mythology and the Greek Family*. Boston: Beacon, 1968.

Slatkin, Laura M. "The Wrath of Thetis." *TAPA* 116 (1986) 1–24.

———. *The Power of Thetis: Allusion and Interpretation in the "Iliad."* Berkeley: University of California, 1991.

Smith, Peter. *Nursling of Mortality, a Study of the Homeric Hymn to Aphrodite (Studien zur klassischen Philologie* 3) Frankfurt: Lang, 1981.

Smith, W. D. "Iphigeneia in Love." In *Arktouros, Hellenic Studies Presented to Bernard M. W. Knox*, ed. G. Bowersock, W. Burkert, and M. Putnam. Berlin: de Gruyter, 1979, 173–80.

Snodgrass, Anthony. *The Dark Age of Greece: An Archaeological Survey of the Eleventh to the Eighth Centuries B.C.* Edinburgh: Edinburgh University Press, 1971.

———. *Archaic Greece: The Age of Experiment*. Berkeley: University of California Press, 1980.

Snyder, Jane McIntosh. *The Woman and the Lyre: Women Writers in Classical Greece and Rome*. Carbondale: Southern Illinois University Press, 1989.

Sokolowski, F. *Lois sacrées des cités grecques*. Paris: De Boccard, 1969.

Solmsen, Friedrich. "The Sacrifice of Agamemnon's Daughter in Hesiod's 'EHOEAE." *AJP* 102 (1981) 353–58.

Sourvinou, Christiane. "Aristophanes, *Lysistrata* 641–647." *CQ* 21 (1971) 339–42.

Sourvinou-Inwood, Christiane. *Studies in Girls' Transitions: Aspects of the Arkteia and Age Representation in Attic Iconography*. Athens: Kardamitsa, 1988.

Stansbury-O'Donnell, Mark D. "Polygnotos' *Iliupersis*: A New Reconstruction." *AJA* 93 (1989) 203–15.

Stehle, Eva. "Sappho's Gaze: Fantasies of a Goddess and Young Man." *differences* 2.1 (1990) 88–125.

Stinton, T.C.W. "Iphigeneia and the Bears of Brauron." *CQ* 26 (1976) 11–13.

Sulzberger, Max. "Ὄνυμα ἐπώνυμον: Les Noms propres chez Homère et dans la mythologie grecque." *REG* 39 (1926) 381–447.

Sutor, Ann. "Aphrodite/Paris/Helen: A Vedic Myth in the *Iliad*." *TAPA* 117 (1987) 51–58.

Suzuki, Mihoko. *Metamorphoses of Helen: Authority, Difference, and the Epic*. Ithaca: Cornell University Press, 1989.

Svenbro, Jasper. *Phrasikleia: An Anthropology of Reading in Ancient Greece*. Trans. J. Lloyd. Ithaca: Cornell University Press, 1993 [Paris, 1988].

Tamburnino, Julius. "Marpessa." *RE* 14.2 (1930) 1916–17.

Thesauros Linguae Graecae (CD ROM). Irvine: University of California, 1985–.

Thiel, Helmut van. *Iliaden und Ilias*. Basel: Schwabe, 1982.

Tod, M. N., and A.J.B. Wace. *A Catalogue of the Sparta Museum*. Rome: Bretschneider, 1968 [Oxford, 1906].

Trendall, Arthur Dale. *Phylax Vases*. 2d ed. (*BICS* suppl. 19) 1967.

———. "Callisto in Apulian Vase-Painting." *AK* 20 (1977) 99–101.

Turner, Judy Ann. *HIEREIAI: Acquisition of Feminine Priesthoods in Ancient Greece*. Ph.D. dissertation, University of California at Santa Barbara, 1983.

Usener, Hermann. *Götternamen: Versuch einer Lehre von der Religiösen Begriffsbildung*. Bonn: Schulte-Bulmke, 1948.

Ventris, M., and J. Chadwick. *Documents in Mycenaean Greek*. Second edition by J. Chadwick. Cambridge: Cambridge University Press, 1973.

Vermeule, Emily. *Aspects of Death in Early Greek Art and Poetry*. Berkeley: University of California Press, 1979.

Vermeule, Emily, and Suzanne Chapman. "A Protoattic Human Sacrifice?" *AJA* 75 (1971) 285–93.

Vernant, J.-P. "Le Mariage en Grèce archaïque." *PP* 28 (1973) 51–74.

———. "Figuration de l'invisible et catégorie psychologique du double: Le Colossos." In Vernant (1981) 2:65–78.

———. "Hestia—Hermès: Sur l'expression religieuse de l'espace et du mouvement chez les Grecs." In Vernant (1981) 1:124–70.

———. *Myth et pensée chez les Grecs*. 2 vols. Paris: Maspéro, 1981 [1965].

———. "At Man's Table: Hesiod's Foundation Myth of Sacrifice." In *The Cuisine of Sacrifice among the Greeks*, ed. M. Detienne and J.-P. Vernant, trans. Paula Wissing. Chicago: University of Chicago Press, 1989 [Paris, 1979] 21–86.

Vidal-Naquet, Pierre. "Slavery and the Rule of Women in Tradition, Myth and

Utopia." In *Myth, Religion and Society*, ed. R. L. Gordon. Cambridge: Cambridge University Press, 1981, 187–200.

Villanueva Puig, Marie-Christine. "A propos des thyiades de Delphes." In *L'Association dionysiaque dans les sociétés anciennes*. Rome: Ecole Française de Rome, 1986, 31–51.

Wagner, R. "Ariadne." *RE* 2.1 (1896) 803–10.

Walbank, Michael. "Artemis Bear-Leader." *CQ* 31 (1981) 276–81.

Webster, T.B.L. "The Myth of Ariadne from Homer to Catullus." *Greece and Rome* n.s. 13 (1966) 22–31.

Wehrli, F. "Leto." *RE* suppl. 5 (1931) 555–76.

Weiler, Ingomar. *Der Agon Im Mythos: Zur Einstellung der Griechen zum Wettkampf.* Darmstadt: Wissenschaftliche Buchgesellschaft, 1974.

Weinberg, Gladys Davidson, and Saul S. Weinberg. "Arachne of Lydia at Corinth." In *The Aegean and the Near East: Studies Presented to Hetty Goldman*, ed. Saul S. Weinberg. Locust Valley, N.Y.: J. J. Augustin, 1956, 262–67; pl. 33–35.

Wentzel, G. "Aiora." *RE* 1 (1894) 1043–44.

Wernicke, K. "Artemis." *RE* 2.1 (1896) 1336–1440.

West, M. L. *Hesiod. Theogony*. Edition and commentary. Oxford: Clarendon Press, 1966.

———. *The Orphic Poems*. Oxford: Clarendon Press, 1983.

———. *The Hesiodic Catalogue of Women: Its Nature, Structure, and Origins*. Oxford: Clarendon Press, 1985.

———. *Hesiodi Opera*. Third rev. ed. Oxford: Clarendon Press, 1990.

Whitehead, David. *The Demes of Attica*. Princeton: Princeton University Press, 1986.

Wilamowitz, U. von. "Die Beide Elektren." *Hermes* 18 (1883) 214–63.

———. *Homerische Untersuchungen*. Berlin: Weidmann, 1884.

Willetts, R. F. *Cretan Cults and Festivals*. London: Routledge and Kegan Paul, 1962.

Wills, Garry. "The Sapphic 'Umwertung Aller Werte.'" *AJP* 88 (1967) 434–42.

Winkler, John J. *The Constraints of Desire: The Anthropology of Sex and Gender in Ancient Greece*. New York: Routledge, 1990.

Wolff, Christian. "Euripides' *Iphigeneia among the Taurians*: Aetiology, Ritual, and Myth." *CA* 11 (1992) 308–34.

Wright, J. C. "The Old Temple Terrace at the Argive Heraeum and the Early Cult of Hera in the Argolid." *JHS* 102 (1982) 186–201.

Wycherley, R. E. *Literary and Epigraphical Testimonia (The Athenian Agora)*. Princeton: American School of Classical Studies at Athens, 1957.

Zeitlin, Froma I. "The Argive Festival of Hera and Euripides' *Electra*." *TAPA* 101 (1970) 645–69.

———. "Travesties of Gender and Genre in Aristophanes' *Thesmophoriazousae*." In Foley (1981) 169–217.

———. "Cultic Models of the Female: Rites of Dionysos and Demeter." *Arethusa* 15 (1982) 129–57.

———. "The Dynamics of Misogyny: Myth and Mythmaking in the *Oresteia*." In Peradotto and Sullivan (1984) 159–94.

———. "Playing the Other: Theatre, Theatricality, and the Feminine in Greek Drama." *Representations* 11 (1985) 63–94.

———. "Configurations of Rape in Greek Myth." In *Rape*, ed. S. Tomaselli and R. Porter. Oxford: Blackwell, 1986, 122–51, 261–64 (notes).

———. *Playing the Other: Gender and Society in Classical Greek Literature*. Chicago: University of Chicago Press, 1996.

Ziehen, L., and G. Lippold. "Palladion." *RE* 18.3 (1949) 171–201.

Zielinski, Thaddeus. "De Helenae Simulacro." *Eos* 30 (1927) 54–58.

NOTE: Appendix citations are not included in the Index Locorum. All **boldface** numbers indicate primary source citations; all others refer to pages in this volume.

General Index

ABOUT THE AUTHOR

Deborah Lyons is Assistant Professor of Classics
at the University of Rochester. She is currently a
fellow of the Center for Hellenic Studies in
Washington, D.C. She is the translator
of *A City of Images*.